Microeconomic Decisions

Microeconomic Decisions

Robert A. Meyer

University of California, Berkeley

Houghton Mifflin Company BOSTON

ATLANTA   DALLAS   GENEVA, ILLINOIS   HOPEWELL, NEW JERSEY   PALO ALTO   LONDON

PRINTED IN THE U.S.A.

Library of Congress Catalog Card Number: 75-30259

ISBN: 0-395-19855-0

To my wife,
Donna Jean (alias "H. Bear")

Contents

Chapter 14   Markets for Inputs to the Productive Process: Perfect Competition

275

Chapter 15   Markets for Inputs to the Productive Process: Imperfect Competition

294

Preface

This text emphasizes the development of microeconomic theory with a view to its applications. The subject is approached both analytically and empirically to use effectively the complementary qualities of microeconomic theory and practical research in an essentially information-building manner. Microeconomic methods are tools for analyzing the types of economic problems arising for producers, suppliers, or consumers. The solutions to problems like pricing, production, investment, inventory control, consumption versus saving, portfolio selection of liability as well as asset composition, and public utility regulation lie at the heart of our interest. Because each new problem one encounters is slightly different from its predecessors, we will isolate the basic common features of decision problems and learn to use them to solve a specific problem. The analysis of such contemporary issues as pollution abatement, rationing of commodities (e.g., gasoline or food), and price/wage/profit limitations brings the usefulness of microeconomic methods into sharper focus.

Empirical studies of market structure and market performance, examples of preference measurement and its application, and capital budgeting and financial decisions add a concreteness to theoretical concepts. Numerical examples illustrate topics like choosing investment projects, evaluating tax benefit effects, and choosing debt or equity financing alternatives. To support the discussion of the formal basis for such concepts as demand and cost, the text includes numerous examples that highlight the importance of problems of economic measurement. Measurement is the key bridge linking the world of models and theory to actual events.

The chapter on linear programming develops many of its key points through a sequence of examples. Although the chapter focuses on the problem-solving ability of the linear programming method using only algebra and diagrams, a detailed appendix illustrates a simple vehicle for organizing, solving, and interpreting problems that cannot be visualized. Problem solving, rather than theory alone, is again the central theme.

Uncertainty is a pervasive characteristic of reality often ignored in micro-economics texts. This aversion is quite understandable—even relatively simple expositions require some probability concepts to which students may not have been exposed. Since uncertainty is an important factor in evaluating alternative policy proposals I have included at the end of most chapters a section that extends discussions into the realm of uncertainty. These sections are marked with an asterisk and may be omitted if student background and/or time prohibit their inclusion. The relevance of uncertainty to actual decision settings and my feeling that the area of uncertainty promises a rich and useful extension of knowledge are the chief reasons for including these sections.

Within each chapter the level of difficulty proceeds from basic concepts through simple applications and then to more difficult material. The broad span in the level of difficulty allows the text to be tailored to the students' background and the instructor's objectives.

The sequence of the chapters is a pattern that has proved its effectiveness. The content of each chapter reflects a balance of emphasis that emerged over the years from the undergraduate microeconomics courses I supervised at Purdue University and the University of California, Berkeley, and the courses I have taught while at Berkeley.

Courses in the principles of economics and college algebra are the pre-requisites to an intermediate microeconomics course. The text presents all basic material in verbal, diagrammatic, and algebraic form to heighten clarity. Diagrams are used extensively to illustrate ideas, but the use of diagrams can imply too much. Therefore, footnotes contain precise restatements of technical details and mathematical versions of arguments. The inclusion of such footnote material again provides a text that can be used at several levels.

Questions at the end of each chapter suggest extensions and additional work that may be used for term papers and/or class discussions. The author's workbook *Problems in Price Theory* offers a further variety of problem sets on tear-out pages that can be selected individually for homework, examinations, and self-test quizzes. An instructor's manual with all solutions is available with the workbook.

Every author knows the heavy debt of gratitude he owes to those who first taught him and to his friends and colleagues who have provided the stimulus for learning as a way of life. For my wife, Donna Jean, a brief acknowledgment is a small token for her encouragement, support and for her willingness to undertake the mammoth job of typing several manuscript revisions. Revisions benefited from comments by M. O. Clement, D. MacFarlane, G. H. Mellish and K. Rethwisch. In addition, I would like to express a special thanks to R. E. Kuenne, Roland Artle, C. A. Knox Lovell, R. D. Peterson, Paul Kohne, and Joseph C. Gallo for their extensive help.

R. A. M.

Berkeley, California

Chapter 1 Introduction

What Is Microeconomics?

The purpose of this book is to provide a student with some basic tools of economic analysis and to illustrate their use in solving decision problems or in appraising the possible outcomes of business or government policy alternatives. Microeconomics is a collection of tools and methods applicable to the actions of individual decision makers. Two broad groups of decisions are studied by microeconomic methods: production and pricing decisions made by firms and consumption decisions made by the individual consumer or household.

Decision-making tools are certainly useful in day-to-day life, but microeconomics has more to offer. Individual decisions become part of a continual flow of economic activity. Microeconomic methods show how individual decisions transmit information through an economy and how and why economic activity is altered by new information. Information, based on the behavior of individual economic agents, determines the passage of resources through the filter created by technology, to the production of the goods and services desired.

How Can Microeconomic Methods Be Used?

The following examples illustrate the types of business and government problems which can be analyzed by microeconomic methods.

Beef and gasoline shortages

The recent shortages of beef and gasoline introduced an aspect of economic life entirely new to those of us born after 1940. These dramatic changes provoke several questions: What causes such shortages? In what sense are they shortages? How can they be alleviated or prevented? How can existing amounts of the scarce commodities be allocated? Simply by allowing prices to rise unchecked? Rising prices tend to curtail existing consumption and inhibit potential consumption as well. Or should the government institute a system of quotas? Ration coupons were used during World War II for food, tires, gasoline, etc. A choice between these two alternatives, establishing quotas for individuals or using a price system, involves explicit or implicit decisions about who is to receive the scarce commodities and who is to go without.

The choice will also have financial consequences for both producers and consumers. For example, during the summer of 1973, the Wage-Price Control Board allowed the gasoline wholesale price to rise. To make this policy acceptable to the consumer, it was argued that retail prices would not rise. The rise in wholesale prices helped the oil companies secure their profits. Following this, the retail supply was contracted. Consumers, harassed by fuel shortages, generated enough political pressure for the retailers to obtain a price increase as well. If the oil companies had originally tried to raise the retail price *and* the wholesale price, they probably would have had little chance of getting the policy approved. Politics and economics are inextricably interwoven. Microeconomic methods make it possible to understand the economic aspect of political decisions and to forecast their probable consequences.

Consider the recent beef shortage from the viewpoint of a producer. When beef prices were frozen in June 1972, cattle firms were already holding stocks of cattle. If they knew that the price freeze was going to be lifted in September, what decision would they make with respect to these stocks? Obviously they would continue to hold them, provided that feed prices, interest costs, and other expenses would not eliminate the potential profit to be made from the higher prices possible in the future. The calculated sacrifice of immediate profits for greater profits in the future is one of the important decisions any business executive must be able to make.

In times of inflation, a beef or gasoline price freeze may make good political sense, but economically it is not always desirable. Microeconomic methods can help politicians to understand the probable effects of alternative policies and to mount the political strength to support reasoned solutions to an energy crisis, a food shortage, or other problems arising in the future.

Urban mass transit

Congestion on urban roads and freeways and the expense of transporting people and products to and from work centers are pressing problems today. Available transportation methods and commuter preferences combine to produce conditions which not only endanger commuters (automobile insurance rates in urban areas are often more than twice as high as in less populated areas) but also waste time which could be spent in leisure or productive activity. Urban mass transit systems are one possible solution to these problems.

If mass transit systems are desirable, what economic policies can be used to promote them? Should excise taxes be enacted to raise the price of gasoline? Should all roads be toll roads, with the prices for traveling on them determined by the time of day and day of the week? The billing price would be highest on the most congested streets and lower on alternate routes.

The impact of proposals for curbing highway congestion and parking problems depends on individual decisions about modes of transportation. Here too microeconomics can provide a framework for answering important questions.

Air and water pollution—problems of the environment

The Environmental Protection Agency (EPA) recently stated that automobile mileage must be cut by as much as 80% in large urban areas such as New York, Chicago, Los Angeles, and San Francisco to reduce vehicle exhaust emissions. The EPA is also urging reduction of parking space in certain urban centers. These recommendations are only part of a pervasive concern for the impact of economic activity on the environment, extending to air and water pollution, the cutting of timber, strip mining, and petroleum and natural gas depletion. The proper management of natural resources requires careful economic analysis.

Decisions by firms to use high-pollution fuels or production methods are influenced by the political and legal environment in which they operate and by the "signals" they are given by current market prices. Technology provides the basic alternatives, but economic considerations dictate the ultimate choice. These decisions can be influenced significantly by public policy.

Business tax policy

Government tax policy plays an important part in business investment decisions. For example, accelerated depreciation in effect gives a firm a subsidy to recover its initial investment outlays in the form of reduced taxes. Alternative depreciation policies offer alternative earnings streams and prices for capital assets. If the government wants to foster growth in a particular industry, accelerated depreciation or special tax credits will reduce the price of the firm's capital, making investment more attractive. Conversely, capital prices and returns on investment provide information relevant in assessing measures to encourage or retard technological change.

The oil depletion allowance has attracted considerable public attention. This tax provision permits a petroleum-producing firm involved in exploration to deduct a percentage of its sales from taxable income as an operating expense. Since the deduction is in no way tied to the actual investment cost, a firm can recover that cost many times over, completely free of taxation. Whether this makes sense economically will depend on its impact on the rate of natural resources depletion and the business condition of the firms involved.

Effects of regulating economic activity

An important area of economic policy deals with regulated industries. Regulation is a fact of life for telephone companies, airlines, railroads, and communication industries. Public utilities operate under several types of regulation, for example, reviews of investment projects and approval of price changes. As a result, long and costly litigation is sometimes required to revise price schedules. The energy crisis precipitated numerous suggestions that regulation should be extended to petroleum firms as well.

Regulation has a direct effect on consumer prices and on the availability of the funds that firms require to meet financial needs. What effect does regulation have on economic decisions? In studying the monopoly market settings which exist in many regulated industries, notably telephone service, electricity, and other public utilities, microeconomic analysis can be applied to determine the influence of different methods of regulation.

Ideally a microeconomics course will provide students with a set of tools that will enable them to analyze the effects of economic policies on decisions relating to a broad range of subjects: career activities and voting, the allocation of consumption over time, or the selection of a stock portfolio. Economic analysis can map out the details of a problem and trace the consequences of each alternative solution.

Production, Consumption, Markets, and Prices

Before looking more closely at the examples given above, it is essential to understand the basic elements of an economy and the role markets play in decision problems. It is easiest to think of an economy as a collection of markets which make up a geo-political unit such as the United States, or Russia, or France and to divide the activity within the economy into two parts: production and consumption. Similarly, all economic decision-making units can be divided into two groups: producers and consumers.

Every economy has a group of resources initially available to it. The major economic decisions then become (1) which resources are to be used by which firms, (2) which goods and services are to be produced by which firms using which production techniques, and (3) how these goods and services are to be distributed among the individuals that make up the economy. These allocation problems are fundamental to every economy and every political ideology. Capitalism, socialism, and communism embody particular schemes for solving identical allocation problems. In the United States, and in many other countries, the most important device for solving these problems is a market system. A market consists of a set of individuals who desire to sell or purchase a particular commodity. Markets solve problems of allocation by using particular kinds of information—*prices*.

A market system generates prices, which then act as signals to producers by indicating which goods are relatively scarce and which are relatively abundant and which goods, consequently, should be produced. The same set of prices gives signals to consumers about the costs of different commodities, thus determining which goods and services they will purchase and the income they will receive.

How does a price system operate? Producers and consumers make decisions based on an initial set of prices. These decisions result in a certain mix of goods and services being produced and consumed. The production side of the economy provides supply information to the market; the consumption side provides demand information. The market fuses these two pieces of information to generate a new set of prices, which triggers the whole chain again. The generation and revision of information for use in solving the three basic allocation problems constitute a dynamic market system. A market system is not the only way of providing this information. The desirability of using an alternative method, such as a central planning agency, to solve allocation problems depends on its cost, measured by the resources spent to generate information, and its efficiency. Since the primary use of resources is to obtain goods and services, the fewer scarce resources spent on intermediary inputs, e.g., information, the better. The resources spent to generate information represent the cost of running a market system. Besides providing information, a market system facilitates the exchange of goods or the title to goods. The various markets used in an economy, together with rules about property rights and contracts, interact to provide the setting in which economic activity is carried on. This economic activity is subject to three major influences: (1) information, (2) legal rules of property and contract, and (3) the political setting of group choice.

The market system outlined above is a *decentralized* method for solving allocation problems. Each decision maker uses only the alternatives and market prices known to him/her. Laws of contract are a necessary adjunct to a decentralized decision process because they reduce the cost of contract enforcement by providing an order and predictability to agreements.

If decision makers could be equipped with a set of prices for all items now *and* in the future all allocation problems would be readily solved. However, the inability of a market system to generate the necessary future information creates an element of uncertainty in an otherwise simple decision process and makes theoretical discussions more complex.

Appraising how well a decentralized decision system works is of basic importance in deciding whether industrial concentration should be encouraged, or restricted by antitrust legislation, and whether the resource allocation achieved by the market system should be adjusted by governmental intervention in the form of wage and price controls, income taxation, funding educational assistance programs, encouraging research, etc.

Empirical Observation and Theories

The economic activity described above and the environment in which it takes place are so complicated that to understand what is going on and why, it is necessary to strip down reality to its essential elements. This approach is widely used in physics, biology, and other disciplines. Starting from empirical observations, major influences are singled out and minor influences are suppressed. This abstracting process leads to models representing a simplified view of certain basic elements or forces. As an example, when analyzing an individual's choice of transportation in the San Francisco area, one might consider the costs and the time requirements of the available alternatives. Data such as the price of orange juice in Chicago and the air temperature in Washington, D.C. are ignored either because they are irrelevant or because their influence is negligible. The simplified models produced by this abstracting process are used to construct theories to explain why certain events occur.

Theories are then subjected to empirical and statistical tests. The results of the statistical tests are used to improve the models, to ensure that they reflect the forces which have a significant influence on the observed events. This process, referred to as *model building*, is actually the application to economics of the scientific method.

With the tools of economic analysis, many of the models discussed in this book can easily be applied to solve decision problems arising in the future. One of the principal aims of this book is to present a method of structuring problems to facilitate solutions and to enhance the power to make decisions based on those solutions.

Models are frequently used in combination with empirical data to make predictions concerning the outcome of certain decisions. How much time, money, and effort should be spent in making predictions of this sort will depend on the potential profits (or losses) resulting from the decision. If a project is large, it makes economic sense to spend more money on narrowing the range of the uncertainty surrounding its outcome. Because empirical observations, theories, and predictions are ways of enhancing our knowledge and improving decision making, they will occupy much of the discussion in this book.

Models of Economic Behavior and Their Analysis

Each of the examples given earlier involves some kind of allocation or *choice problem.*

Choice problems can be divided into two groups: individual choice problems and group choice problems. In group choice problems two or more individual decision makers are involved in forming the choice. By and large, microeconomics is concerned with individual choice problems, and political science with group choice problems. After the individual decisions have been analyzed in detail, we shall see how they fit into the economy as a whole. At this level many questions of group choice appear.

Choice problems may also be categorized according to whether they occur in a deterministic environment or one subject to uncertainty. Most interesting choice problems are characterized by the presence of uncertainty. However, most of the problems to be discussed here, such as pollution control and abatement, production and pricing, will be solved initially in a certainty setting, since the addition of uncertainty elements makes analysis more difficult. Then, at the end of the chapter, we shall usually show extensions that incorporate some elements of each uncertainty.

Time is a crucial element in most economic problems. An investment problem, for example, involves a decision to be made now, yet the outcome of that decision can only be judged *ex post facto* (after the occurrence of future events). A third division can therefore be made between *static problems*, in which time is not a factor, and *dynamic models*, in which its influence is explicitly recognized. The basic decision methods and models covered here deal with static decisions under certainty. Dynamic decisions will also be discussed, but wherever possible a static framework will be used in order to make basic concepts, as well as uncertainty and information aspects, stand out more clearly.

Even without the complicated analysis of dynamic processes, many major economic effects can be isolated by a method called *comparative statics*, which is used throughout the text. Utilizing this method, a choice problem is first solved on the basis of a given set of information. Then one element of the model is altered. Any change in the optimum solution of the problem will then be the result of the change in that element. By changing one piece of information at a time, the effect of many forces can easily be mapped out.

The Elements of a Choice Problem

There are four basic elements to the solution of every choice problem. The first step is to delineate the set from which choices can be made: for an investment problem, the various investments available, for a consumption decision, the commodities that could actually be consumed.

The second step is to identify any constraints on the decisions that must be made. A restriction on the availability of funds or raw material is an example.

The third step, usually the most difficult, is to provide a criterion for ranking the outcomes of the various possible decisions. In the investment example, the ranking criterion might be profit, cost, or time required to recover the initial investment cost. For the consumption problem, possible criteria for a consumer market basket include quantity of commodities, nutrition, or subjective preference. The fourth ingredient is to determine the behavior rule that a decision maker uses to choose among the available alternatives. A behavior rule for a firm might be to choose the most profitable investment project or to choose the one which recovers the initial investment in the shortest period of time.

The following examples illustrate the four elements of a choice problem. Suppose a firm must choose the mix of inputs, say capital and labor, which will allow it to produce a certain quantity of output at minimum cost. The initial set of choices consists of all possible combinations of capital and labor that will produce the given output. The next step is to determine the constraints on decisions. There may be a maximum (or minimum) amount of labor or capital that the firm can use. Technology places certain lower limits on the quantity of inputs required. The third element is to apply the ranking criterion, such as total cost. The behavior rule for the problem is to minimize cost, so the firm will choose the input mix which costs the least while still satisfying the limits set by the constraints.

Now suppose the choice problem is a consumption decision concerning two commodities, cheese and wine. First, list all possible combinations of quantities of cheese and wine. Obviously some budget factor will act as a constraint on total expenditure. The ranking criterion might be an individual's preferences; then the various wine-and-cheese market baskets would be ranked in order from most preferred to least preferred. A behavior rule frequently used for consumption decisions is to choose the most preferred market basket.

The following chapters consider problems like these in greater detail. Chapters 2 through 4 develop concepts of consumption choice and its implications. Once the consumption choice problem is solved for an individual, we can construct the individual's demand schedule for a commodity. This in turn is a building block for constructing a market demand schedule for a commodity. Chapters 5 through 8 consider individual choice problems from the production side of the economy, with the firm as the center of attention. We shall learn methods for deciding what price to charge for output, how much to produce, what mix of goods to produce, and what inputs and technological methods are economically the optimal to use. Once these decisions have been made, we can set up a supply schedule for the firm indicating how much it would be profitable to produce at alternative prices. The supply schedules for the producing firms are the building blocks for the market supply schedule for a particular commodity.

The market demand schedule and the market supply schedule are powerful microeconomic tools. While each represents a very simple concept, they provide a means for analyzing such issues as the effect of excise taxes, quotas on exports or imports, beef or gasoline rationing, mitigation of pollution, and the effect of job training on wages and labor markets. Chapters 9 through 16 apply basic microeconomic analysis to the operation of different types of markets for inputs and outputs.

After looking at individual markets, we shall turn in Chapters 17 and 18 to allocation across different markets with its many interdependent relations, a setting referred to as *general equilibrium*.

Summary

The problems for which microeconomic methods can be used run the gamut from energy and waste management problems to appraising the impact of tax policies. The division of economic activity into production and consumption and the theory of markets and prices form the basic framework of microeconomics.

To obtain a simplified view of the basic elements in a complex problem, models are constructed. Models provide a means of organizing information and drawing logically consistent inferences. Since in the process of simplification it is always possible to overlook relevant factors, it is crucial to compare empirical observations with the predictions obtained from a model. Empirical comparisons also show how a model can be improved. Throughout the following chapters empirical methods will be used to illustrate the concepts and applications of microeconomic methods.

References

Arrow, K. J., "Limited Knowledge and Economic Analysis," *American Economic Review*, 64 (March, 1974), 1–10.

Friedman, M. *Essays in Positive Economics*. University of Chicago Press, 1953.

Harrod, R. F., "Scope and Method of Economics," *Economic Journal*, 48 (1938), 383–412.

Marshall, A., *Principles of Economics*. Macmillan, 1920.

Morgenstern, O., "Thirteen Critical Points in Contemporary Economic Theory: An Interpretation," *Journal of Economic Literature*, 10 (December, 1972), 1163–1189.

Robbins, L., *An Essay on the Nature and Significance of Economic Science*, Second Edition. Macmillan, 1935.

Shubik, M., "A Curmudgeon's Guide to Microeconomics," *Journal of Economic Literature*, 10 (December, 1972), 1163–1189.

Chapter 2 Individual Preferences and Consumption Choice Decisions

Introduction

Decisions concerning which commodities to purchase, when to purchase them, and when to consume them are made in the course of our daily lives with scarcely a second thought. Yet consumption decisions play an important part in economic activity. This chapter develops the basic elements to be used in subsequent chapters, by focusing on the role of individual preferences.

Initially we shall consider the choice between two commodities, for example, beef versus chicken or gasoline versus some other commodity. Once the basic concepts of choice in a two-commodity setting are developed, they can be extended to include many commodities. A particularly interesting use of a two-commodity setting, to be developed in more detail in Chapter 14, treats leisure as one "commodity" and a composite of all other consumption goods as the other.

Analyzing the effect of price changes on the consumption of beef versus chicken or gasoline versus other commodities will enable us to determine the probable effect of levying higher excise taxes on gasoline and of other methods of conserving petroleum, such as rationing. In this analysis gasoline could be replaced by either water or air to give some idea of what would happen if the price of water or air rose to the point where it is no longer available as an essentially free commodity. Understanding how preferences affect demand and how demand affects prices will permit analysis of the effect of changes in preferences, tax schemes, and many other aspects of economic life.

Representing Individual Preferences

Let us begin by looking at the two-commodity consumption choice problem involving beef and chicken. At the outset we need to list all the alternative market baskets of goods, consisting of a certain number of pounds of beef and a certain number of pounds of chicken, that an individual might consume.

One market basket of goods might have one pound of beef and eight pounds of chicken, another may have two pounds of beef and four pounds of chicken, and another nine pounds of beef and four pounds of chicken, etc. Table 2.1 lists several *specific* market baskets, while each point in Figure 2.1 represents a *possible* market basket.

To determine individual preferences, we must next ask someone to rank each basket. Suppose we ask the individual to assign the number 1 to the one preferred least, the number 2 to the next in order of preference, 3 to the next, etc. In each case the individual is describing preferences in a quantitative way by assigning an index number to each market basket. The higher the number associated with a market basket of goods, the higher the basket stands in the individual's preferences. If there are two or more market baskets that he/she feels are equivalent, they are to be assigned the same number. Suppose the result is the rankings listed in the right-hand column of Table 2.1. If we were to repeat this experiment for all possible market baskets of goods, we would have a ranking for every point in Figure 2.1.

Each market basket in Table 2.1 is represented by a point, *A, B, D,* etc. Since the points in Figure 2.1, including the origin and points along the axes, represent all possible consumptions for an individual, they correspond to the list of alternatives described in Chapter 1 as the first element in the solution of a choice problem.

Connecting all points having the same ranking might produce curves such as those in Figure 2.1. On any one of these curves all the points represent

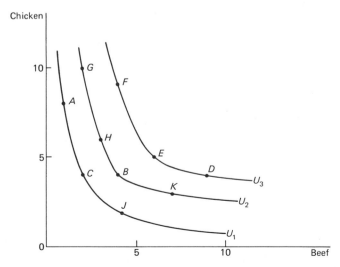

Figure 2.1   Indifference Curves from Market Basket Rankings

Table 2.1   Alternative Market Baskets of Beef and Chicken

BEEF (LBS.)	CHICKEN (LBS.)	RANKING	LABEL
1	8	1	*A*
4	9	3	*F*
2	10	2	*G*
3	6	2	*H*
6	5	3	*E*
2	4	1	*C*
4	4	2	*B*
9	4	3	*D*
7	3	2	*K*
4	2	1	*J*

market baskets which the individual treats as equivalent in terms of preference. Curves such as these are called *indifference curves*. An indifference
curve is defined as a schedule of the market baskets which the individual
treats as equivalent. Indifference curves are *nested*, i.e., they occur in a specific
order. Any commodity bundle that lies on a higher indifference curve is
preferred to any commodity bundle that lies on a lower indifference curve.
Thus any bundle on curve U_3 would be preferred to any bundle on curve U_2.

Indifference curves are simply a device for representing the ranking of
individual preferences. In Figure 2.1 market basket D lies on a higher in-

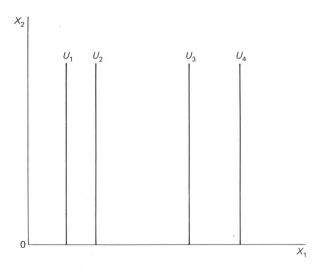

Figure 2.2   Neither Liking nor Disliking for Commodity X_2

difference curve than market basket *B*, which means that the individual prefers *D* to *B*. If both of them were financially feasible, *D* would obviously be
chosen.

Many different preference situations can be described using this technique.
If an individual liked beef but had no strong feelings about chicken, his/her
preferences could be represented by indifference curves like those in Figure
2.2. What curve would represent the situation in which someone liked chicken,
but disliked beef? If the individual kept the same amount of chicken, having
more beef would actually make such a person feel *worse off* than before.

Properties of Indifference Curves

Indifference curves never intersect each other. They are nested very closely
(since every point must lie on *some* indifference curve), but they do not intersect. To prove this, let us assume that the two indifference curves U_1 and U_2
in Figure 2.3 intersect, and then show that this leads to an inconsistency.
Point *A* is a point on U_1, point *C* a point on U_2, and point *B* is the point at
which the two curves intersect. Since the market basket of goods described
by *C* lies on a higher indifference curve than the one described by *A*,
the market basket of goods *C* must be preferred to the market basket of
goods *A*.

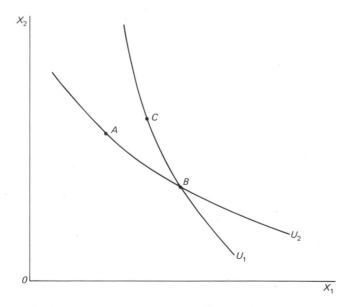

Figure 2.3   Indifference Curves Do Not Cross

But since A and B lie on the same indifference curve, U_1, the individual must regard them as equivalent. The same holds true for B and C, which lie on U_2. If the individual regards A as equivalent to B and B as equivalent to C, this implies that he/she regards A as equivalent to C. But this conclusion contradicts the fact that C is preferred to A. Therefore the initial assumption that the indifference curves intersect must be false.

A second important property of indifference curves is that each point (i.e., each market basket) lies on one and only one indifference curve. The fact that a given market basket lies only on one indifference curve is a corollary from the proof given above. The assertion that every market basket lies on *an* indifference curve proceeds from the assumption that an individual can give a ranking to every market basket, or, formally speaking, that the individual's preferences are *complete*.[1]

The Marginal Rate of Substitution

The negative of the slope at any point along a particular indifference curve is referred to as the *marginal rate of substitution* (MRS). The marginal rate of substitution indicates the rate at which an individual would trade units of one commodity for additional units of another. For example, if the MRS of chicken for beef is 3 at a particular point, this would indicate that the individual would give up 3 units of chicken to get 1 more unit of beef. Since the individual would regard the market baskets possessed before and after the trade as equivalent, they would obviously lie on the same indifference curve.

Another way of indicating the nature of the MRS is to say it is an exchange rate reflecting an individual's indifference to both the market basket of goods acquired after a trade and the original one. The marginal rate of substitution thus describes how much an individual will "pay" in units of one commodity (not in dollar terms) for a unit of another commodity. To know what this means in dollar terms, we simply multiply the MRS by the price of chicken. If the price of a pound of chicken is $1, then an MRS of chicken for beef of 3 means the individual would pay as much as $3 for the next pound of beef.

The numerical value of the MRS at a given point can be determined by constructing a straight line tangent to the indifference curve at that point. To find the MRS at point A in Figure 2.4, construct the tangent line $\overline{BC}$. This line will have the same slope as the indifference curve U_0 at point A, namely $\overline{OB}/\overline{OC}$. The MRS at A is thus $-\overline{OB}/\overline{OC}$.

---

[1] Technically the ordering of alternative choices that is used here is referred to as *partial ordering of alternative consumptions*. In addition to being complete, individual preferences must be transitive and reflexive in order to give rise to a partial ordering. For more details, consult Henderson and Quandt.

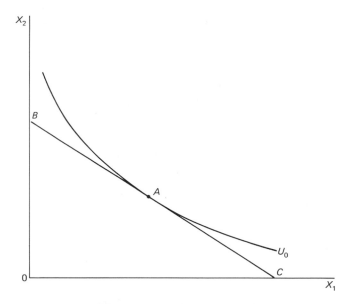

Figure 2.4   Measuring the Marginal Rate of Substitution

Moving along the indifference curve in Figure 2.4, the slope of the curve becomes flatter in one direction and steeper in the other. Since the negative of the slope is the *MRS*, this indicates that the *MRS* diminishes as the individual gets more of either commodity. In other words, in the situation represented in Figure 2.4, an individual who gets more and more of one commodity is willing to pay less and less in terms of the other commodity to get additional units of the plentiful commodity, assuming the level of satisfaction remains constant. If the *MRS* increased with consumption, the indifference curves would look like the ones in Figure 2.5.

The Concept of Utility

Another way of developing the concept of the indifference curve is to introduce the notion of a *utility function*.

Suppose all the different combinations of beef and chicken are written (X_1, X_2), where X_1 is beef and X_2 is chicken. With $X_1 \geq 0$ and $X_2 \geq 0$, the points (X_1, X_2) will represent the market baskets illustrated in Figure 2.1. The ranking of the market baskets (X_1, X_2) might be expressed as an index number assignment rule written $U(X_1, X_2)$. For any given amounts of beef and chicken the expression $U(X_1, X_2)$ provides a number representing the rank of the resulting market basket. $U(X_1, X_2)$ is referred to as a *utility*

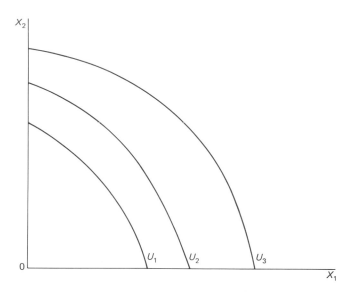

Figure 2.5   A Case of increasing Marginal Rate of Substitution

function. For any two market baskets (X_1^0, X_2^0) and (X_1^*, X_2^*), $U(X_1^0, X_2^0) \geq$ $U(X_1^*, X_2^*)$ implies that the market basket (X_1^0, X_2^0) is liked much more than the market basket (X_1^*, X_2^*). Since the market baskets to which an individual would give the same index value are located along an indifference curve, an indifference curve is simply the graph of the equation $U(X_1, X_2) =$ constant.

The preferences determining the utility function relate only to consumption alternatives. They are independent of market prices of commodities or income. If preferences depended on market prices or income, any attempt to use them as a basis for explaining market prices would lead into a circular trap.

A three-dimensional diagram illustrates the relationship between the utility function and indifference curves. The two bottom axes in Figure 2.6 represent quantities of beef and chicken while the vertical axis represents the numerical value of the index $U(X_1, X_2)$. It is commonly assumed that as an individual consumes more of either commodity the utility index will rise, although the amount of the increase will become successively less as more is consumed. This assumption is represented by having the curve relating utility level to consumption rise more and more slowly as consumption increases. Another way of expressing this result is to say that as an individual consumes more and more the *added* utility, or *marginal utility,* from one more pound of beef or one more pound of chicken

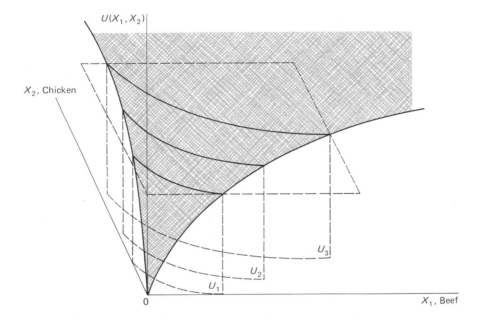

Figure 2.6   Indifference Curves from a Utility Function

diminishes. Geometrically, this means that the slope of the utility surface becomes flatter and flatter as it moves away from the origin.

The marginal utility for the commodity X_1 can be expressed in symbols as

$$MU_{X_1} = \frac{\Delta U(X_1, X_2)}{\Delta X_1} \tag{2.1}$$

for a given level of X_2. The marginal rate of substitution can be represented in another way by using the concept of marginal utility. Any change in the amounts of X_1 and X_2, say ΔX_1 and ΔX_2, will give rise to a change in total utility, ΔU, that can be expressed as[2]

$$\Delta U = MU_{X_1} \cdot \Delta X_1 + MU_{X_2} \cdot \Delta X_2 \tag{2.2}$$

---

[2] If the utility function over n commodities, $U(X_1, X_2, \ldots, X_n)$, is differentiable, then marginal utility is expressed as $MU_i = \partial U / \partial X_i$, $i = 1, \ldots, n$, and equation (2.2) corresponds to taking the total differential

$$dU = \sum_{i=1}^{n} \frac{\partial U}{\partial X_i} dX_i$$

For $n = 2$ along a given indifference curve $dU = 0$,

$$\frac{dX_2}{dX_1} = \frac{\partial U / \partial X_1}{\partial U / \partial X_2} = -\frac{MU_1}{MU_2} = -MRS$$

Along any indifference curve the utility level is constant. Therefore, $\Delta U = 0$, and

$$0 = MU_{X_1} \cdot \Delta X_1 + MU_{X_2} \cdot \Delta X_2$$

or

$$-\frac{\Delta X_2}{\Delta X_1} = \frac{MU_{X_1}}{MU_{X_2}} \tag{2.3}$$

Since $\Delta X_2 / \Delta X_1$ is the slope of the indifference curve and the MRS is defined as the negative of this slope,

$$MRS = -\frac{\Delta X_2}{\Delta X_1} = \frac{MU_{X_1}}{MU_{X_2}} \tag{2.4}$$

Thus the marginal rate of substitution can be expressed as the ratio of the marginal utilities for each pair of commodities.

The combinations of beef and chicken that provide a given level of utility are represented by the corresponding contour of the utility surface. Perhaps the easiest way to represent this geometrically is to pass a horizontal plane through the point U_1 on the vertical axis. Such a plane might look like the dotted plane which cuts through the utility surface in Figure 2.6. The intersection of the plane with the utility surface at level U_1 would look like the curve U_1 in the X_1, X_2 plane.

If this process is repeated for a higher level of utility, say U_2, the new plane would cut through at a higher level on the utility surface, producing a curve of the same shape as U_2 in the X_1, X_2 plane. Repeated over and over again, this would lead to a whole family of nested curves like U_1, U_2, U_3, U_4, etc., in Figure 2.6. The projection of these curves on the X_1, X_2 plane produces the pattern shown in Figure 2.7. Thus the indifference curve map is an equivalent means of expressing the information given by the utility function. The purpose of either approach is to rank consumption alternatives.

Cardinal versus Ordinal Utility: The Question of Measurement

So far the notion of utility has been used only for ranking alternatives. We shall now consider whether utility can be measured in the same sense that temperature is measured and whether measurement of this kind is a necessary part of solving decision problems.

There are two types of ranking: ordinal and cardinal. An *ordinal ranking* classifies any pair of possible choices, A and B, into one of three situations: A is preferred to B, A is indifferent to B, or B is preferred to A. The numerical values assigned to A and B are irrelevant, except that if A is preferred to B the number assigned to A must be larger than the number assigned to B. Fortunately, most decision problems require only the relatively weak condition of ordinal ranking.

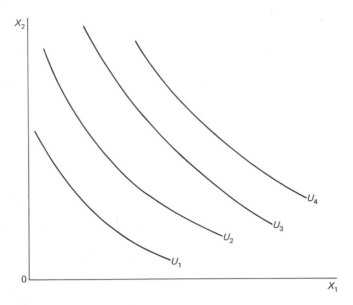

Figure 2.7   Indifference Curves in the X_1, X_2 Plane

Cardinal ranking implies that the numerical values assigned as utilities are unique up to linear transformations. While cardinal ranking is a frequent form of measurement in the physical sciences for temperature, light intensity, etc., the social sciences commonly use only ordinal rankings. An important exception exists for decisions to be made under risk. In this situation, comparative choice experiments will lead to a utility function which is cardinally measurable. Choice under risk is discussed in Chapter 5.

Solution of a Fundamental Choice Problem

The next step in solving the consumption choice problem is to narrow down the choices from all possible consumptions to those which are economically feasible. This is accomplished by adding a *budget constraint*. Let P_1 be the price of a pound of beef, P_2 the price of a pound of chicken, and M be an individual's money income. The budget constraint requires total expenditure on beef, $P_1 X_1$, plus total expenditure on chicken, $P_2 X_2$, to be equal to or less than money income, i.e., $P_1 X_1 + P_2 X_2 \leq M$. This is a very simple budget constraint, since the prices do not depend on the quantity purchased, and money income is given.

As an example, assume that the price of beef is $2, the price of chicken is $1, and the individual has a money income of $12. In Figure 2.8, the shaded area limited by the budget constraint, including the origin and the portion of the axes below the budget constraint, represents all the market baskets that an individual can actually afford. One could not choose the market basket represented by point E, because the cost of that market basket is more than \$12.

The basic elements of the consumption choice problem are, therefore, (1) the individual's preferences, represented by the indifference curves, (2) the prices of each commodity, and (3) the individual's money income. The problem is to choose from all the feasible market baskets of goods the one (or ones) lying on the highest indifference curve, in other words, those market baskets which maximize utility, subject to the budget constraint.

Figure 2.9 illustrates the solution of the choice problem using the numerical example presented earlier. The indifference curves in Figure 2.9 are the same ones shown in Figure 2.1. A market basket represented by a point like N could never be a solution to the problem since there are other market baskets that the individual could still afford to buy which lie on a higher indifference curve. The solution obviously occurs at point H. The optimum amount of beef to purchase is $X_1^0 = 3$ and the optimum amount of chicken is $X_2^0 = 6$.

In Figure 2.9 the variables X_1 and X_2 could represent many other things besides beef and chicken. X_1 could be future consumption and X_2 could be current consumption, in which case the same analysis could be used to solve

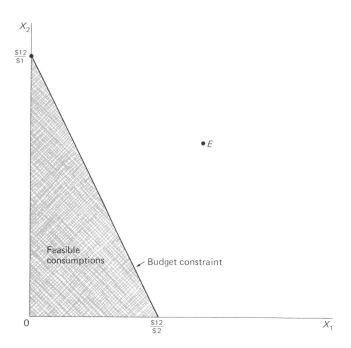

Figure 2.8   The Budget Constraint Defines Economically
Feasible Consumptions

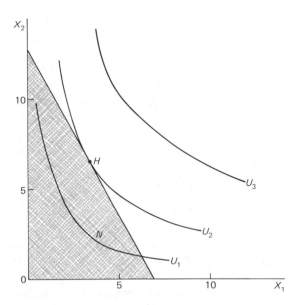

Figure 2.9 Optimum Consumption Choice

the problem of allocating consumption over time. Similarly, X_1 could represent securities paying a steady income and X_2 could represent securities with some measure of risk, so that the same analysis could be applied to a portfolio selection problem. The optimal mix of securities should balance steady return against risks that could lead to higher profits. An indifference curve can describe this type of subjective trade off. In a marketing setting X_1 and X_2 could represent size and color or texture and shape, in which case preferences would be based on the characteristics of a commodity rather than physical quantities. Coupled with market research information about consumer preferences for particular characteristics, this approach could be used to tailor commodities to consumer desires. An empirical experiment studying preferences in this manner is provided in a later section of this chapter.

A Closer Look at the Character of an Optimal Solution

The problem in Figure 2.9 has a unique solution at the point H, but uniqueness is not necessarily a characteristic of the optimal solution to a consumption choice problem. An indifference curve might remain flat for some distance, and the budget constraint might coincide with it over all or a part of that distance. If this happens, there is a well-defined solution to the choice problem. However, a number of different market baskets of goods would all be optimal. In Figure 2.10, for instance, all the points on the line segment $\overline{RS}$

represent optimal solutions. It is usually possible to tell from the shape of indifference curves or the nature of the utility function whether the problem yields a unique solution, several solutions, or an infinite number of solutions.

The indifference curves shown in Figures 2.1 and 2.10 are not the only possibilities. For example, Figure 2.2 represents a case where an individual is always indifferent to X_2, but likes X_1. Figure 2.11 illustrates a case where commodity X_2 is disliked—more X_1 is needed to keep the individual indifferent if more X_2 is consumed. The preferences represented here might correspond to the situation where X_2 is a measure of the pollution level and X_1 is all other goods.

The slope of the budget constraint is the negative of the ratio of the prices of the commodities. This is easily seen from the budget equation $P_1 X_1 + P_2 X_2 = M$, which implies $P_1 \Delta X_1 + P_2 \Delta X_2 = \Delta M$. But with money income constant ($\Delta M = 0$), we obtain $\Delta X_2 = (-P_1/P_2)\Delta X_1$ along the budget constraint. Subsequent discussions will repeatedly focus on *relative prices*, i.e., the ratio of one price to another, rather than the absolute level of prices.

Similarly, money income is not the most significant indicator of an individual's ability to purchase goods. When different prices prevail, the same money income may correspond to a very different *real income*. Real income is *money income relative to the level of prices*.

The importance of relative prices and real income can be seen by analyzing the budget constraint. Solving the budget equation for X_2 gives $X_2 = M/P_2 - (P_1/P_2)X_1$. Notice that the absolute level of income and prices never appears. The first term on the right side measures real income (relative

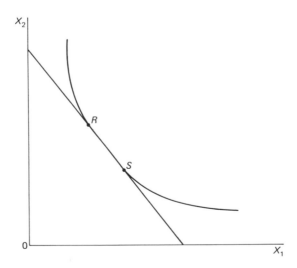

Figure 2.10   A Multiplicity of Optimal Solutions

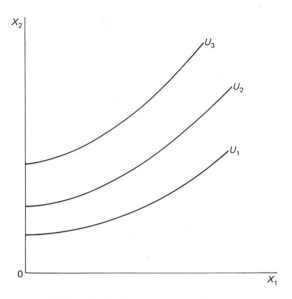

Figure 2.11   Dislike for Commodity X_2

to the price of X_2) and in the second term prices occur only as part of a ratio.

In Figure 2.9 the budget constraint is tangent to the indifference curve at point H, which represents the optimal solution. At this point the slope of the budget constraint is $-P_1/P_2$. The slope of the indifference curve at H is minus the marginal rate of substitution at H. Thus we obtain a fundamental condition which characterizes the optimal solution to this budget problem:[3]

$$\frac{P_1}{P_2} = MRS \qquad (2.5)$$

or, since $MRS = \dfrac{MU_{X_1}}{MU_{X_2}}$,

$$\frac{MU_{X_1}}{P_1} = \frac{MU_{X_2}}{P_2}$$

$$M = P_1 X_1 + P_2 X_2 \qquad (2.6)$$

[3] Using a utility function this problem could be expressed mathematically as

$$\text{Maximize } U(X_1, X_2, \dots, X_n)$$

subject to

$$\sum_{i=1}^{n} P_i X_i \leq M$$

$$X_i \geq 0, \qquad i = 1, \dots, n$$

A particularly elegant way to handle problems of this type is to apply the Kuhn-Tucker

As long as a positive amount of every commodity is consumed, this condition must hold for any optimal market basket. If one or more goods are not consumed in the optimal market basket, then the equality must be replaced by an appropriate inequality.

Although developed in a geometric manner, the condition expressed by Equation (2.5) has a very simple economic interpretation. The left-hand side of the expression is the ratio of the market prices of the two commodities, and therefore the ratio at which quantities of beef could be exchanged for quantities of chicken—a *market exchange rate*. The right-hand side is the marginal rate of substitution, which represents the individual's *subjective exchange rate*. If the equality did not hold for a given market basket, then it would be possible to buy and sell goods at the market prices in such a way as to end up with a market basket on a higher indifference curve. Such a possibility obviously implies that the original market basket could not have been an optimal one.

Theorem for nonlinear programming. This allows one to form a new problem which does not explicitly include constraints by recasting the problem as

$$\phi = U(X_1, \ldots, X_n) - \lambda \left(\sum_{i=1}^{n} P_i X_i - M \right) + \sum_{i=1}^{n} \mu_i X_i$$

and maximizing this with respect to the X_i while minimizing with respect to the Lagrangian multipliers λ and the μ_i. If each $X_i > 0$ at the optimum, then an optimal solution satisfies the conditions.

$$\frac{\partial \phi}{\partial X_i} = \frac{\partial U}{\partial X_i} - \lambda P_i = 0 \qquad i = 1, \ldots, n$$

and with $\lambda > 0$

$$\frac{\partial \phi}{\partial \lambda} = \sum_{i=1}^{n} P_i X_i - M = 0$$

Taking any i and j we have

$$\frac{\partial U}{\partial X_i} - \lambda P_i = 0$$

and

$$\frac{\partial U}{\partial X_j} - \lambda P_j = 0$$

thus

$$\frac{\partial U / \partial X_i}{\partial U / \partial X_j} = \frac{MU_i}{MU_j} = MRS_{i,j} = \frac{P_i}{P_j}$$

which is the same condition developed in the body of the text. Notice that an equivalent way of writing

$$MRS_{i,j} = \frac{P_i}{P_j}$$

is

$$\frac{MU_i}{P_i} = \frac{MU_j}{P_j}$$

for all i and j.

Changing Prices and Changing Market Baskets

Suppose in Figure 2.9 that the price of beef increases to $4 per pound, while the price of chicken remains at $1 per pound and money income remains at $12. What will happen to the optimal market basket of goods?

Increasing the price of beef to $4 affects the budget constraint. Initially the budget constraint was $X_2 = \$12/\$1 - (\$2/\$1)X_1$ while it now has become $X_2 = \$12/\$1 - (\$4/\$1)X_1$. The amount of chicken that could be bought if all income is spent on chicken remains at R (Figure 2.12), but if all income is spent on beef, only 3 pounds can be purchased (point T), although originally $12 would purchase 6 pounds (point S). The original optimum market basket of goods (point H) can no longer be purchased and the new optimum market basket corresponds to point J. Consumption of beef drops from 3 pounds to 2 and consumption of chicken drops from 6 pounds to 4.

What happened to the individual's market basket of goods when the price of beef increased? Faced with an increased price for beef, the best defensive strategy is to substitute commodities which are relatively cheap for those that are relatively expensive. The initial reaction to the price increase is a reduction in the amount of beef purchased, but the market for beef is not the only market that is affected. Even though only the price of beef was

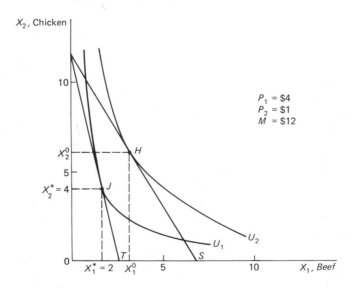

Figure 2.12 Analyzing the Effect of Price Changes

initially changed, there are repercussions in other commodity markets. The consumption of chicken declines even though nothing happened to the price of chicken. The important point to notice is that the quantity of any one commodity consumed depends on *all* prices and income. The next chapter analyzes price change influences in more detail to develop the concept of demand.

Preference Measurement: An Application to Product Design

Even more information can be gleaned from preference rankings of alternative market baskets by the forward-looking management of a firm. Even without considering the use of advertising to sway opinions, we should recognize that market research on individual preferences and the factors influencing them can be an important key to new product design.

Investigation of preferences for different brands shows that each commodity is not viewed as a single entity but rather as a set of attributes. Color, texture, sex appeal, snob appeal, rejuvenating abilities, all play a role.[4] Given a list of a product's attributes, we could determine how an individual would rank it, but it would be still more desirable to know in advance what the characteristics should be to secure a high ranking for the product.

The importance of commodity characteristics is illustrated by the results of a market research study on brand preference and purchase for scouring cleansers and coffee.[5]

The relative weight of each attribute in Table 2.2 is expressed as a percentage of the importance of cleaning ability. Each attribute proved to have a statistically significant impact on preference ranking except harshness. By contrast, in actual purchase decisions only cleansing ability, harshness, and knowledge of price proved to be significant.

Such information is clearly important for marketing and product design decisions. In particular, it might be wiser for a firm to spend more on reducing

Table 2.2   Relative Importance of Scouring Cleanser Attributes

	PACKAGE APPEARANCE	CLEANING ABILITY	GRITTINESS IN USE	HARSHNESS ON HANDS	ODOR	KNOWLEDGE OF PRICE
Preference	0.10	1.00	0.25	0.02	—	0.10
Purchase	0.03	1.00	0.02	0.27	0.14	0.41

[4] This approach was suggested by K. Lancaster. A more detailed discussion of using commodity characteristics as a competitive tool is given in Chapter 12.

[5] Adapted from S. Banks, "Relationships Between Preference and Purchase of Brands," *Journal of Marketing*, 15 (1950), 145–157.

Table 2.3 Relative Importance of Coffee Attributes

	PACKAGE APPEARANCE	FLAVOR	ABILITY TO MAKE MANY CUPS PER LB.	KNOWLEDGE OF PRICE
Preference	0.03	1.00	0.10	0.05
Purchase	0.09	1.00	0.08	0.43

harshness (or playing up mildness to the hands) and to rely less on pretty packages, than initial expressions of consumer preference suggest.

A second study provides interesting data on coffee preferences in Table 2.3. Although preferences appeared to be influenced by all but packaging, purchase decisions were dominated by flavor and knowledge of price.

Each of these examples shows that commodity characteristics play an important role in preferences and ultimate consumption decisions. The potential gains from further knowledge can hardly be ignored. Witness the example of an option-loaded Chevrolet Caprice and a Cadillac. An approximate production cost difference of $300 shows up as a $3,000 difference in market price!

Summary

This chapter has provided a basic introduction to choice problems. The key concepts are the notion of representing preferences by indifference curves or by a utility function, the budget constraint, and the characterization of an optimal solution. Particularly important terms include *marginal rate of substitution, relative prices,* and *real income,* as opposed to nominal or money income.

We noted the empirical study of preferences, their role as determinants of consumption, and the use of preference information in product design decisions and premarket tests.

The next step is to utilize preference information to build the concept of individual demand and draw out its implications. This is the task of the next chapter.

Questions for Study or Class Discussion

1. What difference does it make whether or not preferences depend on commodity prices and income?
2. Suppose that one person's preferences depend on what another person consumes. Could indifference curves be used to represent this situation? Why or why not? How else could it be represented?

3. If an individual's preferences are described by the utility function $U(X_1, X_2) = X_1^2 + 2X_2^2$, graph the indifference curves for $U = 20$ and $U = 40$.
4. Using the data in question 3, find the optimal consumption quantities if $P_1 = \$2.50$, $P_2 = \$7.50$, and $M = \$60$.
5. Do some library research on marketing studies of product design and consumer preferences. List at least five commodity characteristics that appear to influence consumer preference.

References

Friedman, M., and L. J. Savage, "The Utility Analysis of Choices Involving Risk," *Journal of Political Economy*, 56 (August, 1948), 279–294.

Henderson, J. M., and R. E. Quandt, *Microeconomic Theory*, Second Edition. McGraw-Hill, 1971.

Hicks, J. R., *Value and Capital*. Oxford University Press, 1946.

Lancaster, K., "A New Approach to Consumer Theory," *Journal of Political Economy*, 74 (April, 1966), 132–157.

Marshall, A., *Principles of Economics*. Macmillan, 1920.

Samuelson, P. A., *Foundations of Economic Analysis*. Harvard University Press, 1947.

Von Neumann, J., and O. Morgenstern, *Theory of Games and Economic Behavior*. John Wiley & Sons, 1944.

Chapter 3 An Individual's Demand Schedule

Introduction

This chapter develops the basic concept of demand in the context of the choice problem described in Chapter 2. The discussion is couched in terms of the demand for commodities, but virtually all of it is applicable to the demand for assets, including financial assets such as securities, bonds, and money. The individual demand schedule developed here is basic to the market demand concepts presented in the next chapter.

The information contained in individual choices can also be applied to form index numbers, which are widely used to provide summary measures of price changes.[1] Measurement of price changes can be applied to measuring real income. Several examples of this process are given at the end of the chapter.

Individual preferences may change from time to time in either a systematic or a random manner. These changes may add spice and variety to life, but they also introduce uncertainty into a market setting. Consumer demands fluctuate, and as a result selling prices may vary widely. In such a setting information takes on considerable economic importance. This raises interesting questions as to the amount of shopping around that is economically worthwhile, a problem discussed at the end of this chapter.

Individual demand will be significantly influenced by variations in relative prices and money income. This fact is certainly relevant for a firm in choosing its marketing policies. For instance, research may indicate that minor price reductions will substantially enhance sales. On the other hand, if demand is

---

[1] Index numbers are also widely used to measure the volume of production activity.

unresponsive to changes in price, the firm will have to find some other means, perhaps an advertising campaign, to increase sales.

Planning capacity expansion, production scheduling, or inventory growth requires the firm to forecast demand for some time into the future. Alternative forecasts must be made for alternative price policies and for different assumptions about the price policy of competitors. The influence of income growth over time must also be taken into account.

From Choice to the Concept of Demand

The starting point is the individual choice problem discussed in the previous chapter. A family of indifference curves describes an individual's preferences (Figure 3.1) with an initial optimal solution at point A. The optimal market basket consists of X_1^A of beef and X_2^A of chicken. The solution in Figure 3.1 uses three basic pieces of information: (1) individual preferences, (2) the relative prices of commodities, and (3) money income.

Let us begin by developing an individual's *demand schedule* for a particular commodity such as beef. A demand schedule is a list of price and quantity pairs which indicates the quantity an individual would demand at each price. In general, an individual is likely to consume different quantities at different prices.

In Figure 3.1. money income is given at, say, $\overline{M}$ and the price for each commodity is given, say P_1^A and P_2^A. The slope of the budget constraint is the negative of the ratio of the commodity prices, $-P_1^A/P_2^A$. Initially the optimal

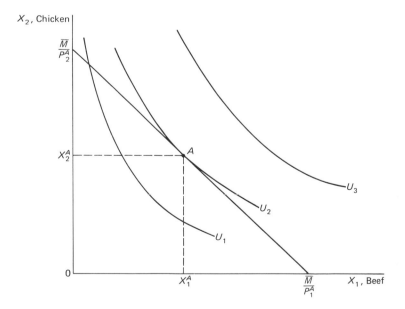

Figure 3.1   Solution of the Fundamental Market Basket Choice Problem

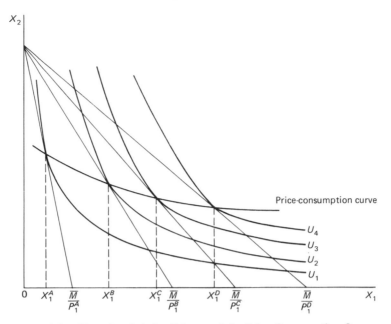

Figure 3.2 Changing Relative Prices and the Price-Consumption Curve

solution is at point A. Suppose now that we successively lower the price of beef and observe how the individual changes his/her choice of market baskets. Decreasing the price of beef to P_1^B results in a new budget constraint represented by the line through B in Figure 3.2. When the price of beef decreases, given a money income of $\overline{M}$, more beef can be purchased if the entire income is spent on beef, but the amount of chicken that can be purchased is unchanged. Therefore the intercept on the vertical axis is still $\overline{M}/P_2^A$ but the slope of the budget constraint is now $-P_1^B/P_2^A$. The intercept on the horizontal axis changes from $\overline{M}/P_1^A$ to $\overline{M}/P_1^B$. The new optimal solution is at B and the new optimal market basket contains X_1^B of beef, while the amount of chicken has fallen to X_2^B. If we repeat this experiment choosing a price even lower than P_1^B, the budget constraint would rotate further so that with a price $P_1^C < P_1^B < P_1^A$ a new optimal solution would arise.

Many replications of the experiment would lead to a series of solutions that might be connected with a curve as in Figure 3.2. The curve connecting the optimal solutions is referred to as the *price-consumption curve*. The price-consumption curve describes the way in which the optimal market basket of goods changes when the price of beef is changed and everything else is held constant. A price-consumption curve describes the way the market basket shifts with changes in the relative price of the commodities. This information may be used to develop an individual's demand schedule.

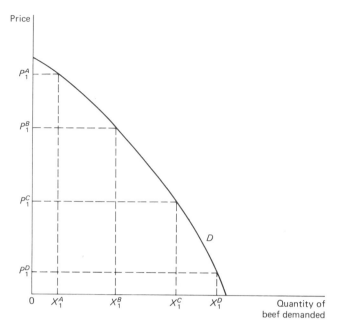

Figure 3.3   Deriving an Individual Demand Curve

Our experiment showed that when the price of beef was P_1^A the individual consumed X_1^A, when the price fell to P_1^B he consumed X_1^B, and when it fell to P_1^C he consumed X_1^C. This information is graphed in Figure 3.3. If the price of beef had been continuously varied, we would have a series of points similar to the curve D in Figure 3.3. This curve is the individual's demand schedule for beef.[2] This schedule depends on four pieces of economic information: (1) the price of beef, (2) the price of chicken, (3) money income, and (4) individual preferences. Changes in prices of commodities other than beef, money income, or preferences will cause the individual demand schedule to shift. Remember that preferences are assumed to be independent of both prices and income.

Notice that if all prices and income are multiplied by a positive quantity both the optimal market basket and the shape of the demand curve remain

---

[2] The demand schedules for each of n commodities can be directly obtained from the solution of the system of equations shown in footnote 3 of Chapter 2. In general, these solutions can be written

$$Q_i = D_i(p_1, \ldots, p_n, M)$$

to indicate that the quantity demanded for each commodity is dependent on *all* prices and income. Since the $n + 1$ equation system is generally nonlinear, the Implicit Function Theorem states the conditions under which it is legitimate to express the Q_i in terms of $p_1, \ldots, p_n$ and M.

unchanged. This again emphasizes the importance of relative prices and real income rather than the absolute level of prices and money income.[3]

Analyzing the Effect of Income Changes

Now let us use the basic choice problem to see how consumption of beef is affected by changes in money income.

If P_1 and P_2 are held constant and money income is increased, how would that change the solution in Figure 3.1? The effect of successive income increases is geometrically represented by a sequence of parallel budget constraints at successively greater distances from the origin. Successive decreases in money income would appear as a successive parallel shift of the budget constraint toward the origin. The shifts are parallel because the slope of the budget constraint is the negative of the ratio of the prices, which are presumed to be constant.

Each level of income determines a new optimal market basket, as represented by points *A*, *B*, *C*, and *D* in Figure 3.4. This leads to a sequence of market baskets which can be represented by a curve such as $\widehat{FF'}$. This curve

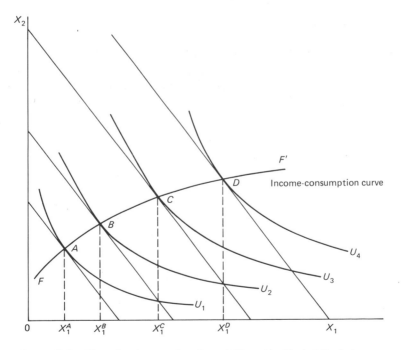

Figure 3.4 Changing Income Levels and Changing Market Baskets

[3] In more technical language demand functions are said to be "homogeneous of degree zero" in prices and income.

is called the *income-consumption curve*. The income-consumption curve describes the way in which the optimal market basket of goods changes when money income changes and relative prices are held constant. As income changes, the proportions of each commodity in the market basket generally change as well as the amounts of each commodity that are purchased.

The income consumption curve is particularly important for forecasting purposes because it allows us to form forecasts of future consumption from forecasts of income and prices. The manner in which the demand for a commodity changes as income changes is summarized in Figure 3.5. In Figure 3.4, the point A is associated with a certain money income M^A, and the individual's optimal consumption was X_1^A. At point B, corresponding to a higher level of money income M^B, optimal consumption rises to X_1^B. The same thing occurs for points C and D. Plotting these points leads to a curve such as $\widehat{HH'}$ in Figure 3.5. This curve is called an *Engel curve*. An Engel curve is a description of the manner in which the optimal consumption of a particular commodity changes as money income changes while relative prices are held constant. The Engel curve for chicken could be constructed in a similar manner.

Normal and Inferior Goods

There are several possible shapes for an Engel curve. In Figure 3.5 the curve slopes upward, indicating that increases in money income are associated with increases in consumption of the commodity. A commodity with an Engel curve like the one in Figure 3.5 (or with a vertical Engel curve, implying that

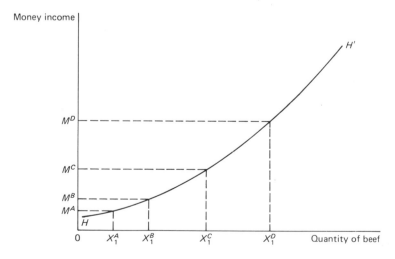

Figure 3.5   Derivation of an Engel Curve

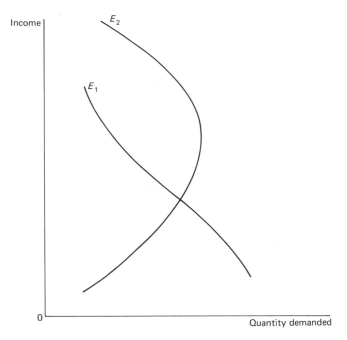

Figure 3.6   Normal and Inferior Ranges of an Engel Curve

increases in money income have no effect on consumption) is referred to as being a *normal* commodity for that range of income. If the Engel curve slopes downward, like the curve E_1 in Figure 3.6, this means that as an individual's money income increases consumption of the commodity decreases, if relative prices are held constant. Commodities with Engel curves like E_1 are said to be *inferior* commodities for that range of income. A commodity may, of course, be normal with respect to some income levels and inferior with respect to other income levels. Such a situation is represented by the Engel curve E_2 in Figure 3.6. For example, margarine would be inferior with respect to income if rising money incomes lead people to purchase butter instead. Yet at very low income levels margarine may be normal with respect to income.

"Normal" and "inferior" are, of course, technical terms and do not imply anything about the physical nature of the commodity.

Analyzing the Effect of Price Changes

The ultimate influence on consumption of any price change depends on two basic effects. The change in consumption caused by change in the relative price of a commodity when real income is held constant is called the *substitution effect*. The *income effect* is the change in the consumption of a commodity caused by a change in real income, when relative prices are held constant.

Consider the reaction to a decrease in the price of a particular commodity such as beef. From market observations, we might determine how much beef was consumed last week at a price of $2.25 per pound. This week, at a price of $2.15 per pound, a new quantity of beef purchases is observed, which we would expect to be larger than last week's purchases. But because there are two forces at work, this will not necessarily be the case.

When the price of beef decreases while the price of chicken stays the same, beef becomes cheaper not only in an absolute sense, but also, more importantly, in a relative sense. But in addition the reduction in the price of beef has increased the consumer's purchasing power. An individual can buy more beef with the same income. In other words, while nominal or money income stays the same, real income has increased. Real income may increase in several ways: (1) money income may increase while prices stay the same, (2) money income may remain constant while prices fall, (3) the rate of decrease in prices may be greater than the rate of decrease in money income, or (4) the rate of increase in money income may be greater than the rate of increase in prices. This latter situation is probably the most common way in which real income increases, since prices generally rise over time.

In Figure 3.7 the change in the relative price of beef is reflected in the

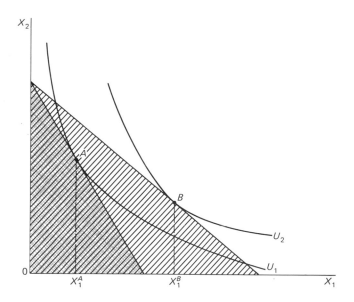

Figure 3.7   Changes in Relative Prices and Changes in Real Income

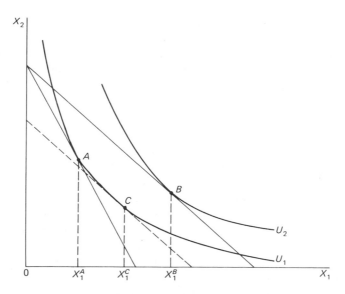

Figure 3.8   Income and Substitution Effects When X_1 Is Normal

difference between the slopes of the budget constraints through A and B. But the fall in the price of beef also means that while initially the consumer could purchase only the market baskets in the shaded area, now, with the same money income, any of the market baskets in the crosshatched area as well can be purchased. This increased choice reflects the increase in real income. How will these two influences—a change in relative prices and a change in real income—affect consumer behavior?

To determine the substitution effect we must ask what the individual would have purchased if confronted with the relative prices resulting from the price change, but with the same real income as before. Suppose this real income is that received at point A in Figure 3.8. It will remain constant so long as the individual achieves the same level of satisfaction; that is, so long as he/she can still purchase a market basket lying on indifference curve U_1. What purchases will the consumer now make if confronted with the set of prices prevailing at B?

To answer this question we draw a budget constraint parallel to the one through B, and tangent to the indifference curve U_1 at point C. Since the slope of the budget constraint through B is the same as the one through C, the consumer is being confronted with the same set of relative prices. The only difference is that at point C the individual has a lower real income. The change in consumption between points A and C, X_1^A and X_1^C respectively, arises solely from the difference in relative prices, since real income is constant. This change is the substitution effect. When beef becomes relatively cheaper, less chicken and more beef is consumed, if real income is constant. By contrast, a change in consumption from X_1^C to X_1^B would be associated with an increase in real income when relative prices are constant. This is the income effect arising from the price change. The total effect $(X_1^B - X_1^A)$ observed in the market data is thus the sum of the income effect $(X_1^B - X_1^C)$ and the substitution effect $(X_1^C - X_1^A)$.

For indifference curves shaped like those in Figure 3.8, the sign of the change in consumption due to the substitution effect will always be opposite to the sign of the change in price, i.e., $\Delta X_1 \cdot \Delta P_1 \leq 0$. The substitution effect reflects the fact that increases in the relative price of a commodity lead to decreases or no change in quantity demanded and decreases in the relative price lead to increases or no change in quantity demanded. Does this mean that if we decrease the price of a commodity, the observed quantity demanded will always increase? The answer is no. We have to consider the income effect.

As we learned earlier, if an increase in income leads to an increase in quantity demanded or to no change in quantity demanded, a commodity is said to be normal in that income range. If an increase in income leads to a decrease in quantity demanded, then the commodity is said to be inferior in that income range. Figure 3.9 illustrates a case in which commodity X_1 is inferior with respect to income. The substitution effect alone would lead to an increase in consumption to X_1^C, but the influence of the income effect

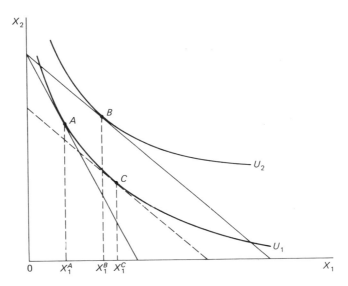

Figure 3.9   Income and Substitution Effects When X_1 Is Inferior

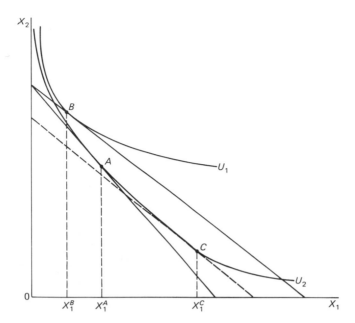

Figure 3.10   Income and Substitution Effects When X_1 Is a
Giffen Good

reduces this to X_1^B. Since the decrease in price is still associated with an increase in quantity demanded, the individual's demand schedule will still
slope downward.

If the income effect is negative and large enough to cancel out the substitution effect, a decrease in price could actually lead to a decrease in the
quantity demanded. This possibility is referred to as the Giffen Case and is
illustrated in Figure 3.10. While the upward-sloping demand schedule that
would arise in this situation is not likely to result from actual market data,
the possibility of its occurrence emphasizes the importance of separating the
income and substitution effects.

The relation of the actual demand schedule to the demand schedule based
only on the substitution effect can be seen in Figure 3.11. If the price of beef
decreases and beef is a normal commodity throughout the relevant income
range, the substitution effect leads to an increase in the consumption of
beef and the income effect causes a further increase. If the price of beef
decreases and beef is an inferior commodity throughout the relevant income
range, then the income effect will have a negative influence on consumption.

It is important to a firm to know whether a commodity is normal or
inferior. If one of its products is inferior, then as consumer income rises over

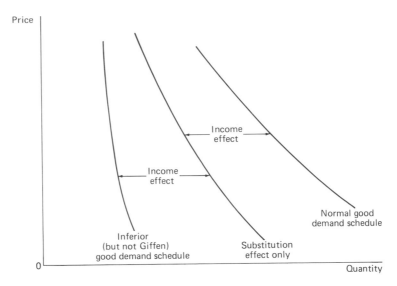

Figure 3.11   Demand Schedules With and Without Income Effects

time the firm will not be able to grow. In addition, failure to recognize income effects could cause major discrepancies between realized sales and estimates.

Consumers' Surplus: A Measure of Maximum Market Value

The maximum price per unit that an individual is willing to pay for a product, as revealed by his/her demand schedule, is certainly an important piece of information for a firm. However, problems in the public sector—transportation, recreation areas, flood control, etc.—frequently do not involve a market in which price can be used as a measurement. The concept of *consumers' surplus* is frequently employed to fill this information gap. Though criticisms of this concept have been many and varied, its recurrent use makes it worthwhile to consider it here.

In Figure 3.12, at the price P^0 an individual purchases Q^0 and pays P^0Q^0. From this we know the quantity Q^0 is valued implicitly at not less than P^0Q^0. But what is its maximum value? Suppose that instead of selling at a constant price, we were to ask the maximum price for the first unit, then the maximum price for the second, etc., moving down the demand schedule D shown in Figure 3.12. For each increment in quantity ΔQ_i we would obtain the maximum price P_1, P_2, etc. Ultimately we would receive a total sum represented by the area under the demand schedule from the origin to Q^0, assuming that any income effect could be ignored. Consumers' surplus is the excess of this total over the amount a firm receives, or, expressed in terms of the areas shown in Figure 3.12, consumers' surplus $= OABQ^0 - OP^0BQ^0 = P^0AB$.

One of the earliest applications of consumers' surplus was to determine the economic feasibility of building a bridge. Presumably the project is worthwhile only if the market value of the services provided by the bridge exceeds its construction cost. If the bridge is built by a private firm which will charge tolls to recover its costs, the only relevant measure of market value is the proceeds that will actually be received by the firm. On the other hand, public authorities frequently estimate market value by adding consumers' surplus to the sums recoverable as tolls. This distinction in investment criteria reflects the fact that the private firm ordinarily cannot afford to incur losses, while a public authority may plan on recovering the costs unrecoverable as tolls from other sources.

It must be remembered that the demand curve used to calculate consumers' surplus must describe marginal, not average, willingness to pay. The measurement of this margin can present substantial difficulties, so that the concept of consumers' surplus should always be applied with caution.

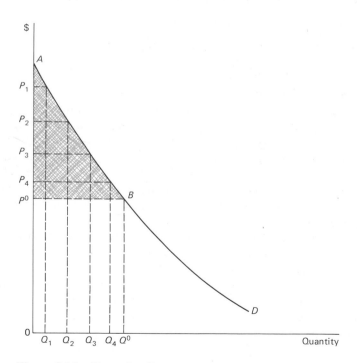

Figure 3.12   **Measuring Consumers' Surplus**

Revealed Preference and Cost of Living Price Indices: An Application

Observations of market prices, incomes, and the market basket of goods chosen by consumers are used to measure price changes, and thus to form measurements of real income. The following discussion of price indices is based on a *revealed preference* approach to demand. Revealed preference is a relatively simple concept with much of the analytic power of more complex mathematical approaches.

To define the meaning of revealed preference, let X_i^0 represent the amount of commodity i purchased when prices $P_1^0, P_2^0, \ldots, P_n^0$ prevail and X_i^1 represent the amount of commodity i purchased when prices $P_1^1, P_2^1, \ldots, P_n^1$ prevail. The market basket X^1 is *revealed preferred* to the market basket X^0 if the individual could have purchased the market basket X^0 at the price P^1, but could *not* have purchased the market basket X^1 at the price P^0. That is, X^1 is revealed preferred to X^0 if

$$\sum_{i=1}^n P_i^1 X_i^1 \geq \sum_{i=1}^n P_i^1 X_i^0 \quad \text{and} \quad \sum_{i=1}^n P_i^0 X_i^0 < \sum_{i=1}^n P_i^0 X_i^1.$$

(The symbol $\sum$ is used algebraically to represent the sum of all terms of a given form. Thus $\sum_{i=1}^n P_i X_i = P_1 X_1 + P_2 X_2 + \cdots + P_n X_n$. For $n = 2$, $\sum_{i=1}^2 P_i^0 X_i^0 = P_1^0 X_1^0 + P_2^0 X_2^0$.) Instead of repeating the subscript notation $i = 1, \ldots, n$ and writing $\sum_{i=1}^n$ in the following discussion we shall simply write $\sum$ and omit the subscripts on prices and quantities.

Since each of the sums $\sum P^0 X^0$ and $\sum P^1 X^0$ represent total money income expended, they can be used to sketch the indifference curves representing the preferences that gave rise to the market observations on which the sums are based. A simple example is given in Figure 3.13. In addition, the basic properties of demand schedules can be derived by using the revealed preference as well as by the preference utility approach used in Chapter 2. Revealed preference also provides a direct route to an important application— measurement by means of index numbers.

A *price index* is a scale which compares the amounts spent to purchase a given quantity of goods at price levels occurring at different points in time. Let us call two such price levels P^0 and P^1.

The two well-known methods used for constructing price indices differ in their choice of the given quantity of goods whose cost at the different price levels is to be compared. The Paasche price index uses the quantity choices observed in the later period, i.e., X_i^1, as the given quantity of goods, and is defined as

$$P = \frac{\sum P^0 X^1}{\sum P^1 X^1} \tag{3.1}$$

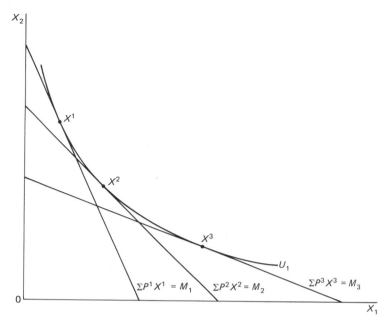

Figure 3.13 Revealed Preference as a Vehicle for Mapping Preferences

In contrast, the Laspeyre price index uses the quantity choices observed in the initial period, i.e., X_i^0, as the given quantity of goods, and is defined as

$$L = \frac{\sum P^1 X^0}{\sum P^0 X^0} \tag{3.2}$$

These two price indices may be used to determine whether or not an individual is better off in the second situation than in the first. Three basic assumptions are made: (1) comparisons refer to a single individual, (2) preferences are the same in both instances, and (3) quality and characteristics of the commodities have not changed.

We shall consider the implications of the Paasche and Laspeyre indices in four cases:

Case 1: Suppose an individual could have purchased X^0 at the prices P^1 but instead purchased X^1, while X^1 could not have been purchased at the prices P^0. This situation is described by the relationships

$$\sum P^1 X^1 > \sum P^1 X^0 \tag{3.3}$$

and

$$\sum P^0 X^0 < \sum P^0 X^1 \tag{3.4}$$

Dividing Inequality (3.3) by $\sum P^0 X^0$ gives

$$\frac{\sum P^1 X^1}{\sum P^0 X^0} > \frac{\sum P^1 X^0}{\sum P^0 X^0} = L \qquad (3.5)$$

and dividing Inequality (3.4) by $\sum P^1 X^1$ gives

$$\frac{\sum P^0 X^0}{\sum P^1 X^1} < \frac{\sum P^0 X^1}{\sum P^1 X^1} = P \qquad (3.6)$$

or

$$\frac{\sum P^1 X^1}{\sum P^0 X^0} > \frac{1}{P} \qquad (3.7)$$

By definition the individual is better off at time 1. From Inequalities (3.5) and (3.7) we can see that this would occur if

$$\frac{\sum P^1 X^1}{\sum P^0 X^0} > L \qquad (3.8)$$

and

$$\frac{\sum P^1 X^1}{\sum P^0 X^0} > \frac{1}{P} \qquad (3.9)$$

Case 2: Now suppose that X^1 can be purchased at price level P^1 but X^0 cannot, while either X^0 or X^1 could have been purchased at P^0. These relationships are represented by

$$\sum P^1 X^1 < \sum P^1 X^0 \qquad (3.10)$$

and

$$\sum P^0 X^0 \geq \sum P^0 X^1 \qquad (3.11)$$

Dividing Inequality (3.10) by $\sum P^0 X^0$ gives

$$\frac{\sum P^1 X^1}{\sum P^0 X^0} < \frac{\sum P^1 X^0}{\sum P^0 X^0} = L \qquad (3.12)$$

and dividing Inequality (3.11) by $\sum P^1 X^1$ gives

$$\frac{\sum P^0 X^0}{\sum P^1 X^1} \geq \frac{\sum P^0 X^1}{\sum P^1 X^1} = P \qquad (3.13)$$

or

$$\frac{\sum P^1 X^1}{\sum P^0 X^0} \leq \frac{1}{P} \qquad (3.14)$$

Here the individual is worse off when prices are at P^1. In terms of the indices this occurs when

$$\frac{\sum P^1 X^1}{\sum P^0 X^0} < L \qquad (3.15)$$

and

$$\frac{\sum P^1 X^0}{\sum P^0 X^0} < \frac{1}{P} \tag{3.16}$$

Case 3: Suppose at P^1 prices the individual can afford the market basket X^1 but could not purchase the market basket X^0, while at P^0 prices he/she can purchase X^0 but not X^1. These conditions are represented as

$$\sum P^0 X^0 < \sum P^0 X^1 \tag{3.17}$$

and

$$\sum P^1 X^1 < \sum P^1 X^0 \tag{3.18}$$

Dividing Inequality (3.17) by $\sum P^1 X^1$ gives

$$\frac{\sum P^0 X^0}{\sum P^1 X^1} < \frac{\sum P^0 X^1}{\sum P^1 X^1} = P \tag{3.19}$$

or

$$\frac{\sum P^1 X^1}{\sum P^0 X^0} > \frac{1}{P} \tag{3.20}$$

while dividing Inequality (3.18) by $\sum P^0 X^0$ gives

$$\frac{\sum P^1 X^1}{\sum P^0 X^0} < \frac{\sum P^1 X^0}{\sum P^0 X^0} = L \tag{3.21}$$

This situation gives us no information about real income since in both situations the individual purchased the cheaper market basket of goods and could not afford the other. In terms of the price indices this occurs when

$$L > \frac{\sum P^1 X^1}{\sum P^0 X^0} > \frac{1}{P} \tag{3.22}$$

Case 4: In this situation the individual purchases X^1 at P^1 prices but could also have purchased X^0, while he/she purchases X^0 at P^0 prices, but could also have purchased X^1. These conditions are represented as

$$\sum P^1 X^1 \geq \sum P^1 X^0 \tag{3.23}$$

and

$$\sum P^0 X^0 \geq \sum P^0 X^1 \tag{3.24}$$

Dividing Inequality (3.23) by $\sum P^0 X^0$ gives

$$\frac{\sum P^1 X^1}{\sum P^0 X^0} \geq \frac{\sum P^1 X^0}{\sum P^0 X^0} = L \tag{3.25}$$

while dividing Inequality (3.24) by $\sum P^1 X^1$ gives

$$\frac{\sum P^0 X^0}{\sum P^1 X^1} \geq \frac{\sum P^0 X^1}{\sum P^1 X^1} = P \tag{3.26}$$

or

$$\frac{\sum P^1 X^1}{\sum P^0 X^0} \leq \frac{1}{P} \tag{3.27}$$

As in Case 3, no conclusive information is obtainable, since the individual apparently considers X^0 and X^1 equally desirable, or else has chosen the more expensive market basket. This occurs when

$$\frac{1}{P} \geq \frac{\sum P^1 X^1}{\sum P^0 X^0} \geq L \tag{3.28}$$

A relationship like Inequality (3.28) suggests either that the consumer's tastes changed, that he/she made an error in choice, or that he/she failed to choose the preferred market basket for some other reason.

Real income measurement is probably the most widely used application for price indices. Newspapers regularly carry reports of both the Consumer Price Index (CPI) and the Wholesale Price Index (WPI). Recent values for these indices are shown in Table 3.1. Each entry in the table shows the average percentage change in prices over those in the base year (1967). For example, the 1972 CPI of 127.3 means that prices rose approximately 27.3% from 1967 to 1972.

Wages, of course, also change over time. Changes in real income, i.e., wages adjusted for price changes, can be estimated by using a price index such as the CPI to "deflate" money wages. Table 3.2 shows average weekly nonagricultural wages for the United States, both in nominal or money terms and in real terms. (The real wage is the nominal wage divided by the CPI, times 100.)

The distinction between money and real wages obviously is an important one. Although money wages rose 28% from 1968 to 1972, real wages rose only 3%. In addition, even though money wages rose from 1968 to 1971, real wages remained virtually unchanged.

Table 3.1   Recent Consumer and Wholesale Price Indices[a]

PERIOD	CPI	WPI
1968	104.2	102.5
1969	109.8	106.5
1970	116.3	110.4
1971	121.3	113.9
1972	127.3	122.9

SOURCE: *Federal Reserve Bulletin*, December, 1973.
[a] 1967 is the base period, i.e., 1967 = 100.0.

Table 3.2   Nominal and Real Wage Rates

	MONEY WAGE	REAL WAGE
1968	$107.73	$103.39
1969	114.61	104.38
1970	119.46	102.72
1971	126.91	104.62
1972	135.78	106.66

SOURCE: *Monthly Labor Review*, December, 1973.

*Uncertain Prices, Market Search, and Random Demand

Information is a vital ingredient of any decision problem—choosing a mix of goods for consumption is no exception. In the foregoing discussion we have implicitly assumed that we knew the prices of each commodity and the individual's income and preferences. Individuals may be presumed to know their likes and dislikes as well as their income, so that our information about these factors can be fairly definite. But prices are another matter. Different sellers offer the same commodity at prices which may differ widely. This is particularly true of consumer durable goods, such as televisions, cars, and major household applicances. The intelligent consumer must therefore adopt a more complicated decision process, based on an information gathering process or *search procedure*.[4] To understand the potential gain from search in an uncertain setting, suppose half the sellers charge $2 and half charge $3 for an item, but it is not initially known which sellers sell at which price. After a consumer visits one store chosen at random the average minimum purchase price expected will be $2.50, since the probabilities are 0.50 and 0.50 that the price found will be $2 or $3. After a second sampling the average expected minimum price will fall to $2.25. Table 3.3 illustrates the results of a hypothetical search. Notice that the rate of decrease in the expected minimum purchase price decreases as the search is extended. The potential gain from searching further successively diminishes.

Searching, however, incurs costs in gasoline, oil, telephone calls, etc. The mere expenditure of time puts a limit on the feasibility of a prolonged search.[5] One rule is to continue the search as long as the added cost of

* Optional material requiring knowledge of probability.
[4] See G. Stigler, "The Economics of Information," *Journal of Political Economy*, 69 (June, 1961), 213, for a more detailed discussion.
[5] Notice that a wealthy individual might pay more because the value of his time makes it uneconomical to spend much time searching.

Table 3.3 Expected Average Minimum Purchase Price

NO. OF SELLERS CHECKED	AVERAGE EXPECTED MINIMUM PRICE
1	$2.50
2	2.25
3	2.125
4	2.062
5	2.00

SOURCE: G. Stigler, "The Economics of Information."

further searching is less than the additional gain to be expected from further searching. Noting that new entrants into markets (e.g., young people) are typically at a disadvantage because they lack information, one author[6] states that

> ... inexperienced buyers (tourists) pay higher prices in a market than do experienced buyers ... and the prices paid by inexperienced buyers will also have a larger variance.

Even if price remains constant, preference uncertainty or income changes can convert a stable demand schedule like the one in Figure 3.3 into a random phenomenon. A given price will not result in a fixed quantity demanded, but rather in a range of quantities whose likelihood of occurrence might be described by a probability density function.

As an example, suppose quantity demanded is given by $D_i(p_i, \ldots, p_n, M) = \bar{D}_i(p_i, \ldots, p_n, M) + u_i$ where $\bar{D}_i$ is the mean (i.e., expected) value of D_i and u_i is a random variable with mean zero and variance σ_i^2. Figure 3.14 illustrates one example of demand volatility. Volatility of this kind, which may be produced by a lack of consumer information as well as other causes, has far-reaching implications for policy questions such as price stability. Uncertain demand prospects also radically affect pricing and production problems for firms. These influences will be explored in detail in Chapters 9–13.

Summary

This chapter has shown how the information used in the solution of an individual choice problem can be used to develop an individual's demand schedule. Both the price-consumption curve and the income-consumption

[6] G. Stigler, *ibid.*

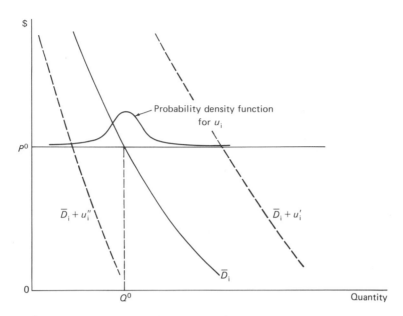

Figure 3.14 An Example of Random Demand

curve describe the influence of basic economic variables on the market basket of goods actually chosen.

Substitution and income effects are basic concepts for analyzing the influence of price changes. With real income held constant, changes in price lead to changes in consumption in the opposite direction. Income changes, relative prices constant, can lead to changes in consumption in the same direction (for normal goods) or to changes in consumption in the opposite direction (for inferior goods).

Index numbers are an important measuring device arising from observed market choices. Perhaps the best-known examples are the cost of living index or Consumer Price Index (CPI) frequently reported in newspapers. The Wholesale Price Index (WPI) reflects the prices of raw materials and other production inputs.

Finally, we observed the significant influence of uncertainty and information on decision processes. The example of price uncertainty and search has a parallel in labor markets in the form of job search and its implications for unemployment, which will be developed in more detail in Chapters 14 and 15.

The next chapter builds on the concepts introduced so far to develop the theory of market demand and then explores the nature of market demand data and its interpretation.

Questions for Study or Class Discussion

1. Why is the concept of real income important? How does it relate to an individual's lifetime financial planning and ultimate retirement?
2. Look up index numbers in the library. List both pitfalls and conveniences associated with index numbers.
3. Collect data on income according to age, sex, years of education, or some other variable. Compute real income and compare it to nominal income over a period of years.
4. How many different ways can you think of to introduce uncertainty into the consumer choice problem? How would you try to solve a decision problem in the face of uncertainty?
5. If information that crucially effects decisions is imperfect, what is the economic value of information? How does your answer accord with your concept of the information that should be used when making commodity purchases or stock or bond purchases?

References

Hicks, J. R., *A Revision of Demand Theory*. Oxford University Press, 1956.

Horowitz, I., *Decision Making and the Theory of the Firm*. Holt, Rinehart and Winston, 1970.

Marshall, A., *Principles of Economics*. Macmillan, 1920.

Stigler, G., "The Economics of Information," *Journal of Political Economy*, 69 (June, 1961), 213–225.

Chapter 4 Market Demand and Its Measurement

Introduction

In the previous two chapters we used a description of an individual's preferences and a budget constraint based on an initial set of prices and money income to solve the problem of choosing among alternative consumption patterns. After allowing one of the prices to vary, we observed the way an individual's choice of a market basket changed as price changed and this information was used to build up the individual's demand schedule for a commodity.

For each price, the individual's demand schedule indicates the quantity of a commodity that an individual demands at that price, given his/her money income and the prices of all other goods. Each individual's demand schedule provides a part of the information needed to determine the aggregate market demand for all purchasers.

The concept of elasticity provides a convenient way of summarizing important pieces of information concerning market demand. After defining and illustrating this concept, this chapter takes up empirical demand measurement and the interpretations of the resulting estimates.

Building the Market Demand Schedule

Let us assume that the individual demand schedules for beef of three consumers are represented by D_1, D_2, and D_3 in Figure 4.1. The corresponding numerical data is given in Table 4.1.

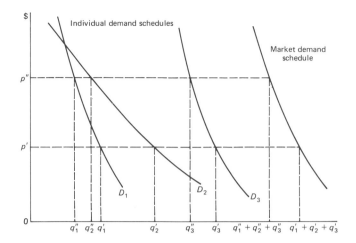

Figure 4.1   Forming Market Demand from Individual Demand

To construct the market demand schedule, we ask: at each price, how much will each individual demand? Starting at the price p', individual 1 will demand q'_1. At the same price, individual 2 will demand q'_2 and individual 3 will demand q'_3. The market demand at the price p' is simply the sum of what all individuals demand, i.e., $q'_1 + q'_2 + q'_3$. The price p' and the quantity $q'_1 + q'_2 + q'_3$ represent one point on the market demand schedule for beef. If we repeat the experiment at a price p'', the sum of the individual quantities demanded would be $q''_1 + q''_2 + q''_3$. This provides a second point on the market demand schedule for beef. Repeated at each price these steps provide the whole market demand schedule.[1]

Table 4.1   From Individual Demand for Beef to Market Demand: A Numerical Example

PRICES PER POUND OF BEEF	QUANTITY OF BEEF DEMANDED BY INDIVIDUAL 1	QUANTITY OF BEEF DEMANDED BY INDIVIDUAL 2	QUANTITY OF BEEF DEMANDED BY INDIVIDUAL 3	MARKET DEMAND FOR BEEF IN POUNDS PER WEEK
0.75	10	11.5	8	29.5
0.90	9	10.5	7.75	27.25
1.00	8	9	7.5	24.5
1.25	7.5	8.5	7	23
1.65	6	8	6.75	20.75
1.85	4	7.5	6.5	18
2.10	2	6	6	14

[1] In slightly more formal style one could begin with the demand schedule of the ith individual given by $D_i(p_1, p_2, \ldots, p_n, M_i)$ and obtain the market demand schedule for the jth commodity from

$$D_j(p_1, p_2, \ldots, p_j, \ldots, p_n, M_1, M_2, \ldots, M_r) = \sum_{i=1}^{r} D_i(p_1, \ldots, p_j, \ldots, p_n, M_i)$$

where r is the number of consumers in the market.

Since the market demand schedule is built up from individual demand schedules, it follows that the major factors affecting market demand are: (1) the preferences of each consumer, (2) the prices of all commodities, (3) total income, and (4) the distribution of total income among individuals.

So far we have assumed that each individual's preferences are independent of the consumption of other individuals as well as independent of prices and income. A keeping-up-with-the-Joneses factor can be incorporated without changing the basic theoretical development outlined in Chapters 2 and 3. The resulting interdependence effect is also referred to as a snob appeal, bandwagon, or Veblen[2] effect. The formal simplicity of adding individual demand curves, as shown in Figure 4.1 and Table 4.1, is no longer possible, but all other essential aspects of market demand remain intact. When random elements exist, they may introduce a similar aggregation problem.

There is an important distinction between two concepts related to demand schedules: the term *quantity demanded* and the term *demand. Change in quantity demanded* refers to the change in quantity associated with a change in price on an existing demand schedule. *Change in demand,* on the other hand, refers to a shift in the whole schedule. If there is a change in total money income or its distribution or in the prices of other commodities, this typically leads to a change in demand—a shift in the whole schedule. Changes in the price of beef alone will not cause the demand for beef to change—only the quantity demanded changes.

A Numerical Example of Choosing a Commodity to Tax

Recently excise taxes have been suggested as one method of rationing petroleum to alleviate possible energy crises. Customs duties, sales taxes, and gasoline taxes are examples of current excise taxes.

There are two principal reasons for taxing a particular commodity. One is to reduce consumption below the level set by its current market price. This might be done to conserve scarce resources or for considerations relating to ethics, morals, or health, as is allegedly true of the taxes on alcohol and tobacco. The other reason is to raise revenue. The success of the tax in either case will obviously depend upon its effect on the quantity demanded of the given commodity. A commodity suitable for raising revenue will have a demand schedule different from that of a commodity whose consumption would be curtailed by the use of excise taxes. This can be illustrated by a numerical example. Suppose the demand schedule for commodity A is $D_A = 400 - 5P_A$ and the demand schedule for commodity B is $D_B = 800 - 40P_B$ (Figure 4.2). Assume the price of commodity A is initially \$5, the price of commodity B is initially \$10, and only one of these commodities

[2] An extended discussion of a theory of consumption built explicitly on interdependent preferences is available in T. Veblen, *The Theory of the Leisure Class.*

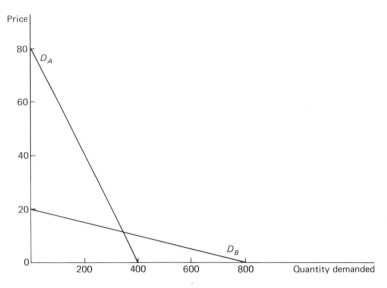

Figure 4.2 Which Commodity to Tax?

can be taxed. One form of excise tax requires payment of a certain amount per physical unit. This type of excise tax is used on gasoline (4¢ per gallon) and cigarettes (approximately 10¢ per package). In addition, suppose that when we levy the tax on either commodity the new prices would be $1 higher than they were initially, thus P_A would be $6 and P_B would be $11. At the pre-tax prices, consumption is 375 units for commodity A and 400 units for commodity B.

If the object of levying this tax is to collect revenue and the tax rate per unit is the same in both markets, then at first glance it might appear desirable to put the tax on commodity B, since its quantity demanded is greater. However, when the tax is levied the response of consumers to a change in price is not the same for both commodities. Raising the price by $1 in both markets causes the quantity demanded of A to decrease by only 5 units while the quantity demanded of B falls to 360—a decrease of 40 units. Commodity A should be taxed, since revenues would be greater ($370 from taxing A as opposed to $360 from taxing B).

Knowledge of the demand schedules was used here in order to determine which commodity to tax, but the basic economic concept which reflects the crucial response element is *elasticity of demand*.

Elasticity: A Key Working Tool

How fast does quantity demanded change with price? How fast does demand change when income changes? The elasticity concept provides the answers.

Such answers can be used for forecasting, for making decisions about price changes as a marketing policy, or for appraising the potential threat of a competitor's marketing policies.

A *demand relationship* indicates that the quantity demanded of commodity A depends on the price of commodity A, the price of other commodities, and money income. The three elasticity concepts which measure the influence of these factors are: (1) the *own-price elasticity* of demand, i.e., elasticity with respect to changes in the price of the commodity itself; for example, the change in demand for gasoline resulting from changes in the price of gasoline, (2) the *cross-price elasticity* of demand for commodity A resulting from changes in the prices of other commodities, and (3) the elasticity of demand with respect to changes in income.

The own-price elasticity of demand is defined as the percentage change in quantity demanded divided by the percentage change in price.

$$\eta_{A,A} = \frac{\% \text{ change in quantity demanded of commodity A}}{\% \text{ change in price of commodity A}} \tag{4.1}$$

or

$$\eta_{A,A} = \frac{\Delta D_A / D_A}{\Delta P_A / P_A} = \frac{\Delta D_A}{\Delta P_A} \cdot \frac{P_A}{D_A} \tag{4.2}$$

ΔD_A represents the change in the quantity demanded of commodity A. Notice that the slope of the demand schedule (as typically graphed) is the change in price divided by the change in quantity, thus the first factor in the elasticity expression is just the reciprocal of the slope of the demand schedule. The second factor in the elasticity expression is determined by the particular point at which the elasticity is calculated. Along any given demand schedule elasticity will in general change. If $\eta_{A,A} = -2.3$ this means that a 1% decrease in the price of commodity A would lead to a 2.3% increase in the quantity demanded for A. Alternatively, a 1% increase in P_A would lead to a 2.3% decrease in quantity demanded.

The cross-price elasticity of demand is defined[3] as

$$\eta_{A,B} = \frac{\% \text{ change in quantity demanded of commodity A}}{\% \text{ change in price of commodity B}} \tag{4.3}$$

or

$$\eta_{A,B} = \frac{\Delta D_A / D_A}{\Delta P_B / P_B} = \frac{\Delta D_A}{\Delta P_B} \cdot \frac{P_B}{D_A} \tag{4.4}$$

If $\eta_{A,B} = +1.5$ this would be interpreted by saying that a 1% decrease (increase) in the price of commodity B would lead to a 1.5% decrease (increase)

---

[3] There are two conventions for defining price elasticity and cross-price elasticity—one uses the definitions given by Equations (4.1) and (4.3) and the other defines these elasticities as the negative of the same quantities. The interpretation and use is the same; simply choose one definition and apply it consistently.

in the quantity demanded for commodity A. Cross-price elasticities are of particular interest to a firm where price competition plays an important role in marketing because they provide a way of judging the economic impact of price changes made by another firm.

In a similar manner, the income elasticity[4] of demand is defined as

$$\eta_{A,M} = \frac{\% \text{ of change in quantity demanded of commodity A}}{\% \text{ of change in money income}} \tag{4.5}$$

or

$$\eta_{A,M} = \frac{\Delta D_A / D_A}{\Delta M / M} = \frac{\Delta D_A}{\Delta M} \cdot \frac{M}{D_A} \tag{4.6}$$

An income elasticity of $+1.6$ is interpreted by saying that a 1% increase in income would lead to a 1.6% increase in quantity demanded for A, even though prices do not change. A negative income elasticity simply means that increases in income are associated with decreases in quantity demanded instead.

In general, the numerical value of price or income elasticities measures the relative responsiveness of quantity demanded to changes in either prices or income at a particular point on a demand schedule. The larger the numerical value of the elasticity, the greater the response. Table 4.2 illustrates the effects of own-price or cross-price elasticities within various numerical ranges.

Table 4.2   Range of Price Elasticities

NUMERICAL VALUE OF PRICE ELASTICITY	DESCRIPTION	EFFECT ON TOTAL REVENUE OF A PRICE DECREASE	EFFECT ON TOTAL REVENUE OF A PRICE INCREASE
$-1 < \eta \leq 0$	inelastic	decrease	increase
$\eta = -1$	unitary elastic	no change	no change
$\eta < -1$	elastic	increase	decrease

NOTE: If the demand curve has a positive slope, i.e., if the commodity is a Giffen good, then all of the above terms apply except that the ranges in question are $1 > \eta \geq 0$, $n = 1$, and $\eta \geq 1$.

[4] Using calculus these elasticities can be expressed as

$$\eta_{A,A} = \frac{dD_A}{dP_A} \frac{P_A}{D_A}, \qquad \eta_{A,B} = \frac{dD_A}{dP_B} \frac{P_B}{D_A},$$

and

$$\eta_{A,M} = \frac{dD_A}{dM} \frac{M}{D_A}.$$

Table 4.3 Ranges of Income Elasticities

NUMERICAL VALUE OF INCOME ELASTICITY	DESCRIPTION
$1 > |\eta| \geq 0$	inelastic
$|\eta| = 1$	unitary elastic
$|\eta| > 1$	elastic

A similar set of information for interpreting income elasticities is given in Table 4.3. The income elasticity can, of course, be positive or negative depending upon the way the quantity demanded changes with income.

Numerical Examples of Elasticity Calculation and Their Interpretation

Example 1: Suppose we have the demand schedule for commodity A, $D_A = 50 - 4P_A + 0.1M$, and we would like to calculate the own-price elasticity of demand and the income elasticity of demand at the price $P_A = 5$ and income $M = 100$ where $D_A = 40$. Using

$$\eta_{A,A} = \frac{\Delta D_A}{\Delta P_A} \cdot \frac{P_A}{D_A} \qquad (4.7)$$

we know D_A and P_A; the only problem is to find $\Delta D_A / \Delta P_A$. If we hold money income constant and change price by a small amount, say ΔP_A, this would lead to a change in quantity demanded of

$$\Delta D_A = -4 \, \Delta P_A \qquad (4.8)$$

or

$$\frac{\Delta D_A}{\Delta P_A} = -4 \qquad (4.9)$$

Substituting this value in Equation (4.7) we obtain

$$\eta_{A,A} = -4 \cdot \tfrac{5}{40} = -0.5 \qquad (4.10)$$

An elasticity of -0.5 indicates that a 1% change in price would lead to a 0.5% change in quantity demanded, where the direction of the change in quantity demanded would be opposite the direction of the change in price.

In general price elasticity changes along a demand schedule. For example, using the demand schedule above but evaluating own-price elasticity at $P_A = 2$, $M = 100$ where $D_A = 40$ gives $\eta_{A,A} = -0.2$. In special cases the elasticity remains contant. Can you find the form of the demand function for which η is a constant?

The income elasticity is computed in a similar manner from

$$\eta_{A,M} = \frac{\Delta D_A}{\Delta M} \cdot \frac{M}{D_A} \tag{4.11}$$

Since we know M and D_A, all we need is $\Delta D_A/\Delta M$. With price held constant, income is changed by a small amount, say ΔM. This leads to a change in quantity demanded of

$$\Delta D_A = 0.1 \, \Delta M \tag{4.12}$$

or

$$\frac{\Delta D_A}{\Delta M} = 0.1 \tag{4.13}$$

Substituting this value in Equation (4.11) gives an income elasticity

$$\eta_{A,M} = 0.1 \cdot \tfrac{100}{40} = 0.25 \tag{4.14}$$

An income elasticity of 0.25 means that a 0.25% change in quantity demanded will arise from a 1% change in money income. If money income were forecast to rise 10%, then the income elasticity would predict approximately a 2.5% increase in quantity sold—even with no change in the market price.

Example 2:   In order to include cross-price elasticities in our analysis, let us consider a demand schedule for commodity B, $D_B = 100 - 5P_B + 3P_C + 10M$, where $M = 10$, $P_B = 10$, and $P_C = 5$. The own-price elasticity of demand for commodity B is

$$\eta_{B,B} = \frac{\Delta D_B}{\Delta P_B} \cdot \frac{P_B}{D_B} \tag{4.15}$$

Using the same reasoning as in Example 1, $\Delta D_B/\Delta P_B$ is found to be -5, thus

$$\eta_{B,B} = -5 \cdot \tfrac{10}{165} = -0.30 \tag{4.16}$$

Demand at this price is inelastic. An own-price elasticity of approximately -0.30 indicates that a 1% decrease in the price of B would be associated with approximately a 0.3% increase in quantity demanded.

The cross-price elasticity of demand for B with respect to C is

$$\eta_{B,C} = \frac{\Delta D_B}{\Delta P_C} \cdot \frac{P_C}{D_B} \tag{4.17}$$

Since $\Delta D_B/\Delta P_C$ is 3, one obtains

$$\eta_{B,C} = 3 \cdot \tfrac{5}{165} = +0.09 \tag{4.18}$$

The cross-price elasticity being so small, i.e., quite inelastic, implies that although a competitor's price reduction would reduce the quantity demanded of B, it would take a 10% price reduction for C to obtain only a 0.9% reduction in the quantity demanded of B. Since the cross-price elasticity is positive in this example this means that a decrease in the price of C would lead to a decrease in the quantity demanded for B.

When the cross-price elasticity is positive, the two commodities are said to be substitutes, while if it is negative they are said to be complements. Beef and chicken or butter and margarine are examples of substitutes, while gasoline and automobiles or tennis rackets and tennis balls are examples of complements.

A Geometrical Calculation of Price and Income Elasticities

The relationship between the slope of a demand schedule and price elasticity can be seen in a geometrical way by considering the demand schedule in Figure 4.3. If we are interested in the price elasticity at point A we can find the slope of the demand curve at this point by constructing a straight line tangent at point A. The slope of the line, $\Delta P/\Delta Q$, is the reciprocal of the slope of the demand schedule, $\Delta Q/\Delta P$, at point A. With an initial price $\bar{P}$ and a quantity demanded of $\bar{Q}$, the price elasticity at this point is

$$\eta = \frac{OB}{OC} \cdot \frac{\bar{P}}{\bar{Q}} \tag{4.19}$$

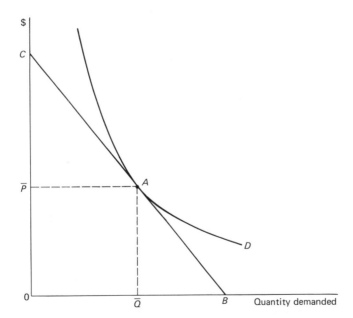

Figure 4.3   Measuring Price Elasticity

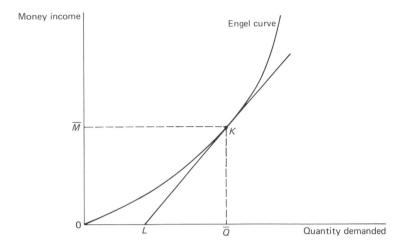

Figure 4.4   Measuring the Response of Purchases to Changes in Income

where OB and OC represent the distances along the horizontal and vertical axes, respectively. Using the geometrical properties for similar right triangles, the price elasticity at point A can also be expressed as AB/CA.

The same geometrical approach can be used to find the relationship between income elasticities and the slope of the Engel curve. If we want to compute the income elasticity at point K in Figure 4.4, we can use the fact that the slope of the Engel curve $\Delta Q/\Delta M$ at K is the reciprocal of the slope of a straight line tangent at K. The income elasticity is found from

$$\eta_{A,M} = \frac{\Delta D_A}{\Delta M} \cdot \frac{M}{D_A} \tag{4.20}$$

The slope of the straight line tangent at K is $O\overline{M}/L\overline{Q}$, thus

$$\eta_{A,M} = \frac{L\overline{Q}}{O\overline{M}} \cdot \frac{\overline{M}}{\overline{Q}} \tag{4.21}$$

Major Factors Affecting the Numerical Value of Elasticities

Three major factors influence the numerical values of price and income elasticities: (1) the number of similar products available which consumers perceive as substitutes, (2) the number of alternative uses that exist for the commodity, and (3) the length of time consumers have to make adjustments in the composition of the purchases.

Generally, the larger the number of competing products and the larger the number of alternative uses in which a commodity might be substituted for others, the more elastic the demand. As an example of the third factor, a sick person is hardly in a position to shop around for a low price on a prescription he or she needs immediately. Similarly, the price elasticity for water is likely to be low in the middle of a desert while it may be almost perfectly elastic at a zero price at the edge of a clear lake.

Over a short interval of time, a rise in the price of fuel oil is unlikely to cause a conversion to gas heating. However, if the price change is large enough and sustained, the demand for fuel oil will become more elastic over a longer period of time. In the same way, although an airline may have a monopoly on service to a small area initially, marked changes in fares may induce other suppliers to enter, altering the elasticities of demand for the original airline's services. The possibility of such entries may well prevent a firm from fully exploiting the revenues forecast by elasticity estimates.

Empirical Measurement of Demand Relationships

Measurement is the means by which the concepts discussed so far are applied to making decisions. It is the step that utilizes statistical techniques to compare empirical observations with economic theories. Demand measurement involves making market observations of prices and quantities, incomes, population, and other demographic statistics and translating these observations into estimates of demand relationships. Statistical measurement is essential when demand information is used for purposes such as forecasting.

Suppose we wish to estimate future prices for food. To do so we must be able to estimate the future demand for food. Management in the construction industry must execute purchase orders for future materials and contract for subsequent deliveries of commodities; therefore the forecasting of housing and other building starts is essential. This involves determining how the demand for housing depends on monetary variables such as interest rates, credit conditions, and down-payment requirements. A hospital scheduling the expansion of its facilities or planning for an added number of beds must forecast the demand for hospital services. A university's plans for staffing and employment, or for negotiating the sensitive political problems involved in securing funds for buildings, depend on the forecast of the demand for educational services.

Knowledge of the demand for waste disposal services is crucial to cities for planning the expansion of capacity for garbage disposal and sewers. Gauging growth accurately is important both for planning city services and for appraising revenue requirements and possibilities. Zoning commissions and real estate interests need some way of forecasting the growth of a city, which is based on the demand for residences. The growth in population of an area implies an economic demand for the services required for living in that area.

It takes anywhere from two to seven years to construct the physical production services needed to generate electricity. Many nuclear plants require a lead time of seven years from the time construction is started to the time the firm can actually produce. Obviously, for business investment problems such as these demand must be forecast for considerable distances into the future.

Each of these examples illustrates important government or business decisions that have to be made now, yet are contingent on future demand.

Interpreting market observations

Let us now take a closer look at the task of estimating the demand for a particular commodity. To solve the measurement problem we may use either *time series data* or *cross-section data*. Time series data are observations on prices, quantities, and other variables at each of a series of points in time, such as demand for airline services two years ago, last year, and this year, while cross-section data are observations of many different economic units at a given point in time. A record of each individual's consumption, the prices he/she was confronted with, and his/her income today, would constitute a cross-section sample. The same data recorded today, next week, and next month, etc., would constitute a time series of cross-sections.

At first glance it might appear market observations could be translated into estimates of demand by taking simple statistical techniques and immediately estimating regressions of quantity demanded on price and income, using a relationship such as $Q = a + bP + cM$, where Q is quantity demanded, P is price, and M is money income, and the unknowns a, b, and c are estimated. Unfortunately, it is not usually possible simply to take time series data on prices and quantities and assume that they represent a demand relationship. The problem that arises is illustrated in Figure 4.5. If points such as A, B, and C are observed, how are we to interpret the information contained in those observations? One interpretation might be that these represent observations on a fluctuating demand schedule and a single stable supply schedule, but this is not the only possibility.

If we have observed this information over time, our observations probably represent some mix of demand changes and supply changes. If so, the three points observed will not be on a single demand schedule, but will represent intersections on three different demand and supply schedules like the solid lines in Figure 4.5. To interpret these observations correctly requires a sophisticated statistical methodology which takes into account not only price and quantity, but also many of the other variables on which demand and supply depend.

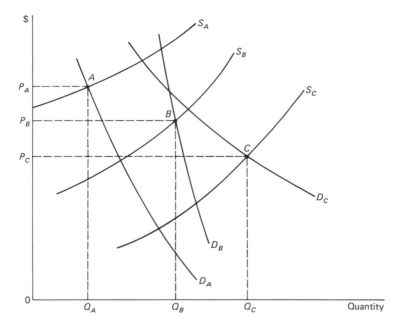

Figure 4.5 The Identification Problem: Are We Observing Demand or Supply or Neither?

To illustrate the identification problem that arises, suppose the market demand and supply schedules for a particular commodity are given by

$$Q_t^d = a + bP_t \tag{4.22}$$

and

$$Q_t^s = c + dP_t + eR_t \tag{4.23}$$

If we assume quantity supplied, Q_t^s, equals quantity demanded, Q_t^d, at time t, given the market price, P_t, and other supply influences, R_t, we can substitute Q_t^d for Q_t^s in (4.23). Multiplying (4.22) by λ and (4.23) by μ gives

$$\lambda Q_t^d = \lambda a + \lambda b P_t \tag{4.24}$$

and

$$\mu Q_t^d = \mu c + \mu d P_t + \mu e R_t \tag{4.25}$$

Adding (4.24) and (4.25) and solving for Q_t^d gives

$$Q_t^d = \frac{\lambda a + \mu c}{\lambda + \mu} + \frac{\lambda b + \mu d}{\lambda + \mu} P_t + \frac{\mu e}{\lambda + \mu} R_t \tag{4.26}$$

Notice that a direct estimate of (4.26) in the form $Q_t^d = A + BP_t + CR_t$ will provide no information about the values of a, b, c, d, or e in either demand or supply schedules: Unscrambling the meaning of the terms A, B, and C requires more detailed information.

A branch of economics and statistics, econometrics, is devoted specifically to the problem of bringing statistical techniques to bear on the interpretation of economic data. Problems of identification and interpretation must be solved as well as problems introduced by aggregation. The estimates that are discussed below come from the application of econometric methods.

Estimates of price and income elasticities and their interpretation

Table 4.4 provides some estimates of elasticities for several commodities and a financial asset. For cigarettes, the price elasticity of demand is in the range -0.3 to -0.4 and the income elasticity is 0.5. Cigarettes have a price elasticity very close to zero. This suggests one reason why a government would levy an excise tax on a commodity like cigarettes. If the purpose of the tax is to raise revenue, it would be futile to levy it on a commodity whose demand is elastic, since the price increase caused by the excise tax would cause demand to drop off quickly, so that little revenue could be raised from after-tax consumption. A commodity's consumption can be limited by an excise tax only if demand is elastic—otherwise the tax would just raise revenues, not decrease consumption. A price elasticity of -0.3 means that even if the price

Table 4.4   Examples of Some Price and Income Elasticities

DESCRIPTION	PRICE ELASTICITIES OF DEMAND	INCOME ELASTICITY OF DEMAND
For Commodities:		
Automobiles	-0.5 to -1.5	3.0
Steel	-0.3 to -0.4	—
Durable consumer goods	-0.5	0.5
Demand for homes	-0.13 to -0.18	—
Cigarettes	-0.3 to -0.4	0.5
Coffee	-0.25	0.3
Liquor	—	1.3
Restaurant services	—	1.85
Meat	-0.28	—
Margarine	-2.67	—
Butter	-0.7	—
For Financial Assets:		
Demand for cash balances	-0.5	1.0

SOURCES: D. Watson, *Price Theory in Action*, Third Edition. H. Wold and L. Jureen, *Demand Analysis*. W. Branson, *Macroeconomic Theory and Policy*.

of cigarettes is raised by 10% this would lead to only a 3% decrease in quantity demanded. The income elasticity of +0.5 indicates that if income rises by 10%, quantity demanded would be expected to rise by 5%. The same principle applies when appraising the usefulness of increasing the price of gasoline or electricity to conserve energy. The short-run inelastic demands observed for these commodities suggest that such policies might only give profits to firms (if prices are increased without a tax) or revenues to governments (if excise taxes are employed). They would *not* necessarily conserve resources!

The income elasticity for liquor of +1.3 indicates that if income grows by 1%, the quantity demanded will grow by about 1.3%. For automobiles, a 1% increase in income would lead to a 3% increase in the number of automobiles demanded, while a 10% growth in income would be expected to lead to approximately a 30% growth in quantity demanded, with no change in prices! If prices dropped, the growth of demand would be stimulated even further.

Distillers might be less interested in the total demand for liquor than in the demand for their particular brand. They would probably also be interested in estimates for each product line, i.e., bourbon, vodka, gin, etc. Some very prestigious brands might have very high income elasticities while other brands might actually have negative income elasticities, indicating that an increase in income would lead to a decrease in quantity demanded.

The income elasticity for restaurant services is well above unity, which means demand is elastic with respect to income. Again, individual types of restaurants, like McDonald's and Kentucky Fried Chicken, might have very different income elasticities from more elegant restaurants.

The price elasticity for coffee, −0.25, is similar to the one obtained for cigarettes. A 5% decrease in price would lead to a 1.25% increase in quantity demanded. Notice that all the price elasticities for food items are relatively inelastic. This means that raising prices would raise incomes of sellers/producers, and shows one economic reason why agricultural interests politically support acreage restrictions and soil bank plans for reducing output. The impact of such policies and the importance of demand elasticity in determining their effectiveness will be discussed in more detail in Chapter 10. Similarly, manufacturing firms may find it desirable to restrict output if they face inelastic demands for their products.

The last example is the demand for money, where the interest rate represents the "price of money." The demand for money appears to be inelastic with respect to changes in the interest rate. At the same time, individuals appear to raise their holdings of money exactly in proportion to their increases in income. Popular rules of thumb that recommend holding cash balances in savings accounts or other liquid assets equal to five to six times the individual's monthly take home pay may partly explain the proportional relationship that has been observed.

income elasticities can be obtained for a wide variety of com-
ices, and assets or liabilities such as stocks and bonds. Demand
mated twenty years ago are not likely to make much sense today.
_st be revised as new market information becomes available.
_millarly, demand estimates from empirical demand functions are most
reliable only if the price, income, or other variables used correspond to the
sample data from which the original estimates are formed.

Estimates of cross-price elasticities and their interpretation

Cross-price elasticities have interesting implications for marketing strategies.
Table 4.5 contains some examples.

The cross-price elasticity for beef with respect to pork of 0.09 indicates
that if pork marketers got together and succeeded in decreasing the price of
pork by 10% the quantity of beef demanded would fall by approximately
0.9%. The fact that the cross-price elasticity is positive means that reductions
in the price of pork are associated with reductions in beef consumption.
Positive cross-price elasticities indicate that the commodities are substitutes.
In the case of beef and pork this certainly corresponds to the choices that
might be made by consumers in meal preparation.

The butter and margarine example emphasizes even more clearly the
strategic value of cross-price elasticities. Notice the extremely high own-price
elasticity of margarine: −2.67 (Table 4.4). For a producer of margarine
interested in increasing sales, what marketing policy might this suggest?
Lowering price by 1% would lead to an approximate increase of 2.7% in
quantity demanded. A 5% price reduction would lead to an approximate
increase of 13.4% in quantity demanded. Since demand is elastic, decreases
in price will also be associated with an increase in total revenue.

On the other hand, look at the cross-price elasticities. If you are producing
butter, should the information contained in Table 4.5 cause you to be concerned about the market power that pricing policies can give margarine
producers? No, because even a 10% reduction in the price of margarine
would change the quantity of butter demanded by only 0.5%. Notice,

Table 4.5 Examples of Cross-Price Elasticities

Beef with respect to the price of pork	0.09
Butter with respect to the price of margarine	0.05
Margarine with respect to the price of butter	1.74

SOURCE: H. Wold and L. Jureen, *Demand Analysis.*

however, that the cross-price elasticities are not symmetrical. Price cutting would not help butter marketers because their own price elasticity is so low (Table 4.4). A price reduction would reduce their total revenue. Margarine producers, on the other hand, do have reason to worry about price cutting by dairy producers. A 1% reduction in the price of butter leads to a decrease of almost 2% in the quantity of margarine demanded. The cross-price elasticity is high, so that dairy producers can draw off competition from margarine and may increase their total income at the same time.

The use of cross-price elasticities is not limited to competition between firms. A meat buyer for a retail food store chain must make estimates of meat use week by week since profit margins are narrow and freezer space for storage may be limited. Excessive carry-over could wipe out any profit, through spoilage. If a buyer is able to secure a special purchase on chicken, which will then be offered at a reduced price, then he/she must adjust beef purchases by means of the cross-price elasticity to be sure that purchases conform to the demand. The same principle applies to an automobile dealer who plans to offer a special on certain models or to a department store intending to give heavy sales promotion to a certain line.

Some estimates of demand relationships

So far we have been measuring demand only in terms of summary elasticities. This section illustrates some estimates of demand relationships in full form, employing the type of demand data used to appraise some of the public policy issues raised by the heavy use of petroleum products and other natural resources. Firms must estimate these relationships in order to plan investment for capacity expansion.

The demand for natural gas[5] has been found to depend basically on its own price, P; per capita income, Y; the change in per capita income, ΔY; population, N; and the quantity consumed in the previous time period, G. The last variable reflects the fact that once gas-using equipment such as a home furnace has been installed only dramatic and sustained changes in the relative cost of alternative methods will cause a switch from gas to some other fuel. The relationship which has been observed is

Natural Gas Consumption = Constant − 0.09 (Price of gas)
$$+\, 0.003 \text{ (Per capita income)}$$
$$+\, 0.017 \text{ (Change in per capita income)}$$
$$+\, 0.004 \text{ (Population)}$$
$$+\, 0.95 \text{ (Gas consumption in last time period)}$$
(4.27)

[5] Adapted from P. Balestra and M. Nerlove, "Pooling Cross-Section and Time Series Data in the Estimation of a Dynamic Model: The Demand for Natural Gas," *Econometrica*, (July, 1966), 585–612.

When evaluated at the average price and income in the sample data above, this estimate indicated a price elasticity of -0.63 and an income elasticity of 0.62. Table 4.6 illustrates how this information could be used to compare alternative estimates of the growth in demand for natural gas.

Another study[6] provides parallel information for the demand for electricity, and also provides an interesting breakdown between classes of customers. The demand for electricity for residential use was found to be approximated by the relationship

$$\begin{matrix} \text{Quantity of Electricity} \\ \text{Demanded for} \\ \text{Residential Use} \end{matrix} = \text{Constant} \cdot \left(\frac{\text{Price of}}{\text{Electricity}} \right)^{-0.41} \cdot (\text{Income})^{0.6}$$

(4.28)

Using a similar form for the demand relationship for commercial use led to the following estimate of the demand by the chemical industry:

$$\begin{matrix} \text{Quantity of Electricity} \\ \text{Demanded for} \\ \text{Chemical Industry Use} \end{matrix} = \text{Constant} \cdot \left(\frac{\text{Price of}}{\text{Electricity}} \right)^{-2.6} \cdot (\text{Output})^{.62}$$

(4.29)

For the textile industry the result was

$$\begin{matrix} \text{Quantity of Electricity} \\ \text{Demanded for} \\ \text{Textile Industry Use} \end{matrix} = \text{Constant} \cdot (\text{Price})^{-1.62} \cdot (\text{Output})^{1.01}$$

(4.30)

Table 4.6 Comparisons of Forecasts of Natural Gas Use for Two Alternative Forecasts of Income and Population Growth

	Forecast 1			Forecast 2		
YEAR	ASSUMED POPULA- TION[a]	ASSUMED PER CAPITA INCOME[b]	ESTIMATED GAS CONSUMPTION[c]	ASSUMED POPULA- TION[a]	ASSUMED PER CAPITA INCOME[b]	ESTIMATED GAS CONSUMPTION[c]
1	31,500	$4,700	212.1	31,500	$4,600	211.8
2	32,100	4,900	348.0	31,700	4,700	343.8
3	32,600	5,200	481.7	31,900	4,800	470.3

[a] In thousands.
[b] In dollars.
[c] In millions of cubic feet.

[6] Adapted from F. M. Fisher and C. Kaysen, *A Study in Econometrics: The Demand for Electricity in the United States.* North-Holland, 1963.

For residential use the price elasticity was -0.4. For commercial use it was -2.6 in the chemical industry and -1.6 for textiles. The income elasticity for residential use was 0.6, while the demand elasticities for changes in output were 0.6 for chemicals and 1.01 for textiles.

The foregoing information might be used by a utility firm forced to raise its rates. Commercial customers generally have alternatives open to them that residential consumers do not. A firm might, for example, be able to generate its own electricity. A residential user typically cannot. The elasticities suggest that raising residential, not commercial, rates would raise total revenues. In fact, it might even be reasonable to lower commercial rates at the same time, since the commercial demand appears to be elastic.

Added information for planning utility expansion is available from the income and output elasticities. Growth in residential uses seems to have less influence than an increase in general economic output. A 10% rise in overall income accompanied by a 10% rise in output in each industry will lead to only a 6% increase in residential use, while the chemical use will rise by 6% and the textile use by 10%. Such information tells the utility not only how much growth in demand to anticipate but also what type of distribution facilities to plan, since residential power is delivered at lower voltage levels than industrial power.

Additional Information from the Market Demand Schedule

As we have seen, demand elasticity may be inelastic, unitary elastic, or elastic. What is the significance of these different ranges of elasticity for a firm planning its price policy?

The firm may well consider the effect of prices on total revenue more important than their effect on quantity sold. It is quite possible for a decrease in price to yield more total revenue than an increase, provided that there is a sufficient corresponding increase in quantity demanded. Obviously price cutting will only enhance profits if it leads to an increase in total revenues. On the other hand, raising prices may increase total revenues in some situations and decrease it in others. It is crucial to know which of these results is going to occur. A simple relationship existing between price elasticity and changes in total revenue is useful in making this determination.

Each point on a demand schedule is associated with a specific total revenue, equal to price times quantity demanded. In fact, a family of three schedules is associated with any market demand schedule. The family consists of a *total revenue (TR) schedule*; an *average revenue (AR) schedule*, $AR = TR/Q$, where Q is the quantity demanded; and a *marginal revenue (MR) schedule*, $MR = \Delta TR/\Delta Q$. The average revenue schedule is the inverse of the demand schedule itself. Since $TR = P \cdot D(P)$, $AR = TR/Q = [P \cdot D(P)]/D(P) = P$, where $Q = D(P)$. Marginal revenue can be interpreted either as the change in total revenue associated with the selling of one more unit or as the amount of revenue that would be lost by selling one less unit. Figure 4.6 illustrates a demand schedule and the associated total revenue and marginal revenue schedules.

In order to derive the relationship between the changes in revenue a firm would experience and price elasticity, suppose that P_0 is the initial price and Q_0 is the initial quantity demanded. If the price P_1 is charged, the quantity demanded will be Q_1. The total revenue at P_0 is $TR_0 = P_0 Q_0$, while at P_1 it is $TR_1 = P_1 Q_1$. Let us write the price P_1 as $P_0 + \Delta P$ and the quantity Q_1 as $Q_0 + \Delta Q$. The change in total revenue will then be

$$\Delta TR = TR_1 - TR_0 = P_1 Q_1 - P_0 Q_0$$

$$= (P_0 + \Delta P) \cdot (Q_0 + \Delta Q) - P_0 Q_0 \qquad (4.31)$$

Expanding Equation (4.31) we obtain

$$\Delta TR = P_0 \, \Delta Q + Q_0 \, \Delta P + \Delta P \, \Delta Q \qquad (4.32)$$

If the price change ΔP is very small we can approximate this by

$$\Delta TR = P_0 \, \Delta Q + Q_0 \, \Delta P \qquad (4.33)$$

Dividing Equation (4.33) by ΔQ gives

$$\frac{\Delta TR}{\Delta Q} \equiv MR = P_0 + Q_0 \frac{\Delta P}{\Delta Q} \qquad (4.34)$$

Factoring out P_0 on the right-hand side, we have

$$MR = P_0 \left(1 + \frac{Q_0}{P_0} \cdot \frac{\Delta P}{\Delta Q} \right) \qquad (4.35)$$

The last term in the parentheses is the reciprocal of the price elasticity of demand evaluated at the point (P_0, Q_0); thus the basic relationship we obtain[7] is

$$MR = P_0 \left(1 + \frac{1}{\eta} \right) \qquad (4.36)$$

If a firm is selling a commodity with a downward-sloping demand schedule, then it can expect to sell more units by lowering the price. However, the

---

[7] Equation (4.33) would be an exact relationship if we had used calculus to derive it, since we can write

$$\frac{dTR}{dQ} = P_0 + Q_0 \frac{dP}{dQ}$$

This is simply the limit of Equation (4.34) as $\Delta Q \to 0$.

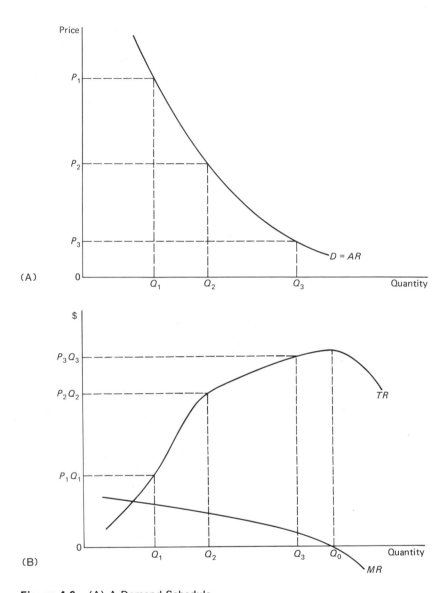

Figure 4.6 (A) A Demand Schedule
(B) Total and Marginal Revenue Schedules

important consideration is whether the marginal revenue is positive, implying that total revenue will increase; zero, implying that there will be no change in total revenue; or negative, implying that total revenue will fall. The information in Table 4.2 provides direct answers for a firm examining policies aimed at increasing profits. If a commodity is in the inelastic or unit elastic range on its demand schedule, then price increases will either raise revenues and reduce costs (both factors tending to increase profits) or will keep revenues unchanged while reducing costs (again increasing profits). On the other hand, if a commodity is in the elastic range of its demand schedule, it may be possible to enhance profits by *reducing* prices, provided the added revenue per unit sold is at least as great as the added production cost. When we have developed the cost and production aspects of a firm in more detail, we will be able to use demand information to make decisions concerning price and production policies.

Colleges and universities considering tuition increases as a means of covering deficits should take special note of price elasticities. Raising tuition will raise total revenues, *provided demand is inelastic*. Whether or not demand for college attendance is inelastic is an open question—one which students might be interested in trying to answer.

Summary

This chapter has developed the concept of market demand by building on the concept of individual demand discussed in Chapter 3. Market demand depends on the preferences of each consumer, the prices of all commodities, and the level and distribution of income among consumers.

The following key concepts were presented: (1) the concept of elasticity— own-price elasticity, cross-price elasticity, and income elasticity; and (2) the family of revenue schedules—total revenue, average revenue, and marginal revenue.

Measurement is the key step in using these concepts as an aid to decision making. The empirical examples discussed in this chapter provide some idea of the range of their applications in organizing information relevant to current problems as well as those which may arise in the future.

Market demand accounts for only one side of market activity. The other side arises from the forces of production, to be studied in the next several chapters.

Questions for Study or Class Discussion

1. Find examples of both cross-section and time series data on quantity consumed, prices, and income.
2. Discuss the problems involved in using the data collected in question 1 to estimate a market demand schedule.
3. List a set of assumptions which will allow you to use the data collected in question 1 to estimate a demand schedule, and do so, using linear regression.

4. Compute and interpret own-price, cross-price, and income elasticities of demand from the results in question 3. Evaluate elasticities at the mean of the sample data.
5. Find the total revenue and marginal revenue schedules associated with the demand schedule in question 3.

References

Branson, W. H., *Macroeconomic Theory and Policy*. Harper and Row, 1971.

Hicks, J. R., *Value and Capital*. Oxford University Press, 1946.

Klein, L. R., *An Introduction to Econometrics*. Prentice-Hall, 1962.

Marshall, A., *Principles of Economics*. Macmillan, 1920.

Schultz, H., *The Theory and Measurement of Demand*. University of Chicago Press, 1938.

Veblen, T., *The Theory of the Leisure Class*. Macmillan, 1899.

Watson, D. S., *Price Theory in Action*, Third Edition. Houghton Mifflin, 1973.

Wold, H., and L. Jureen, *Demand Analysis*. John Wiley & Sons, 1953.

Working, E. J., "What Do Statistical 'Demand Curves' Show?" *Quarterly Journal of Economics*, 41 (1927), 212–235.

Chapter 5 Firm Behavior and Market Environments

Introduction

At this point our focus shifts from the individual consumer, whose behavior we considered in developing a theory of consumption, to the behavior of individual firms, which is fundamental in production.

The firm plays three basic roles in economic activity. First, firms organize the use of resources. The production activity of individual firms results in decentralized decision making with regard to resource use. Next, firms assume economic risks. They acquire resources, invest in plants and equipment, and manufacture new products before it is actually known whether the products will be profitable. Market research studies and attempts to tailor product lines to particular types of consumers can never entirely eliminate the element of risk. Finally, the firm exchanges its obligations—bonds, common stock, and preferred stock—for shares in its profits (or losses). Different classes of obligations carry different degrees of risk of capital loss and opportunity for profit sharing. Returns on each type of financial investment are generally commensurate with the degree of risk taken.

We shall begin by showing how a firm can form input, output, and price decisions, and then use the decisions made by individual firms to develop a supply schedule for an individual firm. Once this has been accomplished, we can aggregate the various firms' schedules to obtain the market supply for a particular commodity. This method of development parallels the development of the market demand schedule in Chapter 4. The diagrams used to illustrate the development of a choice problem for the firm will further reveal the analogy between the consumption choice problem for the individual consumer and the input/output choice problem for a firm.

Alternative Behavior Rules for a Firm

What motivates a firm to undertake its role in transforming resources to outputs? The most common assumption is that a firm makes its input and output choices in such a way as to maximize profits.

Profit maximization

It is not sufficient to say simply that a firm attempts to maximize profits. Do we mean short-term or long-run profits? It may make good economic sense to hold prices and short-term profits down for the time being to retard the entry of competitors. Furthermore, how are we to measure a firm's profits? The problem of measurement is just as important here as it was for demand relationships in the previous chapter.

"Profits" might be defined as profits before or after taxes, as gross revenue less current labor and materials expense, or as gross revenue less labor, materials, and depreciation. Instead of considering only current profits, we might look at the rate of growth of profits over time, the rate of growth of the firm's assets, or the rate of growth of profits per share of stock.

Figure 5.1 sketches the behavior of total revenues, total costs, and profits for a firm as output varies. Profit is the vertical distance between total revenues and total costs and is plotted as a separate function. For simplicity, this sketch is drawn as if the firm produces a single commodity. Multi-product firms require a more complicated diagram with multiple dimensions. Firms with multiple outputs must not only choose the optimal output level, but also the optimal output mix, to be discussed in Chapter 8.

The left part of Figure 5.1 is called a *break-even chart*. The *break-even point* is the output level Q_1 at which the firm first reaches the point where it earns zero profits. If the only output levels at which the firm can produce are less than the break-even point, then the firm would obviously always incur losses. If a firm is to be economically viable, it must ultimately achieve an output level above the break-even point. On the other hand, it would usually not want to exceed the output level at which profits are maximized, represented in Figure 5.1 by Q_0.

In an environment of certainty and many competitors, profit maximization is not a chosen goal, but a condition for economic survival. An absence of competitors permits a firm to seek other goals. Uncertainty creates an attendant risk as well which affects the value of the firm above and beyond the level of profits. This point is discussed in more detail later in this chapter.

The behavior of firms is studied empirically by assuming a particular objective such as profit maximization, deriving its implications, and comparing these implications with market observations. However, no empirical test can prove whether profit maximization or any other goal is actually

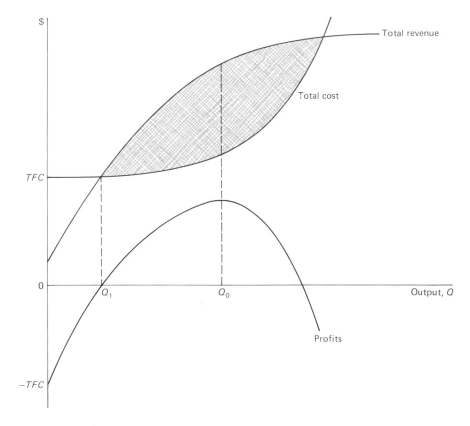

Figure 5.1   The Behavior of Total Revenue, Total Costs, and Profits

pursued by a firm. Empirical evidence can only indicate consistency or lack of consistency with the implications derived from a particular behavioral hypothesis, and it is only sporadically consistent with the existence of a profit maximization goal.

This lack of strong empirical support for the profit maximization hypothesis has led to alternative attempts to explain observed firm behavior.

Sales and output maximization

Perhaps the most popular alternative to profit maximization as a motive for firm behavior is the maximization of either sales (i.e., total revenue) or total output. A graph of total revenue and profits might resemble the curves in Figure 5.2. A firm trying to maximize sales would choose the output level Q'. In general, maximum revenues do not occur at the same point as maximum

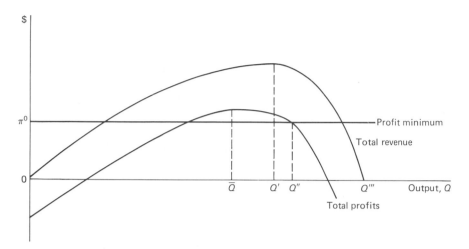

Figure 5.2 Sales or Output Maximization as a Management Goal

profits; in fact, the output which maximizes total revenue is typically greater than the output which maximizes profits. A goal of output maximization, taken literally, would mean expanding output up to Q''', at which the firm is operating at a loss.

A more plausible theory of sales or output maximization supposes that the firm attempts to maximize total sales or output subject to a requirement that total profits (or profits per share) remain at or above some minimum level. If sales are to be maximized subject to a minimum profit of π^0 (Figure 5.2) the desired output level is Q'. A firm trying to maximize output subject to the same minimum profit will expand output until it drives total revenue down to π^0 at the point Q'', which represents the largest quantity the firm can sell if it is to earn total profits of at least π^0.

Growth as a goal

Profit and sales goals are most frequently couched in static terms. In contrast, a firm's management may be primarily concerned with the dynamic objective of *growth*.

Growth may be measured in terms of sales, total assets, number of employees, etc. However it is measured, the policies used to implement it will encompass more than simply price, output, and input. Financial decisions required for expansion will affect the value of the firm, the risk to various classes of creditors, and the firm's ability to attract the funds needed for additional investments. A number of the more interesting aspects of growth elements are discussed in Chapter 16.

Maximization of managerial utility

The managers of a firm may be motivated by other considerations besides profits. As an example, suppose managers are interested in both sales and profits. There is, of course, a trade off between profits and sales, which might be represented by the line AA' in Figure 5.3.

We now need a way of representing the trade off between multiple objectives in terms of a manager's preferences. A utility function serves this purpose. If a manager's preferences are represented by the indifference curves U_1', U_2', and U_3', then the mix of sales and profits that maximizes utility for the manager is given by S', π'. On the other hand, if preferences are reflected in indifference curves U_1, U_2, and U_3, utility maximizing decisions lead to a profit of π^* and a sales level of S^*.

There is a potential lack of consistency between shareholder interest in profit maximization and management interest in other goals such as sales maximization. Sufficiently attractive compensation will presumably induce management to pursue shareholder interests. Table 5.1 gives the results of one study of the determinants of managerial compensation.

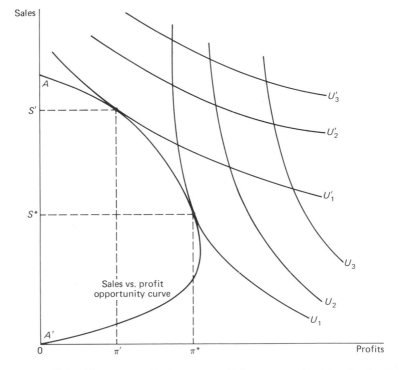

Figure 5.3 Management Preferences and Management Decision Implications

Table 5.1 Determinants of Managerial Compensation

YEAR	EFFECT OF TOTAL ASSET SIZE	EFFECT OF RETURN ON ASSETS	EFFECT OF SALES AS A PERCENT OF TOTAL ASSETS
1957	Significant	Significant	Not Significant
1960	Significant	Significant	Not Significant
1963	Significant	Significant	Not Significant

SOURCE: W. Lewellen and B. Huntsman, "Managerial Pay and Corporate Performance."

In each case sales performance had little weight in determining managerial compensation. On the other hand, since profits appear to have a strong influence on compensation, a manager may well be motivated to pursue shareholder interests, if only as a means of achieving his/her own goals.

Satisficing behavior

The behavior rules discussed above all suppose that a firm is engaged in solving some type of maximum problem. The utility function approach illustrated in Figure 5.3 is a response to the suggestion that observed decisions may not be accurately interpreted as attempts to maximize a single measure of a firm's success.

One alternative is to suppose that management choices are circumscribed by sets of minimum, or *satisficing*, requirements. Using this hypothesis, choices are not necessarily narrowed down to a single optimal solution. There may be many feasible alternatives that are within the chosen limits. Unfortunately, analysis based on satisficing requirements has no predictive content, and prediction is, after all, the basic purpose of constructing models of behavior.

Organizational behavior

Dissatisfaction with explanations of management activity that are based on maximization has given rise not only to the theory of satisficing, but to an entire *behavioral theory of the firm*.[1] A decision is viewed as consisting of four parts: (1) organizational goals, (2) organizational expectations, (3) organizational choice, and (4) organizational control.

The introduction of expectation elements opens up the whole question of the effect of information on decision making—a particularly important

[1] An extensive discussion of this approach is provided in R. Cyert and J. March, *A Behavioral Theory of the Firm*.

element when uncertainty is present. Research on expectation phenomena and information is still a fertile opportunity for inquisitive minds.

Four underlying forces have been suggested as the elements connecting goals, information, and choice: (1) uncertainty avoidance, (2) organizational learning, (3) quasi-resolution of conflict, and (4) problematic search. Newer psychological concepts promise to reveal even more about group decision processes.

The advent of high-speed computers makes it possible to simulate complex decision processes, which cannot be solved explicitly. Many dynamic facets can only be studied in detail by simulating the reactions to alternative decisions. Simulation may therefore be an important management technique in making trial runs of proposed decisions.[2]

*Decisions under uncertainty

What does "uncertainty'" mean? How does it affect the problem of making decisions? The absence of complete information about alternatives and the failure of individual outcomes to correspond to expectations are day-to-day occurrences for consumers and firms alike. Consumers face uncertainty concerning product qualities and price ranges; firms must deal with uncertainties about input and output prices, fluctuations in consumer preferences, and decisions of competitors.

In an uncertain environment it is natural to ask how much information is actually available. Uncertain settings are usually divided into two groups: settings in which we have enough information to describe the possible alternative outcomes and the probability that each outcome will occur, and settings in which no probability distributions over possible outcomes are available.

Approaches to decision making when probabilities are known   Three major approaches are used in decision theory under uncertainty: (1) use of an expected value criterion, (2) use of an expected utility criterion, or (3) use of certainty equivalents.

EXPECTED VALUE CRITERION: This approach supposes that management, taking into account the known probabilities, attempts to maximize the *expected value* of a certain goal, e.g., profits. This, however, represents a drastic oversimplification, since it assumes that management will not consider the risk involved in making a decision. The very essence of decision making under uncertainty is the presence of risk, yet the risk is ignored. Considering only the maximization of expected profits would imply choosing a project

---

[2] An example of this approach can be found in A. Hoggatt, "A Simulation Study of an Economic Model," in *Contributions to Scientific Research in Management*.

* Optional material requiring knowledge of probability.

with an expected profit of $100,000 (but a profit variance of $60,000) over one with an expected value of $95,000 (but a variance of $3,000). For most people this would seem to be taking an unreasonable risk.

EXPECTED UTILITY CRITERION: The most generally accepted approach that explicitly incorporates risk elements is to introduce a utility function defined on the possible outcomes. For example, instead of maximizing expected profits, $E[\pi]$, we would take as an objective $E[U(\pi)]$.[3] The most important aspects of the *expected utility criterion* are: (1) it can be derived rigorously from a set of simple behavioral axioms[4] and (2) it can be quantitatively measured by comparisons of risky choices, in a manner analogous to the representation of consumer preferences by means of indifference curves in Chapter 2.

CERTAINTY EQUIVALENTS: *Certainty equivalents* are defined as sums which management would accept in lieu of undertaking a risky alternative. Typically the certainty equivalent sum will be smaller than the expected value to be realized by assuming the risk. The difference between the expected value to be gained from a risky alternative and its certainty equivalent is an explicit expression of the subjective value placed by management upon taking the risk. The major impediment to widespread use of this approach is that a utility function defined on risky alternatives is needed to define the certainty equivalents.

Approaches to decision making when probabilities are unknown In the following brief discussion we shall introduce four major approaches to decision making when probabilities are unknown: (1) the Bayes-Laplace Principle of Insufficient Reason, (2) minimax, (3) maximax, and (4) the Hurwisz alpha criterion.

BAYES-LAPLACE PRINCIPLE OF INSUFFICIENT REASON: One of the simplest ways to grapple with unknown probabilities is to assign the same probability to each possible event. With N events, assign the probability $1/N$ to each event and proceed as above.

---

[3] Using a simple Taylor series expansion of $U(\pi)$ evaluated at the expected level of profits, μ, we obtain

$$U(\pi) = U(\mu) + \left(\frac{dU}{d\pi}\bigg|_{\pi=\mu}\right)(\pi - \mu) + \frac{1}{2}\left(\frac{d^2U}{d\pi^2}\bigg|_{\pi=\mu}\right)(\pi - \mu)^2 + \ldots$$

Taking expectations we obtain

$$E[U(\pi)] = U(\mu) + \frac{1}{2}\left(\frac{d^2U}{d\pi^2}\bigg|_{\pi=\mu}\right)E[(\pi - \mu)^2] + \ldots$$

Notice that the second term on the right-hand side includes the variance of profits (one measure of risk) since $\sigma_\pi^2 = E[(\pi - \mu)^2]$. If $U(\pi)$ is quadratic, the mean and variance of profits are alone sufficient to order alternatives.

[4] See J. von Neumann and O. Morgenstern, *Theory of Games and Economic Behavior*, for a more detailed specification of the axioms and their implications.

MINIMAX: For each alternative decision look at the range of possible outcomes and assign the worst outcome as the value of the decision. Then make the decision which has the highest minimum payoff. Needless to say, this is an ultra-conservative behavior rule, which basically assumes that "if it's bad and it can happen, it will happen."

MAXIMAX: For each alternative decision assign the value which represents the best possible outcome and make the decision corresponding to the best outcome over all possible decisions. In contrast to the minimax rule, the maximax rule embodies a philosophy equivalent to "live today, for tomorrow we die." Businesses run by such a strategy probably *will* die tomorrow!

HURWISZ ALPHA CRITERION: The Hurwisz alpha criterion attempts to steer a middle course by taking the best and worst outcomes for each possible decision and forming an average by weighting one outcome by α, $0 \le \alpha \le 1$, and the other by $1 - \alpha$. This approach reflects the tendency of risk-averse decision makers to be wary of extremes. Its major drawback is the lack of a suitable means for assigning a numerical value to alpha.

Each of the criteria or goals discussed above may play a part in price and output decisions; however, the market setting in which a firm operates will also exert a powerful influence.

The Market Environment of a Firm

Many economic and legal factors combine to create the environment in which a firm must operate. These include government policy relating to merger activity, potential economies from large-scale production, and the geographical dispersion or concentration of potential buyers for output or supplies. They blend to create *market structures*.

The role of markets

Markets are important not only as vehicles for the exchange of goods and services but also as means of generating information. They create a centralized information exchange for specialized information from buyers and sellers who are interested in trading a particular commodity at a particular time. They provide information that determines which resources are applied to the various lines of production and how much of each commodity is produced.

Markets are an organizational device for carrying out economic activity, just as a firm is an organizational device for achieving the transformation of resources to outputs. Laws governing the rules of exchange, of contract, and of property rights provide the legal framework of a market. Laws define the proper payment for goods and services, and the legal objects of exchange. It seems obvious to say that a person must have a property right in something before he can sell it, but we shall see that the definition of property rights actually creates some of the major stumbling blocks to the effective operation of a market system. Many of the current issues concerning the use of natural resources revolve around questions of property rights. The twin influences of legal and political environments create the setting in which the firm and markets operate.

In discussing the major influences on the decisions made by firms, we shall group topics under four basic market settings. None of these exactly mirror real-life settings, though some come very close. Any specific problem can typically be represented by adapting these basic models. Each of them will be discussed in more detail in subsequent chapters.

Pure competition

Pure competition is characterized by the following five attributes: (1) Every individual and firm in the market has complete information about existing alternatives and prices on all commodities. (2) Within any one market the commodity being traded is homogeneous. This means that the units produced by any one seller are indistinguishable from the units produced by any other seller. There are no brand names associated with goods. (3) Prices are uniform. Each individual and each firm pays or receives the same price for the same commodity. There is no price discrimination between individuals or between firms. In addition, there is a uniformity across quantities. An individual pays the same price for the 15th unit as he/she did for the 2nd; in other words, there are no quantity discounts. (4) There is complete factor mobility. This means that in the long run resources may move without restraints or impediments from one industry to another and from one line of production to another. (5) There are a large number of buyers and sellers in the market, so that prices cannot be influenced by the actions of a single buyer or seller alone.

Commodity exchanges for grain, sugar, and other agricultural products are a close approximation of the pure competition model.

Pure monopoly

The pure monopoly model differs from the pure competition model in two major respects. While there may still be a large number of buyers, there is only one seller. In addition, although resources may still flow freely into or out of the single monopoly firm, no other firms are allowed to produce the commodity it produces. In other words, there are absolute barriers to entry into the industry.

Water and sewage utilities, telephone service, electricity, and natural gas are real-life situations closely approximating the monopoly model. Where the monopoly has been created with a franchise to a specific firm for exclusive sale and distribution in geographical areas, the study of a monopoly market setting can help in determing whether the franchise in question is a desirable method for organizing resource use. Monopolies may also emerge as a consequence of owning patents or specific natural resources, or from the tendency of economies of scale to lead to a single producer. The concept of scale economies is discussed in the next chapter.

Monopolistic competition

Monopolistic competition has the following attributes: (1) Although there may be a large number of buyers, there are fewer sellers than under pure competition. There is no strict quantitative criterion for the number of sellers; markets with ten to thirty sellers might well fit into the monopolistic competition model. (2) The outputs of different sellers are distinguishable. In particular, brand names may exist. With respect to its own brand name, or whatever other characteristics differentiate its commodities from those of other producers, each firm exercises a degree of monopoly. (3) Resources may freely enter and leave the market as new firms are formed or old firms cease production. (4) Firms and consumers each have knowledge of commodity prices and available alternatives. However, despite the fact that each firm's pricing decisions will affect the demand for the products of the other firms, it is assumed that this interdependence is ignored in decision making.

Markets in canned goods and clothing are possible examples of monopolistic competition. Each market has numerous producers, yet each producer is distinguished by the use of a brand name, or some other product characteristic.

Oligopoly—strategic market settings

In an oligopolistic market setting it is assumed that firms are aware of their interdependence and exploit it in decision making. Oligopoly settings permit collusion or open conflict.

The theory of games, in a simplified form, will be an important part of our analysis of strategic decision making in an oligopoly. If there is a pronounced threat of entry by newcomers, existing firms may hold prices particularly low to inhibit this entry. Oligopoly settings have frequently been observed to lead to long periods of price stability. As we shall see, this stability may result from the threat potential of competitors already in the industry.

Oligopoly settings are fairly accurate descriptions of markets for automobiles, steel, glass, chemicals, cigarettes, petroleum, and commodities such as copper, coffee, and rubber.

Public Policy, Market Structure, and Market Performance

One use of the model market settings sketched above in determining public policy is to appraise the desirability of using various market structures as organizing devices for carrying out economic activity, i.e., for carrying out the transformation of inputs to outputs by the firms operating within the economy.

Antitrust laws

Historically, the first major governmental intervention in business was the creation of the Interstate Commerce Commission in 1880, followed by the Sherman Antitrust Act in 1889 and the Clayton Act of 1914. Up to that time the concentration of tremendous amounts of real and potential market power had placed profits in the hands of a few. This kind of concentration tends to result from the interaction of market mechanisms and production technologies. A market system operating over broad geographical areas, together with technologies favoring large-scale production techniques, gives large-scale firms a cost advantage enabling them to sell at lower prices if they want to. The more efficient firms may drive out their competitors completely and establish a monopoly. Alternatively, even after many competitors have been eliminated by price cutting or some other means, the market may still be large enough to support several sizable firms, and the process will terminate in an explicit or implicit collusive agreement.

Firms such as United States Steel, Standard Oil, American Sugar and Refining formed trusts in rail, steel, and petroleum that effectively dominated the production of a whole industry. The Sherman and Clayton acts were sparked by practices such as price discrimination, interlocking corporate directorships (situations in which the same person was a director of two or more corporations so that the policies of one corporation were not formed independently of the policies of the other), and tying clauses in sales agreements (for example, selling duplicating machines subject to a requirement that all supplies be bought from the same manufacturer).

Chapters 10–13 consider in more detail whether monopolies should or should not be permitted in order to solve particular resource allocation problems.

Ownership, control, and profits

Private ownership of productive resources is a characteristic of capitalistic market systems. Ownership, however, may be less important than the control of management decisions. Federal tax laws exert a powerful influence on the form of ownership and control. Together with the limitation on liability provided by the corporate form, they have caused this form to be preferred

Table 5.2   Measures of the Importance of Form of Ownership

OWNERSHIP	NUMBER		EMPLOYEES (1,000s)		WAGES (MILLIONS $)		VALUE ADDED (MILLIONS $)	
Corporate	153,892	82.3%	17,697	97.1%	$119,530	97.8%	$253,261	97.8%
Partnership	6,731	3.6%	193	1.1%	971	0.8%	1,895	0.7%
Sole								
Proprietorship	24,897	13.3%	243	1.3%	1,187	1.0%	2,361	0.9%
Other	1,539	0.8%	94	0.5%	550	0.4%	1,380	0.5%
Totals	187,059		18,227		$122,238		$258,897	

SOURCE: *Census of Manufacturers*, Vol. 1, 1967.

as a general rule to the sole proprietorship and partnership forms. Table 5.2 gives some statistics for corporations, partnerships, and sole proprietorships in the United States for 1967. By all the economic measures used, the corporate form clearly dominates the scene.

What factors influence profitability within the corporate form of organization? Recent studies[5] suggest that total assets, industry growth rates, and the extent of entry barriers are among the major influences on profit rates. In addition, changeover from nonmanagement to management control appears to have a consistent and significant influence in increasing profit rates. This emphasizes the apparent shift in the United States economy toward greater concentration and management (as opposed to shareholder or owner) control of productive activity. Is this tendency desirable? What criteria should be used to answer this question? How are the relevant terms to be defined and measured?

Traditional microeconomic analysis of the firm centers on the process of making efficient allocation decisions—which input mix to use, which output mix to produce. The role of management in organizing responsibility and work flow within a firm has been almost wholly ignored. Several comparisons[6] of the potential gains in productivity resulting from changes in market structure, as opposed to changes in the internal organization of the firm, suggest the latter may exert the most pronounced effect.

Patents and copyrights

Patents and copyrights grant a monopoly in a particular product or technique. Ordinarily one cannot "own" knowledge and, therefore, cannot sell

[5] See D. Kamerschen, "The Influence of Ownership and Control on Profit Rates," *American Economic Review*, 58 (June, 1968), 432–447, M. Hall and L. Weiss, "Firm Size and Profitability," *Review of Economics and Statistics*, 49 (August, 1967), 319–331, and H. O Stekler, "The Variability of Profitability and Size of Firms," *Journal of the American Statistical Association*, 59 (December, 1964), 1183–1193.

[6] See H. Leibenstein, "Allocative vs. 'X-Efficiency,'" *American Economic Review*, 56 (June, 1966), 392–415.

it. What a patent does is create a property right in knowledge that renders it tradable in a market economy. The existence of a property right is a necessary condition for the ability to trade.

Without a potential property right in the fruits of his research, an inventor would have to lay out costs with no guarantee of receiving any benefits even if his research succeeds. Public policy that secures rights in inventions motivates economic agents, principally firms, to carry on innovative activity. Think of the millions of dollars that have undoubtedly been spent on seeking a remedy for the common cold. A successful remedy would probably be more lucrative than the richest gold mine.

Government activity to encourage innovations spurred by profit motivations is not limited to patent and copyright policy. Support of research by grants to universities and private firms and cost-plus incentive contracting are alternative methods for supplementing the outcomes attained by a market system.

Regulation of economic activity

Some of the important policy issues in governmental regulation of the economy are: Which lines of production should be regulated? How much competition should be allowed? If monopoly privileges are granted, should the grantee firm be controlled in any way? If so, how? Alternative methods include controlling profits, prices, or quantity of output. Which should be chosen? What will be the economic consequences of each method? How will the firm's investment decisions and incentives to innovate be affected?

The question of innovation is particularly important since present methods of regulating may tend to make firms slow to introduce new innovations and encourage innovative activity along lines which have little market desirability, but nevertheless raise costs. The profits permitted to a regulated firm are a function of its investment in plant and equipment; thus between two methods of achieving the same goal there may be an incentive to choose the one requiring greater capital expenditures in order to increase allowed profits. This issue is explored further in Chapter 11.

Summary

The firm is a key economic entity in converting resources to outputs. How well firms function depends on the rules they follow or the goals they seek to achieve when making decisions, and on the market environment of which the firm is a part.

Profit maximization, sales or output maximization (with or without other constraints), a managerial utility function, and satisficing behavior are the most popular alternative descriptions of management motivation. Among the more promising recent approaches is to view decisions within a firm as the outcome of a group choice and thus to develop an "economic theory of teams."[7]

The information available to decision makers is only partly produced within the firm itself. Information—its quality, quantity, cost of acquisition, and time lags in receipt—is the life line between the firm's decisions and its environment.

Pure competition, pure monopoly, monopolistic competition, and oligopoly models of a firm's surroundings provide convenient devices for examining pricing, output, and input decisions.

Questions for Study or Class Discussion

1. List a number of goals managers of a business firm might seek. To what extent are these consistent with shareholder interest?
2. List several criteria for making choices under uncertainty. How do they relate to the criteria discussed in this chapter?
3. Think of at least two actual market settings in addition to those mentioned in this chapter which exemplify the four basic market settings described here.
4. Antitrust policy has been a persistent part of United States economic policy. Why? What are the arguments for and against pursuing an antitrust policy?
5. Ownership and firm size seem to effect profit rates. Try to find more evidence of the influence of these factors. What inferences can be drawn from the evidence?

References

Arrow, K. J., "Limited Knowledge of Economic Analysis," *American Economic Review*, 64 (March, 1974), 1–10.

Balderston, F., and A. Hoggatt, *Simulation of Market Processes*. University of California, 1962.

Baumol, W. J., *Business Behavior, Value, and Growth*. Harcourt, Brace and World, 1967.

Coase, R., "The Nature of the Firm," *Economica*, 4 (1937), 386–405.

Cyert, R., and J. March, *A Behavioral Theory of the Firm*. Prentice-Hall, 1963.

Galbraith, J. K., *The New Industrial State*. Houghton Mifflin, 1967.

Hoggatt, A., "An Experimental Business Game," *Behavioral Science*, 4 (1959), 192–203.

Knight, F., *Risk, Uncertainty, and Profit*. Harper & Row, 1964.

Leibenstein, H., "Allocative Efficiency vs. 'X-Efficiency,'" *American Economic Review*, 56 (June, 1966), 392–415.

[7] See R. Radner and J. Marschak, *The Economic Theory of Teams*, Yale University Press, 1972, for a more extended discussion.

Lewellen, W. G., and B. Huntsman, "Managerial Pay and Corporate Performance," *American Economic Review*, 60 (September, 1970), 710–720.

Lintner, J., "The Valuation of Risky Assets and the Selection of Risky Investments in Stock Portfolios and Capital Budgets," *Review of Economics and Statistics*, 47(February, 1965), 13–37.

Machlup, F., "Theories of the Firm: Marginal, Behavioral, Managerial," *American Economic Review*, 57 (March, 1967), 1–33.

Marris, R., *The Economic Theory of "Managerial" Capitalism.* Free Press, 1964.

Scherer, F., *Industrial Market Structure and Economic Performance.* Rand McNally, 1970.

Scitovsky, T., "A Note on Profit Maximization and Its Implications," *Review of Economic Studies*, 11 (1943), 57–60.

Schramm, R., and R. Sherman, "Profit Risk Management and the Theory of the Firm," *Southern Economic Journal*, 40 (January, 1974), 353–363.

Schumpeter, J., *The Theory of Economic Development.* Oxford University Press, 1961.

Williamson, O., *Economics of Discretionary Behavior.* Prentice-Hall, 1964.

Chapter 6   Production Technology and Input Choice Decisions

Introduction

In this chapter we shall describe production technology and input choices, since the cost information a firm needs for decision making is based on the choices available. The basic tools developed will be applied in analyses of alternative pollution abatement policies and of economic incentives to adopt new innovations.

A Basic Description of Production Technology

Production with one variable input

To analyze the choice problem faced by a firm, we have to be able to describe the range of inputs and outputs that the firm can consider and determine any physical constraints such as physical availability of inputs. Let us begin by describing a physical relationship between one variable input, say labor (L), and one output (Q). Total production may depend on two inputs, say land and labor, but the total amount of land is held fixed. The input/output relationship for labor can then be summarized by means of three concepts: the *total product*, TP, associated with each quantity of input; the *average physical product*, APP, which is the total product divided by the quantity of the variable input, $APP = TP/L$; and the *marginal physical product*, MPP, which is the change in total product divided by the change in the variable input, $MPP = \Delta TP/\Delta L$. Marginal physical product can be expressed as the change in total output associated with a one-unit change in the amount of a variable input.

Table 6.1 Production with One Variable Input and One Output

UNITS OF LABOR	TOTAL PRODUCT (OUTPUT)	AVERAGE PHYSICAL PRODUCT	MARGINAL PHYSICAL PRODUCT
10	100	10	—
20	400	20	30
40	1600	40	60
60	2700	45	55
80	3200	40	20
100	3000	30	−10

Table 6.1 provides the basic data for a numerical example. The first two columns of the table describe the way in which total output varies as the amount of labor is changed. This might hold true for an agricultural situation with a farm of a fixed size and output measured by the yield in bushels or pounds. Average physical product is initially 100 divided by 10. The average physical product for the various inputs is shown in column 3, and the marginal physical product is given in column 4. Marginal physical product of labor when input is increased from 10 to 20 units is the change in total product, 300, divided by the change in the number of units of labor, 10, thus $MPP = 30$. For the next change, marginal physical product is the change in output, 1200, divided by the change in the number of units of labor, 20, thus $MPP = 60$.

A graph of the family of product curves is shown in Figure 6.1. The marginal physical product curve rises initially, intersects the average physical product curve at its maximum, and then declines and becomes negative at the turning point of the total product curve. Geometrically, the marginal physical product curve is the slope of the total product curve, since the slope of the total product curve describes the change in total product associated with a change in input. Where total product reaches a maximum the marginal physical product of one more unit of labor is zero.

For the agricultural example, starting with the given farm and no laborers, when the input is increased to one laborer some increase in output will occur. One man cannot effectively utilize all the equipment required to cultivate the entire plot, so that adding one more man yields a further increase in output. As more and more men are added, there will eventually be so many workers on the plot that they will actually begin to trample the crops, decreasing output. This is the situation when marginal productivity begins to decline and ultimately becomes negative.

The information summarized in the total product, average product, and marginal product curves describes the physical limits that the prevailing techniques of the production impose on a firm. A second, entirely new production method that used inputs more efficiently would be represented by a different total product curve such as *TP'* in Figure 6.1. The important point is that information summarized by these curves is a physical relationship between inputs and output, i.e., a physical boundary or upper limit defined by available technologies.

The "law of diminishing returns" and the stages of production

Figure 6.1 illustrates two additional concepts that are frequently useful in describing the behavior of output as an input is varied: (1) the *Law of Diminishing Marginal Returns* and (2) the *three stages of production.* The Law of Diminishing Marginal Returns simply states that for most production techniques, if all other inputs are held constant, and the amount of one input is increased, a point will eventually be reached where further increments lead to smaller and smaller increases in output. In other words, *MPP* ultimately reaches a maximum and then declines. In Figure 6.1 this point is reached after L_1 units of labor are employed.

The phrase "stages of production" refers to the input ranges over which a firm can use a particular input. A firm interested in hiring inputs so as to maximize profits will only operate in Stage 2, Figure 6.1. It is clear no firm would knowingly extend employment past L_2 into Stage 3 since further employees actually cause total output to fall, but it requires a closer look to see

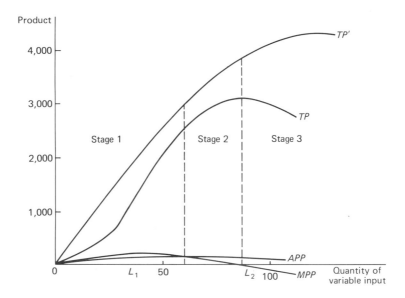

Figure 6.1 Total, Average, and Marginal Physical Product

Table 6.2 Production with Two Variable Inputs

UNITS OF LABOR INPUT	UNITS OF CAPITAL INPUT	OUTPUT
10	60	100
20	80	250
25	25	100
40	50	250
60	20	100
80	40	250

why the firm would not operate in Stage 1. The limit of output expansion occurs at the point where the additional revenue received from the sale of a unit of output just covers the added cost of producing the last unit. If the per unit price of labor is W, then the cost of the last unit of output is W/MPP_L. However, the firm will only extend hiring (and output) to this point if the sales price it receives at least covers its average variable costs. This average variable cost is W/APP_L. Since the sales price of the last unit of output is equal to its cost, W/MPP_L, this condition can be expressed as $W/APP_L \leq W/MPP_L$. Dividing both sides by W and taking reciprocals gives us $APP_L \geq MPP_L$. This is exactly the situation that characterizes Stage 2. In Stage 1, however, $APP_L < MPP_L$, so that the firm would not be recovering its average costs.

Production with two variable inputs

The example given above was based on the use of a single variable input. The description of technologies, however, involves consideration of several inputs. The choice of a technique of production is actually a choice between the various input combinations available to a firm.

Let us take a situation where we have two inputs, say labor and capital, and a single output. Table 6.2 provides the basic data. For each pair of input quantities, the last column indicates the maximum output obtainable from that pair. Alternatively, Table 6.2 could be read as giving examples of minimum input mixes which would produce the output shown in the last column.

The data in Table 6.2 is plotted in Figure 6.2. From a lengthy table of the relationship between input combinations and output, we could plot the combinations of capital and labor for each level of output. Connecting all the input combinations producing the same maximum level of output might yield curves such as the ones for $Q = 100$ and $Q = 250$. Each level of output will have a different curve. This family of curves, one for each level

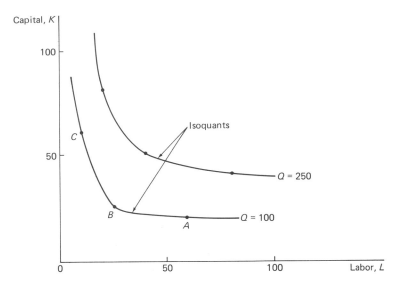

Figure 6.2 Two Members of a Family of Isoquants

of output, is referred to as a *field of isoquants*. Isoquants play the same role in the analysis of a firm's input decision that indifference curves played in the analysis of the consumption decision. In fact, the geometric picture of the input problem for the firm looks very much like the picture we sketched earlier for the consumption problem.

If a firm is trying to produce 100 units of output, then it may choose any input combination *on or above* the isoquant for 100 units of output. The isoquant concept is a way of describing the available techniques of production. Any given isoquant describes the alternative *minimum* mixes of inputs that will yield the same level of output. Analogously, indifference curves describe mixes of commodities, or alternative market baskets, that give rise to the same level of satisfaction.

Input substitution and the marginal rate of technical substitution (*MRTS*)

A concept parallel to the marginal rate of substitution discussed earlier for indifference curves is associated with isoquants. This new concept is called the *marginal rate of technical substitution* (*MRTS*). The marginal rate of technical substitution is defined as the negative of the slope of an isoquant at a given point. Alternatively, the same type of argument used with indifference curves can be used to show that the *MRTS* between any two inputs may be expressed as a ratio of their marginal physical products,[1] $MRTS_{K,L} = MPP_L/MPP_K$. What is the economic significance of the $MRTS$? Suppose we have calculated a marginal rate of technical substitution of capital for labor of 4. This means that the same number of units of output could still be produced if capital were substituted for labor at the rate of 4 units of capital for one unit of labor. The marginal rate of technical substitution is equal to the number of units of one input that must be substituted for one unit of another in order to maintain a constant output.

Moving from left to right along any isoquant in Figure 6.2—for example, moving from B toward A—the curve becomes flatter. This reflects the fact that isoquants like the ones in Figure 6.2 depict a diminishing marginal rate of technical substitution. A diminishing $MRTS$ simply means that for producing a specific amount of this particular commodity, as one hires more and more labor, the amount of the possible reduction in capital becomes smaller and smaller. At a point such as C, if we increase the amount of labor by one unit, a substantial amount of capital can be dispensed with. This might be desirable in order to minimize the cost of production. On the other hand, at a point such as A, adding another unit of labor will not produce as large a reduction in the amount of capital required as occurred at C. If a minimum amount of capital is absolutely necessary the isoquant will eventually become parallel to the axis. The marginal rate of technical substitution of labor for capital is just the reciprocal of the $MRTS$ of capital for labor. A substitution rate of 4 units of capital for one unit of labor is the same as a rate of $\frac{1}{4}$ unit of labor for one unit of capital.

The numerical value of the $MRTS$ is a measure of the ease with which inputs may be substituted for one another. An $MRTS$ of zero implies that no substitution is possible, while a value of unity implies that two inputs may be substituted for each other on a one-for-one basis.

Least Cost Production—Input Choice

This section shows how a firm can solve its input choice problem for the mix of inputs that will minimize production cost. Solution of the optimal

[1] This definition is easily related to the preceding one by considering the production function $Q = F(K, L)$ where $MPP_K = \partial F/\partial K$ and $MPP_L = \partial F/\partial L$. Differentiating the production function totally gives

$$dQ = \frac{\partial F}{\partial K} dK + \frac{\partial F}{\partial L} dL$$

Along a given isoquant $dQ = 0$, thus

$$-\frac{\partial F/L}{\partial F/K} = \frac{dK}{dL} = \text{slope of isoquant}$$

or

$$-\frac{dK}{dL} = MRTS = \frac{\partial F/\partial L}{\partial F/\partial K} = \frac{MPP_L}{MPP_K}$$

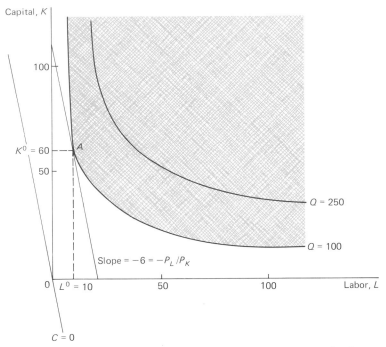

Figure 6.3 Feasible Input Combinations and Least Cost Input Choice

input choice problem is the first step in building the least cost production schedule, which indicates the least total production cost for each output level. This cost function will subsequently be combined with the revenue data built up from our earlier demand analysis to provide the information for the profit function of the firm. The profit function in turn is the basis for solving policy decisions concerning output and pricing.

The isocost curve and optimal input choice

Figure 6.3 represents the isoquant information developed in the previous section. Production is carried out with two variable inputs, capital and labor. Suppose the firm wants to find the mix of inputs which will produce 100 units of output at minimum cost. As we saw earlier, the firm can choose any combination of inputs that lies on or above the isoquant for 100 units of output. The range of input choice is indicated by the crosshatched area in Figure 6.3.

The costs that the firm incurs for any given combination of inputs is the unit price of capital[2] times the number of units employed plus the unit price of labor times the number of units employed.

---

[2] For convenience the *price of capital* might be thought of as a rental rate for a unit period such as a month or a year. The concepts of *cost of capital* and *capital rents* are discussed in detail in Chapter 16.

Let us suppose that the price of capital, P_K, is \$2 and the price of labor, P_L, is \$12. The total cost function for the firm will be $C = 2K + 12L$. In order to graph this cost function in Figure 6.3, let us rewrite it as $K = C/2 - (12/2)L$. This curve represents the alternative combinations of capital and labor that can be purchased for a given total expenditure, C. It is called an *isocost curve*. Graphing the isocost curve for $C = 0$ shows that we cannot buy any positive amount of either input for zero cost. The slope of the isocost curve is -6, which is equal to the negative of the ratio of the input prices, $-P_L/P_K$. The slope of the isocost curve thus reflects the *relative* price of the inputs.

How do we find the minimum expenditure that will allow us to produce 100 units of output? Since $C = 0$ is obviously insufficient we need to raise the level of expenditure, keeping the relative prices of the inputs unchanged. Spending more is represented in Figure 6.3 by a sequence of isocost curves parallel to the one for $C = 0$ and to its right. The level of expenditure must be increased until a point is reached where at least one of the combinations that can be purchased is an input combination lying on the isoquant for $Q = 100$.

For the example given in Table 6.2, the least cost combination is 60 units of capital and 10 of labor. The input combination of $L = 10$, $K = 60$ is the solution to the problem of minimizing the cost of producing 100 units of output for the given prices of capital and labor. Substituting these optimal input levels in the cost expression, we obtain the minimum cost of \$240 = $2(60) + 12(10)$.

Suppose that the price of labor has decreased to $P_L = \$3.50$. How do we describe this decrease in terms of the isocost curve? Since the price of capital remains at \$2 but the price of labor has fallen, the isocost curve becomes flatter. Its slope changes from -6 to $-1.75 = -3.50/2$. The firm's choice will now move from A to the input combination indicated by point B (Figure 6.4). The firm increases the use of that input which has become relatively cheaper, labor, and decreases the use of the input that has become relatively more expensive. This substitution is open to the firm only if its production technologies allow input substitution. This point is developed more fully in the pollution abatement example later in this chapter.

The impact on demand arising from a change in the price of a particular commodity was described in terms of two separate influences: a substitution effect and an income effect (Chapter 3). An analogous pair of concepts exists with regard to input choices, referred to as a substitution effect and an output effect. The analysis described earlier is directly applicable to these concepts; therefore, it will not be repeated here.

The anatomy of an optimal solution

Let us look more closely at the character of the optimal solutions in Figures 6.3 and 6.4. Earlier we defined the concept of a marginal rate of technical substitution as being the negative of the slope of an isoquant at a given point.

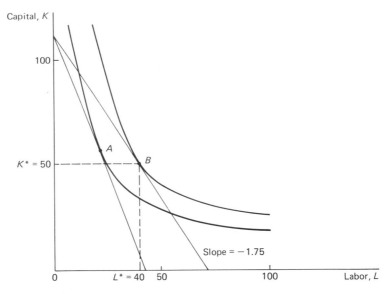

Figure 6.4   Changing Input Prices and Changing Efficient Input Choices

Each of the optimal input mix solutions depicted in Figures 6.3 and 6.4 is geometrically pictured as the point of tangency between the isocost curve and an isoquant. At this point the slope of the isocost curve, which is the negative of the ratio of the input prices, is equal to the slope of the isoquant, which is the negative of the marginal rate of technical substitution at that point. Thus

$$- \frac{P_L}{P_K} = -MRTS_{K,L}$$

or

$$\frac{P_L}{P_K} = MRTS_{K,L} \tag{6.1}$$

Since $MRTS_{K,L} = MPP_L/MPP_K$, Equation (6.1) could be expressed[3]

$$\frac{P_L}{P_K} = \frac{MPP_L}{MPP_K}$$

or

$$\frac{P_L}{MPP_L} = \frac{P_K}{MPP_K} \tag{6.2}$$

[3] In more technical language, the least cost input mix results from solving

$$\text{Minimize } C = \sum_{j=1}^{m} P_j X_j$$

The ratio of input price to *MPP* is the marginal cost of the last unit of output obtainable by using the input in question. Equation (6.2) indicates that for an optimal input mix the marginal cost of one more unit of output is the same for both inputs.

For positive levels of all inputs, the optimal solution is characterized by having the ratio of the input prices equal to the marginal rate of technical substitution.[4] This condition has a simple economic interpretation. The ratio of the input prices indicates the rate at which units of one input can be exchanged for units of another input in the market. The marginal rate of technical substitution indicates the rate at which the inputs can be exchanged for each other technologically. As long as both inputs are used, a firm would substitute one input for another until these two exchange rates were equal, since if they were not, it would always be possible to find a different mix of the inputs which would give a lower cost.

Just as with the consumer budget problem, an optimal solution may use a positive amount of every input, or use one or more inputs at a zero level. Solutions which involve using one or more inputs at a zero level are referred to as boundary solutions.

The expansion path

The *expansion path* directly links the firm's input choices with the least total cost for each level of output. Let us examine the way in which input combinations change with changes in the level of output, when relative input

---

subject to

$$F(X_1, \ldots, X_m) \geq Q^0$$

$$X_j \geq 0, \quad j = 1, \ldots, m$$

Forming the Lagrangian expression

$$\phi = \sum_{j=1}^{m} P_j X_j + \lambda[Q^0 - F(X_1, \ldots, X_m)] + \sum_{j=1}^{m} \mu_j X_j$$

and minimizing with respect to the inputs X_j while maximizing with respect to the Lagrangian multipliers λ and μ_j leads to the conditions:

for $X_j > 0$

$$\frac{\partial \phi}{\partial X_j} = P_j - \lambda \frac{\partial F}{\partial X_j} = 0 \quad j = 1, \ldots, m$$

and for $\lambda > 0$

$$\frac{\partial \phi}{\partial \lambda} = Q^0 - F(X_1, \ldots, X_m) = 0$$

For any j and k

$$\frac{P_j}{P_k} = \frac{\partial F/\partial X_j}{\partial F/\partial X_k} = \frac{MPP_j}{MPP_k} = MRTS$$

The multiplier λ represents the marginal cost of output evaluated at Q^0. Analogous inequality conditions apply if none of an input is used.

[4] If one or more of the inputs is not used at the optimum, then the equality condition is replaced by an inequality condition between any input that is used and one that is not used. Between any pair of inputs that are both used the equality must still hold at the optimum point.

prices are held constant. As output expands, the least cost combination of inputs may change, since different techniques of production become available at one level of output which were not available earlier. Notice that all inputs are regarded as variable.

The information for the expansion path is built up by solving the problem of least cost production at each level of output, Q_1, Q_2, Q_3, Q_4, etc., using the same set of relative prices. Such a sequence of solutions is pictured in Figure 6.5. The solution for Q_1 units of output is point A; for Q_2, point B; for Q_3, point C, etc. The curve connecting all optimal solutions describes the way in which the least cost mix changes as the level of output changes, for a given set of input prices. This curve is referred to as the expansion path.

There are two possible ways in which the usage of an input may change as output changes. If the quantity demanded for an input increases or remains unchanged as the level of output increases, with relative prices held constant, the input is said to be *normal*. The expansion path shown in Figure 6.5 illustrates a case where both capital and labor are normal. It is also possible,

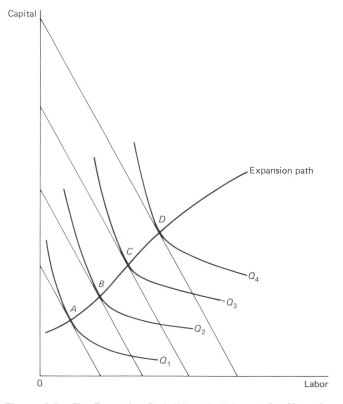

Figure 6.5   The Expansion Path When Both Inputs Are Normal

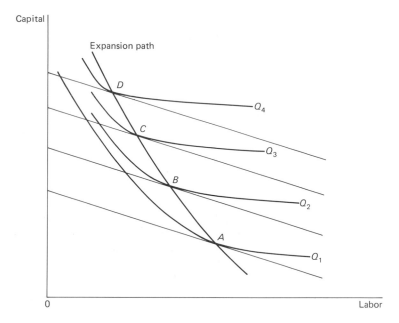

Figure 6.6 The Expansion Path When One Input Is Inferior

however, for one of the inputs, say labor, to be an *inferior* input. This would mean that, when relative input prices are held constant, increases in the level of output cause less and less labor to be used. Figure 6.6 illustrates this possibility. Starting at point A and moving to a higher level of output, less labor is used in the optimum solutions. The expansion path has a negative slope. As with normal and inferior commodities, the terms "normal" and "inferior" refer to particular levels of output. The same input may behave differently at different output levels.

Development of the expansion path concept links the technologically efficient input levels for each level of output with a unique minimum total cost. Although we have followed the steps from efficient input choice to least total cost, the steps are reversible. Given a minimum cost function it is possible to trace a picture of the isoquant field which would give rise to that cost function through solution of a cost minimization problem. This is an application of the powerful tool referred to as *duality*. The information obtainable from production or cost functions either by direct observation or by using their dual nature is particularly useful for empirical measurement.

Derived demand for inputs

Isocost curves like those in Figure 6.3 can be used to develop a firm's demand schedule for inputs. Starting with the optimal solution shown in Figure 6.3

and then successively varying the price of labor would cause the isocost curves to fan out around the intercept on the capital axis, Figure 6.7. Each of the new isocost curves has a different slope, reflecting the difference in the relative cost of capital to labor. From each isocost curve we can read off the optimal amount of labor to hire corresponding to each relative price. This information can be used to build up a firm's *derived demand schedule* for labor.[5] This is used in Chapter 14 when we discuss labor and other input markets.

An Alternative View of Isoquants

Since isoquants play such an important descriptive role, it is worthwhile to consider an equivalent way of obtaining them. At the beginning of this chapter we described the physical limits of input/output relationships in terms of total product curves. Such relationships are referred to as *production functions*. A production function indicates the maximum quantity of output technologically possible for various amounts of each input.

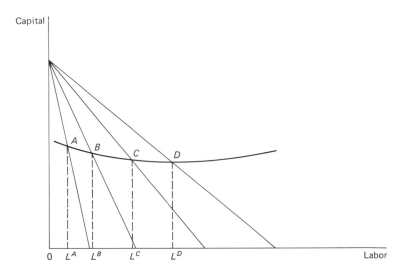

Figure 6.7 Changing Wage Rates and Changing Input Purchases

[5] Using the $m + 1$ equations shown in footnote 4 for $\partial \phi / \partial X_j, j = 1, \ldots, m$, and $\partial \phi / \partial \lambda$, we can formally solve these to express the optimal values of the X_j and λ in terms of the m input prices and Q. This method of solution is valid provided the hypotheses of the Implicit Function Theorem are satisfied. The solutions obtained are the m derived demand functions for each input and an expression for the marginal cost, λ.

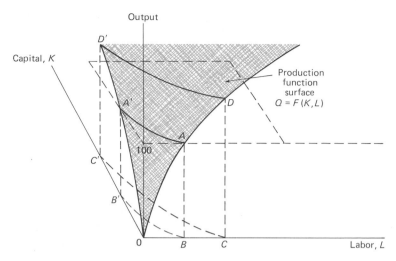

Figure 6.8 A Production Function Surface With Two Inputs

Alternatively, the production function can be used to find the alternative mixes of inputs which are the minimum technological requirements to achieve a given level of output.

Figure 6.8 illustrates a production surface for two inputs, assuming a decreasing marginal physical product for each input and a decreasing marginal rate of technical substitution. As the amount of labor increases, output increases regardless of the amount of capital, producing a bowl-like shape, but the surface tends to flatten out as more labor is used. Since the slope of the surface, parallel to either input axis, is the marginal physical product, the fact that the curve is flattening out reflects the fact that marginal physical product is decreasing. This picture reflects the typical assumption that a production function is a concave function of the inputs.

If we look at all of the combinations of capital and labor associated with a given level of output, we can see the relationship between the production function and isoquants. A plane parallel to the capital and labor plane at 100 units of output cuts through the production surface along the curve AA'. The projection of this intersection in the capital-labor plane is the curve BB'. Repeating this process at many levels of output yields a family of curves in the capital-labor plane. These are the isoquants we obtained earlier. Isoquants represent contours of the production function at various output levels. Both a production function and isoquants are simply means of describing available technologies.

Although all of the isoquants studied so far have been convex toward the origin, this is by no means the only possibility. Figure 6.9 illustrates several

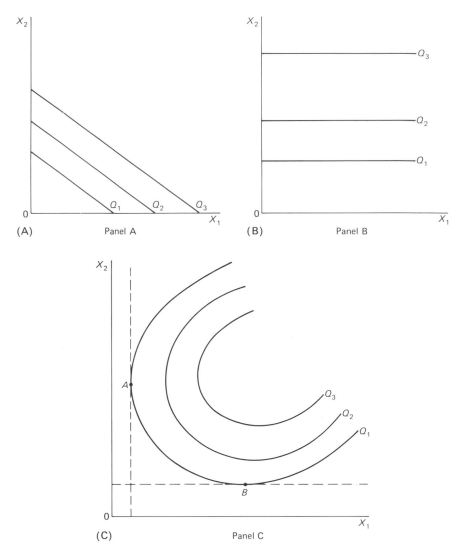

Figure 6.9 Some Alternative Shapes for Isoquants (A) (B) (C)

others. What does each of these alternatives imply about the character of the least cost input mix?

The figure in Panel C illustrates what is referred to as *uneconomic regions* of a production function. As long as the prices of inputs X_1 and X_2 are zero or positive, a solution to the least cost problem for producing Q_1 will always occur on the segment $\widehat{AB}$. Even though the segments above A or to the right of B are part of the isoquant for Q_1 they involve the use of more of both inputs. Combinations of X_1 and X_2 lying on $\widehat{AB}$ will produce Q_1 at less cost.

Empirical Measurement of Production Relationships

The measurement of production functions requires just as much care as the measurement of demand functions.

Table 6.3 lists some of the most common forms used for production functions with the name of each. Economists usually choose the one that seems to provide the best fit to the data for the given inputs and outputs. This variation in the form chosen reflects the different technologies in vogue in different industries or different firms. One or more of these forms typically offers an excellent statistical fit for the data.

Table 6.4 illustrates several empirical applications. The first one is a Cobb-Douglas example for the production of electricity using three inputs: capital, labor, and fuel. The numerical values of the exponents in the Cobb-Douglas form indicate the percentage change in output that would follow from a 1% change in the amount of any one of the associated inputs, i.e., the exponents represent the elasticity of output with respect to each input. For example, the exponent for capital, 0.65, indicates that a 1% increase in the amount of capital employed would lead to a 0.65% increase in the amount of electricity generated, if the amounts of labor and fuel remained constant. From the relative sizes of these elasticities it is clear that adding a unit of capital or fuel increases production more than adding a unit of labor, but

Table 6.3 Some Frequently Used Production Function Forms (For Two Inputs, X_1 and X_2)

NAME	FUNCTIONAL FORM
Cobb-Douglas	$Y = AX_1^{\alpha_1}X_2^{\alpha_2}$
CES[a]	$Y = B[aX_2^\rho + (1 - a)X_2^\rho]^{v/\rho}$
Linear	$Y = C + b_1X_1 + b_2X_2$
Quadratic	$Y = D + c_1X_1 + c_2X_1^2$
	$\quad + c_3X_1X_2 + c_4X_2 + c_5X_2^2$

[a] The letters stand for constant elasticity of substitution.

this does not mean that this is the most economical way of obtaining added output. It all depends on the relative prices of capital, labor, and fuel.

Another example fitting the Cobb-Douglas form is the production of metal and machinery in the U.S. economy. As in the previous example, the exponents represent the elasticity of output with respect to the input. The exponent for labor, 0.71, implies that a 1% change in labor would lead to approximately a 0.71% change in the output of metals and machinery. The third Cobb-Douglas example for coal illustrates the marked difference between the roles capital and labor play in the technologies used for metals and machinery production and coal production.

In the fourth example, a CES production function was applied to the production of bushels of corn. Input X_1 is gallons of water per acre and input X_2 is pounds of nitrogen per acre.

Many production function forms other than those in Table 6.3 might be used in particular applications. The last example in Table 6.4 illustrates another function for corn production using different inputs from those in the CES example.

Table 6.4 Empirical Examples of Production Functions

OUTPUT	FORM USED	ESTIMATED RELATIONSHIP
Electricity[a]	Cobb-Douglas	$Q = \text{constant} \cdot (\text{capital})^{0.65} \times (\text{labor})^{0.15} \cdot (\text{fuel})^{0.73}$
Metals/Machinery[b]	Cobb-Douglas	$Q = \text{constant} \cdot (\text{labor})^{0.71} \cdot (\text{capital})^{0.26}$
Coal[c]	Cobb-Douglas	$Q = \text{constant} \cdot (\text{labor})^{0.29} \cdot (\text{capital})^{0.79}$
Corn[d]	CES	$Q = \text{constant} \times [0.47 \, (\text{water per acre})^{-0.54} + 0.53 \, (\text{nitrogen per acre})^{-.54}]^{-0.89/0.54}$
Corn[e]	other	$Q = \text{constant} - 0.316 \, (\text{pounds of nitrogen}) + 0.635 \, \sqrt{\text{pounds of nitrogen}} + 8.516 \, \sqrt{\text{pounds of phosphate}} + 0.341 \, \sqrt{\left(\begin{array}{c}\text{pounds of}\\\text{nitrogen}\end{array}\right) \cdot \left(\begin{array}{c}\text{pounds of}\\\text{phosphate}\end{array}\right)}$

SOURCES:
[a] M. Nerlove, "Returns to Scale in Electricity Supply," in C. Christ, ed., *Measurement in Economics*. Stanford University Press, 1963.
[b] M. Bronfenbrenner and P. Douglas, "Cross-Section Studies in the Cobb-Douglas Production Function," *Journal of Political Economy*, 47 (December, 1939), 761–785.
[c] K. S. Lomax, "Coal Production Functions for Great Britain," *Journal of the Royal Statistical Society*, 113 (1950), 346–351.
[d] R. Meyer and K. Kadiyala, "Linear and Nonlinear Estimation of Production Functions," *Southern Economic Journal*, 40 (January, 1974), 463–472.
[e] E. Heady, "An Econometric Investigation of the Technology of Agricultural Production Functions," *Econometrica*, 25 (April, 1957), 249–268.

Returns to Scale

A concept directly related to the production function, which becomes useful in analyzing policy problems where production is concentrated in the hands of a few firms, is referred to as *returns to scale*. The returns to scale associated with any particular production function measure the percentage change in output associated with a given percentage change in *all* of the inputs.

In the first empirical example in Table 6.4, the degree of returns to scale would be found by asking by what percentage the number of kilowatt hours of electricity generated would increase if we increased capital (K) by 10%, labor (L) by 10%, and fuel (F) by 10%. In order to measure returns to scale, one considers increases or decreases for *all* inputs in the *same* proportion. If we multiply the amount of capital employed by λ, the amount of labor employed by λ, and the amount of fuel employed by λ, we obtain

$$A(\lambda K)^{\alpha_1}(\lambda L)^{\alpha_2}(\lambda F)^{\alpha_3} \tag{6.3}$$

or

$$\lambda^{\alpha_1+\alpha_2+\alpha_3}AK^{\alpha_1}L^{\alpha_2}F^{\alpha_3} = \lambda^{\alpha_1+\alpha_2+\alpha_3}Q \tag{6.4}$$

The term which determines the effect on output involves the sum of the exponents. If λ is greater than zero, then the sum of the exponents indicates whether output changes at the same rate, at a slower rate, or at a faster rate, than the increase or decrease in inputs.

The case where the sum of the exponents $\alpha_1 + \alpha_2 + \alpha_3$ is unity is referred to as *constant returns to scale*. This means that the technologies in use have the property that if all of the inputs are increased in a given proportion, then output increases in the same proportion. For example, multiplying all of the inputs by two increases output by two; increasing all inputs tenfold increases output tenfold, etc. The case where the sum of the exponents is greater than unity is referred to as *increasing returns to scale*. In this situation a 10% increase in all of the inputs increases output by more than 10%. The electricity example in Table 6.4 is a case of increasing returns, and Table 6.5 provides examples for several other industries. The third situation occurs when the sum of the exponents is less than unity. This is referred to as *decreasing returns to scale*. Doubling all input quantities, for instance, would lead to less than twice as much output.

The existence of economies of scale suggests that there may be cost advantages from large-scale operations. Thus production in industries whose technology exhibits increasing returns to scale is likely to be concentrated in a few firms. In the same way, returns-to-scale information is relevant to the investment choice between building one very large plant or several smaller ones.

Table 6.5   Estimates of Returns to Scale

INDUSTRY	RETURNS TO SCALE EXPONENT
Electric power[a]	1.53
Coal[b]	1.08
Natural gas[c]	0.93
Paper[d]	1.08
Sugar[d]	0.92
Metals and Machinery[e]	0.97

SOURCES:
[a] See M. Nerlove footnote to Table 6.4.
[b] See K. S. Lomax footnote to Table 6.4
[c] M. J. Verhulst, "Pure Theory of Production Applied to the French Gas Industry," *Econometrica*, 16 (1948), 295–308.
[d] V. N. Murti and V. K. Sastry, "Production Functions for Indian Industry," *Econometrica*, 25 (1957), 205–221.
[e] See M. Bronfenbrenner and P. Douglas footnote to Table 6.4.

The phenomena of returns to scale is actually implicit in the previous illustrations of isoquants. With constant returns, the isoquants for, say, 100, 200, 300, etc., are all equally spaced apart since increasing all inputs by the same proportion increases output by the same proportion. In contrast, for decreasing returns the isoquants for 100, 200, 300, etc., would be spaced farther and farther apart since proportionately larger inputs are needed to achieve equal increases in output. With increasing returns the isoquants for 100, 200, 300, etc., will become closer together as output increases.

Elasticity of Input Substitution

There is one other concept associated with the production function that is useful in decision making, the concept of *elasticity of input substitution* (or elasticity of factor substitution). The elasticity of input substitution is defined as the ratio of the percentage change in the input ratio divided by the percentage change in the marginal rate of technical substitution, when output is held constant. In symbols, using the familiar two-input setting with capital and labor,

$$\sigma = \frac{\Delta(K/L)/(K/L)}{\Delta MRTS/MRTS} \tag{6.5}$$

Although this looks rather complicated, it has a simple economic interpretation. It measures the ease with which one input may be substituted for another along a particular isoquant. Like any elasticity, it has three ranges:

Table 6.6   Some Estimates of the Elasticity of Capital/Labor Substitution

INDUSTRY	σ
Coal Mining	0.93
Petroleum and Natural Gas	1.71
Textiles	0.80
Chemicals	0.90
Electric power	0.82
Transportation	1.74

SOURCE: K. J. Arrow, H. B. Chenery, B. S. Minhas, and R. M. Solow, "Capital-Labor Substitution and Economic Efficiency," *Review of Economics and Statistics*, 43 (August, 1961), 225–250.

an inelastic range, an elastic range, and a unit elastic range. The CES shown in Table 6.3 as the name of a production form stands for Constant Elasticity of Substitution.[6] The CES form has the property that for any level of the inputs, σ is a constant.

The ease with which inputs can be substituted for one another is important in determining how easy it would be to change the technique of production. If this elasticity of factor substitution is zero this indicates that, for technological purposes, the firm is unable to change the mix in which it uses inputs. Even if the relative prices of inputs change, the production technologies will not allow the firm to take advantage of the change. The value of σ therefore roughly indicates which industries will be able to hold their costs down in the face of rising relative input prices by changing techniques of production and which industries will incur increases in production costs which must ultimately reduce profits or increase output prices. The greater the value of σ the better the industry is able to protect consumers against product price increases.

Since σ measures the ease of input substitution it is related to the shape of an isoquant. If isoquant surfaces are smooth, with slopes defined at all points (which implies that *MRTS* and σ are defined at all points), then the closer σ is to zero the more the isoquants resemble right angles. As σ becomes very large the isoquants look more like the straight-line isoquants shown in Panel A of Figure 6.9.

Table 6.6 contains some empirical estimates of σ using two inputs: capital and labor. What information about available technologies is given by the data in Table 6.6? In the petroleum and natural gas example, an elasticity of 1.71

[6] Recent research has emphasized more flexible production function forms which allow the elasticity of substitution to vary with input ratios and/or output. See C. A. Knox Lovell, "Estimation and Prediction with CES and VES Production Functions," *International Economic Review*, 14 (October, 1973), 676–692, for an extended discussion and comparison.

indicates that it is technologically feasible to substitute capital for labor in petroleum extraction. Comparing coal and petroleum, the influence of the different technologies used in these two extractive industries becomes apparent. The possibilities of substituting capital for labor while maintaining output constant appear better in petroleum than they do in coal extraction. If wage rates in the economy rise substantially, while the price of capital does not, then the petroleum industry is better able to take advantage of this since its technologies allow it to substitute the relatively cheap capital for the relatively expensive labor. The coal industry is less able to buffer itself against production cost increases occasioned by the rise in wage rates.

Policy Evaluation for Pollution Control

Let us take the concept of least cost input choice and put it to work in solving a pollution control example. Suppose a firm uses two inputs: a waste disposal service, W, and a second input or group of inputs, I. This might apply to a manufacturing situation where the waste is polluted water discarded into a lake or river or smoke, unburnt fuels, and odorous gases. Alternatively, one input might be high sulfur content fuel and the other low sulfur content fuel. Then the problem is the one faced by a public utility attempting to produce electric power at least cost. High sulfur content fuel oil or coal may cost less, but its use leads to high pollution discharges unless steps are taken to "clean" the smoke.

An important part of the pollution problem is to describe the techniques available to the firm. Let us define a technique of production as the ability to use inputs in a particular ratio. The phrase refers to a situation in which one can use inputs only in a specific ratio of one to the other. The existence of technique options means that the firm has the technological possibility of using inputs in different proportions. The geometrical picture of a technique, as defined above, is a ray starting at the origin with the slope of the ray equal to the ratio in which the two inputs may be used (Figure 6.10). If technique T_1 is one in which inputs must be used in the ratio 2 units of X_2 to 1 unit of X_1, then this would be represented by the ray T_1 whose slope is 2. In technique T_2, 1/3 unit of X_2 is used for every unit of X_1.

To build up the isoquants associated with these techniques we pick out the input levels along each ray associated with each level of output. Suppose that for technique T_1 points A, C, and D are the minimum input requirements for producing 100, 200, and 300 units of output, respectively, and that points B, E, and F are the corresponding minimum requirements for technique T_2. With only two available techniques, the associated isoquants will appear as in Figure 6.10. They are not the smoothly curved isoquants sketched earlier. Instead, each isoquant is *piecewise linear*—composed of a sequence of flat surfaces. The explanation for the vertical line above point A on $Q = 100$

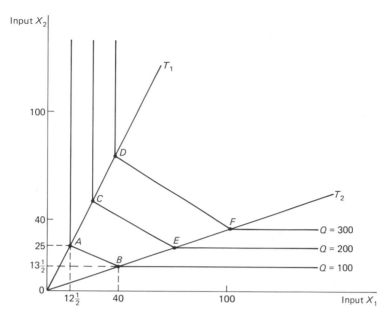

Figure 6.10   Techniques of Production and Piecewise Linear Isoquants

is that, with only $12\frac{1}{2}$ units of X_1, adding more than 25 units of X_2 will not produce further output because the inputs must be used in fixed proportions to one another. The same reasoning applies for points on $Q = 100$ to the right of point B. So long as there are only $13\frac{1}{3}$ units of X_2, more X_1 does not provide any further productive potential.

It is not true, however, that production on $Q = 100$ above A or to the right of B will never occur. This is an important point in analyzing solutions to economic problems like the pollution example.

What is the economic interpretation of the line segments AB (or CE or DF) that join the two techniques? Our ability to join the two techniques in this manner stems from the assumption that either or both techniques can be used and that using one does not interfere with the other. Points on the line segment represent the various combinations of the two techniques that might be used. At point A technique T_1 is being used 100% of the time, and at B technique T_2 is being used 100% of the time. Along the segment from A to B, T_1 is used for a successively smaller percentage of the time and T_2 is used for the rest of the time. Regardless of the percentage mix, output remains constant along a given isoquant.

Suppose in our example that the firm wants to solve the problem of producing 100 units of output at least cost. If there are no regulations about the disposal of wastes, what input mix should be chosen? With P_W the price of waste disposal service and P_I the price of the other inputs, total costs are

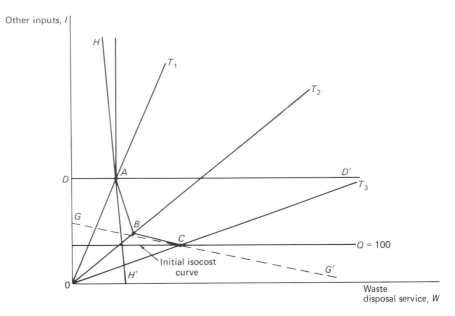

Figure 6.11 Input Choice for Alternative Pollution Policies

$P_W W + P_I I$. With no disposal regulations, what are the costs of these inputs? The price of the other input, P_I, whether it is labor, materials, fuel, or capital, is generally nonzero. However, with pollution or discharges, a private property rights system imputes its own price. A property right may convey the right to use a resource at a zero cost. The perceived cost of using the air or the water of a lake or a river as a vehicle for waste disposal is zero!

Assuming a zero cost for waste disposal, the isocost curve will be parallel to the horizontal axis. Any input combination at C (Figure 6.11) or to the right of C is an optimal input choice. The firm is limiting the use of costly inputs and making the greatest possible use of any input which is available at zero cost, or relatively cheap, and yet has a productive use. Without any controls or regulations, the firm is led to exploit the use of inputs which have zero prices or at least inputs which are *relatively* the cheapest. The fact that high-grade hard coal has a very high price but a low sulfur content, while soft coal, which has a higher sulfur content, has a lower price, explains why firms may make choices that tend to pollute at a high rate.

Suppose the choice made by the industry leads to an undesirable degree of pollution. How might the solution pictured in Figure 6.11 be improved? One possibility is to order a firm not to produce at C, but to produce at A when output is 100 units. This simply prohibits the use of technique T_2 or T_3. The firm would still be confronted by the relative costs represented by the isocost curve through *C*, but it would be producing at *A*. The new isocost curve is *DD'*.

This solution, however, forces the firm to increase the amount of other inputs. This means that the effect of reducing the amount of pollution by this particular policy is an increase in the total production costs borne by the firm. Increasing the cost of an average unit of output means that two things may happen: profits may fall, in which case the burden of cleaning up the pollution problem is borne by the firm, or the increased costs may be passed on to consumers through increases in commodity prices. The cost of cleaning up the environment is ultimately shared between the firm, through reduced profits, and the consumers of the commodity, through increased product prices.

A second alternative might be to have a public body pay a subsidy to a firm to produce at *A* instead of *B*. We can easily see how large this subsidy must be to induce the firm to operate at *A*. If the firm would otherwise produce at *C* at the prevailing set of prices, the total cost would be C_C. Producing at *A* involves a total cost of C_A. The question is how much one has to offer the firm in order to induce it to voluntarily choose to produce at point *A*. Any subsidy larger than $C_A - C_C$ will produce a perceived total cost of producing at *A* which is less than that at *C*.

The two policies we have considered so far have very different distributional effects. In the first case, the cost is borne by the firm and/or the consumers of the commodity. In the second case, the firm's profits could actually be enhanced, if the firm kept the cost savings. Alternatively, it might pass some of the cost savings on to consumers through reduced commodity prices. However, an added cost is being borne by the public treasury. This added cost must be made up by revenue, drawn not merely from the consumers of the commodity in question, but from the whole population of taxpayers. The second policy may be preferred to the first largely because its indirect influence makes it difficult to determine who is paying and how much.

In examining the two previous policy alternatives we did nothing to disturb the initial relative prices created by the market. Waste disposal (polluting) cost nothing while the other input(s) had a strictly positive market price. As a third policy, consider inducing the firm to curtail the use of an input by increasing the relative cost of using it, possibly by levying a per unit tax or penalty on the amount of the input used. For example, an "effluent discharge price" of so many dollars per hundred gallons of discharge might be charged to firms pumping waste into a river. Or the volume of gaseous discharges might be taxed at so many dollars per hundred cubic feet of discharge. The important question is whether this will solve the problem.

Levying taxes or other charges on the act of polluting will not necessarily solve the problem; in fact, it may have no effect at all! To see how this may occur, we draw a new isocost curve *GG'* (Figure 6.11) which reflects a positive price for the waste disposal service. This isocost curve is no longer parallel to the horizontal axis and its slope determines which solution actually occurs. If its slope is only slightly negative, it is quite possible that the firm will still find the optimal combination at point C. Raising P_W further might lead to an isocost curve that is tangent along the face of the flat segment between B and C, in which case any of the input combinations between and including B and C are optimal. An excise or penalty tax will be effective only when it is raised sufficiently high to force a change in production technique. The operation of such a tax might be reflected by the isocost curve HH'.

Notice in this example the extreme importance of alternative techniques for production. The isoquants that we used in early descriptions of the input choice problem were smoothly shaped, while the ones we are using are angular. Instead of having input usage change continuously with relative input prices, we encounter critical changeover points, while at other times no change in input occurs over a wide range of changes in relative prices. Starting out with a single technique of production, the isoquants will be right angles like the ones in Figure 6.12. With two techniques of production, the isoquants are similar to those in Figure 6.13. Ten techniques of production will be represented by ten rays and each isoquant face will be composed of many flat segments. As the number of techniques is increased to the point where there is an indefinitely large number of input ratios, the limiting shape for the isoquants will be the smoothly curving isoquants illustrated earlier.

In practice firms are not confronted with an indefinitely large number of techniques, but with a small finite number. This means that the most realistic descriptions of a firm's input choice problems are probably isoquants with flat faces that, therefore, do not permit continuous substitution of inputs.

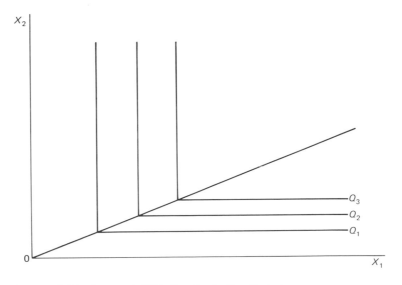

Figure 6.12   Isoquants With One Production Technique

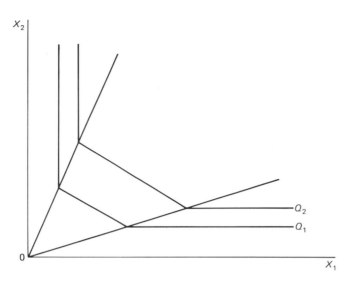

Figure 6.13   Isoquants With Two Production Techniques

This is extremely important in appraising the impact of alternative policies, as in the pollution control example.

Let us consider another example: Labor groups in favor of raising the minimum wage might argue as follows: increasing the minimum wage will raise the incomes of workers and, as a result, their demand for commodities. Commercial interests might counter with the argument that such a policy would reduce employment. The resolution of this argument basically depends on the technological possibilities for substituting capital and labor. If it is technologically possible for each industry to substitute capital for labor, then a large enough increase in the price of labor would cause a substitution, and employment would, in fact, be reduced. On the other hand, where technological possibilities do not permit this substitution, total payments to labor would increase without a decrease in employment *provided* the resulting increased product prices or reduced profits do not lead to a reduction in output. The issue must therefore be resolved for each industry individually, depending on the available technologies for that industry and on demand elasticities.

Determining the Economic Feasibility of an Innovation

Industry is constantly in search of new techniques to improve its efficiency in the use of resources. New techniques must be not only technologically feasible, but economically feasible as well.

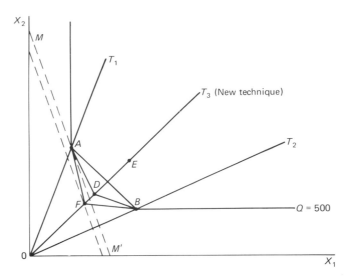

Figure 6.14   Economic Feasibility for a New Production Technique

Let us start with a situation where there are only two techniques of production, T_1 and T_2, and with a firm producing 500 units of output at point A.
The initial isocost curve is MM'. Suppose a new technique, T_3, now becomes
available. We need to find the minimum input combination for T_3 that
corresponds to an output level of 500. If a point like E in Figure 6.14
happens to be the minimum input level, there will never be a set of relative
input prices for which it will be optimal to use technique T_3. So long as the
isoquant lies on the flat segment between A and B, it will be preferable to
use either T_1 or T_2 or some combination of the two. No one will spend the
extra money to use the input levels required by technique T_3 at E.

On the other hand, suppose the input level necessary for an output of
500, using T_3, corresponds to point D. If the relative prices stay as they are
at A, the firm will not immediately change its production techniques. However,
if a new set of relative prices causes the slope of the isocost curve to change,
then it is possible that technique T_3 will be used. If, with T_3, the minimum
input level occurs at point F, T_3 will be adopted immediately, because at the
set of relative prices prevailing at A the firm can reduce total expenditure
by switching to the input combination associated with point F.

When technique T_3 is economically feasible it will either be implemented
immediately, as at point F, or implemented only if the relative prices change
sufficiently, as at point D.

The information in Figure 6.14 can be used not only to appraise an existing
technology, but also to define the minimum efficiency that a new technique

must have before it would be economically feasible to use it in place of existing technologies. Such information can be used also for allocating research and development funds, or for appraising the economic feasibility of a proposed new technique from drawing board sketches.

*Uncertainty in the Production Function

Treating the production function as a known determinant relationship is convenient but not necessarily very accurate. Inputs may vary in quality from one purchase to the next and the vagaries of equipment failure and defect rates all contribute uncertain elements.

One way of introducing uncertainty is to add a random input. If the uncertainty element is regarded as additive, its influence on output may be reflected in a function such as $Q = F(X_1, \ldots, X_m) + u$; if uncertainty is multiplicative, the function would be $Q = F(X_1, \ldots, X_m) \cdot u$. A more general function is $Q = F(X_1, \ldots, X_m, u)$, where no specific relationship for u is assumed.

The introduction of uncertainty fundamentally changes the character of input choice problems. The least cost problem now has a constraint that involves a random variable. This means that least cost must be replaced by a new objective—perhaps minimizing expected cost. The derived demand functions will now be random demand functions analogous to the random derived demand for commodities illustrated in Chapter 3. The formal solution of problems with random terms in the constraints will be taken up in Chapter 8.

Summary

Apart from restrictions on available inputs, the fundamental limitation on a firm's production decisions is imposed by technology. At each output level the firm must choose the technique that best suits the current economic situation. Input and technology choice decisions provide the basic bridge between production technologies and the cost schedules a firm uses in forming output and pricing decisions.

The key concepts included (1) the concept of total product, (2) average physical product, (3) marginal physical product, (4) isocost curve, (5) the expansion path, (6) the production function, (7) the marginal rate of technical substitution, (8) returns to scale, and (9) the elasticity of factor substitution. These concepts summarize the economic factors influencing management

* Optional material requiring knowledge of probability.

decisions with regard to inputs, and may also be used to analyze the effect of new policies.

The next chapter is devoted to the cost implications of production choices, which are crucial to a firm's ability to compete.

Questions for Study or Class Discussion

1. What difference does it make whether isoquant faces are smooth or piecewise linear?
2. What would the derived demand for labor input look like if contract terms specified minimum employment levels? Show how to derive a demand schedule from the least cost production choice problem.
3. Using input prices P_1 and P_2 and the Cobb-Douglas production function $Q = AX_1^{\alpha_1}X_2^{\alpha_2}$, find the derived demand functions for X_1 and X_2.
4. List several factors which would introduce uncertainty elements in the least cost production problem. How could each of these elements be incorporated into the solution of the problem?
5. Suppose in question 3, that production function is $Q = AX_1^{\alpha_1}X_2^{\alpha_1}u$, where u is a random element. Assume the expected value of u is unity and its variance is σ^2. How would this change the character of the derived demand functions? If contractual agreements prevent the firm from protecting itself from uncertainty by adjusting inputs, how will this affect profit and loss?

References

Arrow, K. J., H. B. Chenery, B. S. Minhas, and R. M. Solow, "Capital-Labor Substitution and Economic Efficiency," *Review of Economics and Statistics*, 43 (August, 1961), 225–250.

Ferguson, C. E., *The Neoclassical Theory of Production and Distribution*. Cambridge University Press, 1969.

Hicks, J. R., *Value and Capital*. Oxford University Press, 1946.

Klein, L. R., *An Introduction to Econometrics*. Prentice-Hall, 1962.

Lovell, C. A. Knox, "Estimation and Prediction with CES and VES Production Functions," *International Economic Review*, 14 (October, 1973), 676–692.

Meyer, R. A., and R. Kadiyala, "Linear and Nonlinear Estimation of Production Functions, *Southern Economic Journal*, 40 (January, 1974), 463–472.

Walters, A. A., "Production and Cost Functions: An Econometric Survey," *Econometrica*, 31 (January–April, 1963), 1–66.

Chapter 7 Costs as a Basis for Decisions

Introduction

The foundation for the cost concepts discussed here lies in the optimal input decision problem developed in Chapter 6. Production cost data are fundamental for sound decision making. We shall begin by describing the distinctions made in economics between various types of costs.

Short-run versus long-run costs

There is a basic distinction between costs incurred during a period over which at least one input—for example, plant and equipment—remains constant, which are referred to as *short-run costs*, and costs incurred over longer periods of time when the firm can vary all its inputs, which are referred to as *long-run costs*.

The significance of this distinction will be clearer after we discuss the short-run and long-run output decisions in Chapters 10-13.

Opportunity costs: accounting versus economic costs

The second important distinction is between accounting costs and economic costs. Accounting costs include all those expenses the average person would consider as costs: labor costs, insurance, materials, equipment, etc. In reckoning economic costs, however, one more element must be added: *opportunity cost*. Opportunity cost is a measure of the best return that a resource could obtain in an alternative use. The opportunity cost for a self-employed man is the highest salary he could otherwise earn. The opportunity cost of capital invested in steel production is the highest earnings that it could achieve in some other use. The opportunity cost for money invested in a bond is the highest return it could earn if invested otherwise, for example, in common or preferred stock.

To illustrate this distinction, suppose that a lawyer who is self-employed earns $9,000 in a particular year and that the maximum salary he could have earned if he had been working for a law firm is $12,500. Although in accounting terms he has earned $9,000, in economic terms he has incurred a loss of $3,500, equal to $9,000 less his opportunity cost, or $9,000 − $12,500. In general, economic profit or loss can be calculated by the following scheme:

Total Revenues	$ xxx
Less: Accounting Costs	xxx
Accounting Profit (loss)	$ xxx
Less: Opportunity Cost	xxx
Economic Profit (loss)	$ xxx

An *economic profit* will be realized only when the amount earned exceeds the earnings available from the best alternative. To say that a firm is earning zero economic profit, does not mean that it ought to go out of business, but that it is earning the same return for invested resources in its current line of activity as is available in the best alternative activity. From here on the words *costs* and *profit* will mean economic costs, not accounting costs, and economic profit, not accounting profit.

Private versus social costs

The third basic distinction is between private cost and social cost. *Private cost* is the cost an individual or firm actually incurs when making purchases in the market. *Social cost* includes private cost plus the difference between market price and the full cost *to the economy* of using a particular commodity. Ideally market prices reflect the full cost of resource use, but in real life they commonly exceed or fall short of the true cost to the economy. Therefore, the term *social cost* is used to describe the cost of using a particular commodity to the economy as a whole. The difference between private costs and social costs or between private benefits and social benefits is sometimes given the name *externality*.

The use of soft coal, with its high sulfur content, provides both heat energy and a discharge of sulfur particulants into the air. The private cost of using the soft coal is measured by the market price per ton, while the social cost is the market price per ton plus the "disutility" of the emitted sulfur. Since high sulfur content in the air leads to more rapid deterioration of paint surfaces and the darkening of stone, the disutility might be measured by the cost of cleaning discharges of sulfur particulants. The disposal of waste products in the form of either gaseous air pollutants or as liquid pollutants are examples of cases where private and social costs diverge from one another. Many of the frequently cited examples of pollution problems arise because private cost is less than social cost.

Private cost is not always less than social cost. University tuition in this country is substantially below the costs of educating an individual. This is justified by the assumption that a democratic society benefits from having educated members. This is particularly true for democratic political systems. If students had to pay for the full cost of their education, an economically rational student would end his education when the added cost to himself was equal to the benefit he could realize from it. Since the benefit to society is probably greater than the direct benefit perceived by the student, most students would probably stop too soon. Low tuitions place the private cost below the social cost, but the social benefit is believed to be higher than the private benefit.

Since it is difficult to measure social costs precisely, the following discussion will refer only to private cost. However, decisions based only on private cost are likely to produce results which are not ideal from the point of view of society. Many forms of regulation arise from an attempt to "correct" decisions based on private cost alone.

Some of the market failures introduced by externalities will be illustrated in Chapter 17.

Basic Cost Concepts

Cost schedules match a given output level with the least cost necessary to achieve that output. These costs, however, depend on time. In the short run a firm may be locked into expenditures for one or more factors regardless of whether or not the factors in question are needed for current operations. Over longer periods of time all inputs become variable and the firm will generally be able to reduce its costs. Analysis of minimum total costs will provide several useful decision-making tools.

Total cost (TC) is actually composed of two major elements: *total fixed cost* (TFC), and *total variable cost* (TVC), $TC = TFC + TVC$. Total fixed costs consist of payments for all inputs which must be maintained at fixed quantity levels. For example, in the short run a firm must pay a certain amount for insurance, real estate taxes, and maintenance charges on its plant and equipment. Total fixed costs are incurred whether the firm operates or not.

Total variable costs are payments for all inputs whose level may be varied with the level of output. For example, if a firm can afford to hire more workers or buy more material, then these inputs are variable and their costs are variable costs. Notice that since all inputs are variable in the long run, long-run total fixed costs will be zero, so that long-run total cost and long-run variable cost will be the same.

Average total cost (ATC) is defined as total cost divided by output,

$ATC = TC/Q$. Average fixed cost is total fixed cost divided by output, TFC/Q, and average variable cost is total variable cost divided by output, TVC/Q. It is easy to see that average total cost is composed of average fixed cost plus average variable cost. Dividing the expression $TC = TFC + TVC$ by Q, we obtain $TC/Q = TFC/Q + TVC/Q$ or $ATC = AFC + AVC$.

Marginal cost (MC) is defined as the change in total cost divided by the change in the level of output, $MC = \Delta TC/\Delta Q$. Marginal cost may be interpreted in either of two ways: (1) as the increase in total cost associated with an increase in output of one unit or, alternatively, (2) as the decrease in total cost associated with a decrease in output of one unit.

A Numerical Example

Suppose that we have a single output and a single input, labor. The output that results from hiring various numbers of units of labor is given by the second column in Table 7.1. Total fixed costs are $65, which, of course, remains constant regardless of the level of output. Since total fixed costs are greater than zero, this example occurs in a short-run setting. Column 4 shows the total variable cost associated with hiring the amount of labor shown in column 1. Columns 3 and 4 are added to obtain the total cost given in column 5. Figure 7.1 illustrates the behavior of TC, TFC, and TVC.

Average variable cost is the total variable cost given in column 4, divided by output in column 2. For one unit of labor total variable cost is $115 divided by an output of 15, thus average variable cost is $7.67 = $115/15. The total variable cost for two units of labor is $175. Dividing by an output of 30 gives an average variable cost of $5.83 = $175/30. Average total costs can be computed either by adding average fixed costs to average variable costs, or alternatively, by taking total costs and dividing by output. The average total cost shown in column 8 is obviously just column 6 plus column 7.

Marginal cost is shown in the last column. Notice that even in the short run, marginal cost includes only variable costs. Marginal cost is defined

Table 7.1 An Illustration of Cost Calculations

NUMBER OF UNITS OF LABOR	QUANTITY OF OUTPUT	TOTAL FIXED COST	TOTAL VARIABLE COST	TOTAL COST	AVERAGE FIXED COST	AVERAGE VARIABLE COST	AVERAGE TOTAL COST	MARGINAL COST
0	0	$65	0	$ 65	—	—	—	—
1	15	65	115	180	$4.33	$7.67	$12.00	$7.67
2	30	65	175	240	2.17	5.83	8.00	4.00
3	50	65	310	375	1.30	6.20	7.50	6.75
4	65	65	442	507	1.00	6.80	7.80	8.80
5	85	65	680	745	0.76	8.00	8.75	11.90
6	100	65	935	1000	0.65	9.35	10.00	17.00

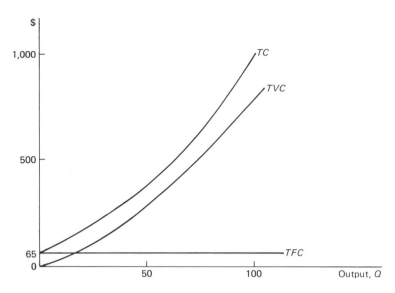

Figure 7.1 The Behavior of Total Cost and Its Components

as the change in total cost; therefore, by definition, fixed cost elements will never be included in it. Figure 7.2 illustrates the behavior of the *AFC, AVC, ATC*, and *MC* schedules shown in Table 7.1.

From Least Cost Production to Cost Schedules

We are now ready to use the least cost production information developed in Chapter 6 to construct the total cost schedule which underlies a firm's decision-making process. First, we will derive the short-run total cost curve assuming that capital is fixed and only labor varies. Next we will allow both inputs to vary and derive the long-run cost schedule from the expansion path.

Figure 7.3 illustrates a situation where the amount of capital is held fixed at K^0. The isoquant map describes the usual input/output alternatives, but these alternatives are really only available *ex ante*. Actually, in the short run, a firm will always be locked into a particular level of one or more inputs.

Since capital is fixed at K^0, the solutions to the least cost input choice problem occur at the points *H, J*, and *K* in Figure 7.3, for output levels Q_1, Q_2, and Q_3, respectively. Notice that the isocost curve could be pushed lower if capital could be varied, so that the firm is being forced to pay—in a literal sense—for its past decisions. Instead of being able to achieve costs of C_1, C_2, and C_3, the higher costs represented by C_1', C_2', and C_3' are the best short-run solutions. Figure 7.4 graphs the output and cost information derived from the solutions arrived at in Figure 7.3.

124   MICROECONOMIC DECISIONS

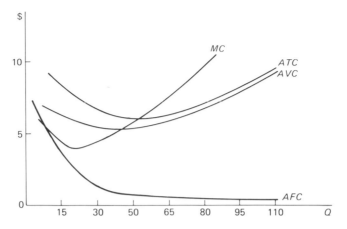

Figure 7.2   The Behavior of Average Total Cost, Average Variable Cost,
Average Fixed Cost, and Marginal Cost in the Short Run

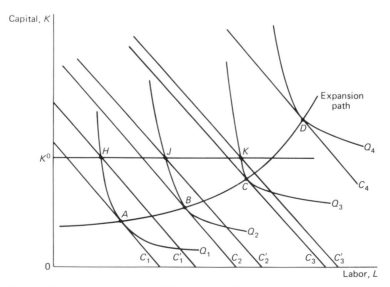

Figure 7.3   Least Cost Input Choice in the Short Run and the Long Run

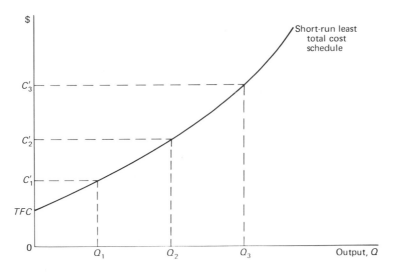

Figure 7.4 Derived Short-Run Least Cost Schedule

Figure 7.3 also illustrates the long-run choices. If capital is allowed to vary, least total cost at the output levels $Q_1, \ldots, Q_4$ is achieved at the input levels corresponding to points *A*, *B*, *C*, and *D*. The expansion path *ABCD* traces the minimum cost input combination for any given level of output, given the relative input prices. To construct the long-run cost schedule we simply read off the information along the expansion path. For Q_1 the optimal inputs multiplied by the prices per unit of each input gives the minimum total cost, C_1. The same calculation can be repeated for each output level. For the solutions *A*, *B*, *C*, and *D* we obtain the least costs C_1, C_2, C_3, and C_4. Figure 7.5 shows a graph of these costs versus output.[1]

The derivation of the long-run cost schedule shows important duality existing between available technologies and the function describing the least cost for the efficient input choices. That is, equivalent economic information can be derived from studying either the best technologies for given input prices or the least cost functions. Empirical estimates of the parameters in the production functions illustrated in Chapter 6 can be obtained indirectly from the least cost function associated with the production relationship.

[1] Formally the long-run cost function implied by a particular production function may be found by solving for the derived input demand functions (which depend on input prices and output level) and then substituting these into the total cost expression. If the derived demand functions are $X_j^* = h_j(p_1, \ldots, p_n, Q)$, then minimum cost is given by

$$TC = \sum_{j=1}^{n} P_j X_j^*$$

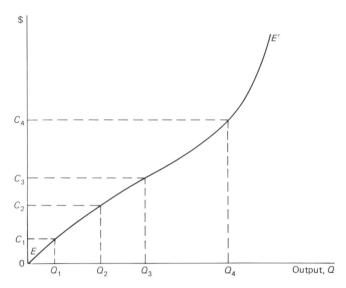

Figure 7.5   Derived Long-Run Least Cost Schedule

This shortcut was used in some of the empirical studies illustrated in Chapter 6 and later in this chapter.

Cost and Supply Schedules

The firm's short-run supply schedule

Figure 7.6 illustrates a short-run average total cost curve, $SRATC$, short-run average variable cost curve, $SRAVC$, and a short-run marginal cost curve, $SRMC$, as they might typically appear for a firm.

Suppose the firm wants to choose the level of production that will maximize profits when the market price for its output is P_2 per unit. Assume the firm can sell as much as it desires at the price P_2, but that this market price must be held constant for the time being, possibly due to competitive pressures from other firms. To maximize profits, the firm must determine (1) its price policy, (2) its production schedule, and (3) the optimal production technique and the corresponding inputs.

Total profits are just total revenues minus total costs, $\pi = TR - TC$, so that changes in profit, $\Delta\pi$, are equal to changes in total revenues minus changes in total cost, $\Delta\pi = \Delta TR - \Delta TC$. Dividing by the change in output, ΔQ, we obtain the following expression for the *marginal profit*, $\Delta\pi/\Delta Q$:

$$\frac{\Delta\pi}{\Delta Q} = \frac{\Delta TR}{\Delta Q} - \frac{\Delta TC}{\Delta Q} \tag{7.1}$$

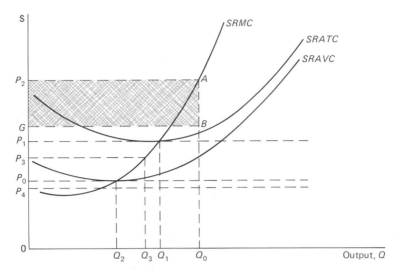

Figure 7.6 Determining the Optimal Short-Run Production Decision for a Profit-Maximizing Firm

Since $\Delta TR/\Delta Q$ is marginal revenue and $\Delta TC/\Delta Q$ is marginal cost, we obtain

$$\text{Marginal Profit} = \frac{\Delta \pi}{\Delta Q} = \frac{\Delta TR}{\Delta Q} - \frac{\Delta TC}{\Delta Q} = MR - MC \qquad (7.2)$$

From any initial output level, the firm can increase profit by expanding output provided marginal profit is positive. In other words, adding one more unit of output will increase total profits, provided that the resulting contribution to total revenue exceeds the increase in total cost. However, the firm can also increase profit by cutting back output, so long as the reduction in total costs is greater than the reduction in revenue.

Let us now return to the example illustrated in Figure 7.6. Since we have assumed that the market price is fixed at P_2, the price policy is already determined. The next task is to choose the optimal level of output.

The firm can either produce nothing or some positive amount. If it produces nothing it will incur a loss equal to its total fixed cost. It will never be economically sensible to produce and yet lose more than total fixed cost, so this sets an upper limit on losses. This provides some insight into why a firm would try to keep overhead costs to a minimum—this reduces the risk of high losses if the firm is shut down by labor strikes or other adversity.

Since we know that a firm will expand output if marginal profit is positive, we can take as a starting point the output levels at which marginal cost equals marginal revenue, i.e., where marginal profit is zero. We know marginal cost from the schedule in Figure 7.6, but how can we find marginal revenue?

The fact that the price P_2 is fixed implies that the additional revenue from selling one more unit is P_2. In general, marginal revenue is equal to the price received for the next unit *minus* the reduction in total revenue resulting from the overall price reduction necessary to sell one more unit. (In order to sell more units, it is usually necessary to reduce the price on all units.) Suppose the initial selling price on the demand schedule shown in Figure 7.7 is $\bar{P}$. Let $\bar{Q} + 1$ be the next unit sold when the price is reduced to $\bar{\bar{P}}$. The marginal revenue of the $\bar{Q} + 1$st unit is equal to the price $\bar{\bar{P}}$, *minus* the difference in revenue between selling $\bar{Q}$ units at $\bar{P}$ and selling $\bar{Q}$ units at $\bar{\bar{P}}$, or $(\bar{P} - \bar{\bar{P}})\bar{Q}$. The marginal revenue of the $\bar{Q} + 1$st unit is $\bar{\bar{P}} - (\bar{P} - \bar{\bar{P}})\bar{Q}$. Since in the example it was assumed that the firm could sell as much as it wishes at P_2, MR is obviously equal to P_2, and the second term in the marginal revenue expression is zero.

With marginal revenue always equal to P_2, it first becomes equal to the marginal cost at the output level Q_0 (Figure 7.6). Before concluding that the output level Q_0 maximizes short-run profits, an important second test must be made. Marginal cost equals marginal revenue not only at profit maximum points, but also at profit *minimum* points. The necessary second check is made by considering small increases and decreases in output away from the points for which $MR = MC$, in order to be sure that marginal cost exceeds marginal revenue for output levels above Q_0 and that marginal revenue exceeds marginal costs at output levels below Q_0, in other words, that profits decrease on either side of Q_0. If this condition is satisfied, Q_0

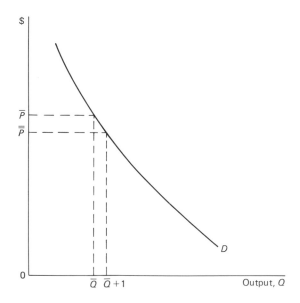

Figure 7.7   A Market Demand Schedule

must be a maximum, rather than a minimum. If more than one output level passes the second test, it is necessary to calculate total profit at each level in order to choose the best one.

Applying the second test in Figure 7.6, Q_0 proves indeed to be a maximum point. At Q_0, the average revenue, P_2, is greater than average total cost by the vertical distance AB. Total economic profits are represented by the cross-hatch area in Figure 7.6, average profits times output. If price is P_1, the firm earns zero economic profits. For any price above P_1 the firm earns positive economic profits.

Would the firm produce if the price is less than P_1? Suppose the market price is P_3. Repeating the $MR = MC$ test and the second check indicates that Q_3 might be an optimal output, but at Q_3 average revenue is less than average total costs, thus average (and total) profits are negative! Why would a firm produce in the short run if it is earning an economic loss? If the firm produced nothing, its short-run loss would be its total fixed cost. A firm would never operate in a situation where losses *exceeded* total fixed cost, but as long as the firm can defray some portion of its total fixed cost it is worthwhile to continue operating and attempt to minimize losses. Therefore, the firm will operate in the short run with a market price less than P_1 and earn an economic loss, provided the loss is less than total fixed costs. If the price is P_4, on the other hand, there is no output level at which the firm can even recover the costs described by the short-run average variable cost curve. Below a price of P_0, our cost information indicates the economically optimal decision is to shut down. Between P_0 and P_1 the firm operates, but earns zero economic profits or losses that are less than total fixed costs. For prices above P_1 the firm earns economic profits in the short run. Table 7.2 summarizes these decision rules.

The decision to terminate production after output has dropped to Q_2 (Figure 7.6) corresponds to the rule developed in Chapter 6 requiring a firm to operate only in Stage 2. The amount available to defray fixed cost is the excess of average revenue over average variable cost. With only one variable input purchased at a given price per unit, W, $AVC = W/APP$, thus AVC reaches a minimum where APP reaches its maximum. Since at the output level Q_2 average revenue is exactly equal to average variable cost, this level corresponds to the dividing point between Stage 1 and Stage 2.

Another way of interpreting the information in Figure 7.6 is to say that so long as the firm sells at constant market prices its short-run supply schedule will correspond to its short-run marginal cost schedule above the point of minimum average variable cost, because it would never produce for any prices below minimum average variable cost. This relationship between the firm's marginal cost schedule and the firm's short-run supply schedule is based on the assumption the firm sells at constant market prices and we will augment or qualify this relationship as needed later.

Table 7.2   Some Production Decision Rules

SHORT-RUN MARKET PRICE	SHORT-RUN PROFIT MAXIMIZING DECISION	OPERATING RESULTS
Below P_0	Shut down production	Losses; however, shutdown limits losses to total fixed costs
Equal to or above P_0, but below P_1	Produce at output level where marginal revenue equals marginal cost[a]	Losses occur, but they are less than or equal to total fixed costs; or zero economic output occurs
Equal to or above P_1	Produce at output level where marginal revenue equals marginal cost[a]	Firm earns positive economic profits

[a] If there are multiple output levels for which $MR = MC$, choose the one with the smallest loss or maximum profit.

The short-run market supply schedule

The short-run supply schedule for an individual firm illustrated in Figure 7.6 can be used to judge the response of an individual firm to changing market prices for output, but it is also the basic building block for the short-run market supply schedule.

Figure 7.8 shows the portion of three firms' short-run supply schedules above the point of minimum average variable cost. To obtain the market supply schedule, all we have to do is determine the amount each firm will find it optimal to produce at each price. At a price of P', $SRMC_1$ shows that firm 1 will supply Q_1'. Similarly, firm 2 will decide to produce Q_2' and firm 3, Q_3'. Total market supply at the price P' is simply the sum $Q_1' + Q_2' + Q_3'$ indicated by point A. Similarly, total market supply at the price P'' is $Q_1'' + Q_2'' + Q_3''$, indicated by the point B. Repeating the above steps for each price, we will obtain a curve such as CC' which is the *short-run market supply curve*. This simply horizontal summation of the relevant part of each individual firm's MC schedule implicitly assumes all inputs have perfectly elastic supply schedules.

In the next chapter the market supply schedule will be combined with the market demand schedule developed in Chapter 4 to determine market prices for commodities.

The firm's long-run cost and supply schedule

Each choice relating to plant size or technology which a firm can make has its own short-run average total cost schedule. In the short run this is the only relevant set of costs for a firm, but in the long run the firm has the option

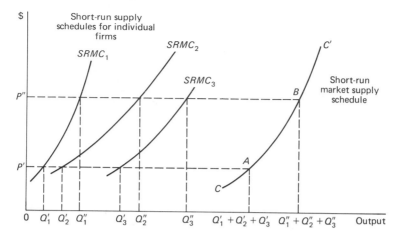

Figure 7.8 Deriving Short-Run Market Supply for the Short-Run Supply Schedule of Individual Firms

of switching to a different plant size or technology. Long-run decisions involve choosing from a family of short-run average total cost curves the one which will maximize profits (or achieve some other goal) under the market conditions the firm believes it will be confronted with. This family of *SRATC* schedules forms the basis for the firm's *long-run average total cost curve* or *planning curve*.

Figure 7.9 illustrates five different *SRATC*s, each representing a different plant or technology choice. The decisive information for the firm is the minimum average total cost at the desired level of output. For example, for Q_1 the firm would make the choice associated with $SRATC_1$. The curve which describes the least *ATC* for each level of output is the lower "envelope" of the five *ATC* curves in Figure 7.9. This curve, *ABCDE*, is referred to as the *long-run average total cost schedule (LRATC)*. Associated with the *LRATC* is a *long-run marginal cost schedule (LRMC)* which is shown in Figure 7.10.[2]

---

[2] If all alternative technologies are reflected in a production function $Q = F(X_1, X_2, \ldots, X_n)$ then the least total cost for each output level can be found from the solution of the problem

$$\text{Minimize } TC = \sum_{j=1}^{n} P_j X_j$$

$$\text{subject to } F(X_1, X_2, \ldots, X_m) \geq \bar{Q}$$

$$X_j \geq 0, \quad i = 1, m$$

In Lagrangian form, we minimize

$$\phi = \sum_{j=1}^{n} P_j X_j - \lambda[\bar{Q} - F(X_1, X_2, \ldots, X_m)]$$

with respect to the inputs, X_j, and maximize with respect to λ. The Lagrangian multiplier, λ, represents the long-run marginal cost at the output level $\bar{Q}$.

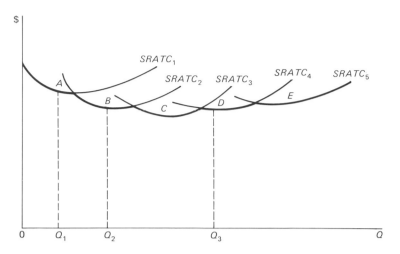

Figure 7.9   Deriving the Long-Run Average Cost Curve from Short-Run Alternatives

While *ABCDE* has a scalloped shape because we used only five alternative choices, as the number of choices open to the firm increases the *LRATC* may become a smooth curve such as the one shown in Figure 7.10.

The shape of short-run and long-run cost curves

By definition, a short-run decision problem presupposes fixed input levels for at least one factor. Attempts to expand output ultimately encounter the Law of Diminishing Returns for those inputs which can be varied. The result is sharply rising costs. The rising right-hand portion of the U-shaped *ATC* curve reflects the assumption that marginal returns ultimately diminish.

The shape of the *LRATC* reflects the plant size and technology choices available and the production costs they imply for a given set of input prices. Since a firm can presumably increase all inputs in proportion, the Law of Diminishing Returns will not affect the shape of the *LRATC*. With constant input prices and constant returns to scale, *LRATC* will be horizontal. With increasing returns to scale *LRATC* decreases as output rises, and with decreasing returns to scale *LRATC* rises as output rises. Now suppose that input prices change. If the price of certain inputs rises or falls as a greater quantity is purchased, then the returns to scale phenomena which influence input markets will also affect a firm's *SRATC* and *LRATC*. Even though some inputs can be replicated, the diminishing ability of management to

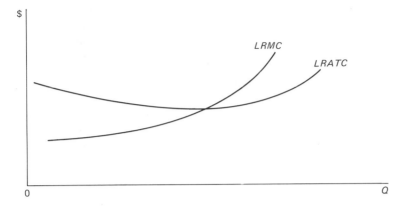

Figure 7.10   Long-Run Average and Long-Run Marginal Costs

organize and control an increasingly large firm may cause the *LRATC* to turn up in the end, even though it has a long trough.

More Numerical Examples

The first of the two examples in this section illustrates the relationship between the *MR* = *MC* rule and the goal of maximizing total profit, assuming the profit, cost, and revenue functions are "well-behaved." The second example uses total revenue and total cost functions to illustrate the solution of the same type of decision problem algebraically.

Example 1: The *MR* = *MC* rule

Suppose a firm is confronted with the revenue and cost data given in Table 7.3. Profit at each output level is shown in the column at the far right. An output level of 500 yields the highest profit. The total revenue and total cost data from Table 7.3 are graphed in Figure 7.11. The profit maximizing output level is the level at which the vertical distance between total revenue and total cost is a maximum. Notice that this occurs at the output level where the tangents to these curves, *CC′* and *DD′*, are parallel to one another. Recall that the slope of the line tangent to the total cost schedule is equal to the change in total cost over the change in output, or the marginal cost. Similarly, the slope of the total revenue schedule is equal to marginal revenue. Therefore, to say that the tangents to the total cost and total revenue curves are parallel at a given level is equivalent to saying that marginal cost equals marginal revenue at that level. This is confirmed by the numerical data in Table 7.3.

Table 7.3 A Numerical Example of Total Revenue, Total Cost, and Profit

OUTPUT	TOTAL REVENUE	MARGINAL REVENUE	TOTAL COST	MARGINAL COST	PROFIT
100	$10,000	—	$12,000	—	− $2,000
200	12,000	$20.00	12,500	$5.00	− 500
300	13,750	17.50	13,250	7.50	+ 500
400	15,250	15.00	14,250	10.00	+ 1,000
500	17,500	12.50	15,500	12.50	+ 2,000
600	18,500	10.00	17,300	18.00	+ 1,200

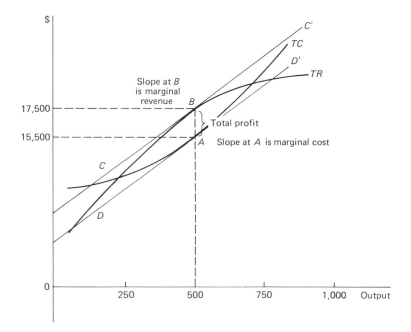

Figure 7.11   Total Revenue, Total Cost, and Profit

Example 2: An algebraic example of revenues, costs, and profits

Assume a firm's estimate of its total revenue function is

$$TR(Q) = 6Q \qquad (7.3)$$

A careful cost study suggests that total costs are related to output by

$$TC(Q) = 200 + 0.03Q^2 \qquad (7.4)$$

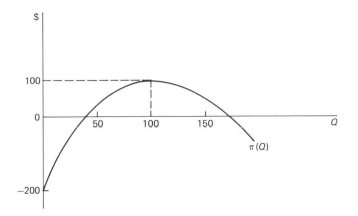

Figure 7.12   The Behavior of Profit as a Function of Output

Total profits are $\pi = TR - TC$ or

$$\pi(Q) = 6Q - 200 - 0.03Q^2 \qquad (7.5)$$

which is a quadratic function. Since the coefficient of Q^2 is negative, profits will rise to a maximum point and then fall. We want to find the production level that will maximize profits.

There are two possibilities: either produce nothing or produce at a positive level of output. If nothing is produced the firm loses $200, its total fixed cost. We can search for candidates for positive output levels by finding those outputs for which $MR = MC$. Marginal revenue is 6 and marginal cost is $0.06Q$.[3] Equating MR and MC and solving for Q, we obtain a possible solution at $Q = 100$. When we check for outputs on either side of $Q = 100$, profits decline as required. Therefore, maximum total profits are

$$\pi(100) = 6(100) - 200 - 0.03(100)^2 = \$100 \qquad (7.6)$$

Figure 7.12 is a graphical solution of this problem.

Empirical Examples of Cost Functions

Just as in the case of production functions, the first step in the empirical evaluation of cost functions is to choose an appropriate form for the function. Frequently used forms include the linear form, $TC = a_1 + a_2Q$, the quadratic, $TC = b_1 + b_2Q + b_3Q^2$, and the cubic, $TC = c_1 + c_2Q + c_3Q^2 + c_4Q^3$. Whether or not the form of the cost function is derived explicitly by minimizing cost using a specific production function form, such as the Cobb-

---

[3] $MR = dTR/dQ = 6$; $MC = dTC/dQ = 0.06Q$.

Douglas or CES, it will always depend ultimately on the available technological alternatives.[4]

Let us first estimate the cost function for producing electricity using a modified quadratic cost curve.[5] The estimated relationship is

$$\text{Total Cost} = \text{Constant} + 1.694 \cdot (\text{Output})$$
$$- 0.043 \,(\text{Output squared})$$
$$- 0.247 \,(\text{Time trend}) \tag{7.7}$$

Total cost is expressed as a function of output, but there is a second variable, time. This cost function was estimated from time series data. The negative term involving time implies the cost schedule is declining over time, due to the use of newer technologies or changing input prices. Average total cost is

$$ATC = \frac{\text{Constant}}{Q} + 1.694 - 0.043Q - 0.247 \,(\text{Time}/Q) \tag{7.8}$$

A second example is drawn from the manufacturing data of a hosiery mill[6] using a linear total cost curve. The estimated relationship is

$$\text{Total Cost} = \text{Constant} + 2.0 \,(\text{Output}) \tag{7.9}$$

thus average total costs fall as output rises.

$$ATC = \frac{\text{Constant}}{Q} + 2.0 \tag{7.10}$$

Another example,[7] this time based on a cross-section sample, illustrates the dependence of total costs on input prices. The total cost expression is

$$\text{Total Cost} = (\text{log base})^{\text{Constant}} \cdot (\text{Wage Rate})^{0.483}$$
$$\cdot (\text{Price of Capital})^{0.496} \cdot (\text{Output})^{0.723} \tag{7.11}$$

By taking logarithms of both sides of (7.11) we obtain

$$\log (\text{Total Cost}) = \text{Constant} + 0.483 \log (\text{Wage Rate})$$
$$+ 0.496 \log (\text{Price of Capital}) + 0.723 \log (\text{Output}) \tag{7.12}$$

---

[4] As an example, in a two-input setting a Cobb-Douglas production function
$$Q = AX_1^{\alpha_1} X_2^{\alpha_2}$$
with input prices p_1 and p_2 implies the cost function
$$TC = r[A\alpha_1^{\alpha_1}\alpha_2^{\alpha_2}]^{-1/r} P_1^{\alpha_1/r} P_2^{\alpha_2/r} Q^{1/r}$$
where $r = \alpha_1 + \alpha_2$.

[5] Adapted from J. Johnston, *Statistical Cost Analysis,* McGraw-Hill, 1960.

[6] Adapted from J. Dean, "Statistical Cost Functions of a Hosiery Mill," *Journal of Business,* supplement 1941.

[7] Adapted from M. Nerlove, *Estimation and Identification of Cobb-Douglas Production Functions,* Rand McNally, 1965.

In general, the cost functions are based on a given set of relative input prices. If the relative input prices change, then the cost function changes. This dependency on price is reflected in the wage and capital terms in (7.11).

Tables 7.4–7.6 indicate a wide range of applications of cost studies and the principal results.

Table 7.4   Some Examples of Cost Studies of Particular Industries

RESEARCHER (DATE)	INDUSTRY	PERIOD[a]	RESULT
Bain (1956)	Manufacturing	L	Small economies of scale of multiplant firms.
Eiteman and Guthrie (1952)	Manufacturing	S	*MC* below *AC* at all outputs below capacity.
Hall and Hitch (1939)	Manufacturing	S	Majority have *MC* decreasing.
Lester (1946)	Manufacturing	S	Decreasing average variable cost to capacity.
Moore (1959)	Manufacturing	L	Economies of scale generally.
Temporary National Economic Committee, Monograph 13	Various industries	L	Small or medium-size plants usually have lowest costs. Blair (1942) draws different conclusions.
Alpert (1959)	Metal	L	Economies of scale to 80,000 lbs./month; then constant returns.
Johnston (1960)	Multiple product	S	Direct cost is linearly related to output. *MC* is constant.
Dean (1936)	Furniture	S	*MC* constant. *SRAC* "failed to rise."
Dean (1941)	Leather belts	S	Significantly increasing *MC*. Rejected by Dean.
Dean (1941)	Hosiery	S	*MC* constant. *SRAC* "failed to rise."
Dean (1942)	Dept. store	S	*MC* declining or constant.
Dean and James (1942)	Shoe stores	L	*LRAC* is U-shaped (interpreted as not due to diseconomies of scale).
Holton (1956)	Retailing (Puerto Rico)	L	*LRAC* is L-shaped. But Holton argues that inputs of management may be undervalued at high outputs.
Ezekiel and Wylie (1941)	Steel	S	*MC* declining but large standard errors.
Yntema (1940)	Steel	S	*MC* constant.
Ehrke (1933)	Cement	S	Ehrke interprets as constant *MC*. Apel (1948) argues that *MC* is increasing.
Nordin (1947)	Light plant	S	*MC* is increasing.

SOURCE: A. A. Walters, "Production and Cost Functions: An Econometric Survey," *Econometrica*, 31 (January–April 1963), 1–66.
[a] Time period: L = long run, S = short run.

Table 7.5 Some Examples of Cost Studies for Public Utilities

RESEARCHER (DATE)	INDUSTRY	RESULT
Lomax (1951)	Gas (U.K.)	*LRAC* of production declines (no analysis of distribution).
Gribbin (1953)	Gas (U.K.)	,, ,,
Lomax (1952)	Electricity (U.K.)	,, ,,
Johnston (1960)	Electricity (U.K.)	,, ,,
Johnston (1960)	Electricity (U.K.)	*SRAC* falls, then flattens, tending toward constant *MC* up to capacity.
McNulty (1955)	Electricity (U.S.A.)	Average costs of administration are constant.
Nerlove (1961)	Electricity (U.S.A.)	*LRAC* excluding transmission costs declines, then shows signs of increasing.
Johnston (1960)	Coal (U.K.)	Wide dispersion of costs per ton.
Johnston (1960)	Road Passenger Tpt. (U.K.)	*LRAC* either falling or constant.
Johnston (1960)	Road Passenger Tpt. (U.K.)	*SRAC* decreases.
Johnston (1960)	Life Insurance	*LRAC* declines.

SOURCE: A. A. Walters, "Production and Cost Functions: An Econometric Survey," *Econometrica*, 31 (January–April 1963), 1–66.

Table 7.6 Some Examples of Cost Studies for Railroads

RESEARCHER (DATE)	COUNTRY	RESULT
Borts (1952)	U.S.A.	*LRAC* either constant or falling.
Borts (1960)	U.S.A.	*LRAC* increasing in East, decreasing in South and West.
Broster (1938)	U.K.	Operating cost per unit of output falls.
Mansfield and Wein (1958)	U.K.	*MC* is constant.

SOURCE: A. A. Walters, "Production and Cost Functions: An Econometric Survey," *Econometrica*, 31 (January–April 1963), 1–66.

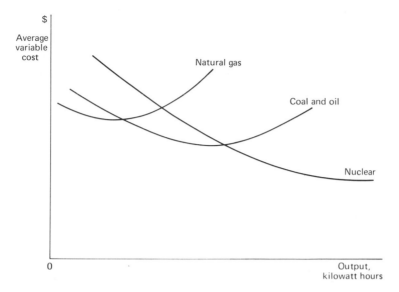

Figure 7.13 Comparisons of Average Variable Costs for Alternative Production Technologies for Electricity

An Empirical Example of Average Costs from Different Technologies

Electricity can be generated by turbines driven by steam or water. Suitable hydroelectric sites are insufficient for expansion purposes. The standard steam generator uses a heat source to produce the steam that is used to drive the turbines. The basic heat sources are natural gas, oil, coal, and nuclear energy. Each represents a different technology with its own initial investment requirements and operating costs. In making investment decisions the firm must look at the *SRATC* associated with each technology for generating facilities of various sizes.

Figure 7.13 provides a rough idea of the average variable cost curves for these alternatives. Notice that for very low output levels nuclear power is not economically feasible, but is superior to other technologies at high output levels. While natural gas facilities can be built in a relatively short period of time (about 2 years) at relatively low capital costs, their operating costs are higher. In contrast, the low operating costs of nuclear plants come at a high capital investment, a wait of 6 to 7 years for construction, and the possibility of radiation and/or thermal pollution. The "correct choice" for a particular firm depends on the market size it must serve, expected future growth, and other political as well as economic pressures.

An Application of Costs to a Public Utility Pricing Problem

It is sometimes suggested that the long-run average and marginal cost schedules for public utilities, instead of being U-shaped, tend to fall as output rises, due to the high economies of scale inherent in the available technologies. Typical curves of this sort are illustrated in Figure 7.14.

An important aspect of public utility policy is the determination of appropriate pricing rules. It has frequently been suggested that firms should set prices equal to marginal cost. What would happen if a firm with the cost schedules shown in Figure 7.14 priced at marginal cost? At Q_0, if the firm sets a price at the marginal cost, C', average revenue will be less than average total cost by the amount $C'' - C'$, and the firm will incur a loss equal to the crosshatched area. A marginal-cost pricing rule therefore presupposes that the firm is able to make up these deficits, possibly by subsidies from the public treasury.

A subsidy enabling the firm to sell more output at lower prices is implicitly an income transfer to the consumers of the commodity, since the subsidy is paid out of general tax revenues. The question is whether the larger consumption resulting from pricing at marginal cost is worth the cost of a redistributional tax and financing plan. Pricing below average total costs, running a deficit, and then drawing on general tax revenues for support is typical of virtually all public schools and state universities. The social benefits are presumed to justify such a pricing scheme.

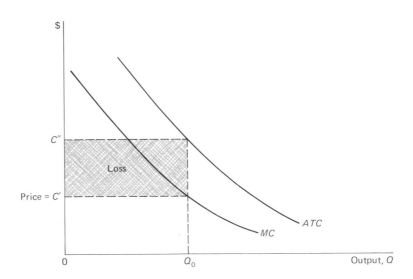

Figure 7.14   Marginal Cost Pricing With Decreasing Costs

On the other hand, if *MC* is rising a marginal-cost pricing rule may result in large profits.

When a firm has multiple classes of customers (e.g., residential users and commercial users, children and adults, poor and rich, daytime users and nighttime users, or summer users and winter users) there is the possibility that losses on sales at prices below average total costs to one or more groups may be made up by sales at prices above average total costs to another. Pricing schemes of this kind embody a cross-subsidization between customers. This is an important issue in tariff cases for public utilities. It is discussed further in the context of monopoly and price discrimination in Chapter 11.

*Uncertain Input Prices, an Uncertain Production Function, and Uncertain Costs

The theory of cost developed at the beginning of this chapter is set in an environment of certainty. Uncertain input prices, an uncertain production function, even sporadic departures from least cost production decisions, all impart an unstable character to cost functions.

The formal development of a random cost function begins by introducing the relevant random elements into the least cost production setting described in Chapter 6. Both short-run and long-run cost concepts can then be derived, but the implied cost function will be random. The precise form in which randomness enters the cost function will, of course, influence the way randomness enters the least cost problem.

Empirical studies use relatively simple random elements in order to introduce statistical methods for estimation and testing. The most common practice is to add a random error term to the cost function obtained from a static setting. This practice has no formal justification. The analysis of uncertainty and its implications for both theoretical and empirical results is an open area for inquiry.

Summary

Production costs are among the main pieces of economic information used by management in decision making. Along with the distinctions between short-run and long-run costs, economic and accounting costs, and private and social costs, the key concepts introduced in this chapter were (1) total cost, (2) average total cost, (3) average variable cost, (4) average fixed cost, and (5) marginal cost.

* Optional material requiring knowledge of probability.

By combining cost information with market demand information and a behavior rule for the firm such as profit maximization, we can find the schedule of outputs a firm will produce at each market price. This supply schedule for an individual firm in turn forms the basis for the market supply schedule.

Questions for Study or Class Discussion

1. Would it ever be economically sensible to operate and still sustain losses? Why?
2. How would short-run market supply be derived if there are technological interdependences between firms, that is, if costs for one firm depend on output of other firms? Can you think of examples where this might occur?
3. How can the short-run and long-run effects of a new technology be represented and analyzed?
4. Distinguish between the terms *technological externality* and *pecuniary externality*. How would each of these influences show up in cost information?
5. Using the derived input demand functions for the two-input Cobb-Douglas setting used in the questions at the end of Chapter 6, derive the implied random long-run cost function.

References

Ellis, H., and W. Fellner, "External Economies and Diseconomies," *American Economic Review*, 33 (1943), 493–511.

Johnston, J., *Statistical Cost Analysis*. McGraw-Hill, 1960.

Klein, L., *An Introduction to Econometrics*. Prentice-Hall, Inc., 1962.

Knight, F., "Some Fallacies in the Interpretation of Social Cost," *Quarterly Journal of Economics*, 38 (1924), 582–606.

Nerlove, M., *Estimation and Identification of Cobb-Douglas Production Functions*. Rand McNally, 1965.

Staehle, H., "The Measurement of Statistical Cost Functions," *American Economic Review*, 32 (1942), 321–333.

Stigler, G., *The Theory of Price*. Macmillan, 1966.

Viner, J., "Cost Curves and Supply Curves," reprinted in American Economic Association, *Readings in Price Theory*. Richard D. Irwin, Inc., 1952.

Chapter 8 Linear Programming as an Aid to Decision Making

Introduction

The preceding discussions illustrated the general form of cost and input choice problems and their application in solving decision problems for a firm. What we need now is a way of solving choice problems to obtain quantitative answers.

Virtually all of the problems that we have discussed can be expressed mathematically as the maximization or minimization of a given objective subject to a series of constraints. Problems structured in these forms are referred to as *mathematical programming problems*. While formal mathematical programming can be very detailed, it provides a powerful method of computing solutions to complicated problems. This chapter deals with a type of mathematical programming problem that has been used widely in solving decision problems—*linear programming* (*LP*).

The General Form of a Linear Programming Problem

An economic problem suitable for solution by linear programming involves an objective that is a linear combination of the variables and constraints that are also linear in the variables and stated as inequalities. An example with two variables, X_1 and X_2, might be:

$$\text{Maximize } Z = 10X_1 + 3X_2 \qquad (8.1)$$
$$X_1, X_2$$

143

subject to

$$X_1 \leq 50 \tag{8.2}$$

$$9X_1 + 4X_2 \leq 250 \tag{8.3}$$

$$X_1 \geq 0, \qquad X_2 \geq 0 \tag{8.4}$$

A minimum problem with three variables to be chosen might be:

$$\underset{U_1, U_2, U_3}{\text{Minimize}} \; W = 2U_1 + 3U_2 + 11U_3 \tag{8.5}$$

subject to

$$5U_1 + \tfrac{1}{2}U_2 + U_3 \geq 86 \tag{8.6}$$

$$U_1 \geq 0, \qquad U_2 \geq 0, \qquad U_3 \geq 0 \tag{8.7}$$

Examples of practical problems that can be cast in this form are choice of the profit-maximizing product mix for a firm that has multiple outputs or choice of a shipping and warehousing scheduling plan that minimizes transportation costs. Business firms frequently need a scheduling plan that routes salespeople through various sales areas on prescribed schedules so as to minimize the time that they spend traveling, and maximize the time spent in contact with prospective buyers. Another example would be choosing a combination of nutrients for fertilizing various agricultural crops or for feeding chickens or cattle or people in order to minimize the cost of the food or fertilizer, while still meeting minimum constraints on the nutritional content of the diet. Each of these problems can be quickly solved when cast in a linear programming form.

Numerical analysis of linear programming techniques will not be emphasized here. An appendix to this chapter gives simple steps for solving any linear program that can easily be programmed for a computer. Instead, we shall discuss the skill required to translate a business problem into a linear programming form. This is a powerful tool both for simulating policy alternatives and for aiding in choice decisions.

There are four basic assumptions employed in formulating a linear program:

1. *Linearity.* All variables to be chosen must be linear in the objective function and all constraints must have exponents of unity, and none of them may be multiplied together.
2. *Continuity.* All variables to be chosen must be capable of taking any numerical value. Fractions as well as whole numbers are permissible as answers.[1]

---

[1] It is very tempting to conclude that an optimal answer expressed in integer values can be obtained by just rounding off all initial answers. Unfortunately, this result is only obtainable by integer programming methods except in special cases and these more elaborate methods are beyond the scope of this text.

3. *Additivity and Independence.* The amount for any one variable may be chosen arbitrarily, without reference to the level chosen for any other variable (within the limits imposed by the constraints). Total resource use (or output) is found by adding the use (or output) for each individual activity.

4. *Proportionality.* The amount of each input used per unit of output must be constant for every level of output. For example, if it took two working hours to produce one pottery vase, it would be assumed to take twenty working hours to produce ten.

Although these limitations may seem rigid, some of the requirements can usually be dodged by rephrasing the form of the initial linear program.

Linear Programs and Their Duals

All linear programs, in fact all mathematical programs, come in pairs. Every problem in which some quantity is maximized with a set of constraints has associated with it another problem called its *dual*. The dual problem for every maximum problem is a minimum problem and the dual of any minimum problem is a maximum problem.

The concept of a dual can be illustrated by the following example. Suppose a firm wants to maximize the profits arising from two products, output 1 and output 2, where the profit, or market value added, from selling a unit of output 1 is c_1 and the profit from selling a unit of output 2 is c_2. In addition, assume that there are two resources, capital and labor, available only in limited amounts: an amount b_1 of capital and an amount b_2 of labor.

In order to produce one unit of output 1 we need a_{11} units of capital, thus the total capital requirement to produce an amount X_1 of output 1 is $a_{11}X_1$. It takes a_{12} units of capital to produce each unit of output 2; therefore the total amount of capital used to produce X_2 units is $a_{12}X_2$. The total amount of capital used must be equal to or less than the capital available; i.e., $a_{11}X_1 + a_{12}X_2 \leq b_1$. In the same manner the total amount of labor used in the production of output 1 plus the total amount of labor used for the production of output 2 must be equal to or less than the total amount of labor available; i.e., $a_{21}X_1 + a_{22}X_2 \leq b_2$. The problem of maximizing profits given the resource limitations then has the form:

$$\text{Maximize } Z = c_1 X_1 + c_2 X_2 \qquad (8.8)$$
$$\underset{X_1, X_2}{}$$

subject to

$$a_{11}X_1 + a_{12}X_2 \leq b_1 \qquad (8.9)$$

$$a_{21}X_1 + a_{22}X_2 \leq b_2 \qquad (8.10)$$

$$X_1 \geq 0, \quad X_2 \geq 0 \qquad (8.11)$$

The dual to this maximum problem is to minimize the value of the resources that are used in the production of X_1 and X_2. The problem of maximizing profits given certain amounts of resources is essentially equivalent to the problem of minimizing the value of the resources drawn into the production of outputs with given market values. This illustrates the fact that every dual problem provides quantitative measures of the opportunity costs associated with decisions. The variables in the minimum problem, U_1 and U_2, are sometimes referred to as *imputed values*, or *implicit prices*, or *shadow prices* per unit of the resource. These terms are used because resources do not have a value in and of themselves; they derive their value from the value of the goods into which they can be transformed. This is why the U's are called imputed or implicit values.

The constraints for the minimum problem are that the value of the labor and capital resources used to produce commodity 1 must be at least equal to the value added by producing the commodity, i.e., c_1. Since a_{11} is the amount of capital needed to produce one unit of commodity 1 and U_1 is the imputed price per unit of capital, then $a_{11}U_1$ is the imputed value of the capital used to make one unit of commodity 1. In the same manner, since a_{21} is the amount of labor used to make one unit of commodity 1, thus the imputed value of the labor services for producing one unit of commodity 1 is $a_{21}U_2$. By the same reasoning, the imputed value of the capital required to produce one unit of commodity 2 is $a_{12}U_1$, and the imputed value of labor is $a_{22}U_2$, while their sum must be at least equal to c_2. The form of the minimum problem that is the dual of the profit maximization problem above is

$$\text{Minimize } W = U_1 b_1 + U_2 b_2 \qquad (8.12)$$
$$\scriptstyle U_1, U_2$$

subject to

$$a_{11}U_1 + a_{21}U_2 \geq c_1 \qquad (8.13)$$

$$a_{12}U_1 + a_{22}U_2 \geq c_2 \qquad (8.14)$$

$$U_1 \geq 0, \qquad U_2 \geq 0 \qquad (8.15)$$

Although this example has only two variables in the maximum problem, and two variables in the minimum problem, much larger problems can be solved. Some applications have literally hundreds of variables and hundreds of constraints.

Solving Linear Programs

Let us now work some specific problems to illustrate both the method of solution by linear programming and the types of problems to which it may be applied.

Example 1: A petroleum product mix problem   Suppose a petroleum refiner sells two products, gasoline and fuel oil, and wishes to find the most profitable mix when faced with limitations on refining capacity and storage facilities. Let X_1 represent the amount of gasoline and X_2 represent the amount of fuel oil. Assume the net profit from gasoline is \$16 per barrel and the net profit from fuel oil is \$8 per barrel. We are trying to maximize profits, which are equal to $16X_1 + 8X_2$. There are two sets of constraints. Storage tank capacity is limited to 5,000 gallons for gasoline and 12,000 gallons for fuel oil. The distillation process used in refining allows the plant a maximum of 27,000 units of capacity. Each gallon of gasoline requires 3 units of productive capacity while each gallon of fuel oil requires 2 units. Our problem can now be written as

$$\text{Maximize } Z = 16X_1 + 8X_2 \qquad (8.16)$$
$$\underset{X_1, X_2}{}$$

subject to

$$X_1 \leq 5,000, \qquad X_2 \leq 12,000 \qquad (8.17)$$

$$3X_1 + 2X_2 \leq 27,000 \qquad (8.18)$$

$$X_1 \geq 0, \qquad X_2 \geq 0 \qquad (8.19)$$

The easiest way to begin solving this problem is to graph the constraints, so that we can see what choices are actually available. In Figure 8.1, the constraint requiring gasoline production to be equal to or less than 5,000 is

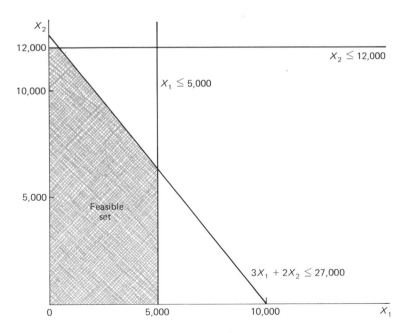

Figure 8.1   Constraints Define Feasible Choices

represented by a linear constraint perpendicular to the horizontal axis at the level 5,000. The 12,000-gallon limit on fuel oil is represented by a line perpendicular to the vertical axis at 12,000. The technological constraint is also represented in Figure 8.1, by the graph of the equation $3X_1 + 2X_2 = 27,000$. The points that satisfy the inequality are those on the graph and below it. The axes represent the requirement that production be nonnegative. The area that represents the feasible output choices consists of the points which simultaneously satisfy each constraint. All of the points in the crosshatch area in Figure 8.1 and those on the boundary, including the origin, therefore represent mixes of gasoline and fuel oil which are possible solutions to the maximization problem.

We now want to find the solution that maximizes profits. The profit function, $Z = 16X_1 + 8X_2$, can be written in the form $X_2 = Z/8 + (-16/8)X_1$. For profits of zero, $Z = 0$, this line passes through the origin and has a slope of -2. Obviously producing zero of both commodities is not the optimal solution. We want to push this isoprofit line as far from the origin as we can while still keeping at least one point in the crosshatched area representing the feasible set. This process gives a solution at point A in Figure 8.2, at which the optimal produce mix is: $X_1^* = 5,000$ and $X_2^* = 6,000$. The maximum profit can be found by substituting back into the profit function to obtain $Z^* = \$16(5000) + \$8(6000) = \$128,000$.

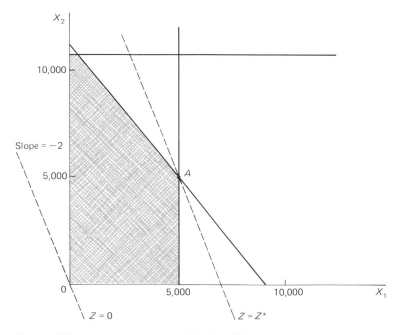

Figure 8.2   Determining Optimal Product Mix

If we had five outputs, obviously the problem could not be solved with a diagram, but the same method applies to solving problems for any finite number of outputs (see the appendix).

Considering the recent gasoline and fuel oil shortage, it is interesting to see what effect the relative profitability of gasoline to fuel oil has on a firm's decision with regard to the use of a barrel of crude oil. During the price-control period the wage-price council permitted an increase of 2¢ per gallon for fuel oil while ordering a decrease of 1¢ per gallon for gasoline. This made fuel oil relatively more profitable than before. Whether this is sufficient to alter the choices petroleum producers make is not clear, but it is clear from Figure 8.2 that if the slope of the objective function is changed enough, firms will find it advantageous to alter the mix of outputs. The effect of imposing excise taxes on one output, but not the other, can be analyzed in a similar way.

Example 2: Choice of production method to minimize production cost Let us consider an extension of the pollution example discussed earlier in Chapter 6 in which linear programming is used in locating efficient input combinations and choosing production techniques in order to minimize production costs.

Suppose we have two types of labor: high-skilled labor, U_1, costing \$40 per day, and low-skilled labor, U_2, costing \$24 per day. We want to minimize $W = 40U_1 + 24U_2$. There are, however, certain limitations on our choice: first, a production requirement of 500 units of output which requires either $\frac{1}{5}$ unit of high-skilled labor or $\frac{1}{2}$ unit of low-skilled labor per unit of output. This can be expressed by the production function constraint $5U_1 + 2U_2 \geq 500$. In addition, we have available no more than 80 high-skilled laborers and no more than 200 low-skilled laborers. Furthermore, a labor union has negotiated a contract which specifies that the firm must employ at least 150 laborers with high-skilled laborers in a ratio of 2-to-1 to low-skilled laborers. This constraint can be approximated by $\frac{1}{2}U_1 + U_2 \geq 150$. The problem can now be written

$$\text{Minimize } W = 40U_1 + 24U_2 \qquad (8.20)$$
$$\scriptstyle U_1, U_2$$

subject to

$$U_1 \leq 80, \qquad U_2 \leq 200 \qquad (8.21)$$

$$\tfrac{1}{2}U_1 + U_2 \geq 150 \qquad (8.22)$$

$$5U_1 + 2U_2 \geq 500 \qquad (8.23)$$

$$U_1 \geq 0, \qquad U_2 \geq 0 \qquad (8.24)$$

A graph of the resource constraint for 80 or less high-skilled laborers is a vertical line at 80 (Figure 8.3), and the constraint for 200 or less low-skilled laborers is the horizontal line at 200. The graphs of labor union constraint and the production function are both linear and are also illustrated in

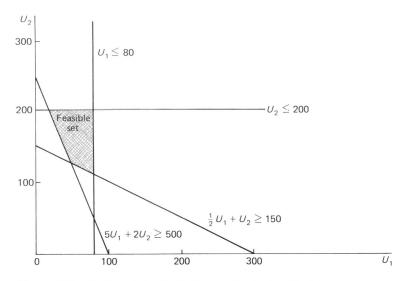

Figure 8.3   Outline of the Limitations on Production Decisions

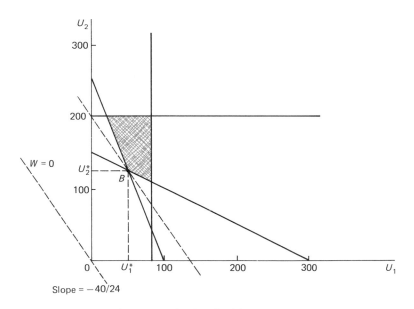

Figure 8.4 · An Efficient Production Decision

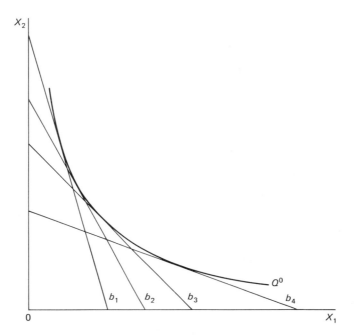

Figure 8.5 Approximating an Isoquant by Linear Constraints

Figure 8.3. The points that represent the feasible choices open to the firm lie below the labor resource limits but above the technological and labor union constraints. These choices are represented by the crosshatch area.

We want to find the solution which minimizes cost. Rewrite the cost expression as $U_2 = W/24 - (40/24)U_1$. For $W = 0$, the isocost line passes through the origin with a slope of $-(40/24)$. Finding an expenditure level that is just sufficient to reach a point in the feasible area is accomplished by pushing this isocost curve out from the origin to point B, Figure 8.4. The optimal solution is $U_1^* = 50$, $U_2^* = 125$ and the minimum cost is $W^* = 40(50) + 24(125) = \$5,000$.

Linear programming may be readily applied to the problem of minimizing the cost of the inputs required to produce a given level of output and its dual of maximizing the level of output for a given total expenditure. An isoquant initially given as a smooth curved surface can be approximated to any desired degree of accuracy by a set of linear constraints as shown in Figure 8.5. In this manner the original problem is reduced to a readily solvable form. At the same time, this example illustrates that duality between maximum and minimum problems in programming terms has a direct analog to the duality between the least cost function and the feasible input levels for any given level of output.

Example 3: "Make versus buy" decisions   A firm frequently must decide whether to purchase particular components or to manufacture the components themselves. This is a so-called make versus buy decision. This problem might be encountered by an optical firm constructing cameras which has to decide whether to make lenses or buy them from an outside firm, or by an electronics firm contemplating making all tubes and transistors for a television set itself or subcontracting some part of the equipment.

Let U_1 be the number of parts the firm purchases and U_2 the number of component pieces that the firm makes itself. Suppose the market price is $1.50 for purchased components while the cost of making the part is only $1 per unit. Noting the cost difference does not solve the decision problem since there are limitations on the decisions open to the firm. First of all, it needs 2,000 parts. The sum of the amount purchased plus the amount made by the firm must satisfy $U_1 + U_2 \leq 2,000$. On the other hand, the firm has a manufacturing capacity of only 1,250 pieces, and a storage limit on in-shipments so that no more than 1,500 units bought from outside suppliers can be stored. The problem can now be written

$$\text{Minimize } W = 1.50U_1 + 1.00U_2 \qquad (8.25)$$

subject to

$$U_1 \leq 1,500, \qquad U_2 \leq 1,250 \qquad (8.26)$$

$$U_1 + U_2 \geq 2,000 \qquad (8.27)$$

$$U_1 \geq 0, \qquad U_2 \geq 0 \qquad (8.28)$$

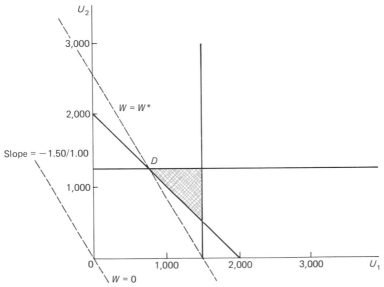

Figure 8.6   Feasible Choices for the Make versus Buy Problem

Each of the constraints is graphed in Figure 8.6. The feasible choices open to the firm are indicated by the crosshatched area. The objective function $W = 1.50U_1 + 1.00U_2$ is an isocost curve which can be rewritten as $U_2 = W/1.00 - (1.50/1.00)U_1$. If we graph this isocost line for $W = 0$, it passes through the origin with a slope of -1.5. To find the optimal mix of manufactured and purchased products, we have to increase expenditures just enough to purchase one of the mixes in the shaded area. Moving the isocost curve out from the origin we find it first touches the feasible area at point D, Figure 8.7. The optimal decision is to purchase 750 units, $U_1^* = 750$, and to make as many as the manufacturing capacity will allow, $U_2^* = 1,250$. The total cost of meeting the requirements constraint is thus $2,375 = \$1.50(750) + \$1.00(1,250)$.

The dual of this example provides information about the marginal cost of meeting the requirements constraint. Details are given in the appendix.

Example 4: Scheduling use of manufacturing capacity and investment and labor purchase decisions A firm often needs to schedule the use of its facilities in order to produce several different product lines from a given set of resources. The solution to this problem may necessitate decisions about expanding capacity or negotiating new contracts for input purchases. We shall develop the usefulness of the dual problem for studying this second type of decision in the next section.

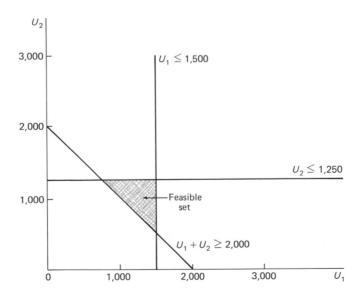

Figure 8.7 The Least Cost Decision for Make versus Buy

Suppose that a firm produces two outputs: cars, X_1, and trucks, X_2, and that production and sale of one car results in a net profit of \$400 while production and sale of one truck results in a net profit of \$450. The firm desires to maximize net profits which are $Z = \$400X_1 + \$450X_2$. There are the following limitations on output choices: first, a constraint on the production line limiting the volume of vehicles that can be processed per day; second, a constraint on the worker-hours available in the paint shop. Each of these constraints is a technological constraint representing part of the production function facing the firm. In addition, assume there is a constraint on parts assembly; and finally a constraint on the total amount of labor that may be used. These constraints are listed as follows:

Production line capacity	$X_1 + 2X_2 \leq 1{,}500$
Paint shop	$2X_1 + (\frac{4}{3})X_2 \leq 2{,}000$
Parts assembly	$(\frac{1}{5})X_1 + X_2 \leq 600$
Labor limit	$(\frac{2}{3})X_1 + X_2 \leq 1{,}000$

The problem can be written

$$\underset{X_1, X_2}{\text{Maximize}} \; Z = 400X_1 + 450X_2 \tag{8.29}$$

subject to

$$X_1 + 2X_2 \leq 1{,}500 \tag{8.30}$$

$$2X_1 + (\tfrac{4}{3})X_2 \leq 2{,}000 \tag{8.31}$$

$$(\tfrac{1}{5})X_1 + X_2 \leq 600 \tag{8.32}$$

$$(\tfrac{2}{3})X_1 + X_2 \leq 1{,}000 \tag{8.33}$$

$$X_1 \geq 0, \qquad X_2 \geq 0 \tag{8.34}$$

Figure 8.8 shows the graph of each of these constraints. The feasible set is represented by the crosshatch area in Figure 8.8.

To solve for the optimal production plan, we rewrite the profit expression as $X_2 = Z/450 - (400/450)X_1$ and graph this equation for profits of zero. For $Z = 0$ the curve passes through the origin with a slope of $-400/450$. We want to push this profit contour out as far as possible from the origin, while still remaining within the feasible set. The solution is represented by the point E in Figure 8.9. The optimal number of cars is $X_1^* = 750$, and the optimal number of trucks, $X_2^* = 375$. The profit at the optimum is $\$468{,}750 = \$400(750) + \$450(375)$.

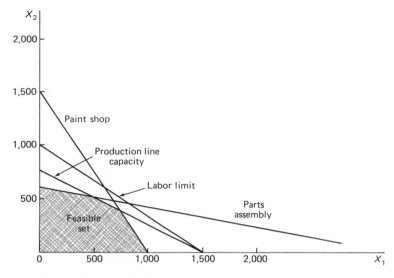

Figure 8.8   Production Limitations/Profit Possibilities

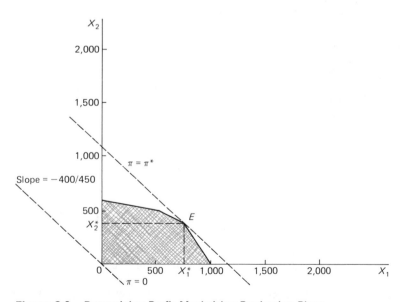

Figure 8.9   Determining Profit Maximizing Production Plans

The Economic Interpretation of the Dual of a Linear Programming Problem

A dual problem has one variable for each constraint in the associated maximum problem, and each variable in the maximum problem corresponds to a constraint in its associated dual problem. For instance, in the dual problem for Example 4, there is one dual variable for the labor constraint, one for the parts assembly constraint, one for the paint shop constraint, and one for the production line constraint.

The numerical value of each dual variable represents the maximum increment in profit which could be obtained by relaxing the associated constraint by one unit. For example, if the dual variable associated with the labor constraint has a value of $25 this would mean that one more unit of labor would lead to an increment in profit of at most $25. The dual variables are the imputed or implicit prices for each resource. Knowledge of the imputed price for a unit of labor is useful in labor negotiations. A firm would be willing to hire more worker-days of labor provided that the contribution to revenues is at least as great as the cost in wages. In terms of Example 4, this means that the firm will buy more labor provided that the market price of labor is equal to or less than $25 per day.

Dual variables associated with other resources have similar implications for purchase contract negotiations, since a firm would never bid more than the imputed price of a given resource. If, in Example 4, it costs $500 to add a unit of equipment in the parts assembly area, then a dual variable for the parts assembly constraint of $625 indicates that the firm should make the investment.[2]

Although we cannot illustrate the full solution of the dual problem for Example 4 in a graph because it has four variables, it can be written

$$\text{Minimize } W = 1,500U_1 + 2,000U_2 + 600U_3 + 1,000U_4 \qquad (8.35)$$
$$\underset{U_1,U_2,U_3,U_4}{}$$

subject to

$$U_1 + 2U_2 + 0.2U_3 + (\tfrac{2}{3})U_4 \geq 400 \qquad (8.36)$$

$$2U_1 + (\tfrac{4}{3})U_2 + U_3 + U_4 \geq 450 \qquad (8.37)$$

$$U_1 \geq 0, \qquad U_2 \geq 0, \qquad U_3 \geq 0, \qquad U_4 \geq 0 \qquad (8.38)$$

Notice that Constraints (8.36) and (8.37) correspond to the two variables in Example 4. The first constraint simply indicates that the imputed value of the resources used to make a car must be at least equal to the increase in the market value of these resources when incorporated in a car—$400. The

---

[2] Interpretation for investment decision use actually involves more detailed analysis, which is taken up in Chapter 16.

second constraint indicates that the imputed value of the resources used to make a truck must be at least equal to the increase in the market value of those resources when incorporated in a truck—$450. The computational method in the appendix may be used to find the actual values of U_1, U_2, U_3, and U_4 at the optimal solution.

A Closer Look at the Character of an Optimal Solution

The solutions in Figures 8.2 and 8.4 both occur at an extreme point, or "corner" of the feasible set. This common characteristic suggests an easy method for solving linear programs. It is *not* true that every optimal solution occurs on a corner, but it is true that if there exists an optimal solution, then a corner will be optimal. This method, first discovered by the mathematician George B. Dantzig, is called the *Simplex Method*. It solves a given problem by studying the polyhedron formed by the constraints. We start at one corner and evaluate the objective at that point. Next we can look at the adjacent corners. If one of them has a higher value for the objective (if the problem is a maximum problem) or a lower value (if it is a minimum problem), then we move on to that corner. We then ask again: does an adjacent corner give a higher (or lower) value for the objective? If one does, we move again. Once a corner is found for which no adjacent corner gives a higher (or lower) value, then that corner represents the optimal solution. The steps from corner to corner in this search are the steps of the *Simplex Algorithm*.

*Uncertainty and the Solution of Linear Programs

In practice, many of the elements of a linear program may not be known with certainty. Although most practical applications are set up and solved as certainty problems, various kinds of uncertainty can easily be introduced without affecting the computational simplicity which is so important for applications.

There are three pieces of information used in an *LP* problem—the c's, the b's, and the array of technological coefficients given by the a's.

If the c's are random variables in the maximum problem while the other terms are known with certainty, we might substitute an objective representing the expected value (i.e., the mean) in place of the original objectives. The reduced problem is then recast in the form of an *LP* problem under certainty. This procedure, unfortunately, assumes that the decision maker is indifferent between varying degrees of risk, which hardly seems desirable. Typically the

---

* Optional material requiring knowledge of probability.

introduction of risk will require a nonlinear objective function,[3] but some computational simplicity might be recovered by using linear segments to approximate the nonlinear function.

Uncertainty about the b's in the maximum problem can be handled in a simple way which retains the risk elements of the problem. Suppose that a firm wants its decisions to incorporate a specified probability that a constraint will not be violated. For instance, in Example 1 the refiner might want to schedule gasoline and fuel oil production so that the probability that production exceeds the storage tank capacities is equal to or less than p, $0 \leq p \leq 1$. This means that Constraint (8.18) would be written

$$\text{Prob } (X_1 > b_1) \leq p$$

or equivalently

$$\text{Prob } (X_1 \leq b_1) \leq 1 - p \tag{8.39}$$

If Inequality (8.39) can be reduced to an equivalent linear form, then the familiar solution method can be employed.

Let $\bar{b}_1$ be the expected value of b_1 and σ_1 be its standard deviation. Subtracting $\bar{b}_1$ from both sides of the inequality on the left side of Inequality (8.38) and then dividing by σ_1 yields

$$\text{Prob } \left(\frac{X_1 - \bar{b}_1}{\sigma_1} \leq \frac{b_1 - \bar{b}_1}{\sigma_1} \right) \leq 1 - p \tag{8.40}$$

Since the random variable b_1 is now in standardized form we can use probability tables to find the value of $(b_1 - \bar{b}_1)/\sigma_1$ which will satisfy Equation (8.40). If this number is 2.5, for example, then Equation (8.40) can be written

$$\text{Prob } (X_1 \leq \bar{b}_1 + 2.5\sigma_1) \leq 1 - p \tag{8.41}$$

Instead of using the constraint $X_1 \leq b_1$ where b_1 is random, we substitute the equivalent of Inequality (8.39), i.e.

$$X_1 \leq \bar{b}_1 + 2.5\sigma_1 \tag{8.42}$$

and proceed as before.

The procedure just outlined is referred to as chance-constrained programming and was suggested by A. Charnes and W. W. Cooper. Although the illustration developed above is in terms of the b's for a maximum problem, the same idea can be used for the c's in a minimum problem as well.

Summary

This chapter has illustrated the application of the linear programming method of solving decision problems. The important topics were (1) how to set up a problem so that it can be solved as a linear program and (2) how to

---

[3] See Chapter 5 for a more detailed discussion of decision criteria under uncertainty.

interpret the solution to a linear program, particularly its dual. The dual variables frequently contain as much or more economic information than the solution of the original problem. The ease with which some aspects of uncertainty can be included in problems solvable by linear programming adds to its usefulness as an aid to decision making.

Questions for Study or Class Discussion

1. How can *LP* methods be used to derive the cost functions referred to in Chapter 7?
2. What is the relationship between Example 2 and the discussion of isoquants and isocosts in Chapter 6?
3. Why is the dual of economic importance? What information does it contain?
4. Variables in linear programs are typically constrained to be non-negative. How could a problem be set up so that a variable could take on negative values? How could you require a variable to be between 72 and 107?
5. List at least five problems, in addition to those listed in the text, that could be solved by means of a linear program. Be specific about the objective and constraints.

Appendix

Each of the examples in Chapter 8 had a sufficiently small number of variables so that we could easily graph the problem to find the solution. This approach, however, is not particularly accurate, will not handle two or more variables, and will not provide the dual variables or imputed prices on the constraints. To circumvent these drawbacks we shall illustrate a more general tool that is easy to apply. The following discussion restates the form of maximum and minimum problems and their solution. Examples 1 and 3 are then reworked to illustrate each step. The solution to Example 4 is indicated along with its initial setup.

The general form of a linear maximum problem is

$$\underset{X_1,\ldots,X_n}{\text{Maximize }} Z = c_1 X_1 + c_2 X_2 + \ldots + c_n X_n \tag{A8.1}$$

subject to

$$a_{11} X_1 + a_{12} X_2 + \ldots + a_{1n} X_n \le b_1$$
$$a_{21} X_1 + a_{22} X_2 + \ldots + a_{2n} X_n \le b_2$$
$$\vdots \qquad \vdots \qquad \qquad \vdots \qquad \vdots$$
$$a_{m1} X_1 + a_{m2} X_2 + \ldots + a_{mn} X_n \le b_m \tag{A8.2}$$

$$X_j \ge 0, \qquad j = 1, \ldots, n \tag{A8.3}$$

and the general form of a linear minimum problem is

$$\underset{U_1,\ldots,U_m}{\text{Minimize }} W = U_1 b_1 + U_2 b_2 + \ldots + U_m b_m \tag{A8.4}$$

subject to

$$a_{11}U_1 + a_{21}U_2 + \ldots + a_{m1}U_m \geq c_1$$
$$a_{12}U_1 + a_{22}U_2 + \ldots + a_{m2}U_m \geq c_2$$
$$\vdots \qquad \vdots \qquad \qquad \vdots \qquad \vdots$$
$$a_{1n}U_1 + a_{2n}U_2 + \cdots + a_{mn}U_m \geq c_n \qquad \text{(A8.5)}$$
$$U_i \geq 0, \qquad i = 1, \ldots, m \qquad \text{(A8.6)}$$

The U_i in the minimum problem are the dual variables for the m constraints in the maximum problem and the X_j are the dual variables for the n constraints in the minimum problem. The following discussion assumes $n \geq m$.

To use the Simplex Method to solve a linear program we simply set up the required information in a *tableau* and then apply a set of rules to connect the initial tableau to a new one. We then check to see whether a stopping test is met, and if not we apply the same rules again to yield a third tableau. This process is repeated until checking indicates either that no solution exists or that an optimal solution has been found. The final solution is read from the last tableau.

The starting tableau is formed by setting up the data for the maximum or minimum problem in the following block form:

X_1	X_2	$\ldots X_n$	U_1	U_2	$\ldots$	U_m	
$-c_1$	$-c_2$	$\ldots -c_n$	0	0	$\ldots$	0	0
a_{11}	a_{12}	a_{1n}	1	0	0	0	b_1
a_{21}	a_{22}	a_{2n}	0	1	0	0	b_2
$\vdots$	$\vdots$	$\vdots$	$\vdots$	$\vdots$	$\vdots$	$\vdots$	$\vdots$
a_{m1}	a_{m2}	a_{mn}	0	0	0	1	b_m

$$\text{(A8.7)}$$

The a's, the c's, and the b's are the basic pieces of information for either the maximum or minimum problem. The whole block has $m + 1$ rows and $n + m + 1$ columns. *Warning:* Notice that for the maximum problem the a's in the first constraint are the a's in the first *row* in the block array, but for the minimum problem the a's in the first constraint are the a's in the first *column* of the block array. Check this statement by a careful reading of the subscripts on the a's in the block above and in the constraints for the general form for the maximum and minimum problem.

Once the data is set up in the block array three tools are used in solving a problem:

1. a rule to tell us when to stop calculations and read the answers
2. rules for constructing a new tableau from an old one if the solution is not complete
3. a rule to locate the answers in the last tableau when the solution is complete.

Each step is described for the Primal Simplex Method. Consult one of the references for the Dual Simplex variation.

Stopping rule

The entries in the top row of the block just below the columns labeled $X_1, X_2, \ldots, X_n, U_1, U_2, \ldots, U_m$ are a set of *signals*. The last column entry is not used so there is a total of $n + m$ signals. The stopping rule is to stop when all of the signal entries are zero or positive. If any signal entry is negative a new tableau must be constructed.

Rules for constructing a new tableau

There are three steps for constructing a new tableau from an old one—an *entry criterion*, an *exist criterion*, and a *transformation rule*.

Entry criterion: The first step for constructing a new tableau is to choose a column in the block which has a negative signal over it. We shall arbitrarily choose the column headed by the negative signal with the highest absolute value. This column will be called the *pivot column*. If one of the signals is negative, and all of the entries in that column (below the first row) are zero or negative, then the linear program has no solution.

Exist criterion: The second step is to compute the ratio of each entry in the last column on the right to the entry in the same row of the *pivot column*. We do this, however, only for rows below the top row and only if the entry in the *pivot column* is positive. For example, initially the last column contains the b's. If we had chosen column 4 as the pivot column then we would compute $b_1/a_{14}, b_2/a_{24}, b_3/a_{34}, \ldots, b_m/a_{m4}$ for all rows where $a_{i4} > 0$. We choose as the *pivot row* the row which has the smallest ratio.[4] It is assumed all b's are non-negative.

Transformation rule: The element common to the *pivot row* and the *pivot column* is called the *pivot element*. The transformation process is accomplished in two steps:

1. Divide every entry in the pivot row by the pivot element, and replace the pivot row by the resulting row.
2. For every row except the pivot row, replace each entry in the old tableau by a new entry computed as follows:

$$\text{new entry} = \text{(old entry)} - \text{(the entry in the pivot column}$$
$$\text{which is in the same row as the old entry)}$$
$$\cdot \text{(the entry in the new pivot row which is}$$
$$\text{in the same column as the old entry)} \qquad \text{(A8.8)}$$

---

[4] It is technically possible to be led into a circular sequence which never arrives at a final solution. This problem is known as degeneracy. Fortunately, it is not an obstacle to practical computations.

Some examples will show that these rules are much less involved than they appear at first glance. After a few applications, the steps become almost automatic.

An illustration of the Simplex computations

Example 1 can be written

$$\text{Maximize } 16X_1 + 8X_2 \qquad (A8.9)$$

subject to

$$X_1 \leq 5{,}000, \qquad X_2 \leq 12{,}000 \qquad (A8.10)$$

$$3X_1 + 2X_2 \leq 27{,}000 \qquad (A8.11)$$

$$X_1 \geq 0, \qquad X_2 \geq 0 \qquad (A8.12)$$

The Simplex Method has a built-in device for keeping all variables non-negative, so only the first three constraints must be included explicitly. In tableau form this information can be written

X_1	X_2	U_1	U_2	U_3	
-16	-8	0	0	0	0
1	0	1	0	0	5,000
0	1	0	1	0	12,000
3	2	0	0	1	27,000

$$(A8.13)$$

Notice that since X_2 does not appear in the first constraint we enter a coefficient of zero for X_2 in row 2 and similarly for X_1 in the second constraint.

The first step is to see whether the stopping rule is met. Since two of the signals are negative we must continue. Using the entry criterion we choose column 1 as the pivot column. Since two of the entries in column 1 *below* the first row are positive we initially compute the ratios $5{,}000/1 = 5{,}000$ and $27{,}000/3 = 9{,}000$. We choose row 2 as the pivot row since it has the smallest ratio.

To transform the initial tableau to a new one, we begin by dividing all the entries in row 2 by the pivot element. Since the pivot element is unity, row 2 of the new tableau will be the same as row 2 of the initial tableau.

To find the new row 1 we need to take each entry in the old row 1 and subtract the entry in row 1 in the pivot column times the entry in the transformed pivot row which is in the same column as the old entry. The entries in the old row 1 are

$$-16 \qquad -8 \qquad 0 \qquad 0 \qquad 0 \qquad 0 \qquad (A8.14)$$

The entry in this row which is in the pivot column (column 1) is -16; thus we must subtract -16 times the corresponding entry in the transformed pivot row from these entries to find the new row 1. The entries in the transformed pivot row (row 2) are

$$1 \qquad 0 \qquad 1 \qquad 0 \qquad 0 \qquad 5{,}000 \qquad \text{(A8.15)}$$

Multiplying by -16 gives

$$-16 \qquad 0 \qquad -16 \qquad 0 \qquad 0 \qquad -80{,}000 \qquad \text{(A8.16)}$$

Subtracting these values from the old row 1, we have:

$$
\begin{array}{rrrrrr}
-16 & -8 & 0 & 0 & 0 & 0 \\
(-)-16 & 0 & -16 & 0 & 0 & -80{,}000 \\
\hline
0 & -8 & 16 & 0 & 0 & 80{,}000
\end{array}
\qquad \text{(A8.17)}
$$

as the new row 1.

Initially row 3 is

$$0 \qquad 1 \qquad 0 \qquad 1 \qquad 0 \qquad 12{,}000 \qquad \text{(A8.18)}$$

and the entry in the pivot column of row 3 is zero; thus the new row 3 is the same as the old row 3.

The old row 4 is

$$3 \qquad 2 \qquad 0 \qquad 0 \qquad 1 \qquad 27{,}000 \qquad \text{(A8.19)}$$

The entry in the pivot column is 3. The new row 4 is thus the old row 4 minus the terms found by multiplying 3 times the transformed pivot row. Subtracting gives:

$$
\begin{array}{rrrrrr}
3 & 2 & 0 & 0 & 1 & 27{,}000 \\
(-)3 & 0 & 3 & 0 & 0 & 15{,}000 \\
\hline
0 & 2 & -3 & 0 & 1 & 12{,}000
\end{array}
\qquad \text{(A8.20)}
$$

The new tableau is

X_1	X_2	U_1	U_2	U_3	
0	-8	16	0	0	80,000
1	0	1	0	0	5,000
0	1	0	1	0	12,000
0	2	-3	0	1	12,000

$$\text{(A8.21)}$$

Since one of the signals is still negative, we have not passed the stopping rule, so we choose column 2 as the new pivot column. There are two elements below the first row in column 2 which are positive. Row 4 becomes the pivot row and 2 becomes the pivot element.

Transformation to tableau 3 begins by dividing the pivot row (row 4) by the pivot element to give the new row 4:

$$0 \qquad 1 \qquad -\tfrac{3}{2} \qquad 0 \qquad \tfrac{1}{2} \qquad 6{,}000 \qquad \text{(A8.22)}$$

The new row 1 is found by multiplying the element in row 1 which is in the pivot column, -8, times the transformed pivot row and subtracting this from the old row 1. Subtracting gives:

$$
\begin{array}{cccccc}
0 & -8 & 16 & 0 & 0 & 80{,}000 \\
(-)0 & -8 & 12 & 0 & -4 & -48{,}000 \\
\hline
0 & 0 & 4 & 0 & 4 & 128{,}000
\end{array}
\qquad \text{(A8.23)}
$$

The new row 2 is found by multiplying the element in row 2 which is in the pivot column, 0, times the transformed pivot row, and subtracting this from the old row 2:

$$
\begin{array}{cccccc}
1 & 0 & 1 & 0 & 0 & 5{,}000 \\
(-)0 & 0 & 0 & 0 & 0 & 0 \\
\hline
1 & 0 & 1 & 0 & 0 & 5{,}000
\end{array}
\qquad \text{(A8.24)}
$$

The new row 3 is found from

$$
\begin{array}{cccccc}
0 & 1 & 0 & 1 & 0 & 12{,}000 \\
(-)0 & 1 & -\frac{3}{2} & 0 & \frac{1}{2} & 6{,}000 \\
\hline
0 & 0 & \frac{3}{2} & 1 & -\frac{1}{2} & 6{,}000
\end{array}
\qquad \text{(A8.25)}
$$

thus the new tableau is

X_1	X_2	U_1	U_2	U_3	
0	0	4	0	4	128,000
1	0	1	0	0	5,000
0	0	$\frac{3}{2}$	1	$-\frac{1}{2}$	6,000
0	1	$-\frac{3}{2}$	0	$\frac{1}{2}$	6,000

$$\text{(A8.26)}$$

In this tableau all the signals are zero or positive. It is time to stop and read off the solution. To find the optimal quantity for X_1, look down the column with the heading "X_1." If there is only a 1 in one row, then the optimal quantity for X_1 is read from the entry in the column on the far right in the same row as the 1. In this case $X_1^* = 5{,}000$. The same procedure is followed for X_2. In this case $X_2^* = 6{,}000$. For every j, if there are any entries in the column headed "X_j" other than just a single 1 and zeros, then the optimal value, X_j^*, is zero. The optimal values for the U_i are found just beneath their column labels in the first row; e.g., $U_1^* = 4$, $U_2^* = 0$, and $U_3^* = 4$. The optimal value of the objective function, regardless of whether the problem is a minimum or a maximum problem, is found in the far right column in the top row; $Z^* = \$128{,}000$. Compare these answers with the ones we obtained earlier.

New information is now available concerning the value of the dual variables. Remember that each dual variable, or imputed price, represents the maximum change in the objective function that could be achieved by relaxing the constraint associated with it by one unit. We interpret $U_1^* = \$4$ as meaning that profits would rise by approximately $4 if the constraint on fuel storage could be increased to 5,001 gallons. If it would cost $2.75 to add one unit of capacity, then we would invest since we realize a net gain in profits of $1.25.

Example 3 is a minimum problem, and it is worthwhile to look closely at the set-up of the initial tableau. Once the tableau is set up all computations proceed as outlined above. The problem is

$$\text{Minimize } \$1.50U_1 + \$1.00U_2 \tag{A8.27}$$

subject to

$$U_1 \le 1,500 \tag{A8.28}$$

$$U_2 \le 1,250 \tag{A8.29}$$

$$U_1 + U_2 \ge 2,000 \tag{A8.30}$$

$$U_1 \ge 0, \qquad U_2 \ge 0 \tag{A8.31}$$

We can again ignore the constraints $U_1 \ge 0$ and $U_2 \ge 0$ since these are insured by the Simplex Method. Before setting up the problem in its initial tableau, notice that the first and second constraints are not in the standard form outlined earlier, since the first and second inequalities point the wrong way. To correct this we can multiply both sides by -1 to give

$$-U_1 \ge -1,500$$
$$-U_2 \ge -1,250$$
$$U_1 + U_2 \ge 2,000 \tag{A8.32}$$

as the constraints.

The initial tableau is

X_1	X_2	X_3	U_1	U_2	
$-1,500$	$1,250$	$-2,000$	0	0	0
-1	0	1	1	0	1.50
0	-1	1	0	1	1.00

$$\tag{A8.33}$$

The second tableau is

X_1	X_2	X_3	U_1	U_2	
$1,500$	-750	0	0	2,000	2,000
-1	1	0	1	-1	0.50
0	-1	1	0	1	1.00

$$\tag{A8.34}$$

and the final tableau is

X_1	X_2	X_3	U_1	U_2	
750	0	0	750	1,250	2,375
-1	1	0	1	-1	0.50
-1	0	1	1	0	1.50

$$\text{(A8.35)}$$

The optimal values indicate that the firm should purchase $750(U_1^* = 750)$ and make $1,250(U_2^* = 1,250)$. Total cost is \$2,375. The values of the dual variables are $X_1^* = 0$, $X_2^* = \$0.50$ and $X_3^* = \$1.50$. Notice that these are determined by examining the columns under the X labels. Column 1 does not have a single 1 and zeros, thus X_1^* is zero, X_2^* and X_3^* are read from the far right column. The dual variables indicate that the cost saving from relaxing the manufacturing constraint is \$0.50 per unit, which is exactly the cost saving achieved by making rather than buying. The \$1.50 imputed price on the total production constraint indicates the marginal saving which could be achieved by reducing the constraint one unit. This is \$1.50 since the marginal units are being bought from outside at a cost of \$1.50 each.

Example 1 could have been solved twice by means of a diagram—once for X_1^* and X_2^* and a second time for the dual variables U_1^*, U_2^*, and U_3^*. However, this method could not be used to obtain the dual variables in Example 4, where there are four constraints, and a four-dimensioned diagram would be needed. In this case we must use the computation method illustrated above. The initial tableau for Example 4 is

X_1	X_2	U_1	U_2	U_3	U_4	
-400	-450	0	0	0	0	0
1	2	1	0	0	0	1,500
2	$\frac{4}{3}$	0	1	0	0	2,000
$\frac{1}{5}$	1	0	0	1	0	600
$\frac{2}{3}$	1	0	0	0	1	1,000

$$\text{(A8.36)}$$

To make sure you understand the Simplex computations, solve this problem and show that the solution is $X_1^* = 750$, $X_2^* = 375$, and that the imputed prices on the constraints are $U_1^* = \$137.50$, $U_2^* = \$268.75$, $U_3^* = 0$, and $U_4^* = 0$.

References

Baumol, W. J., *Economic Theory and Operation Analysis.* Prentice-Hall, 1961.
———, "Activity Analysis in One Lesson," *American Economic Review,* 48 (December, 1958), 837–873.

Charnes, A., and W. Cooper, *Management Models and Industrial Applications of Linear Programming*, Volumes I and II. John Wiley & Sons, 1961.

———,"Chance-Constrained Programming," *Management Science*, 6 (October, 1959), 73–79.

Dorfman, R., "Mathematical or 'Linear' Programming: A Non-Mathematical Exposition," *American Economic Review*, 43 (December, 1953), 797–825.

———, P. Samuelson, and R. Solow, *Linear Programming and Economic Analysis*. McGraw-Hill, 1958.

Kemeny, J., A. Schliefer, J. Snell, and G. Thompson, *Finite Mathematics with Business Applications*. Prentice-Hall, 1962.

Chapter 9 Market Equilibrium and Price and Production Stability

Introduction

In the previous chapters we developed the concept of demand, both individual and market demand, and the concept of supply by an individual firm and by the market. We can now bring these two concepts together to analyze market equilibrium. In particular, we can discuss methods of determining market price and total quantity traded. We can also analyze policies designed to alter market price through changes in supply or demand.

At the outset we need to introduce two important concepts. *Equilibrium price* is defined as a price at which quantity demanded is equal to quantity supplied. The quantity at the equilibrium price is the *equilibrium quantity*. If quantity demanded exceeds the quantity supplied, then there is *positive excess demand* at that price. If the quantity demanded is less than the quantity supplied, there is *negative excess demand* at that price. In a given supply and demand situation there may be more than one equilibrium price; however, we will usually be considering markets where there is a unique equilibrium price.

Equilibrium and the role of time

In analyzing market equilibrium, time is usually divided into three periods. The first is referred to as the *market period* or the *instant period*. The second is referred to as the *short run* and the third the *long run*. The distinction between these three periods reflects the ability of firms to respond to changes in their market environment by altering production. During the market, or instant, period firms are already supplying a particular quantity to the market with no possibility of altering that quantity. As a result, during this period, the market supply schedule is perfectly inelastic. In the short run, the relevant supply schedule is the market supply schedule developed in Chapter 7. In the long run it is possible for new firms to enter an industry. We will therefore require a new concept, *the long-run industry supply schedule*, developed in more detail in Chapter 10.

Partial and general equilibrium

There are two main methods of analyzing market equilibria—*partial equilibrium analysis* and *general equilibrium analysis*. Partial equilibrium analysis examines equilibrium price and equilibrium quantity in one market at a time, while general equilibrium analysis considers the equilibrium in every market at the same time. In this chapter, and for several subsequent chapters, we shall be using partial equilibrium analysis. General equilibrium is introduced in Chapter 17.

The comparative statics method

Comparative statics is a powerful technique for partial equilibrium analysis. We begin by setting up an initial problem and solving it. Then we allow one of the initial conditions for the problem to change and solve the resulting new problem to obtain a new solution. The difference between the two solutions obtained is easily traced to the single element of the initial problem that was changed. This provides an easy way to understand the influence of different factors.

For example, the comparative statics method can be applied to analyze the effect of a change in the level or distribution of consumer incomes on an initial market equilibrium. Income changes typically alter demand, thus giving rise to a new equilibrium price and quantity. When we re-solved the consumer equilibrium problem after changes in price or income in Chapters 2 and 3, we were also using comparative statics. Similarly the least cost production problem in Chapter 6 was re-solved for repeatedly changing outputs to develop the cost functions in Chapter 7.

Notice that the comparative statics method compares two equilibrium situations. It does not determine either the length of time required to reach a new equilibrium after an initial change, nor the path of price or quantity from one equilibrium to another. Later in this chapter we can explore the dynamics of change in more detail.

Market Equilibrium: A Numerical Example

Let us begin with a numerical example of market equilibrium. Assume the market demand schedule is $D = 200 - 4P$ and the market supply schedule is $S = -120 + 6P$, where P is price per unit and D and S represent quantity demanded and supplied, respectively. These schedules are represented by the negatively sloped demand curve and the positively sloped supply schedule shown in Figure 9.1.

Using the definition of equilibrium, it is easy to see that equilibrium points are geometrically represented by intersections between supply and demand schedules, since an intersection corresponds to a price for which the quantity demanded is equal to quantity supplied. In Figure 9.1, the quantity demanded at the price P_1 is less than the quantity supplied. The horizontal distance AB is the negative excess demand at the price P_1. In a similar way, at a price P_2 the quantity demanded exceeds the quantity supplied by the horizontal distance CF. In this case, excess demand is positive.

Equilibrium prices or quantities can be found either geometrically or mathematically. As we have seen, asking whether or not an equilibrium price exists is equivalent, in geometric terms, to asking whether or not the supply and demand schedules intersect.[1] The above problem is treated mathematically by solving the two equations simultaneously for the price P.

$$D = 200 - 4P = -120 + 6P = S \tag{9.1}$$

$$P = \frac{320}{10} = \$32 \tag{9.2}$$

$$Q = 200 - 4(\$32) = \$72 \tag{9.3}$$

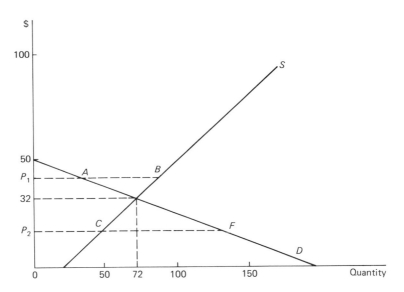

Figure 9.1   Supply, Demand, and Market Equilibrium

[1] In mathematical terms the existence of equilibria depends on whether or not two equations (a supply function and a demand function) can be simultaneously solved.

Though analysis of equilibrium prices is important if prices are to be the information signals of a market system, it must be remembered that in practice the system is constantly adjusting to the changes introduced by day-to-day events.

The Impact of Excise Taxes: An Application of Market Equilibrium Analysis

Excise taxes are frequently levied on commodities such as gasoline, cigarettes, telephone service, and automobiles. All sales taxes are excise taxes, as are customs duties. For policy decisions one needs to be able to analyze what effect such taxes may have on market price and quantity. We can simulate policies by using supply and demand analysis tools before actually implementing them.

Excise taxes typically take one of two forms: (1) a specific amount of tax per unit of the commodity or (2) an ad valorem excise tax, specified as a certain percentage of the price. The latter includes the federal excise tax on the price of the interstate telephone calls, customs duties, and sales taxes.

The effect of levying an excise tax of an amount T per unit is illustrated in Figure 9.2. The market demand schedule is D and the supply schedule is S,

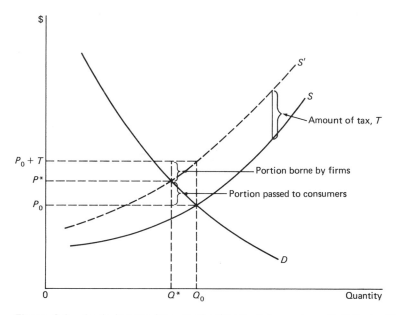

Figure 9.2 Analyzing the Impact of a Constant Amount per Unit Excise Tax

with an initial equilibrium price P_0 and equilibrium quantity Q_0. If we levy a tax, for example an added gasoline tax, then we must add an amount equal to the tax to every price along the supply schedule. If initially suppliers would have supplied 100 gallons at 65¢ per gallon and the tax is 4¢ per gallon, then the new supply schedule shows 100 gallons at 69¢ per gallon. Adding a specific amount excise tax is therefore represented by a vertical shift in the supply schedule equal to the amount of the tax, T.

Who bears the burden of this tax? One possibility is for the tax to be paid entirely by consumers in the form of higher prices. In economic terms, this would mean that the tax is entirely shifted forward to consumers through a new equilibrium price exactly T higher than the initial equilibrium price. Alternatively, the tax might be borne entirely by firms in the form of reduced profits or output. Reduced output might result in reduced employment for the inputs in the industry affected. In this case, some portion of the tax is said to be *shifted backward*, meaning that it is borne by the factors of production. The "incidence" of any excise tax can be broken down into a portion that is passed forward in the form of price increases and a portion shifted backwards to be borne by the factors of production, through reduced profits and/or by decreased employment.

Looking at Figure 9.2 we can measure the magnitude of these effects. The new supply schedule S' yields a new equilibrium price of P^*, which is higher than the initial price, and a reduction in output to Q^*. There is some forward shifting of the tax burden through an increase in price, but part of

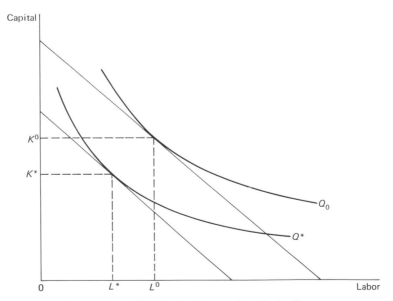

Figure 9.3 Backward Shifting Incidence of an Excise Tax

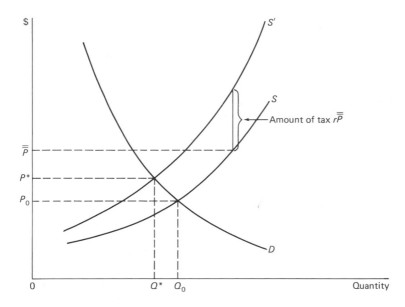

Figure 9.4   Analyzing the Impact from Levying an Ad Valorem Excise Tax

the burden is also borne either by the firms or by inputs. The portion of the tax that is shifted forward is the difference between the new equilibrium price and the old one, $P^* - P^0$. Notice that in this situation not all of the tax is shifted forward.

If the demand is completely inelastic, the effect of levying an excise tax is entirely shifted forward to consumers. On the other hand, if demand is perfectly elastic, the entire burden of the tax is shifted backwards to the firm and other factors of production. How much of the tax is shifted forward, and how much is shifted backward, thus depends upon the interaction of the elasticity of supply and the elasticity of demand. In Figure 9.2, the reduction in output from Q_0 to Q^* reflects the backward shifting. How much of this impact is borne by any one input depends on the technologies available for production—in other words, on the shape of the isoquants. Figure 9.3 illustrates the quantitative measurement of this effect.

In the case of a specific amount of excise tax levied on alcohol or cigarettes, where demand is quite inelastic, one might expect that the impact is largely borne in the form of an increase in price. This also means that if one is interested in cutting back the consumption of such products, excise taxes will not be effective in doing so unless they are very large. Since the tax is shifted forward, it does not give producers any incentive to contract output.

How is the effect of an ad valorem excise tax described geometrically? Since the ad valorem tax is a percentage of the price, the old supply schedule S and the new one S' must diverge as price increases. Figure 9.4 illustrates the effect of levying an ad valorem tax at the rate r. As an exercise, work through the analysis in Figure 9.4 to determine the forward or backward shifting of the tax effect and find the magnitudes of the respective shifts.

A Comparison of Methods for Solving Gasoline and Energy Shortages: A Second Application

This example illustrates the different effects of several popular alternatives for solving the problem of allocating scarce goods among consumers. Supply and demand analysis is based on the use of prices to perform a rationing role. Manufacturing quotas or ration coupons could also be used to limit consumption.

Suppose we want to restrict the use of gasoline to a level $\bar{Q}$ (Figure 9.5) and are considering accomplishing this by a quota, excise taxes, or price increases without taxes. Analysis will show that the distributional impact of these alternatives is quite different.

In the case of a production quota, limiting demand to $\bar{Q}$ requires either raising the price to $\bar{P}$ (Figure 9.5) or finding some other method to allocate goods, since without a price increase the quantity demanded will exceed $\bar{Q}$. The question is, who will benefit from the institution of the quota? A manufacturing quota system, accompanied by price increases, transfers income from consumers to suppliers. Such a policy has a very explicit income

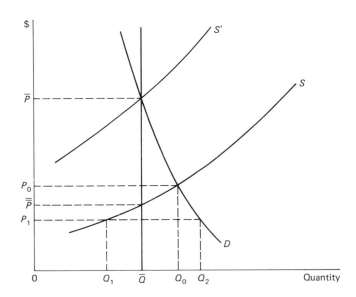

Figure 9.5 Restricting Consumption by a Quota versus an Excise Tax

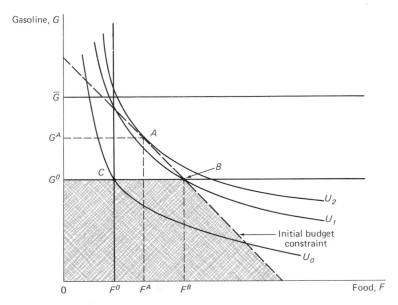

Figure 9.6 Effect of Rationing on Consumption Choice

redistributional component to it. Similarly quotas on imported goods take money from consumers who would buy the cheaper imported goods, and transfer it to domestic suppliers producing goods in competition with the imported products.

Now suppose we achieve the same objective by using a specific amount excise tax of $\bar{P} - \bar{\bar{P}}$ per unit. In this case money is not transferred from consumers to firms, but from consumers to the government treasury.

If prices are limited to less than equilibrium price, for example by a price ceiling on beef or gasoline, then an explicit or implicit rationing scheme is needed to cope with the excess demand at the legal price. At a price of P_1 (Figure 9.5) the quantity demanded is Q_2 while the quantity supplied is only Q_1, resulting in an excess demand of $Q_2 - Q_1$. In the same way, instituting a quota of $\bar{Q}$, while prohibiting price increases, creates an incentive for an illegal market in the commodity because individuals are willing to pay more than the legal price.

For an alternative view of rationing, let us return to the graphs used for the consumer budget analysis. Suppose a consumer is initially choosing between two commodities, food and gasoline, at the equilibrium point A in Figure 9.6, where he/she is consuming G^A of gasoline and F^A of food. If we institute a quota limiting the amount of gasoline to G^0, but leaving market prices and income the same, we force the individual to move along the budget constraint from A to B. Notice that the consumer will undergo a decrease in utility as a consequence of any quota less than G^A. The new feasible budget set is represented by the crosshatch area in Figure 9.6. An additional quota on food of $F^0 < F^B$ would force the individual below his/her budget constraint to the solution at C.

Adjustment Paths: The Cobweb Example

Each of the foregoing examples compared an initial equilibrium to an equilibrium achieved after a specific change. Let us turn to an example which emphasizes the adjustment process from one equilibrium to another. Agricultural markets have from time to time been plagued by unstable output prices which lead to unstable farm incomes. Stability of farm income is one of the objectives of government agricultural price support programs and of soil bank projects, which take acreage out of productive use. Hogs, beef, corn, wheat, and soy beans are examples of outputs characterized by a substantial growing season that requires production decisions a year or more in advance. The lags in adjustment introduced by a long production period play a crucial role in price, production, and employment stability.

The simplest illustration of the problems introduced by adjustment lags is provided by a model known as the *cobweb adjustment process*. The model derives its name from the adjustment path that prices and/or output take in their movement toward or away from equilibrium. The model provides a clear illustration of the importance not only of equilibrium but also of time in the process of adjustment toward equilibrium.

Suppose the quantity demanded at time t is $D_t = c + dP_t$, $d < 0$, and the quantity supplied at time t is $S_t = a + bP_{t-1}$, $b > 0$. Notice that although the demand schedule is a single downward sloping schedule, the quantity supplied at time t is a fixed amount plus b times the price that prevailed during the previous period. In an agricultural context, this reflects the fact that in the spring farmers may base their planting decisions on the price which prevailed at the last harvest. This is the first time that we have explicitly introduced forecast information or expectations into a decision problem.[2] The forecast used in the cobweb model is simply that the current expected price is the price that prevailed last period. Such forecasts are sometimes called *naive forecasts*. We could easily use more sophisticated forecasting forms such as averages of past prices, e.g., a distributed lag (or weighted average) such as $P_t^* = a_1 P_{t-1} + a_2 P_{t-2} + \cdots a_m P_{t-m}$.

Figure 9.7 illustrates the kind of adjustment that arises from the cobweb process. Suppose the initial price is P_1. The quantity demanded is Q_2, but

[2] The fact that current decisions depend on future events immediately introduces uncertainty elements since the unknown future data must be replaced by forecast information. Statistical forecasts, of course, are random phenomena.

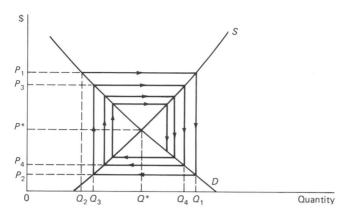

Figure 9.7 An Example of Stable Cobweb Adjustment

the quantity supplied will be Q_1. The only way the market can be made to absorb a quantity Q_1 is by offering it at the price P_2. P_2 now becomes the basic piece of information for the production decision in the next time period. Firms find that at a price of P_2 their most profitable strategy is to supply Q_3, but for that quantity individuals would be willing to pay P_3. At P_3, firms will supply Q_4, but when Q_4 is supplied, that, in turn, leads to a new market price P_4, etc.

Successive adjustment leads to a sequence of prices. The graph of the path of equilibrium prices looks rather like a maze (Figure 9.7). Notice that each new price is closer than the preceding one to the equilibrium price P^*. Figure 9.7 shows a cobweb adjustment process that leads to a convergent sequence of prices. It is also possible, however, for a cobweb process to lead to a divergent sequence of prices, where each successive price is further away from the equilibrium point. Figure 9.8 illustrates this possibility. The major economic factors determining not only stability or instability, but also the speed at which prices change, are the slopes of the supply and demand schedules.

The path of prices may also be derived mathematically. The price at time t is given by[3]

$$P_t = \left(P^1 - \frac{c - a}{b - d} \right)\left(\frac{b}{d}\right)^t + \frac{c - a}{b - d} \tag{9.4}$$

where P^1 is the initial price shown in Figure 9.8. Notice that the slopes of the supply and demand schedules, b and d, are the crucial elements. If

---

[3] Equation (9.4) can be obtained by equating supply and demand and solving the resulting linear difference equation. A good elementary introduction can be found in S. Goldberg, *Introduction to Difference Equations*, John Wiley & Sons, 1961.

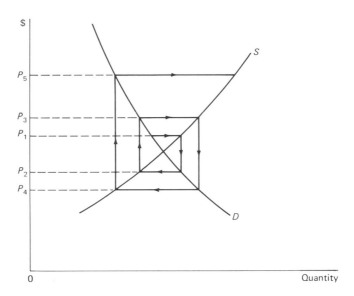

Figure 9.8   An Example of Unstable Cobweb Adjustment

$|b/d| < 1$ the process converges; if $|b/d| = 1$ the process oscillates indefinitely; and if $|b/d| > 1$ the process diverges.

The cobweb example emphasizes the role played in actual market out-comes by price expectations and the formation of forecasts. Forecasts frequently involve past data, thus introducing a lagged adjustment process into the equilibrium problem. Expectations are also important in financial markets for funds to be used as loans. There is a supply of funds available for loans and a demand schedule for loans, much like those depicted in Figure 9.1, only in this case the price on which the quantity supplied and demanded depends is the interest rate. The expected rate of inflation alters the interest rate at which firms will be willing to lend and also effects the determination of the amounts individuals will wish to borrow. The stability of the interest rate is directly dependent on individual expectations about the rate of inflation, just as in the cobweb example.

Stability of Equilibria

Once the existence of an equilibrium has been determined, whether geo-metrically or mathematically, the next question concerns its stability. The stability of an equilibrium has direct implications for the stability of market prices and consequently for the stability of production as well. Production stability, in turn, affects the stability of employment. Apart from its theoretical

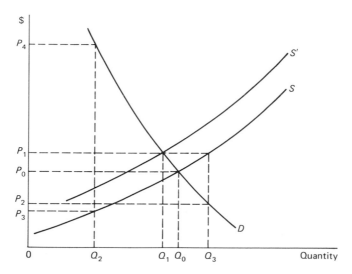

Figure 9.9 An Example of a Market That Is Both Marshallian and Walrasian Stable

interest, the study of the stability of market equilibria is therefore connected with the desire to stabilize prices, employment, or the incomes of producers and laborers.

Figure 9.9 shows a demand schedule on which quantity demanded increases with decreases in price and a supply schedule on which quantity supplied increases with increases in price. This represents a typical picture of market equilibrium. It is also possible to have negatively sloped supply schedules, as shown in Figures 9.10 and 9.11, and positively sloped demand schedules (for Giffen goods).

Initially we need to define what we mean by the stability of an equilibrium. The stability of an equilibrium depends on the tendency of prices or quantities once they depart from an initial equilibrium. A market is said to be stable if, for small changes in price away from the initial equilibrium, there is an adjustment process that establishes a new equilibrium.[4] The stable market represented in Figure 9.9 is initially in equilibrium at the price P_0. When supply changes to S', it generates information in an adjustment process which leads to the new equilibrium price P_1. A market is said to be unstable if, for small changes away from an initial equilibrium price, the market processes information in a way that leads to a sequence of new prices which, instead of leading to a new equilibrium, depart further from equilibrium.

---

[4] Technically this is referred to as *stability in the small* as opposed to convergence to an equilibrium from an arbitrary disequilibrium starting point, which is called *stability in the large*. See P. A. Samuelson, *Foundations of Economic Analysis*, Harvard University Press, 1947, for a more formal discussion.

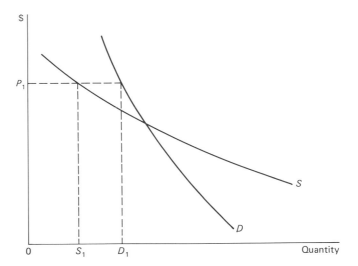

Figure 9.10 An Example of a Market That Is Marshallian
Stable, but Walrasian Unstable

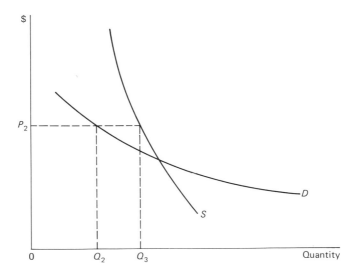

Figure 9.11 An Example of a Market That is Walrasian Stable,
but Marshallian Unstable

Prices and quantities are actually only in equilibrium for relatively short periods of time, if at all. Thus, the process of adjustment from one equilibrium to another is a basic part of the ongoing dynamics of a price system.

Let us look at two specific examples of adjustment processes, a *Walrasian adjustment process* and a *Marshallian adjustment process*. $E(p) = D(p) - S(p)$ is the *Walrasian measure of excess demand* at an initial price p. The Walrasian adjustment process is defined by the adjustment rule $\Delta E / \Delta P \geq 0$. Translated in terms of price changes, the rule indicates that if excess demand is positive, prices are revised upward and if excess demand is negative, prices are revised downward. In Figure 9.9 there is positive excess demand at the price P_2 and the Walrasian adjustment rule indicates prices should be revised upwards. Notice that this change is in the direction of P_0 (using curves D and S).

The Walrasian adjustment process uses prices as the adjusting force. In contrast, the Marshallian adjustment process is based on quantities as the adjusting mechanism. The Marshallian measure of excess demand price is defined at any quantity Q by $F(Q) = D^{-1}(Q) - S^{-1}(Q)$. $D^{-1}(Q)$ represents the maximum price per unit individuals will offer for the market quantity Q. $S^{-1}(Q)$ is the minimum price per unit necessary to induce producers to supply the market quantity Q.

The Marshallian adjustment rule is $\Delta F / \Delta Q \geq 0$. This implies that if F is positive, quantity will increase and prices will fall and if F is negative, quantity will decrease and prices will rise. To apply the Marshallian concept geometrically we simply read the quantity along the horizontal axis and measure the excess demand price by the vertical distance between the demand and supply schedules. For the Walrasian concept we read the price from the vertical axis; the excess quantity demanded is the horizontal distance between the demand and supply schedules.

Let us look at specific supply and demand schedules and apply both stability concepts to see whether or not the market is stable. First, look at Figure 9.9. We know the initial equilibrium price and quantity are P_0 and Q_0. At a disequilibrium price such as P_1, excess demand is negative. Decreasing the price, as the Walrasian adjustment rule requires, leads back toward equilibrium. If the initial disequilibrium price is below equilibrium excess demand is positive, and a price increase leads toward equilibrium, again in accordance with the Walrasian adjustment rule.

The same procedure can be repeated using the Marshallian rule. If we start out at quantity Q_2, the price that individuals are willing to pay is P_4, while Q_2 would be supplied for a price P_3; thus $F = P_4 - P_3$. Since F is positive, output should increase and prices fall, which leads in the direction dictated by the Marshallian rule. In the same way, if we are initially at the quantity Q_3, where the supply price exceeds the demand price, F is negative and decreasing quantity, with consequent price increases, leads toward equilibrium.

The Walrasian and Marshallian adjustment processes both lead to a stable market for supply and demand schedules like those in Figure 9.9, but this is not always true. As an exercise in applying the adjustment rules, satisfy yourself that in the situation depicted in Figure 9.10 the equilibrium is stable in the Marshallian sense, but unstable in the Walrasian sense, while the equilibrium depicted in Figure 9.11 is stable according to the Walrasian adjustment rule but unstable according to the Marshallian one.

The stability of prices and production depends ultimately on the way in which the market participants respond to situations that are not initially in equilibrium. It may be more important to understand how long it takes to achieve equilibrium than to know the equilibrium price ultimately arrived at. Time and information are basic to all adjustment processes.

*Information, Uncertainty, and the Concept of Market Equilibrium

To say that the equilibrium market price occurs at the intersection of supply and demand schedules suggests that its actual determination is an elementary procedure. But this is misleading. Even with the introduction of time lags and adjustment processes, the determination of market price poses complex problems whose solutions are far from clear.

Microeconomics begins by studying individual decision makers and deriving decision rules based on various assumptions about their behavioral objectives. But how do individual decision makers act if they have incomplete knowledge of market prices? To answer this question formally we must extend the setting for decision making to include the simultaneous determination of all prices, incomes, and choices. This process is illustrated in Chapter 17. But even the creation of a general equilibrium setting will not explain how market prices are actually determined under uncertainty.

The transition from individual behavior to aggregate market activity has been traditionally represented by a situation in which buyers and sellers present the offers they would make at a given price to be tallied by a hypothetical auctioneer. If the quantities demanded and supplied at the given price are equal, trading commences; otherwise, a new price is set and the bidding process is repeated.

The essence of this view is the requirement that no trading take place until equilibrium is determined and the equilibrium price is known to all participants. Convenient as the auction description may be for theoretical explanations, day-to-day activity obviously involves trades at many different prices. In fact, disequilibrium trading probably plays the dominant role in bringing about the evolution of prices over time.

* Optional material requiring knowledge of probability.

Disequilibrium trading typically occurs because information is imperfect or nonexistent and costly to acquire. The moment information imperfections are introduced the concept of equilibrium must be reexamined.

Understanding decision processes under uncertainty requires a study of two phenomena: (1) individual behavior rules for choice and (2) the lack of complete accurate information that gives rise to uncertainty. A number of behavior rules were outlined in Chapter 5. The absence of complete information necessitates undertaking a search to acquire it, as illustrated in Chapter 2.

Since no market participant can afford the expense of an indefinite search, trading will occur at different prices. Information imperfections thus tend to replace the concept of a single market equilibrium price with the notion of an *equilibrium distribution of prices*. A particular commodity no longer has a fixed price, but, instead, an expected price and a variation about the expected price.

Discussions of equilibria and their stability under certainty occupy a large part of economic literature. Only recently has attention turned to disequilibrium processes and the role of uncertainty. Concepts of equilibrium based on probability and investigation of the economic implications of decisions under uncertainty represent the most promising areas of contemporary economics. Hopefully such studies may lead to an understanding of inflation.

Summary

This chapter has brought together two of the basic tools of microeconomic analysis—supply and demand—and illustrated their interaction in the formation of market prices. The existence and stability of market equilibrium prices were demonstrated in a numerical example and by the application of the Walrasian and Marshallian adjustment rules.

Several of the examples in this chapter illustrate methods for translating proposals for dealing with such contemporary problems as food and fuel shortages into diagrams which highlight their major economic impacts.

We can now turn to more concrete applications of market equilibrium in particular market settings. The following chapters utilize the concepts of demand, cost, and equilibrium to study environments confronting a firm with different degrees of competition. We shall also analyze the impact of imperfect information.

Questions for Study or Class Discussion

1. What influences are suppressed by partial equilibrium analysis?
2. Why are behavior rules for economic agents relevant to a discussion of market equilibrium?

3. What information is relevant to achieving a market equilibrium? How might information imperfections alter market adjustment?
4. "Raising gasoline and electricity prices through excise taxes will lead to resource conservation." Evaluate this statement. What other alternatives are available?
5. What is the economic value of information? How does this influence the equilibrium market price of information services such as newspapers, financial advice, and magazines like *Newsweek* or *Consumer Reports*?

References

Arrow, K. J., "Limited Knowledge and Economic Analysis," *American Economic Review*, 64 (March, 1974), 1–10.

Henderson, J. M., and R. E. Quandt, *Microeconomic Theory*, Second Edition. McGraw-Hill, 1971.

Hicks, J. R., *Value and Capital*. Oxford University Press, 1946.

Marshall, A., *Principles of Economics*. Macmillan, 1920.

Samuelson, P. A., *Foundations of Economic Analysis*. Harvard University Press, 1947.

Smith, V., "Experimental Auction Markets and the Walrasian Hypothesis," *Journal of Political Economy*, 73 (August, 1965), 387–393.

Stigler, G., "The Economics of Information," *Journal of Political Economy*, 69 (June, 1961), 213–225.

Chapter 10 Pricing and Production Decisions in Pure Competition

Introduction

This chapter deals with the first of the specific market settings for a firm outlined in Chapter 5—pure, or perfect, competition. The word *competition* has at the same time acquired two almost entirely different connotations. On the one hand, competition is viewed as a desirable attribute of economic activity providing advantages for consumers through the interfirm rivalry it generates. On the other hand, competition is frequently cited as the bane of any business executive faced with the problem of meeting the challenges produced by rivals. The word *competition* is used here in a special sense that does not exactly coincide with either of the colloquial usages of the term. Pure competition is a model of a business environment. It is a model just as the models of monopoly, monopolistic competition, and oligopoly discussed in the following chapters are also models, or abstractions, intended to simplify the complexities of the real world. Models provide a vehicle for studying economic activity in a way simple enough to gain insight into what happens, yet realistic enough to solve problems.

A market setting is perfectly competitive if it has the following characteristics: (1) There are a large number of buyers and sellers, no one of which is sufficiently large enough to influence market price independently. (2) The product of each seller is indistinguishable from the commodity produced by any other seller. In other words, output is homogeneous. (3) All buyers and sellers have complete information, including the prices of alternative com-

185

modities, quantities bought and sold, demand conditions, and costs.[1]
(4) Resources are freely mobile. This means resources can flow from one
industry to another or from use in one technique of production to another.
No rigidities prevent resources from flowing into an industry and none prevent them from flowing out of one.

Actual market settings that approximate the purely competitive model
include securities markets for stocks and bonds, and agricultural markets for
corn, wheat, or soybeans. Each of these markets are examples that, while not
exactly meeting the strict definition of perfect competition, come close
enough so that the model of a perfectly competitive market is a useful tool
for solving policy problems.

Purely competitive market analysis can occur within the three familiar
time periods: the market period, the short run, and the long run. Within each
period it can be applied to the entire market or to each individual firm.

Market Equilibrium in the Market Period

The market period is an interval of time during which firms cannot respond
to price changes by adjusting output levels or even by hiring other variable
inputs. This is illustrated in Figure 10.1 by a perfectly inelastic supply
schedule at the quantity Q^0. With a demand schedule D', the equilibrium
market price in the market period is P'. If demand changes to D'', then the
equilibrium market price rises to P''. Consequently, during the market period,
equilibrium market price is entirely determined by demand.

Market Equilibrium in the Short Run

From the viewpoint of each firm, the basic difference between the market
period and the short run is whether or not they have enough time to respond
to changing market demand conditions. In general, if even a brief period of
time elapses, there will be some inputs that the firm can vary in order to
respond to changes in demand. In Figure 10.2, instead of facing a perfectly
inelastic supply schedule, as in Figure 10.1, each firm is able to move along
its own short-run supply curve. We know from the discussion in Chapter 7
that a firm's short-run supply schedule is its short-run marginal cost schedule
above the point of minimum average variable cost. The upward slope of the

---

[1] In a riskless setting, an economic agent is said to possess "complete information" if
it knows (1) its own transformation possibilities from resources to outputs, (2) its own
preferences, and (3) market information such as prices and quantities. In a competitive
setting decentralized decision-making units are used to economize on the expense of
information acquisition and distribution, since each agent does not need to possess all
information in existence.

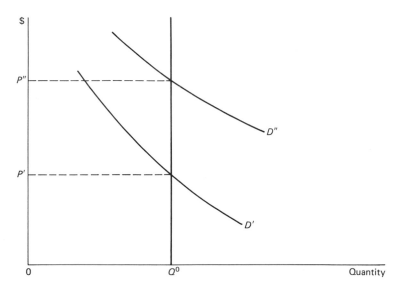

Figure 10.1 Market Equilibrium in the Market Period

short-run market supply schedule reflects the assumption that in the short run firms are able to alter production only at increasing marginal cost.

Let us assume that the schedules shown in Figure 10.2 are the short-run market supply and demand schedules. This leads to a stable short-run market equilibrium at the price P^* and the total market quantity Q^*.

The Firm's Pricing and Production Decisions in the Short Run

We know from the first requirement for a purely competitive market setting that no one decision maker is large enough to influence the market price. We shall now use this assumption to derive the short-run equilibrium analysis for a typical firm.

Each firm knows the short-run equilibrium price, P^*, and assumes that at this price it can sell as many units of outputs as it wishes to produce. If a firm sells one unit of output it will receive a revenue of P^* and when it sells 500 units of output the added revenue from the 500th unit will still be P^*. This means that even though the market demand schedule actually slopes downward, the individual firm perceives its own demand curve (which is equivalent to the average revenue schedule) as being horizontal at the market price P^*. In fact, since increases in sales can be achieved without a reduction

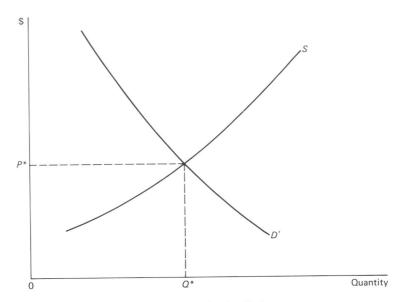

Figure 10.2   Short-Run Equilibrium for the Market

in price, marginal revenue remains constant and is also equal to P^*, i.e., $MR = P^* = AR$.

The short-run production decision for the firm is to find the output level and the associated input levels which achieve the objective it desires, for example, to maximize profits. Figure 10.3 illustrates how the cost data developed in Chapter 7 provides a foundation for a firm's decisions. In the short run, the firm should either shut down and produce zero, or produce a positive level of output. If it shuts down, its total losses equal its total fixed costs. If it produces, we know from Chapter 7 that optimal output occurs at a point where marginal revenue equals marginal cost.

In Figure 10.3, marginal revenue equals marginal cost for one output level Q^0. We are assured that the firm will produce a positive output because P^* is above minimum average variable cost. The optimum short-run production decision will not be to shut down unless market price is below minimum average variable cost. At Q^0 the firm receives an amount $\overline{AE}$ in excess of its average variable cost, which means that losses will be less (or profits higher) than could be achieved by shutting down and producing nothing.

For small increases in output above Q^0, marginal cost is above average revenue, which means that profits would decrease. For output levels below Q^0 marginal revenue is greater than marginal cost. It would not make sense to cut back production of units whose marginal revenue is greater than marginal cost, since marginal profit on such units is positive. Cutting back

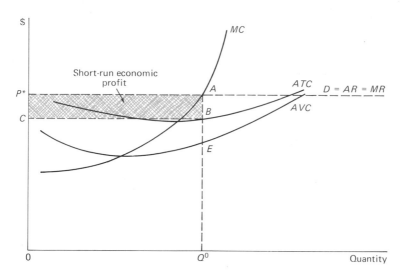

Figure 10.3 Short-Run Equilibrium Production and Pricing for an Individual Firm

production below Q^0 would also reduce profits, therefore Q^0 must be an optimal level of output.

In the short run, by definition, there are some resources that cannot be varied, among them plant and equipment; thus a firm may earn an economic profit, which, as we have seen, means a return on investment over and above the next best alternative available in the economy as a whole. In Figure 10.3, short-run economic profit is indicated by the crosshatch area. Average profit is the distance $\overline{AB}$, which equals average revenue, $\overline{OP^*}$, less average total cost, $\overline{OC}$. Multiplying average profit by the total quantity Q^0 gives total profit.[2]

---

[2] Alternatively, we can restate the firm's decision problem as

$$\text{Maximize } \pi = P^*Q - C(Q)$$
$$\text{\small Q}$$

subject to

$$Q \geq 0$$

where $C(Q)$ represents total cost. Differentiation with respect to Q gives

$$\frac{d\pi}{dQ} = P^* - C'(Q) = 0$$

which is the familiar $MR = MC$ rule. To insure we are at a local maximum point requires

$$\frac{d^2\pi}{dQ^2} = -C''(Q) < 0$$

This condition is clearly satisfied if marginal cost is increasing ($C''(Q) > 0$) as shown in Figure 10.3.

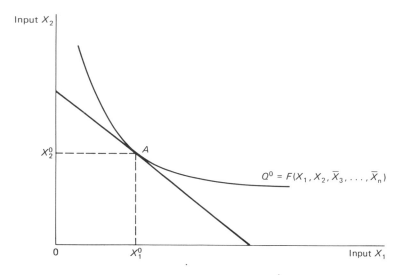

Figure 10.4   Finding the Short-Run Optimal Input Decision for
Variable Inputs

The short-run optimal input decision for variable inputs at output level Q^0 is illustrated in Figure 10.4. If we assume that X_1 and X_2 can be varied while inputs $X_3, \ldots, X_n$ are fixed, then the isoquants correspond to the production function $Q = F(X_1, X_2, \overline{X}_3, \ldots, \overline{X}_n)$. Once market price and output have been chosen total revenue is fixed, thus the firm can maximize profits for given input prices by minimizing total production costs. Least cost production occurs at point A. The firm employs X_1^0 units of input X_1 and X_2^0 units of input X_2.

Market Equilibrium and the Firm's Pricing and Production Decisions in the Long Run

Over longer periods of time resources can move from one technique of production to another within an industry, and even from one industry to another. As long as resources are freely mobile, they will be drawn toward areas of production in which previous resource commitments are earning economic profits, and away from industries which are earning economic losses.

This process is analogous to the way water seeks its own level, gradually flowing out of high places (locations of short-run economic losses) and toward low areas (locations of short-run economic profits) until it achieves a uniform level, which corresponds to long-run equilibrium for an economy. In other

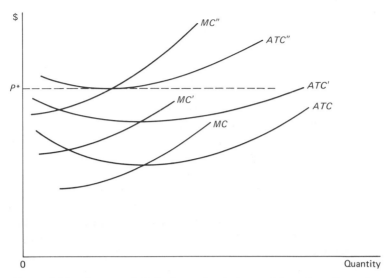

Figure 10.5 Entry and Exit from the Industry May Alter Costs for Individual Firms

words, resources will continue moving until each firm in the industry is earning zero economic profits. (Remember, however, that this does not mean that resources are earning no returns, but that the return in their current use is the same as the return from the best alternative use.)

The flow of resources into areas of high economic profit will cause increases in supply and possibly in the prices of inputs as well. Bidding up the prices of inputs changes costs for each firm.

Figure 10.5 illustrates another possible effect of the flow of resources, the entry of new firms in the market. The entry of new firms may increase, decrease, or leave unchanged the costs of each firm. Elasticities of supply for inputs used in the industry are critical economic factors determining whether costs change (and in what direction). Relatively inelastic input supply schedules with positive slopes imply sharply rising costs while falling input supply schedules imply that the entry of new firms would confer a benefit on existing firms through reduced costs of inputs.[3] Whether the output of a particular firm rises or falls obviously depends on the combined influence of changes in market prices and production costs.

Apart from its influence on the costs of individual firms, drawing resources into an industry can dissipate short-run economic profits in another way. Using the market demand schedule in Figure 10.2, added resources drawn

---

[3] Costs or benefits transmitted by the market are sometimes referred to as *pecuniary externalities*, as opposed to *technological externalities*.

into an industry means an expansion of supply, like the move from S to S' in Figure 10.6. This will drive the short-run equilibrium market price down from P^* to P'. If economic profits are still earned at the new equilibrium price P', then they will continue to draw resources into the industry. Supply might then increase to S'', which will drive the short-run equilibrium price still lower.

Bringing resources into an industry thus may cut away economic profits both by driving the market price down, and by driving short-run average costs up. The long-run supply adjustment for the individual firm is illustrated in Figure 10.7. In the long run the firm typically has more than one technological possibility. It therefore faces a long-run average cost curve, $LRATC$, which is the lower envelope of all the short-run average total cost curves for possible technologies, as shown in Chapter 7. The long-run equilibrium adjustment for the individual firm will result in an output at the minimum of its long-run average total cost curve, P'. If the long-run equilibrium price were greater than P', say P^*, then there would exist output levels and technological combinations which could produce economic profit, but that would draw more resources into the industry. If the market price is below P', say $\bar{P}$, then losses would occur regardless of which technology was employed, and the firm would be forced to leave the industry.

Figure 10.7 provides a clue as to which firms will enter the market and which will leave. The $LRATC$ of any particular firm reflects market input

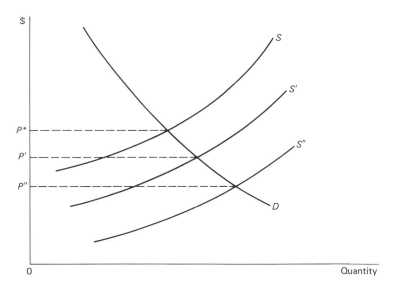

Figure 10.6 Entry or Exit From the Industry Alters Market Supply and Thus Market Price

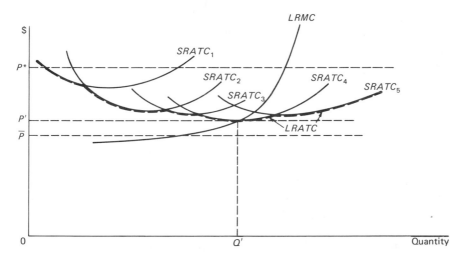

Figure 10.7 Long-Run Equilibrium Production for an Individual Firm

prices, which are presumed to be accessible to all firms, and the available technologies. Competition forces the firm to adopt least cost technologies as a condition for economic survival. Firms that fail to adopt cost-cutting innovations or are poorly organized internally will continue to earn economic losses until they are forced out by firms using resources more efficiently.

The basic characteristic of long-run equilibrium is that the economic profit of each producing firm is zero. The situations illustrated in Figures 10.3 to 10.6 show short-run economic profits; therefore, resources will flow into the industry. If there had been short-run economic losses, the reverse would occur. Resources flowing out of an industry or rising input costs from entry would change supply from S to $\bar{S}$ (Figure 10.6). The exit of firms from the industry may cause a reduction in the demand for inputs, causing cost curves to fall and supply to increase.

Long-run equilibrium for the firm in pure competition is characterized by: (1) market price equal to minimum long-run average total cost ($P =$ min $LRATC$), (2) market price equal to long-run marginal cost ($P = LRMC$), (3) output at the minimum of the relevant short-run average total cost curve ($P =$ min $SRATC$), and (4) market price equal to short-run marginal cost ($P = SRMC$). Figure 10.7 illustrates these conditions.

Notice that nothing in the foregoing discussion precludes a firm from experiencing constant $LRATC$. If $LRATC$ is constant and less than or equal to the market price, then the equilibrium level of output for an individual firm is either indeterminate or indefinitely large. A decreasing $LRATC$ raises the possibility of an individual firm driving out all competitors, contradicting the assumption of a purely competitive setting. In fact, decreasing *LRATC* may well lead to one of the "natural monopolies" discussed in the next chapter.

Long-Run Industry Supply

Suppose the market is initially in long-run equilibrium (Figure 10.8) with demand D_1 and supply S_1 and that demand then increases to D_2. Initially the long-run equilibrium price is P_1 with an equilibrium market quantity Q_1. In the market period, the price must rise to P_2, but in the short-run period, after firms have had a chance to respond, it will fall back to a short-run equilibrium market price of P_3. The problem is to predict what will happen in the long-run.

There are three possibilities for the new market supply schedule arising in response to the increase in demand. If it turns out to be like S_2, in Figure 10.9, the new long-run equilibrium price will be the initial price, P_1. If within a given industry input costs and production technologies permit

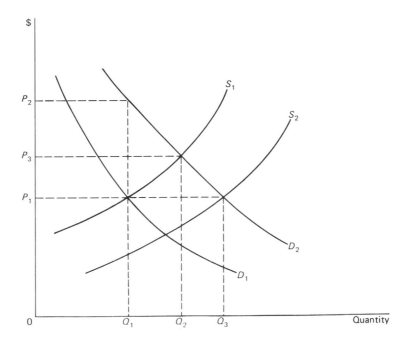

Figure 10.8 Long-Run Market Equilibrium and Supply Response to Changing Demand for a Constant Cost Industry

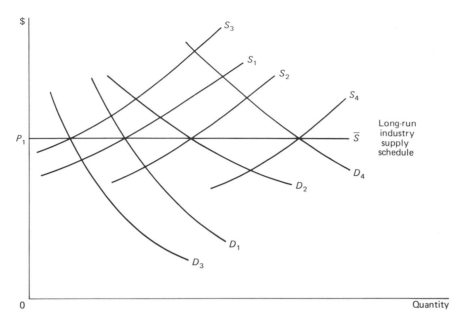

Figure 10.9   Deriving the Long-Run Industry Supply Schedule for a
Constant Cost Industry

successive adjustments of quantity to changes in demand so that the equilibrium price always returns in the end to the initial price P_1, then the industry
is said to be a *constant cost industry*. This means that the industry has the
ability to respond to increases or decreases in demand in such a way that
even though in the market period and in the short run, price deviates from
the long-run equilibrium price, ultimately it returns to P_1. The total market
output level may, however, change even though the long-run market equilibrium price does not.

The long-run industry supply schedule is defined as the locus of the market
equilibria that occur as the industry supply schedule shifts to its successive
new long-run positions. For a constant cost industry the long-run supply
schedule is horizontal, as in Figure 10.9. S_1, S_2, S_3, and S_4 represent the
industry short-run supply schedules resulting from successive long-run
adjustments.

Since the long-run equilibrium market price always returns to P_1, this
implies that the *LRATC* for each firm in the industry has its minimum at the
same cost level. This does not mean the *LRATC* for each firm cannot change,
for it may shift laterally as shown in Figure 10.10. The important point is
that the minimum is achieved at the same cost level, although possibly at a
different output level. Constant returns to scale technology, coupled with

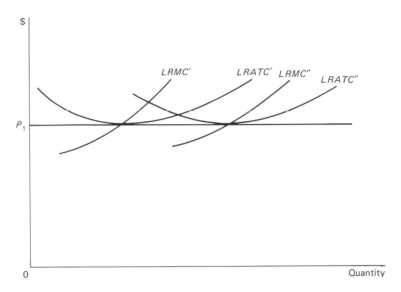

Figure 10.10   *LRATC* Curves for a Firm Constant Cost Industry

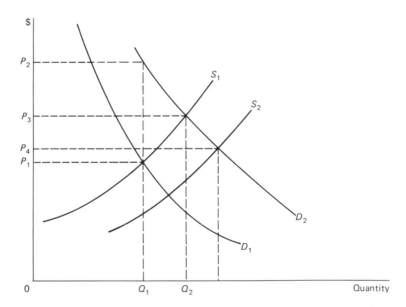

Figure 10.11   Long-Run Market Equilibrium and Supply Response to Changing Demand for an Increasing Cost Industry

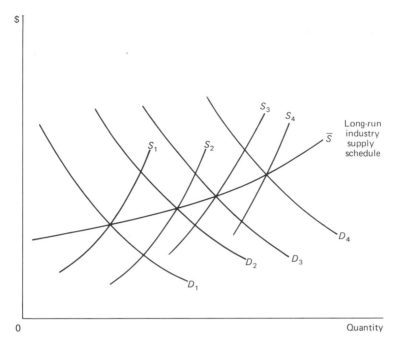

Figure 10.12 Deriving the Long-Run Industry Supply Schedule for an Increasing Cost Industry

perfectly elastic input supply schedules, is sufficient to produce constant cost conditions, although they may also be the net result of input price changes and changing technology choices.

Now suppose that long-run equilibrium price ultimately fails to return to its initial level. In Figure 10.11, although we start with the same situation depicted in Figure 10.8 and the same increase in demand to D_2 causing short-run market price to rise to P_2, the long-run adjustment leads to a supply schedule like S_2; then the new long-run equilibrium price P_4 is above P_1. Successive long-run supply adjustments of this sort will produce a long-run supply schedule like $\bar{S}$ in Figure 10.12, which slopes upward. Industries responding in the manner illustrated in Figures 10.11 and 10.12 are called *increasing cost industries*.

The third possibility is that increases in demand lead to successive *decreases* in long-run equilibrium price, as illustrated in Figure 10.13. In the short run the increase in demand from D_1 to D_2 leads first to a rise in price from P_1 to P_2 and then a decline to P_3. If supply expands as far as S_2, the new long-run equilibrium price, P_4, will be less than P_1. Successive supply responses of this sort result in long-run equilibria which yield a decreasing long-run

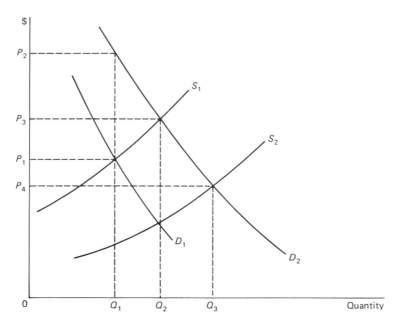

Figure 10.13   Long-Run Market Equilibrium and Supply Response to Changing Demand for a Decreasing Cost Industry

industry supply schedule like the one illustrated in Figure 10.14. Industries which behave in this way are referred to as *decreasing cost industries*.

Let us now consider the effect of economic and technological forces in producing increasing or decreasing long-run industry supply schedules. A constant returns to scale technology, coupled with rising input supply schedules (or even with input supply schedules falling at a moderate rate of speed), can lead to a rising long-run industry supply schedule. Similarly, increasing returns to scale, coupled with perfectly elastic input supply schedules (or with sharply falling input supply schedules) can create a falling long-run industry supply schedule.

A long-run decrease in average cost may seem improbable at first, but it is thought to be characteristic of the communications, transportation, and (until recently) electricity industries. In these cases, as the volume of goods produced increases, the available technologies allow firms to move to different methods of production thus experiencing increasing returns to scale.

Empirical Measures of Supply

This section contains some empirical estimates of industry supply functions and short-run and long-run supply elasticities.

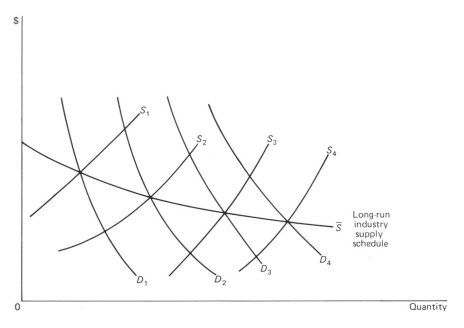

Figure 10.14 Deriving the Long-Run Industry Supply Schedule for a Decreasing Industry

The short-run supply schedule for beef has been estimated[4] as

Steers = Constant + 0.096 (Price of Beef/Price of Corn)
        + 0.495 (Stock on Hand at End of Previous Period)   (10.1)

with an elasticity of supply of 0.16 with respect to the price of beef. In other words, if the price of beef rises by 10%, the quantity of beef supplied will increase by only about 1.6%. This shows clearly how a relatively small surge in demand can increase the market price dramatically.

As you might expect supply becomes more elastic over a longer period of time. Table 10.1 illustrates the marked difference between short-run and long-run supply elasticities for United States agriculture. Notice the contribution of individual inputs to the overall response. Table 10.2 illustrates the short-run versus long-run elasticity comparison for several agricultural products.

[4] Adapted from S. Reutlinger, "Short-Run Beef Supply Response," *Journal of Farm Economics*, 48 (November, 1966), 909–919.

Table 10.1   U.S. Agricultural Supply and Its Components

INPUT	Contribution to Aggregate Supply Elasticity	
	SHORT RUN	LONG RUN
Fertilizer and lime	0.03	0.14
Machinery expense	0.06	0.28
Feed, seed, livestock	0.06	0.18
Other expenses	0.03	0.23
Crop and livestock inventories	0.01	0.10
Machinery inventory	0.02	0.26
Labor	0.03	0.25
Real estate	0.03	0.08
Total Elasticity	0.27	1.52

SOURCE: L. G. Tweeten and C. L. Quance, "Positivistic Measures of Aggregate Supply Elasticities: Some New Approaches," *American Economic Review Papers and Proceedings*, 59 (May, 1969), 175–183.

Table 10.2   Estimated Supply Elasticities for Selected Products

PRODUCT	Price Elasticity of Supply	
	SHORT RUN	LONG RUN
Carrots	0.14	1.00
Lettuce	0.03	0.16
Tomatoes	0.16	0.90
Cauliflower	0.14	1.10
Cucumbers	0.29	2.20

SOURCE: M. Nerlove and W. Addison, "Statistical Estimation of Long-Run Elasticities of Supply and Demand," *Journal of Farm Economics*, 40 (November, 1958), 861–880.

Agricultural Price Supports and Farm Income: An Application

Two types of agricultural policies have frequently been followed in the United States. One is a price support policy in which the federal government agrees either to purchase a particular commodity, such as corn or wheat, at a particular price if the market price falls below a certain level or to pay a subsidy equal to the difference between the support price and the actual market price multiplied by the quantity sold. The other policy is the well-known soil bank plan, in which farmers receive payment for not planting crops on

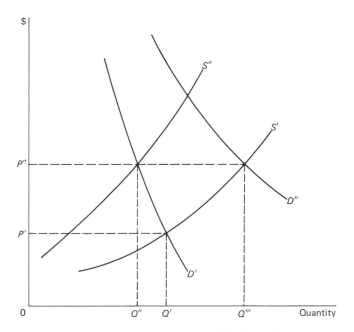

Figure 10.15 Analyzing the Impact of Soil Banks and Price Supports

a certain acreage. Directly or indirectly, each of these policies is aimed at stabilizing or raising farm income.

The impact of an effective soil bank policy is shown in Figure 10.15. Initially the equilibrium market price is P'. A soil bank plan causing a restriction in supply from S' to S'' raises the price, and output falls from Q' to Q''. Alternatively, the price received by farmers could be raised to P'' by instituting a price support at the price P''.

These policies cause an implicit income redistribution tending to increase farm incomes. Since the demand for agricultural products is generally inelastic, raising their price raises farm income.

As with the examples in Chapter 6, these alternative income raising policies may have quite different side effects. In both cases, if the actual market price rises to P'', individual demand is restricted to Q''. With soil bank restrictions, consumers pay all of the higher price P''. Under a price support scheme farmers might continue to sell at the initial market price P', but they would receive a subsidy equal to the difference between P' and the support price, P'', times the quantity sold. The total subsidy would be $(P'' - P')Q'$. This amount comes out of the public treasury and must be made up from income taxes or other revenue sources.

A third method for raising the price to the support level is through government purchases that effectively increase demand to D'' (Figure 10.15). The government actually buys the corn, wheat, or soybeans, and may store them, in which case it incurs not only the cost of purchasing the commodity, but the cost of storing it as well. It may easily happen that the net effect of attempting to increase farm incomes by having the government purchase enough to raise the market price, may actually raise farm incomes by *less* than the purchase cost plus the cost of storage! In other words, the government might have produced the same increase in farm income at lower cost by giving farmers the money directly. Economic rationality is not, of course, necessarily the same as political feasibility, which undoubtedly accounts for numerous roundabout policies of this kind.

But what happens in the long run? In the short run incomes (and presumably profits) to farmers engaged in agricultural production increase. This may create positive economic profits, which encourage entry into the industry in the long run. If this occurs, even more extreme policies are needed to prevent market prices from falling again. Presumably the reason for instituting the policy originally was that overproduction at existing market prices was keeping farm incomes too low, but a low return may well encourage consolidation to larger units where more efficient technologies may be employed. Subsidies, price supports, and the rapid rise in food prices in 1972 and 1973 may only hinder long-run adjustments needed to provide sufficient food for growing populations.

Analyzing the Impact of Profit Taxation

In the short run, profit taxation reduces the revenue remaining after variable inputs and fixed contractual obligations have been paid for. If the firm desires to maximize profit and is subject to a profit tax of 30%, instead of solving the problem

$$\text{Maximize } \pi(Q) \qquad\qquad (10.2)$$
$$\text{\scriptsize Q}$$

subject to

$$Q \geq 0 \qquad\qquad (10.3)$$

the firm must now solve the problem

$$\text{Maximize } \bar{\pi}(Q) = \pi(Q) - \text{Tax} = \pi(Q) - 0.30\pi \qquad (10.4)$$

subject to

$$Q \geq 0 \qquad\qquad (10.5)$$

In a riskless setting, the solutions to these two problems are exactly the same, since maximizing a constant times profit leads to the same output as maximizing profit alone. This means that, in the short run, output level is affected neither by a profit tax imposed as a percentage of profit nor by the level of fixed costs. Under pure competition, the only effect of these two elements is on the level of profits left in the hands of the firm.

In the long run, profit taxes may reduce the funds available to pay dividends on invested capital. If they reduce these funds below the level that can be achieved elsewhere in the economy, capital will flow out of the industry. This is particularly likely when effective profit tax rates differ from one industry to another as a result of special tax provisions such as the depletion allowances available to the oil and mining industries. In the short run, however, profit taxation which takes less than all short-run net revenues will not alter a firm's decisions.

*Price Uncertainty and Production Decisions

Uncertainty as to market price is common in agricultural and other markets. The introduction of price uncertainty can cause pervasive changes in the results obtained in a riskless setting.

Assume that the firm's total costs are composed of total variable costs, $C(Q)$, and total fixed costs, B, and that price can be either $(1 + a)P$ or $(1 - a)P$ with equal probability, $0 \leq a \leq 1$.[5] Expected profit is

$$E[\pi] = \tfrac{1}{2}(1 + a)PQ + \tfrac{1}{2}(1 - a)PQ - C(Q) - B \qquad (10.6)$$

where Q is output and P and a are given. Increasing a increases price volatility, while $a = 0$ corresponds to a riskless setting. For the moment let us assume the firm seeks to maximize expected profits, and that it must make its production decision before price is known. If decisions can be postponed until *after* the random event occurs, then substantial reduction in profit risk can be achieved, but the essence of a risky planning problem is removed. Although we will not pursue their ramifications, other elements of uncertainty problems also change the character of the results one obtains. How does uncertainty influence price, quantity demanded, or cost? What is the objective of the firm? Are we considering a single production period or a sequence of periods where inventories may be carried over from period to period? Each of these questions must be answered in more complicated problems.

Maximizing expected profits requires

$$\frac{dE[\pi]}{dQ} = \tfrac{1}{2}(1 + a)P + \tfrac{1}{2}(1 - a)P - C'(Q) = 0 \qquad (10.7)$$

where $C'(Q)$ is marginal cost and the first two terms on the right-hand side

---

* Optional material requiring knowledge of probability.
[5] The following analysis can be repeated using a probability distribution of prices, without changing the important implications.

of Equation (10.7) are the expected selling price. If the expected price is equal to P, the condition expressed in Equation (10.7) is satisfied at the same level of output as in a riskless setting. If the firm commits itself to this level, it will be unable to expand output to take advantage of the higher price of $(1 + a)P$, and will produce in excess of demand when the price is $(1 - a)P$. Therefore, expected profits will be less than the profit that could be achieved under certainty. In addition, as the variation in price increases (i.e., as a increases), expected profits decline, thus creating an economic value for information, which would reduce the degree of uncertainty.

The foregoing results are based on the assumption that the firm seeks to maximize expected profits. Notice that variance in profits is not even considered. Obviously this is an important omission. Most decision makers will pass by an alternative offering the prospect of a $1,000 gain or no gain with equal probability, for one which offers the prospect of a $600 gain or a $400 gain with equal probability. In both cases the expected gain is $500, but the degree of risk (at least measured by variance) is much lower for the latter. As we learned in Chapter 5, we can use a utility function as a vehicle for incorporating this kind of risk aversion (or even risk preference) into decisions.

Using the criterion of maximizing expected utility instead of expected profit above, i.e., taking $E[U(\pi)]$ as the objective, the problem becomes

$$\text{Maximize } E[U(\tfrac{1}{2}(1 + a)PQ + \tfrac{1}{2}(1 - a)PQ - C(Q) - B)] \qquad (10.8)$$
$$\text{\scriptsize Q}$$

subject to

$$Q \geq 0$$

Maximizing (10.8) with respect to Q requires

$$E[U'(\pi)(\bar{P} - C'(Q))] = 0 \qquad (10.9)$$

where $\bar{P}$ is expected price and $U'(\pi)$ represents the marginal utility of profit. Now we must ask whether the marked difference between riskless and risky decisions applies to these results as well as to those observed using the expected profit criterion.

Though a detailed development is beyond our scope, the major implications of price uncertainty for a purely competitive firm may be summarized as follows:

1. For the risk-averse firm, optimal output is less than under certainty.
2. Fixed costs are no longer irrelevant. Increased fixed costs will normally lead to a decrease in optimal output.
3. Increasing marginal cost is no longer a necessary condition for a finite optimal production level nor, consequently, for a determinate firm size.
4. For a risk-averse firm, an optimal production plan is characterized by *ATC less* than expected price.

Fixed costs become relevant when risk is introduced, since a firm will want to provide a margin for possible losses by keeping fixed costs down. Result 4 indicates that expected economic profits will be positive, not zero, in equilibrium; in fact, they will increase as the firm assumes more risk. This result corresponds to the common assumption that risk taking is a valuable economic function which should command a positive market price.

Summary

The market setting of perfect competition has a prominent place in microeconomic analysis. The basic concepts of a market period, the short run, and the long run provide a simple and yet powerful vehicle for judging the probable impacts of alternative policies or decisions.

Each of the three time period analyses is composed of two parts: an analysis of market price and output adjustment and an analysis of the impact on a typical firm. Applications to agricultural price supports and profit taxation are examples of the policies we can analyze with microeconomic methods.

Although limited in scope, the discussion of price uncertainty in a purely competitive setting emphasized the gross errors—both theoretical and practical—that can result from ignoring risk elements.

Questions for Study or Class Discussion

1. What role does resource mobility play in long-run adjustments? If resources are not freely mobile what influence would this have on profits, prices, and output?
2. How does demand price elasticity influence price changes as a firm moves from adjustment in the market period to a long-run setting?
3. "It does not make good sense to operate if the firm sustains an economic loss." Is this correct? When? Why?
4. How would the emergence of new technologies be reflected in a firm's long-run planning information? Which costs would be affected? How? Would a new technology always be economically feasible? Why or why not?
5. How could uncertainty about costs be illustrated in a diagram? If the firm seeks to maximize expected profits, how will output decisions be affected? What output choices will a risk-averse firm make when costs are uncertain?

References

Ellis, H., and W. Fellner, "External Economies and Diseconomies," *American Economic Review*, 33 (1943), 493–511.

Henderson, J., and R. Quandt, *Microeconomic Theory*, Second Edition. McGraw-Hill, 1971.

Knight, F., *Risk, Uncertainty, and Profit*. Harper & Row, 1921.

Marshall, A., *Principles of Economics*. Macmillan, 1920.

Oi, W., "The Desirability of Price Instability Under Perfect Competition," *Econometrica*, 29 (January, 1961), 58–64.

Samuelson, P. A., *Foundations of Economic Analysis*. Harvard University Press, 1947.

Sandmo, A., "On the Theory of the Competitive Firm Under Price Uncertainty," *American Economic Review*, 61 (March, 1971), 65–73.

Scitovsky, T., *Welfare and Competition*. R. D. Irwin, 1951.

Stigler, G., "Perfect Competition, Historically Contemplated," *Journal of Political Economy*, 65 (1957), 1–17.

Tisdell, C., "Uncertainty, Instability, Expected Profit," *Econometrica*, 31 (January-April, 1963), 243–247.

Chapter 11 Pricing and Production Decisions in Monopoly Market Settings

Introduction

The word *monopoly* in a business context frequently suggests such evils as conspiracy, prohibition of competition, and predatory price cutting. In an economic context, however, pure monopoly is a market situation that has one and only one seller. Instead of having free resource mobility, pure monopoly sustains itself by the existence of either legal or economic inhibitions that are absolute barriers prohibiting entry into the industry.

Much of the interest in studying monopoly market settings stems from the fact that many business firms operate in a setting closely parallel to the model that we will develop here. Telephone companies, natural gas companies, and electricity are examples of pure monopolies. Most utilities are provided by a single producer. A single transit authority frequently provides the rail service or bus service. On some routes even air carriers are granted a single producer status. In addition to having such single producer status, many monopolies operate in regulated settings as an adjunct to receiving monopoly privileges.

After examining the origins of monopoly, we shall discuss pure monopoly by developing equilibrium for the monopolistic firm in the short run and in the long run.

Barriers to Entry and the Existence of a Monopoly

The origins of a monopoly may be *legal* or *technological*.

Public utilities are examples of monopolies created by law. A franchise to the firm gives it the exclusive rights to supply a prescribed market area.

Theoretically, such franchises avoid the economic costs of duplicate facilities when production involves increasing returns to scale. Though this sounds plausible, it is important to note that increasing returns to scale do not necessarily imply decreasing average costs.

Franchises are not the only legal means of creating a monopoly. Patents and copyrights also create a monopoly for specified periods of time. Title to specialized resources, such as a specific type or grade of mineral or a specific piece of property, gives the owner a monopoly in the resource or location.

Economic forces can also create a monopoly or dissipate the power of an existing monopoly. Increasing returns to scale and/or constant or declining input supply schedules can lead to decreasing average costs. A firm can then achieve larger profits by driving out competitors through price cutting or some other means. In addition, the sheer size a new firm must have to compete with an existing firm can create an economic barrier that is just as rigid as a technological one.

Equilibrium for the Market and the Firm in the Short Run

The essential distinction between the discussion of pure monopoly and discussion of the purely competitive setting is that under pure monopoly the market and the firm are one and the same. There is no short-run industry supply curve, and, in fact, there is no short-run supply curve for the firm either. In addition, the demand curve perceived by the firm is identical with the demand curve in the market.

Initially, let us assume the monopolist produces a single output and must charge a single price to all purchasers. Figure 11.1 illustrates a market demand schedule and its relationship to a marginal revenue schedule. The inverse of the demand schedule is simply the schedule of average revenue. The fact that the marginal revenue schedule lies below the demand schedule follows from the relationship derived earlier: $MR = P(1 + 1/\eta)$, where η is the elasticity of demand. For demand schedules that are less than perfectly elastic, marginal revenue is less than price, i.e., average revenue. The cost curves in Figure 11.2 represent the short-run average total cost curve, short-run average variable cost curve, and a short-run marginal cost curve for a particular technology and plant size. Just as in the perfectly competitive example, the firm is locked into a particular set of cost schedules in the short run by its previous choice of plant and technology.

In the short run a monopolist trying to maximize profits must still choose three policies: a short-run price policy, a short-run output policy, and a short-run input policy. Like the purely competitive firm, a monopolist can can either produce nothing or produce some positive output level. Profit

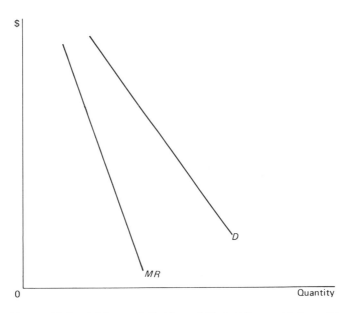

Figure 11.1   A Monopolist's View of Market Demand Information

maximizing possibilities will again occur at the positive output levels for which marginal revenue is equal to marginal cost, such as Q^* in Figure 11.2.[1]

As in Chapter 10, to make sure that profits are maximized at Q^*, we still have to examine the profits earned at levels slightly above or below Q^*. Increasing output slightly above Q^* involves a marginal cost greater than marginal revenue, thus profits would decrease. Decreasing output slightly

---

[1] The monopolist's short-run decision problem can be formally restated as

$$\text{Maximize } \pi = P \cdot D(P) - C(Q)$$
$$P, Q$$

subject to

$$P \geq 0, \qquad Q \geq 0$$

In a riskless setting $D(P) = Q$. We can write $P = D^{-1}(Q)$ where $D(P)$ is the market demand schedule and D^{-1} is the inverse demand schedule. A maximization of profit for $Q > 0$ requires

$$\frac{d\pi}{dQ} = D^{-1}(Q) + Q \frac{dD^{-1}}{dQ} - C'(Q) = 0$$

where C' is marginal cost. Using the relationship between price and marginal revenue this expression may be rewritten

$$\frac{d\pi}{dQ} = MR - MC = 0$$

The second order test for maximization can be expressed mathematically by the requirement

$$\frac{d^2\pi}{dQ^2} < 0$$

below Q^* involves giving up units for which marginal revenue is greater than marginal cost, thus profits would again decline. This test, however, only insures we have found a local profit maximum, not necessarily the global maximum. If there are several output levels for which $MR = MC$ and each passes the local maximum test, then we must evaluate profit at each level to find the best one.

Once the profit maximizing output level has been found, at what price should the firm sell? The competitive firm, of course, sold at a price determined by the market. A monopolist, on the other hand, has some degree of latitude in setting prices. We can determine the optimal price policy from the optimal output Q^*, by using the *inverse demand function*, $P = D^{-1}(Q)$ derived from $Q = D(P)$. At Q^* the firm will not charge more than P^* since demand would be less than output and there would therefore be unsold output. On the other hand, the firm will not sell at a price below P^* because this would reduce total revenue.

P^* is therefore the average revenue at the output level Q^*. Average total cost, C, can be read off from the average total cost schedule. Average profit is the distance $\overline{AB}$. Total profit is represented by the crosshatch section in Figure 11.2. In the short run, a monopolist's profit-maximizing (or loss-minimizing) strategy is to produce at a positive level as long as average revenue is not less than average variable cost. Otherwise, losses will be minimized by shutting down and losing only total fixed costs.

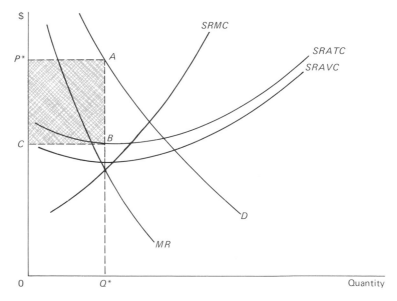

Figure 11.2 Short-Run Equilibrium for a Monopolist

Notice that the monopoly short-run equilibrium problem does not involve any supply schedules. The only relevant pieces of information are contained in the market demand schedule and the monopolist's cost schedule. The monopolist's short-run marginal cost schedule is a critical element.

Equilibrium for the Market and the Firm in the Long Run

In a purely competitive setting, the existence of short-run economic profit or loss causes a shift of resources either into or out of the industry. The mobility of resources acts as an equilibrating force, expanding supply and driving prices down or costs up. In a monopoly setting, even if there are economic profits in the short run, other firms are not allowed to enter the industry. A telephone company, for instance, might earn economic profits in the short run, but this would not cause the government to franchise other firms in the same marketing area.

The only long-run adjustments that a firm is likely to make are a decision to leave the industry entirely or a change to a plant size-technology mix with lower costs (Figure 11.3). A monopolist will not necessarily adopt other

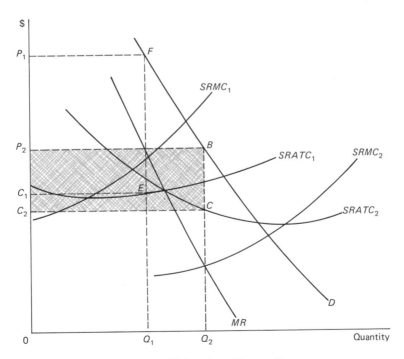

Figure 11.3 Long-Run Equilibrium for a Monopolist

technologies, try innovations, or change plant size unless such changes will enhance the firm's profits.

Figure 11.3 illustrates the kinds of changes a monopolist might make in the long run. Assume the firm's initial short-run cost schedule is $SRATC_1$ and that it chooses to produce output level Q_1 at a price P_1. Suppose in the long run the monopolist has a second production possibility described by the cost schedule $SRATC_2$ and the marginal schedule $SRMC_2$. If the firm switches to this possibility, optimal output will be Q_2 and optimal price, P_2. The firm would receive an average profit of $\overline{CB}$, and a total profit equal to Q_2 times $\overline{CB}$ (represented by the crosshatch area). If the firm makes no change, optimal output is Q_1, average profit is $\overline{EF}$, and total profit is given by $\overline{EF}$ times Q_1. The long-run decision for the monopolist is based on a comparison of these two total profits, choosing whichever plant size-technology combination yields the largest profit. Alternatively, the firm's $LRATC$ and $LRMC$ can be used to locate the maximum profit plant size-technology mix as in Figure 11.4.

In pure competition, the mere existence of new technologies offering lower costs would guarantee their adoption by the industry, since a firm that failed to adopt them would be sacrificing a competitive advantage and encouraging the entry of competitors using the new technology. There is no such guarantee under monopoly. If the monopolist does not adopt a new technology or different plant size there is not as direct an economic threat.

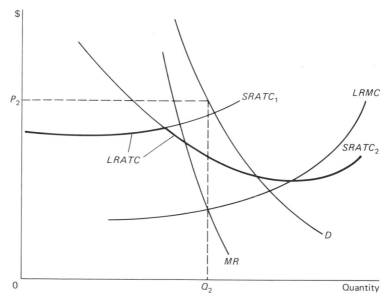

Figure 11.4   Long-Run Monopoly Plant and Technology Choice

There is thus a potential threat in the competitive market that is absent in monopoly. Freedom of entry turns out to be a potential threat *even if it is never exercised.* The mere existence of the potential threat guarantees that certain types of economic decisions occur in its presence that might not otherwise occur. Inertia on the part of a monopolist can also be the result of pursuing nonprofit goals.

If satellite communication provides a more economically sound method of communication than cable telephone, nothing will compel a firm to switch to the newer technology. In fact, a regulated environment together with a monopoly setting may encourage firms to do the exact reverse, and resist innovation. A monopoly setting therefore does not produce benefits without economic costs, which may be subtly hidden. The nonimplementation or nonadoption of a new technology *is* a cost if more efficient resource use could otherwise have been achieved.

Price Discrimination and Optimal Marketing Strategy

Monopoly permits a firm to use a strategy that is never possible in a purely competitive environment—*price discrimination.* For economic purposes, price discrimination is defined as selling a given commodity to different individuals at different prices even though costs remain the same throughout.

Figures 11.1–11.4 showed situations in which there was a single market demand. In practice, it is much more likely that the market can be divided into groups of potential buyers, each with its own demand schedule. For example, there might be one demand schedule for buyers located in San Francisco, a different one for buyers in Chicago, and yet another for buyers in Miami. Different demand groups need not be defined only in geographic terms. One could also consider high and low income individuals or individuals demanding electricity in the winter and in the summer, or telephone service during the day and at night or on a weekday and on a weekend.

If demand can be divided into groups the firm is likely to offer its product or services to different groups at different prices. Airlines offering special prices for young travelers, as opposed to regular customers, are certainly another example. Airlines also have first-class and coach-class service. Movie theaters have a child's ticket, a youth ticket, and an adult ticket. These examples illustrate methods of dividing the total market into different groups by offering a slightly differentiated product to different individuals and charging the maximum each group can be expected to pay. Notice that the cost of providing the product or service in each case is almost identical. This reflects the fact that price discrimination is based on differences in price elasticities, not on cost differences.

When would a firm find price discrimination desirable? When is it economically feasible? How can it be carried out? Price discrimination is viable if the commodity sold can be neither stored nor traded, for either physical or legal reasons. Services are obvious examples of commodities that cannot be traded. For example, telephone services in daytime and at night are physically non-retradeable.

In Figure 11.5 the firm has divided its customers into two groups, with demand schedules D_1 and D_2. The policy problems will be similar to those posed by a single class of demand. We begin by solving for total production in order to find marginal cost. Using MC we can maximize profit in each market individually.

The marginal cost schedule is part of our initial information. The next step is to form an aggregate marginal revenue schedule from the individual marginal revenue schedules for each market. A marginal revenue of a' (Figure 11.5) is associated with sales of q'_1 in market 1 and q'_2 in market 2. The aggregate quantity yielding a marginal revenue of a' is thus $q'_1 + q'_2$. This information provides one point on the aggregate marginal revenue schedule, point A. A marginal revenue of a'' is associated with sales of q''_1 in market 1 and q''_2 in market 2. At each level of marginal revenue, we find the total sales associated with that particular level of marginal revenue. Geometrically, this is equivalent to adding the two marginal revenue schedules

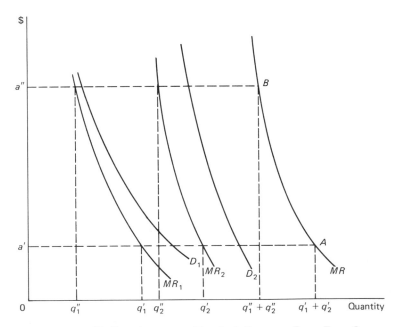

Figure 11.5 Finding Aggregate Marginal Revenue From Two Groups of Purchasers

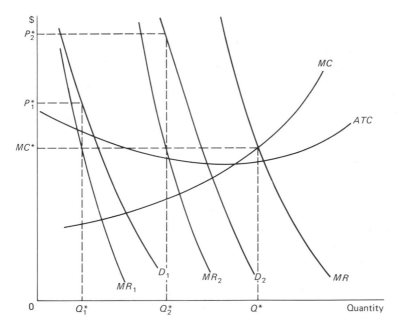

Figure 11.6 Price Discrimination Between Two Markets (or Two Classes of Customers)

horizontally. The aggregate marginal revenue schedule, MR, contains the information we need to solve for optimal total output.

The aggregate marginal revenue and marginal cost schedules show that the output level which maximizes total profit is Q^* (Figure 11.6).[2] At Q^* marginal cost is C^*. To determine how to divide Q^* between the two markets to achieve maximum profit we simply maximize profits in each market one at a time. By equating marginal costs with marginal revenue in market 1 we

---

[2] With two classes of customers, the monopolist's decision problem can be cast in the form

$$\text{Maximize } \pi = P_1 Q_1 + P_2 Q_2 - C(Q)$$
$$Q_1, Q_2, Q$$

subject to

$$Q_1 + Q_2 \geq Q$$
$$Q_1 \geq 0, \qquad Q_2 \geq 0, \qquad Q \geq 0, \qquad P_1 \geq 0, \qquad P_2 \geq 0$$

Letting $Q_2 = Q - Q_1$ (since it will not be optimal to produce more than is sold) and letting MR_1 and MR_2 represent the marginal revenues from groups 1 and 2, the necessary conditions for maximum profit can be written

$$MR_1(Q_1) = C'(Q_1 + Q_2)$$
$$MR_2(Q_2) = C'(Q_1 + Q_2)$$

These conditions correspond to the steps shown in Figure 11.6. The second order profit maximum check (Footnote 1) must also be satisfied in each market.

find that the maximum profit occurs at the output level Q_1^*. The demand curve for market 1 shows that the optimal price to charge is P_1^*. In the same way, equating marginal revenue with marginal cost in market 2 leads to an optimal quantity Q_2^* and an optimal price P_2^*.

Notice that as long as the firm can divide its customers into groups with different demand schedules, price discrimination is the optimal policy to maximize profits. In other words, as long as one can divide customers into different groups and they cannot resell among themselves, it generally is possible to extract larger profits by price discrimination. This observation suggests why one observes adult, youth, and child prices in the movie theaters. For a long period of time, prices for movie tickets were simply divided into two groups—adult tickets and children's tickets. Dividing the market into a third segment obviously yields higher total revenues. Adding a third airline class, youth fares, undoubtedly serves a similar purpose. Even though the demand schedule for aggregate use of airline passage may be inelastic, airlines appear to believe that they are on a fairly elastic segment in the youth market, where price reductions will lead to higher total revenues.

To emphasize the potential gains from price discrimination, let us look at a specific numerical example with two demand groups. Demand for group 1 is given by

$$Q_1 = 1,000 - 2P_1 \qquad (11.1)$$

and for group 2 by

$$Q_2 = 1,200 - 3P_2 \qquad (11.2)$$

Total cost is given by

$$C(Q_1 + Q_2) = 350 + 2(Q_1 + Q_2) + 0.5(Q_1 + Q_2)^2 \qquad (11.3)$$

Case 1: Charge all purchasers the same price   First suppose the monopolist is obliged to charge the same price to all customers. Profit for the firm is

$$\pi = P_1 Q_1 + P_2 Q_2 - C(Q_1 + Q_2) \qquad (11.4)$$

Since $P_1 = P_2 = P$ the problem becomes

$$\underset{P}{\text{Maximize }} \pi = P(1,000 - 2P) + P(1,200 - 3P) - 350$$
$$- 2(1,000 - 2P + 1,200 - 3P)$$
$$- \tfrac{1}{2}(1,000 - 2P + 1,200 - 3P)^2 \qquad (11.5)$$

Optimal price must satisfy the condition[3]

$$35P = 2,210 + 11,000 \qquad (11.6)$$

---

[3] The necessary conditions are found by differentiating π with respect to the variables to-be chosen. We will assume that there is a unique profit maximum—an assumption which can be verified, but is not essential to the discussion.

which implies $P^* = P_1^* = P_2^* = \$377$. Sales to customers in market 1 are

$$Q_1^* = 1,000 - 2(377) = 246 \qquad (11.7)$$

and to market 2 are

$$Q_2^* = 1,200 - 3(377) = 69 \qquad (11.8)$$

Total profit is easily found by substituting into Equation (11.5):

$$\pi^* = 377(246) + 377(69) - 350$$
$$- 2(315) - \tfrac{1}{2}(315)^2 = \$68,162 \qquad (11.9)$$

Case 2: Different prices may be charged each class of customer Now, let us allow price discrimination. We can use the original Equation (11.4). Solving Equation (11.1) for P_1 and Equation (11.2) for P_2 and substituting, we obtain as the new profit function

$$\pi = (-Q_1/2 + 500)Q_1 + (-Q_2/3 + 400)Q_2$$
$$- 350 - 2(Q_1 + Q_2) - 0.5(Q_1 + Q_2)^2 \qquad (11.10)$$

The conditions which Q_1 and Q_2 must satisfy to maximize (11.10) are

$$-2Q_1 - Q_2 = -498 \qquad (11.11)$$

$$-Q_1 - \tfrac{5}{3}Q_2 = -398 \qquad (11.12)$$

Optimal outputs for market 1 and market 2 are 185 and 128, respectively. The optimal prices will be \$408 and \$357. Notice that it is advantageous to offer a price in one market below the one obtained in Case 1 and to increase price dramatically in the other. The new profit level is \$71,215. No wonder firms find price discrimination an attractive marketing strategy!

These examples provide an insight into the strategy referred to as *price lining*. A dress manufacturer divides the same or very similar garments into one line of \$50 dresses, another line of \$40 dresses, a line of \$20 dresses, and another line of \$9 dresses, differentiated by appropriate labels from one with a prestige image to one with a discount store image. Basically the firm produces the same commodity but creates product image differences in the eyes of the consumer. The firm thus segments the market on the basis of snob appeal and/or ability to pay.

Types of Price Discrimination

The kind of discrimination described above is referred to as *third degree price discrimination*. Within each group of purchasers everyone pays the same price for every unit sold. In this section we shall discuss first and second degree price discrimination.

Under *first degree price discrimination*, instead of charging each individual the same price per unit, a firm charges the maximum price that can be obtained for each unit sold. In Figure 11.7, a monopolist firm starts off at Q_1 and sells at the maximum it can get for that unit. Then it considers selling the Q_1-plus-first-unit. But when it does so, it again sells at the maximum price obtainable. Every unit is sold to the highest bidder and then the next unit is sold. The firm will continue selling in this fashion until the price of the last unit sold is equal to the marginal cost: in Figure 11.7, the output level Q^*.

The firm can expand output level up to the point Q^* because selling one more unit does not require an adjustment of the price charged to previous buyers. The average revenue schedule thus in effect becomes the relevant marginal revenue schedule. Normally, marginal revenue is less than average revenue, because the reduction needed to sell one more unit must be applied to all units sold. Since demand is usually less than perfectly elastic, marginal revenue falls below average revenue.

Notice that while third degree discrimination involves separate demand schedules, first degree discrimination can be pictured as operating along a single market demand schedule. A firm can rarely achieve first degree

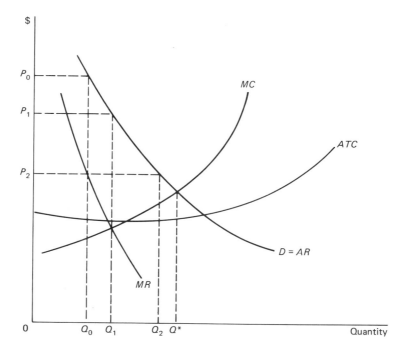

Figure 11.7   Output and Pricing under First and Second Degree Price Discrimination

discrimination in practice because of the magnitude of the information required. However, the difficulties involved in using individual prices at each unit can be avoided by establishing *price blocks*. For example, in Figure 11.7 a price P_0 would apply for quantities zero to Q_0, a price P_1 from Q_0 to Q_1, and a price P_2 from Q_1 to Q_2, etc. With a first degree pricing scheme the firm's customers will exhibit total willingness to pay (measured by the area under a marginal demand schedule); the price-block scheme, known as *second degree price discrimination*, secures results that are almost as good. The smaller the block quantity width the closer the firm will come to obtaining the whole area. Telephone charges which involve a monthly charge plus charges for additional message units represent a version of second degree price discrimination and so do many kinds of electric utility charges such as declining block tariffs.

Limits on Price Differentials

Are there any limits on the difference in prices that may exist between different groups of purchasers? Or would a monopolist always be able to impose whatever price differential it considered profitable? Suppose that D_1 represents the market for refrigerators in San Francisco and D_2 represents the demand for refrigerators in Chicago, what determines the manufacturer's ability to impose a price differential? If people in both markets know what the prices are in the other markets and the commodity is tradeable, like refrigerators, what would be the upper limit to the difference in price? The major factor would be the cost of transporting a refrigerator between Chicago and San Francisco. The elements that determine the permissible difference in prices are therefore transport cost, information cost, and other transaction costs.

Trading prices on the New York Stock Exchange and a Pacific Coast Exchange involve transaction costs. Many securities are listed on both markets, but not always at the same price. However, the price differential between the two markets will hardly ever be greater than the transaction cost. If it costs 10¢ per share to execute a buy or sell, then when the price differential rises above 20¢, traders can buy in one market and sell in the other to achieve a profit. This process is called *arbitrage*. Arbitraging takes place in domestic and international security and bond markets, commodity markets, and money markets.

A Comparison of Purely Competitive and Monopoly Price and Production Decisions

Newspaper reports and antitrust policies often give the impression that monopoly is "bad" and competition (presumably meaning a perfectly competitive market setting) is "good." Which setting is actually more desirable?

To make a valid comparison, we need to assume that a firm in a purely competitive environment would adopt the same technology as a firm in a monopoly environment and that the two firms have the same input costs. This implies that they both have the same average and marginal cost schedules. Figure 11.8 contrasts the solutions obtained under monopoly and under perfect competition. In the long run under purely competitive conditions price is driven down to the point of minimum average total cost. The long-run price ultimately arrives at P^*, and output is Q^*. On the other hand, a monopolist faced with the market schedule D and an associated marginal revenue schedule MR will maximize profits by choosing the output Q^0 and a price of P^0. The monopoly setting leads to lower output and a higher price than would be achieved under pure competition.

From Figure 11.8 it is clear that there may be economic arguments in favor of a purely competitive environment and against a monopoly setting, but notice that part of the argument against monopoly is dependent on the assumption that the two firms have the same costs. The information in Figure 11.8 indicates that if there is an economic argument for monopoly, it does not arise from a setting in which both purely competitive and monop-

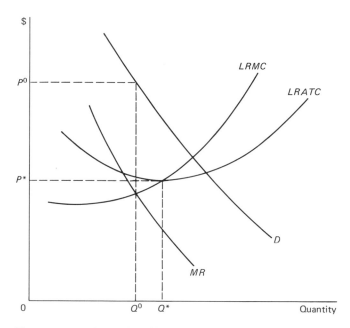

Figure 11.8 Comparing Monopoly and Perfectly Competitive Solutions When the Same Costs are Incurred

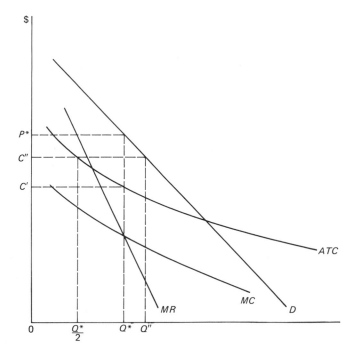

Figure 11.9 Monopoly Pricing and Output with Decreasing Costs

olistic firms are adopting the same technology and paying the same input costs.

Now, however, suppose that average total costs decline as illustrated in Figure 11.9, presumably as a result of adopting more sophisticated types of technology. Many economists believe that public utilities do, in fact, have declining average costs, at least for the relevant ranges of output, although ultimately, of course, they will reach some lower limit.

With declining costs a purely competitive market form cannot be sustained. If every firm is faced with declining costs, then every possible scheme for dividing the total market among the firms will lead to production at higher average costs than if one firm supplied the whole market. For example, suppose that in Figure 11.9 two firms each sell half the monopolist's optimal output of Q^*. Average costs for producing the same total quantity are driven up from C' to C''. Enforcing competition under these conditions purchases "competition" at the price of the increase in the average cost of resources needed to produce each unit of output.

Figure 11.9 illustrates a basic public policy problem. For some industries costs and technologies may well be such that the minimum average resource use per unit of output is achieved by letting one firm produce for the whole market. On the other hand, a single producer will not necessarily pass on to the consumer the efficiency in resource use that it is able to achieve. In fact, the price that consumers must pay to a monopoly is usually higher than if the economy was *less* efficient in resource use! The trade off involved is thus resource use for commodity prices.

Up to now we have assumed that all firms produced a commodity of equal quality. However, recent work suggests that a monopolist may also exploit its market position by producing less reliable products.[4]

A Business Pricing and Investment Example: Peak Load Pricing

Let us apply the monopoly model to a situation that actually occurs quite frequently in several types of business environments—the *peak load pricing problem*. At a given set of prices the quantity of electricity demanded varies by day, week, month, and year. Figure 11.10 illustrates the variation in the demand for electricity at the various hours of the day, assuming that the price of electricity remains constant regardless of whether one buys electricity at 5 a.m., 10 a.m., or 9 p.m.[5] Empirical data for electricity, telephone, natural gas, and air transportation also resemble the demands curve shown in Figure 11.10.

Irregular demand creates problems both for investment in capacity and for pricing. One possible solution to the investment problem is to gauge investment solely by the peak demand, Q^*. If this policy is followed, capacity, once available in electrical generators or telephone lines or gas or oil pipelines, will be fully utilized only in the peak period.

Suppose that, instead of investing for peak demand and using prices that are uniform for all times of day, the firm charges different prices at different times of day or different times of year. In particular, we might decrease the price substantially for periods when the demand for electricity is much less than capacity to encourage utilization, while increasing the price in peak periods, thus reducing capacity investment costs. To accommodate the peak volume of telephone calls during the daytime, a firm may be obliged to allow as much as 80% of its capacity to sit idle at night.

---

[4] Suggestions to this effect can be found in D. Levhari and T. N. Srinivasan, "Durability of Consumption Goods: Competition Versus Monopoly," *American Economic Review*, 59 (March, 1969), 102–107, and R. Schmalansee, "Regulation and the Durability of Goods," *Bell Journal of Economics and Management Science*, 1 (Spring, 1970), 54–64.

[5] Actually utility tariffs are quite complicated and vary by class of customer, volume of demand, etc. For simplicity we will assume that initially everyone pays the same price.

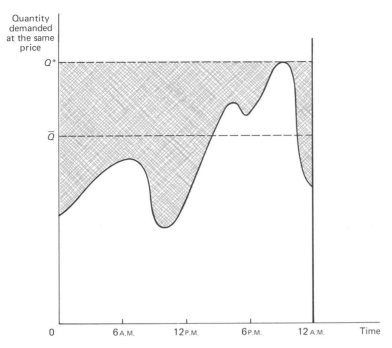

Figure 11.10 An Example of Demand Variation over Time at a Given Price

Given the day and night demands in Figure 11.11, let us try to find the most efficient set of prices and the optimal capacity level. These curves might represent telephone services demanded in the daytime, $Q_d = D_d(P_d)$, and those demanded at night, $Q_n = D_n(P_n)$, where P_d and P_n are the day and night prices. Assume costs are given in the following form: (1) average variable cost is a constant, b, which is therefore equal to marginal cost and (2) fixed costs (capacity investment cost) are β per unit of capacity, Q. Solving an optimal pricing problem simultaneously solves the related optimal investment problem.

Since it will never be optimal for the firm to sell at a price below average variable cost, b, the only admissible prices are either equal to or above b. (Any price below b involves giving a subsidy to customers.) The amounts contributed by customers to defray the costs incurred to provide capacity will be equal to the average revenue the firm receives minus average variable cost. The daytime demand schedule can be written $Q_d = D_d(P_d)$ or $P_d = D_d^{-1}(Q_d)$. The net contributions by day purchasers will be $d_d(Q_d) = P_d - b = D_d^{-1}(Q_d) - b$. Similarly, $d_n(Q_n) = P_n - b = D_n^{-1}(Q_n) - b$ will be the net contribution from night purchasers. It is only these *net demand schedules* d_d and d_n which are relevant to solving the optimal capacity problem.

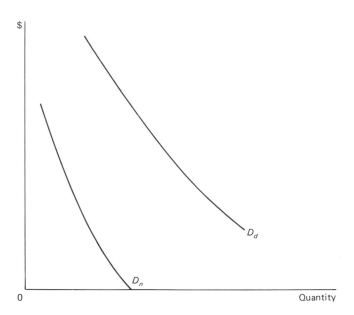

Figure 11.11 Demand Schedules for a Peak Load Pricing Problem with Two Periods

A particular capacity level is economically feasible to install provided the net amount collected per unit during both periods is at least equal to the cost, β, per unit of capacity. For it to be profitable to install the capacity $\bar{Q}$ in Figure 11.12 the price charged at night, P_n, minus average variable cost, b, plus the price charged in the daytime, P_d, minus average variable cost, b, must equal β. Geometrically this sum is represented by adding the two net demand curves vertically to produce the *demand schedule for capacity*. For example, when we add the two amounts for $\bar{Q}$ we obtain the point A in Figure 11.12. The demand schedule for capacity is the vertical sum of the net demand curves. For each level of plant capacity it costs β dollars for providing one unit which is shown by the horizontal line in Figure 11.12. The horizontal line intersecting the y-axis at β is an input supply schedule. The optimum level of investment is therefore Q^*, the level at which the supply schedule intersects the demand schedule for capacity.

We can now solve for the optimal set of prices corresponding to Q^*. Notice that even if we charge a net price of zero at night (i.e., $P_n = b$) the quantity demanded will still be less than capacity. On the other hand, in order to limit demand to capacity we have to raise the daytime price to the point where the net demand price will reduce the quantity demanded to Q^*. The optimal price to charge in the daytime is therefore $P_d^* = b + \beta$ and the

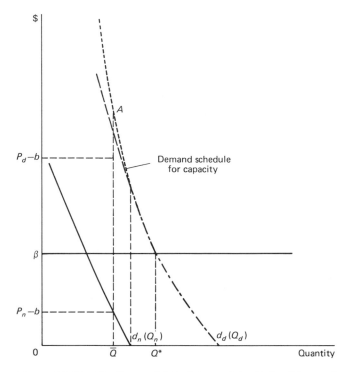

Figure 11.12 Net Demand Schedules and the Derived Demand for Capacity Schedule

optimal price to charge at night is $P_n^* = b$. Notice that $(P_d^* - b) + (P_n^* - b) = \beta$.

Ideally, a firm would alter its prices so as to produce a uniform demand over time of day, corresponding to the dotted line at $\bar{Q}$ in Figure 11.10. In practice this ideal is rarely possible, but any reduction in demand at the peak will reduce investment cost. The peak-load pricing problem can be extended to analyze the pricing policies of telephone companies, natural gas companies, and electricity firms that must sell to various groups of customers at different times.

Regulation of Economic Activity: An Application

We saw earlier that in the presence of decreasing costs there may be some economic arguments in favor of establishing a monopoly. Unfortunately, we also saw this could lead to a situation in which a firm charges unduly high prices. The usual response to this is to place such firms in a regulated environment. The most common types of regulation limit either prices, by means of tariff schedules, or profits. In some cases, for example in the airline industry, prices are regulated, earnings are reviewed, and quantities are controlled by allocating specific routes to specific airlines.

For an example of regulation let us study a simple monopoly setting where the firm is producing a single output, Q, charging a single price, P, using two inputs, capital (K) and labor (L), and desires to maximize profits. Assume that w is the price of labor, that r is the rental price of capital,[6] and that the firm has a technological constraint in the form of a production function, $F(K, L)$. If a firm is an unregulated monopoly, then the basic decision problem for choosing output, price, and inputs might be stated as:

$$\text{Maximize } \pi = PQ - wL - rK \qquad (11.13)$$
$$\small P, Q, K, L$$

subject to

$$Q \leq F(K, L)$$
$$Q \geq 0, \qquad K \geq 0, \qquad L \geq 0$$
$$P = D^{-1}(Q), \qquad P \geq 0 \qquad (11.14)$$

Since in this problem it is not economically sensible to produce more than can be sold nor to sell at less than the highest price consumers will pay, we can replace the inequality in the production constraint by an equality. Then, using the inverse demand function, we can rewrite the profit function as

$$\pi = D^{-1}(Q)F(K, L) - wL - rK$$

or

$$\pi(K, L) = D^{-1}(F(K, L)) \cdot F(K, L) - wL - rK \qquad (11.15)$$

These substitutions reduce the problem to one involving only two variables, rather than four.

We can obtain a clearer picture of the solution to (11.15) by maximizing with respect to one variable at a time. Thus

$$\text{Maximize } \pi(K, L)$$
$$\small K, L$$

can be written

$$\text{Maximize } \bar{\pi}(K) \qquad (11.16)$$
$$\small K$$

where

$$\bar{\pi}(K) = \text{Maximize } \pi(K, L) \qquad (11.17)$$
$$\small L$$

The graph of the profit function $\pi(K)$ might be like the one in Figure 11.13. An unregulated firm will choose the level of capital which maximizes profits, K^*, and achieve profits of π^*. Output and price can be found from $Q^* = F(K^*, L^*)$ and $P^* = D^{-1}(Q^*)$, and L^* is found from the conditions defined by (11.17).

---

[6] See Chapter 16 for an extended discussion of the concepts of cost of capital and rental price of capital.

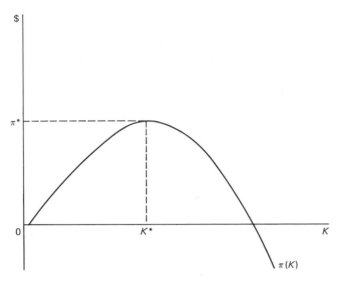

Figure 11.13 Finding an Unconstrained Monopoly Profit Maximum

Regulated firms, including almost all utilities, are frequently allowed to earn no more than a given rate of return on investment. AT&T is allowed to earn approximately 8% on its investment; other rates of return established by regulatory commissions vary between 6.5% and 9%. Such a situation may obviously affect the unconstrained profit function depicted in Figure 11.13.

A simple form for a profit constraint requires profits divided by the value of invested capital to be equal to or less than some allowed rate of return, β:

$$\pi(K)/cK \leq \rho \qquad (11.18)$$

The c in the above expression is a price term which might be current market value, original cost, or some other valuation of plant and equipment. For simplicity, assume that c is unity since its actual value will not influence the basic result which follows. Multiplying (11.18) by cK, we can write the constraint in the form

$$\pi(K) \leq \rho cK = \rho K \qquad (11.19)$$

thus profits must be equal to or less than ρK. The graph of the right hand side of this profit constraint is a straight line whose slope is ρ, as shown in Figure 11.14. The levels of profit which satisfy the regulatory constraint are those that lie on the constraint or below it. It is clear that for the value of ρ illustrated in Figure 11.14 the firm cannot choose the unregulated profit maximizing level of capital because profits are greater than permitted by the regulatory constraint. The best the firm can achieve is a level of profits π^0. Notice that π^0 is associated with a level of capital K^0 which is *greater* than K^*. The rate-of-return method of regulating a firm gives the firm an economic incentive to overinvest in capital!

There is another way of using economic analysis to reach the same conclusion. In an unregulated setting, the monopolist pays a market price for every unit of capital, which reduces its profits by r. However, if the firm is regulated, buying one more unit of capital still increases cost by r, but the firm is now permitted to earn more profits. If $c = 1$, then buying a unit of capital costing r causes the "rate base" to increase by r. Allowed returns are ρ times the rate base; therefore allowed returns will increase by $r\rho$. Under regulation the firm will perceive the net price of capital as being equal to r minus $r\rho$, while in the unregulated case the net price of capital was r. Under rate-of-return regulation the firm perceives a price of capital which is less than the market price of capital. The price of labor, however, is still w. The effect of decreasing the relative price of capital leads to a substitution in its favor. Figure 11.15 illustrates this point.

Output is greater in a regulated setting than in an unregulated setting. The only drawback is that the higher output (and lower price) must be paid for by an inefficient use of resources. In addition, a regulated setting may cause the firm to inflate costs and underutilize resources in the short run in the hope of driving down observed rates of return so that it can obtain higher tariffs. The challenge is to develop a method of regulation which encourages efficient resource use while preventing the inflated prices that are likely to

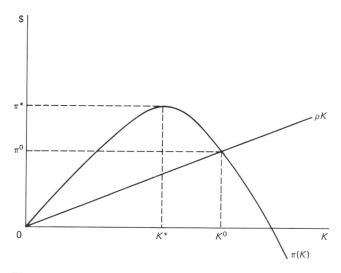

Figure 11.14   Analyzing the Impact of Rate-of-Return Regulation

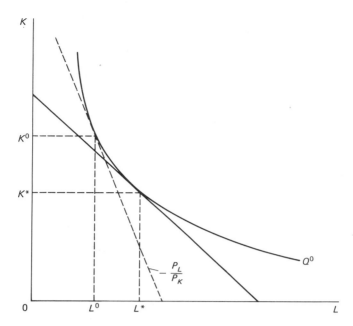

Figure 11.15 Influence of Rate-of-Return Regulation on a Firm's Choice of Inputs and Technology

occur when monopolies are completely unfettered. An ideal method of regulation would provide just enough economic profits to persuade a firm to introduce new, cost-cutting technologies and new products.

Should regulatory agencies permit a certain amount of competition in order to create incentives in a monopoly setting? Utilities such as AT&T have fought several battles to prohibit alternative suppliers from entering their markets. Some economists are now asking whether the benefits that supposedly accrue to consumers from regulating prices might not be less than the costs of the regulatory process, so that an unregulated monopoly might actually require less total resource use.

*Uncertainty and Monopoly Pricing

Uncertainty confronts a monopolist just as it does a competitive firm. Suppose a monopolist faces a random market demand schedule $D(P) = \bar{D}(P) + u$ where $\bar{D}(P)$ is the expected value of demand (equal to riskless demand) and u is a random component with zero mean, variance σ^2, and

---

* Optional material requiring knowledge of probability.

probability density $f(u)$. In addition, assume the firm must choose production and price before demand is known, with production costs given by $C(Q) = bQ$. Marginal and average costs are thus constant.

Ignoring risk-averting behavior, assume price and production policies are chosen to maximize expected profits. Since costs will be fixed once output is chosen, the only random factor will be revenue. Total revenue depends on *both* the choice of price and production since the amount produced sets an upper limit on the amount the firm can sell. If the quantity demanded is less than output, then expected total revenue is formed by weighting each possible level of revenue by the probability of occurrence and summing:

$$\text{Expected Total Revenue if } D(P) < Q = \int_{-\infty}^{Q} P[\bar{D}(P) + u]f(u)\, du \quad (11.20)$$

If quantity demanded exceeds output, total revenue will be PQ. Since the probability that quantity demanded exceeds Q is given by

$$
\begin{aligned}
\text{Prob } [\bar{D}(P) + u > Q] &= \text{Prob } [Q - \bar{D}(P) < u] \\
&= F[Q - \bar{D}(P)] \\
&= \int_{-\infty}^{Q - \bar{D}(P)} f(u)\, du
\end{aligned}
\quad (11.21)
$$

expected total revenue if quantity demanded exceeds Q is $PQF[Q - \bar{D}(P)]$.
Expected profits can now be expressed as

$$
E[\pi] = \begin{array}{l}
\text{Expected Total Revenue} \\
\text{If Quantity Demanded is} \\
\text{Equal to or Less than } Q
\end{array}
$$

$$
\begin{array}{l}
\text{Expected Total Revenue} \\
+ \text{ if Quantity Demanded is} \\
\text{Greater than } Q
\end{array}
$$

$$- \text{ Total Cost}$$

or

$$E[\pi] = \int_{-\infty}^{Q} P[\bar{D}(P) + u]f(u)\, du + PQF[Q - \bar{D}(P)] - bQ \quad (11.22)$$

Maximizing (11.19) with respect to price and production[7] results in an optimal pricing and production rule

$$P^* = b/\{1 - F[Q^* - \bar{D}(P^*)]\} \quad (11.23)$$

where the starred values of P and Q indicate their optimal values.

[7] These conditions assume that the optimal values of P and Q are positive and that the relevant second order conditions are satisfied.

The pricing rule in Equation (11.23) can be contrasted with the riskless monopoly pricing rule

$$P^0 = \frac{\eta}{1 + \eta} \, b \tag{11.24}$$

where η is the elasticity of demand evaluated at the optimal price. A more extended argument shows[8] that in general $P^* \leq P^0$, but no specific answers can be given for the relationship between riskless and risky production unless more information is provided about the probability distribution of demand. In addition, different ways of introducing the random component, for example multiplicatively, can influence whether P^* is less than, equal to, or greater than P^0.

Summary

In a market setting of pure monopoly we were able to analyze several business pricing and investment problems, including price discrimination, price lining, peak-load pricing and investment, and rate-of-return regulation. Price policy for public utilities and the influence of regulation on firms utilizing natural resources will obviously continue to receive close attention in a period of energy crises.

The example of public utility regulation highlighted the potential dangers which may stem from regulation. However, it is still not clear whether monopoly formation should be encouraged or inhibited. What is the cost of monopoly? The available evidence[9] is limited and certainly subject to question, but it suggests that the potential gains from eliminating monopolies may be relatively meager. However, efficiency may not be as important a criterion as the degree of economic power amassed in one entity, which may have a destabilizing effect on the economy as a whole. The concentration of economic activity is studied in Chapter 13.

Questions for Study or Class Discussion

1. If a monopolist sells to m different groups of customers and the demand schedule for each group depends on the prices charged to the other groups, find the expression for marginal revenue for the ith group.
2. "A monopolist's profit-maximizing price is always at a point on the elastic part of a demand schedule." Show that this statement is correct if only one demand schedule is involved. Does the statement always hold if there are several groups of customers? Why or why not?

---

[8] See the discussion by S. Karlin and C. Carr cited in the References.
[9] See the discussions by A. Harberger, D. Schwartzman, and H. Leibenstein cited in the References.

3. A monopolist has two groups of customers with demand schedules $D_1 = 100 - 2P_1$ and $D_2 = 300 - P_2 - 2P_1$ and total costs $C(Q) = 50 + 2Q^2$, where Q is total output. Find the optimal prices and resulting profit if it practices third degree price discrimination.
4. What conditions might make it economically desirable to permit a monopoly to exist? Desirable from whose standpoint?
5. Look up financial data from several regulated firms and several unregulated firms. How do their financial structures (i.e., composition of assets and liabilities) differ? How do their earnings compare? How do their rates of return to shareholders compare?

References

Averch, H., and L. Johnson, "Behavior of the Firm Under Regulatory Constraint," *American Economic Review*, 52 (December, 1962), 1052–1069.

Dhrymes, P., "On the Theory of the Multiproduct Firm Under Uncertainty," *International Economic Review*, 5 (September, 1964), 239–257.

Harberger, A., "Using the Resources at Hand More Effectively," *American Economic Review, Papers and Proceedings*, 59 (May, 1959), 134–147.

Hicks, J., "Annual Survey of Economic Theory: The Theory of Monopoly," *Econometrica*, 3 (1936), 1–20.

Kaldor, N., "Market Imperfections and Excess Capacity," *Economica*, 2 (1935), 33–50.

Karlin, S., and C. Carr, "Prices and Optimal Inventory Policy," in *Studies in Applied Probability and Management Science*, edited by K. J. Arrow, S. Karlin, and H. Scarf. Stanford University Press, 1962.

Leibenstein, H., "Allocative Efficiency and 'X-Efficiency'," *American Economic Review*, 56 (June, 1966), 392–415.

Machlup, F., "Characteristics and Types of Price Discrimination," in *Business Concentration and Price Policy*, 400–423. Princeton University Press, 1955.

Mansfield, E., *Monopoly Power and Economic Performance*. W. W. Norton, 1968.

Marshall, A., *Principles of Economics*. Macmillan, 1920.

Mills, E., "Uncertainty and Price Theory," *Quarterly Journal of Economics*, 73 (February, 1959), 116–130.

Robinson, J., *The Economics of Imperfect Competition*. Macmillan, 1933.

Scherer, F. M., *Industrial Market Structure and Economic Performance*. Rand McNally, 1970.

Schwartzman, D., "The Burden of Monopoly," *Journal of Political Economy*, 68 (December, 1960), 727–729.

Steiner, P. O., "Peak Loads and Efficient Pricing," *Quarterly Journal of Economics*, 71 (November, 1959), 585–610.

Westfield, F. M., "Regulation and Conspiracy," *American Economic Review*, 55 (June, 1965), 424–443.

Chapter 12 Pricing and Production Decisions in a Monopolistically Competitive Market Setting

Introduction

The previous two market structures discussed in Chapters 10 and 11 have polar properties. Either there is a large number of firms in the industry with each individual firm having no control over market price and products that are homogeneous—the purely competitive case—or we find a single seller with virtually absolute control—pure monopoly. A description of a monopolistically competitive market represents the first step towards understanding a market setting closer to the environment that many firms actually experience.

Although monopolistic competition shares some of its features with pure competition, such as free entry into the industry, free resource mobility, and complete information for buyers and sellers, it differs by allowing the output of one seller to be distinguished from the output of another seller, in particular, by means of brand names. There may be many sellers, but each one possesses a quasi-monopoly over his/her particular product. However, as the products of other sellers are considered close substitutes by consumers, the degree of monopoly power is limited. In this setting, we can begin for the first time to examine the influence of interdependent decisions.

Clothing, canned goods, frozen goods, and educational services are examples of commodities produced and marketed in what is essentially a monopolistically competitive setting.

Equilibrium for the Market and the Firm in the Short Run

In monopolistic competition, each firm uses advertising or some other marketing strategy to induce consumers to attach specific attributes to its output. Since each firm has a monopoly in its own special product, its short-run demand schedule is equivalent to the market demand schedule for that product.

The firm is confronted with demand information, average cost schedules, and a marginal cost schedule which it will use to (1) form a price policy, (2) find the proper level of output, and (3) make input choices. To maximize profits in the short run, the firm will produce a positive level of output as long as its average revenue is at least as great as minimum average variable cost. In Figure 12.1, since average revenue is simply the inverse demand schedule, there are obviously many output levels that satisfy this condition. However, the only level at which marginal revenue equals marginal cost is Q_0. The market price at Q_0 is obtained from the demand schedule. The short-run equilibrium for each producing firm occurs at an output level for which marginal revenue is equal to short-run marginal cost, and average revenue is equal to or greater than minimum average variable cost.

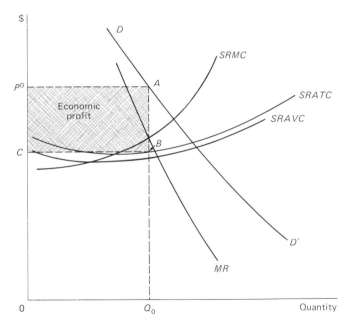

Figure 12.1 Short-Run Pricing and Production Decisions for the Monopolistically Competitive Firm

Analysis of the short-run equilibrium and pricing and production decisions for a firm are thus basically the same as for a monopoly. This is illustrated in Figure 12.1. However, in a monopolistic setting, the demand for each firm's product depends not only on thé price the firm charges and the prices of all other commodities, but also on the prices being charged by competitors. Dependence of each firm's demand schedule on its competitors' pricing decisions is not explicitly recognized by the firm itself. As a result, each firm sees its demand schedule as more elastic than it really is. As we shall see, this fact helps to explain certain long-run adjustments.

Equilibrium for the Market and the Firm in the Long Run

As in the purely competitive setting, economic profits in the short run under monopolistic competition cause long-term adjustments in the firm's policies. However, while economic profits in a purely competitive setting were eroded primarily by the entry of other firms, in monopolistic competition there are at least four possible means by which long-run adjustment is achieved, including (1) short-sighted price cutting, (2) entry or exit, (3) product differentiation costs, and (4) selling costs.

Short-sighted price cutting

As we saw in the preceding section, under monopolistic competition failure to recognize the effect of competitors' pricing decisions may well cause a firm to perceive demand for its product as more elastic than it is in fact. Such a firm will frequently cut prices in order to increase profits, since a high elasticity implies a positive marginal revenue (see Chapter 4). The result is illustrated in Figure 12.2. Although the actual demand schedule is DD', the firm acts as if its demand schedule is initially d_1d_1'.

The resulting price cuts produce a new perceived demand schedule, d_2d_2'. Since this schedule also suggests a high elasticity, the firm may make further price cuts until point A is reached. Price reductions below P_3 will lead to economic losses. The sequence of short-sighted price-cutting maneuvers has thus led to a long-run equilibrium in which the firm earns zero economic profit.

Notice in the long-run equilibrium represented in Figure 12.2 that while $LRATC = AR$ and $MR = MC$, it is not true that $AR = P = MC$ (except in the special case where DD' is perfectly elastic). In addition, the long-run optimal output for the firm does not correspond to the minimum of the $LRATC$ curve. Long-run equilibrium for each firm is characterized by a tangency of its perceived demand curve and its $LRATC$ schedule, with $MR = MC$.

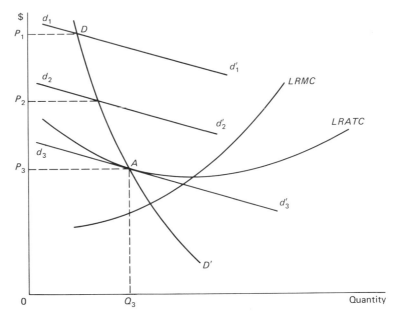

Figure 12.2 Short-Sighted Price Cutting Drives Economic Profits to Zero in the Long Run

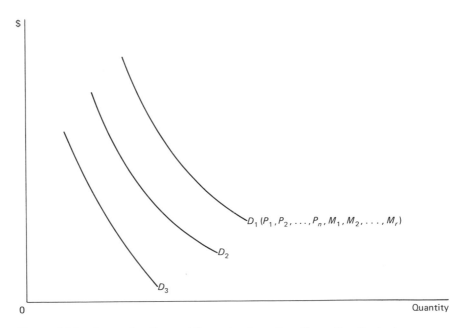

Figure 12.3 Decreasing Demand Stemming from New Competing Products

Entry or exit

The movement of competitors in and out of the industry in the long run has two possible effects on an individual firm: (1) The entry of new firms increases the number of products on the market causing a dilution of total market demand and a potential reduction in the market share captured by any one firm. This effect is illustrated in Figure 12.3. (2) Other firms entering the industry may bid up input prices, causing increases in long-run average total costs for existing firms, as shown in Figure 12.4. The impact of entry (or exit) on costs is, of course, dependent on available technologies and the elasticity of input supply schedules, as we saw in Chapter 10.

If economic losses cause firms to leave the industry, the number of competing products is reduced, which tends to increase demand for the products of the firms remaining. In addition, the demand for inputs may fall, reducing equilibrium input prices and leading to a decrease in long-run average total costs.

Whether firms enter the market as a result of short-run economic profits or leave it in response to short-run economic losses, the adjustment process again leads to zero economic profits in the long run, as shown in Figure 12.5, with output at Q^* and a price of P^*. If demand is perfectly elastic, when economic profits reach zero the demand schedule will be tangent to the

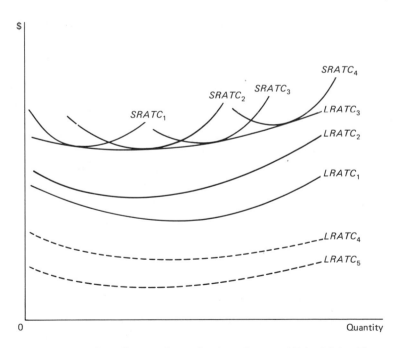

Figure 12.4 Cost Changes Stemming from Entry and Exit of Other Firms

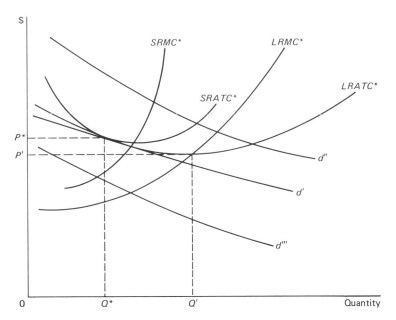

Figure 12.5 Long-Run Equilibrium Adjustment Through Entry or Exit of Firms

minimum point on the firm's *LRATC* schedule with an output level *Q'* and a price *P'*.

If a demand schedule lies above the *LRATC* curve, like *d"*, there will always be some output level at which the firm can earn an economic profit. If so, further adjustment will take place. If a demand schedule lies below the *LRATC* curve at all points, like *d'''*, no output levels exist that yield an average revenue at least as great as average total costs, so that the firm will incur economic losses. This is also inconsistent with long-run equilibrium. *Q** and *P**, therefore, represent the only possible solution.

Long-run equilibrium for a firm in monopolistic competition satisfies the following conditions: (1) Price is equal to long-run average total costs. This condition guarantees that the firm is making zero economic profits. (2) Price is also equal to the relevant short-run average total cost, but not necessarily to short-run marginal costs. With demand and costs like those in Figure 12.5, equilibrium occurs at a lower output and a higher price than associated with minimum *LRATC*.

Product differentiation and the role of advertising

Advertising becomes economically sensible for an individual firm within an industry only when that firm's product can be differentiated in the market.

It therefore plays a much more prominent role in monopolistic competition than in pure competition or monopoly, where the only motive for advertising is to attract consumers to one industry as opposed to another. Although it might pay for groups of purely competitive firms to enter a cooperative industry advertising campaign, it never would pay a single firm in pure competition to advertise. The monopolist could advertise in an attempt to attract purchasers to its commodity but there really is no competitive motive for advertising vis-a-vis firms in the same industry.

In monopolistic competition, demand depends not only on the prices of other goods and the level and distribution of consumer income but also on the characteristics a commodity possesses.[1] The firm may either alter the characteristics of its commodity physically by changing the production process, or alter its consumer image through advertising. Each characteristic— size, smell, shape, etc.—can be varied for marketing purposes, and each has a cost associated with it. The way in which characteristics enter an individual's utility function is frequently taken as given. However, advertising opens up the added possibility of changing the individual's preferences by operating on his/her utility function, perhaps by changing the way the individual perceives the characteristics, i.e., creating product "images." A firm's demand schedule still depends on prices, but now price policy is only one of an array of alternative marketing policies. The desirability of using price policy as a way of attracting customers has to be weighed against the other alternative policies open to the firm. It could alter characteristics of a particular commodity, which we might call C_{11}, C_{21}, etc., but the firm could also operate by altering the level of advertising expenditures. Demand also depends on competitors' advertising and commodity characteristics C_{12}, $C_{22}, \ldots, C_{1n}, C_{2n}, \ldots$, where C_{ij} denotes the ith characteristic on the jth product. Of course demand still depends on consumer incomes, $M_1, M_2, \ldots,$ M_r, but we have now embellished the number of influences substantially. Instead of a single demand schedule and one set of costs, a monopolistic firm must reckon with a group of cost and demand schedules determined by the particular mix of characteristics chosen.

If we increase the level of advertising expenditures from A' to A'' this produces another average cost schedule which lies above the initial one, like *LRATC''* in Figure 12.6. Such an increase is naturally intended to raise the demand schedule also. In the same way, changes in commodity characteristics will generally shift the demand curve, but with accompanying changes in production costs.

The long-run equilibrium adjustments are more difficult to diagram, since they involve not only the variation in price, but also all variations in com-

---

[1] For K. Lancaster's detailed analytical development of this view of demand theory see the References.

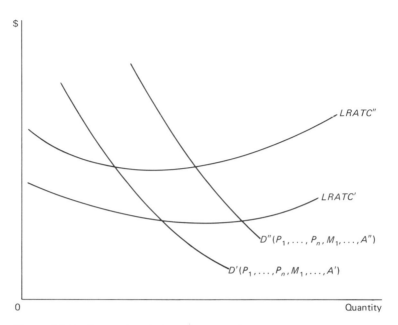

Figure 12.6 Demand and Cost Changes Stemming from Changes in Product Characteristics

modity characteristics and advertising expenditures. However, if we allow only advertising expenditures to vary, while holding other factors constant, we can determine the optimal amount of advertising from the demand schedule.

Suppose the effect of advertising is measured by market observations comparing quantity sold with pages of advertising. Assume the total revenue schedule in Figure 12.7 is associated with a price policy, $\bar{P}_1$, and a particular set of commodity characteristics, $\bar{C}_1, \bar{C}_2, \ldots, \bar{C}_m$. Advertising expenditure is the only variable. The marginal revenue schedule associated with changes in advertising expenditure and the marginal cost schedule of changes in advertising are given for an amount of advertising measured in pages and advertising costs of \$100 per page. The optimal amount of advertising is indicated by the point A^*, where the marginal revenue equals marginal cost.

The analysis described in Figure 12.7 can be used for any commodity characteristic. Holding the price policy and all other commodity characteristics constant, one can trace the way in which total revenue changes as one changes a particular commodity characteristic. From production information the relevant marginal cost schedule indicates the cost of imbuing a product with various levels of a particular attribute. The optimal amount of

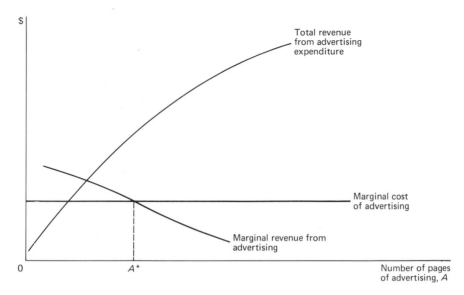

Figure 12.7 Determining the Optimal Amount of Advertising

each attribute will occur at the point where its marginal revenue is equal to its marginal cost.[2]

Optimum product quality can be determined in a similar manner. The optimum quality level will depend on the degree of consumer sensitivity

---

[2] If only advertising and price policy can vary, then the firm's decision problem can be written as

$$\text{Maximize } \pi = PD(P, A) - C(Q, A)$$
$$P, A, Q$$

subject to

$$Q = D(P, A)$$

$$P \geq 0, \qquad Q \geq 0, \qquad A \geq 0$$

where A represents advertising and P and Q represent price and output choices. Since price can be determined once Q and A are chosen, the profit maximizing level of Q and A must satisfy

$$\frac{\partial \pi}{\partial Q} = \frac{\partial TR}{\partial Q} - \frac{\partial C}{\partial Q} = 0$$

and

$$\frac{\partial \pi}{\partial A} = \frac{\partial TR}{\partial A} - \frac{\partial C}{\partial A} = 0$$

provided $A > 0$, $Q > 0$. The first condition expresses the familiar requirement that marginal revenue be equal to marginal cost. The second condition requires $\partial TR/\partial A$, the marginal revenue from added advertising, to be equal to $\partial C/\partial A$, the marginal cost of additional advertising. A more detailed discussion by R. Dorfman and P. Steiner is cited in the References.

to variations in quality and price, and the effect of changes in quality attributes on average costs.

Regardless of whether we view these adjustments as product characteristic variations or as selling cost variations, the result is the same. Demand and/or costs are altered until economic profits are squeezed out and the firm arrives at a long-run equilibrium solution like the one in Figure 12.5.

Comparison of Pure Competition and Monopolistic Competition in Long-Run Equilibrium

Suppose that two representative firms have the same total costs, but that one operates under pure competition and the other in a monopolistic setting, and let us compare their respective long-run equilibrium solutions.

In pure competition the firm's demand schedule is horizontal at the long-run equilibrium market price and tangent to the average total cost curve at its minimum point. The firm would therefore produce at the output Q' and the price P' in Figure 12.5. This solution would occur in monopolistic competition only in the extreme case where demand is perfectly elastic. For any other case the long-run equilibrium solution occurs when marginal revenue equals marginal cost and the long-run average total cost curve is tangent to the firm's demand schedule at an output level less than Q'. The equilibrium output for a firm maximizing profits under monopolistic competition will therefore be lower than under pure competition, and the equilibrium price will be higher.

Remember, however, that a monopolistic setting produces a degree of variety not found under pure competition. That such variety is purchased at the cost of higher price and lower output should be neither surprising nor distressing. Consumer tastes may be better satisfied by a variety of products than a single model.

Comparison of Pure Monopoly and Monopolistic Competition in Long-Run Equilibrium

A similar comparison can be made between monopoly and monopolistic competition. The solution in Figure 12.1 could just as easily have been a long-run solution under monopoly as a short-run solution under monopolistic competition. However, a monopoly's short-run price and output choice do not necessarily change in the long run, and only by accident would it ever earn zero long-run economic profits. Unlike the monopolistic firm, its demand schedule will not necessarily decline in the long run, nor will its costs necessarily change. Explicit comparisons of price and output are not possible, since the monopolist supplies the entire market demand for a commodity, not just the demand for a single differentiated product.

Product Characteristics: Some Empirical Examples

The following examples illustrate the influence of advertising, brand names, and commodity characteristics used as marketing devices.

Washing machines and cameras: an example of product reliability

The name Maytag is part of a quality image for washing machines, dryers, and dishwashers. Average selling prices for Maytag products are above the average prices on similar products by as much as 20%. Such a price differential expresses the consumers' willingness to pay the added price for the added quality they believe is inherent in the product.

Reliability is a particularly important characteristic, as reflected in television advertisements you have seen for color television sets and automobiles.

Certain brands of cameras such as Leica, Hasselblad, Nikon, and Rolliflex have high reputations for reliability and photographic quality. There are substantial differences in price between one camera and another depending not only on perceived quality, but also on special features like automatic exposure settings and interchangeable lenses.

Reliability is purchased at a cost of increased materials and inspection labor. Optimum reliability from an economic standpoint, therefore, is not necessarily the same as maximum engineering reliability. If service and repair costs are low it may not be economically optimal to spend the extra money to purchase or produce a product with high reliability. On the other hand, as repair costs rise it becomes worthwhile to invest more to acquire a more reliable product initially. If the difference in the price between two washing machines is $40, and repair charges are $3 per call, the lower-priced machine may still be the best buy, even though the higher-priced one needs to be repaired less often. If repair charges rise to $12.50 or $15.00 per call, the more reliable machine may be much more economical.

Retail gasoline sales

A difference in prices is not necessarily associated with physically tangible characteristics as with cameras and washing machines. For example, price differences between independent brand gasolines and producer brands, such as Shell, Texaco, and Standard, may range from as little as 1¢ to 2¢ to 10¢ or more per gallon, yet they seem to be based simply on brand names. While brands of gasoline may have slight chemical differences resulting from additives, the products themselves are virtually indistinguishable from one another.

Indeed, if the nearest supply point in a particular area is a Union Oil refinery, it is not uncommon for retail stations in the area to buy from the Union Oil terminal. Agreements for swapping truck loads or rail tank loads of fuel often exist between major oil companies. Gasoline price differentials are largely based on a perceived difference created by advertising, although the location of service stations is also significant.

Toothpaste

Though choices of toothpaste are probably made principally on the basis of brand names, consumers may also respond to such intrinsic qualities as fluoride content, texture, color, and taste—characteristics that can be varied by the producer.

Empirical Estimates of the Cost of Advertising

A Department of Health and Welfare study[3] on prescription drugs found that in 1968 major drug firms spent approximately $4,500 per physician each year to extol the virtues of their products. This amount reflects the fact that it is the physician, not the ultimate consumer, who chooses which brand to use.

A *Business Week* survey[4] on the use of gasoline station games cites an expenditure of $85 million in 1966–1967 for games and prizes. Advertising accounts for slightly over $44 million of the total. It is hard to imagine that such campaigns lead to an increase in the aggregate volume of gasoline purchased, but individual stations report sales increases of 15–50% associated with games and price offerings. If individual firms perceive a potential gain, yet in the aggregate consumers use the same volume of gasoline, what social value corresponds to the enormous cost of the resources consumed by advertising?

Table 12.1 shows the relative importance of advertising in certain industries, measured as a percentage of total sales volume. Observe the wide spread in relative expenditures. Even for those commodities with a comparatively small percentage of a sales dollar spent on advertising, remember that the volume of sales is generally very large, so that the amount spent on advertising is also large. Table 12.2 shows the average percentage of the selling price for selected food products spent on advertising and other promotion expenses.

---

[3] *U.S. Task Force on Prescription Drugs: Final Report*, HEW, 1968.
[4] "Why Gas Stations Keep Up Games," *Business Week*, September 21, 1968.

Table 12.1 Selected Advertising/Sales Ratios in 1957

COMMODITY	ADVERTISING/SALES RATIO
Perfumes	14.7%
Drugs	10.3
Soap	7.9
Beer	6.9
Cereals	4.8
Appliances	3.3
Costume jewelry	2.5
Liquor	2.4
Carpets	2.1
Dairy products	1.9
Women's clothing	1.3
Men's clothing	0.9
Motor vehicles	0.9

SOURCE: L. Telser, "Advertising and Competition," *Journal of Political Economy*, December, 1964.

Table 12.2 Relative Importance of Advertising and Promotion Expenses as a Percentage of Selling Price (1964 data)

COMMODITY	ADVERTISING AS PERCENTAGE OF RETAIL PRICE
Breakfast cereals	20.0%
Canned corn	6.3
Ice cream	4.9
White bread	4.8
Milk	3.4
Eggs	3.3
Beef	2.8

SOURCE: U.S. Department of Labor, *Food From Farmer to Consumer*, June, 1966.

Designing Product Lines for Optimal Price and Quality

Recalling the gains a monopolist was able to realize by charging different prices to different classes of customers, you can see that the same principle can be applied by developing product lines with actual or apparent hierarchies for a product. Automobiles, kitchen appliances, stereos, radios, televisions, etc. are examples of commodities offered in multiple models tailored to different segments of the market with different brand names and images. The marketing function of a brand name is precisely to divide the market by creating brand preferences.

Summary

Monopolistic competition is a market setting in which a firm enjoys a quasi-monopoly over a product with particular characteristics, yet is subjected to the competitive pressures resulting from free resource mobility and complete information. Advertising plays a prominent role both in disseminating information about products and in developing "brand loyalty." This marketing term actually expresses a reduction in the cross-price elasticity of demand, only now the cross-elasticity influences include other characteristics as well as price.

Compared to a perfectly competitive or monopoly setting, monopolistic competition provides product variety instead of product homogeneity. This variety may, however, be purchased in the long run at the price of higher average total costs and resulting higher market prices. This is not unambiguously "good" or "bad"—it simply represents a choice.

Long-run equilibrium is characterized by average total cost equal to average revenue. Price competition, entry, exit, technological conditions, supply elasticities for inputs, product characteristics, and variations in selling cost combine to drive economic profit to zero in the long run. All of these forces operate in an environment in which firms do not engage in strategic planning, despite the interdependencies among them. The next chapter examines the implications of explicitly interdependent pricing and production decisions.

Questions for Study or Class Discussion

1. List at least five products other than those mentioned in the text which are marketed in a monopolistically competitive setting.
2. Does the long-run optimal price and output level for a monopolistically competitive firm imply the existence of inefficiency or excess capacity? Why or why not?
3. Suppose in the short run the demand schedule for a monopolistically competitive firm is $D = 400 - 3P + 2A$, where P is price and A is advertising cost. With total costs given by $C(Q) = 25 + 3Q^2 + 4A$, find the optimal price, output, and advertising levels.
4. List at least five products and at least three characteristics of each product which could be altered by the producer. Think of recent product advertisements you have seen, read, or heard.

5. Look up some frequency of repair data by brand name or model for household appliances or automobiles. (Consult *Consumer Reports* as a start.) What does the data suggest about the degree of built-in product "quality"? How could a product be "designed to fail" in order to encourage replacement? Does the repair data you have suggest how long these replacement cycles might be?

References

Chamberlin, E., *The Theory of Monopolistic Competition*. Harvard University Press, 1933.

Dorfman, R., and P. Steiner, "Optimal Advertising and Optimal Quality," *American Economic Review*, 44 (December, 1954), 826–836.

Kaldor, N., "Market Imperfection and Excess Capacity," *Economica*, 2 (1935), 33–50.

Lancaster, K., "A New Approach to Consumer Theory," *Journal of Political Economy*, 74 (April, 1966), 132–157.

Machlup, F., *The Economics of Sellers' Competition*. The Johns Hopkins Press, 1952.

Robinson, J., *The Economics of Imperfect Competition*. Macmillan, 1933.

Scherer, F. M., *Industrial Market Structure and Economic Performance*. Rand McNally, 1971.

Telser, L. G., "Advertising and Competition," *Journal of Political Economy*, 72 (December, 1964), 537–562.

Triffin, R., *Monopolistic Competition and General Equilibrium Theory*. Harvard University Press, 1949.

Chapter 13 Oligopoly Market Settings

Introduction

"People of the same trade seldom meet together but the conversation ends in a conspiracy against the public, or in some diversion to raise prices." This forceful accusation sounds like a quote from the morning newspaper, but in fact it is found in Adam Smith's famous treatise *The Wealth of Nations* published in 1776! It describes the most important setting for economic activity, *oligopoly*, a situation in which a small number of firms, each producing differentiated or identical products, know their rivals.

In an oligopoly setting we can introduce for the first time the possibility that firms make strategic decisions with respect to pricing, marketing, and production policies, based on explicit consideration of the actions and reactions of other firms in the market.

A clear example of strategic maneuvering in an oligopoly setting occurs each September when the automobile manufacturers introduce their new models. One company announces that the list price of its new cars will show increases of $180. A few days later a second company announces list price increases of only $80, and a third announces increases of $91. Suddenly there is a news flash from the first firm. A horrible error has been made! Their prices will increase not by $180, but by $71 instead. At this point other firms may discover similar "errors," and announce still smaller price increases. This type of behavior is a strategic interactive decision setting unlike any discussed in earlier chapters. In our discussion of monopolistic competition we pointed out that the demand schedule facing any one monopolistic competitor depends on the prices that other competitors name for their products, but we did not discuss the whole decision process as a simultaneous interactive one.

In addition, we shall introduce methods of representing uncertainty about the strategies an opponent will follow. The principles involved carry over to other aspects of decision making including uncertainty about costs and demand, about government decisions, about natural phenomena like storms and droughts, or even about the effects of an advertising campaign.

Unlike pure competition, monopoly, and monopolistic competition, oligopoly theory does not consist of a single model, but a group of alternative descriptions concentrating on one or more aspects of actual business decision settings. Thus one model might be more appropriate to a specific market than another.

After a discussion of the major models of oligopoly behavior, the remainder of the chapter is devoted to empirical aspects of oligopoly markets. Important public policy issues include the degree of industrial concentration, its impact on inflationary tendencies, and the economic value of barriers to entry.

Interdependent Decisions: The Cournot Model

We shall illustrate the type of interdependence common to an oligopoly market by means of a numerical example using a *Cournot model* of oligopoly behavior. Suppose we have a market setting with two firms where the market price for the commodity is given by the demand curve $P = 500 - 25(Q_1 + Q_2)$, where Q_1 and Q_2 are the outputs of firm 1 and firm 2, respectively. Notice that the market price for both firms depends on the quantity they both produce. This means that, as we shall prove, the profit for each firm is linked directly to the profit of the other.

Assume firm 1 has a cost function which depends only on what it produces, $C_1(Q_1) = 400 + 25Q_1$, and that firm 2 has its own cost function, $C_2(Q_2) = 100 + 50Q_2$. Different cost functions imply different payments for inputs or the use of different production techniques. There is no necessity that both firms be operating with the same costs and the same technology. The profit function for firm 1 is

$$\pi_1(Q_1, Q_2) = PQ_1 - C_1(Q_1) \tag{13.1}$$

After substituting the cost function for firm 1 and using the market demand function we obtain

$$\begin{aligned} \pi_1(Q_1, Q_2) &= [500 - 25(Q_1 + Q_2)]Q_1 - 400 - 25Q_1 \\ &= (475 - 25Q_2)Q_1 - 25Q_1^2 - 400 \end{aligned} \tag{13.2}$$

Firm 1's profit depends on its own output level, but it also depends on firm 2's output level. The same thing is true for firm 2:

$$\begin{aligned} \pi_2(Q_1, Q_2) &= PQ_2 - C_2(Q_2) \\ &= (450 - 25Q_1)Q_2 - 25Q_2^2 - 100 \end{aligned} \tag{13.3}$$

Graphing profit for firm 1 for a specific value of firm 2's output, say $\bar{Q}_2$, the profit function might resemble the one shown in Figure 13.1. If firm 2 chose some other output level, say $\bar{\bar{Q}}_2$, then the profit function might change to the dotted line in Figure 13.1. For each level of firm 2's output, firm 1's profit function shifts. The same is true for firm 2, as shown in Figure 13.2. Neither firm can determine its optimal output level without taking into account the behavior of the other firm.

The Cournot solution of the oligopoly problem is based on the profit function for firm 1 given by Equation (13.1) and the assumption that firm 1 will treat the current level of firm 2's output as constant and choose the value of Q_1 that maximizes π_1. Firm 2 is assumed to proceed in the same way. Needless to say, the assumption that one firm will make no change in output no matter what the other firm decides to do is very naive. Next we must consider equilibrium price and market sharing under the Cournot model.

Strategic Policy Reactions

For every level of firm 2's output, firm 1 determines its profit-maximizing output by solving the problem

$$\underset{Q_1}{\text{Maximize }} \pi_1(Q_1, Q_2)$$

subject to

$$Q_1 \geq 0 \tag{13.4}$$

Notice that each solution depends on the value for Q_2. Suppose we write the optimal output for each value of Q_2 as $Q_1^* = g_1(Q_2)$.

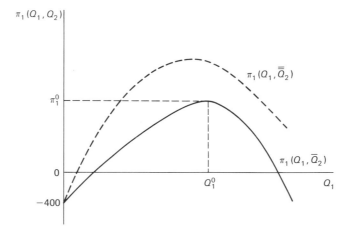

Figure 13.1   Firm 1 Profit as a Function of Firm 2 Output

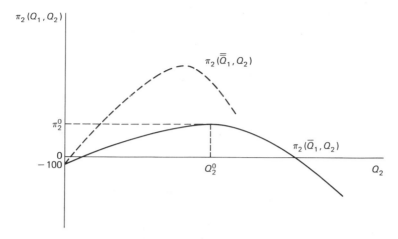

Figure 13.2 Firm 2 Profit as a Function of Firm 1 Output

Now solve for firm 2's profit-maximizing output at every possible output firm 1 might choose. Firm 2 must solve the problem

$$\text{Maximize } \pi_2(Q_1, Q_2)$$
$$Q_2$$

subject to

$$Q_2 \geq 0 \tag{13.5}$$

Firm 2's optimal output is a function of the output level chosen by firm 1. We can express this as $Q_2^* = g_2(Q_1)$.

The two functions g_1 and g_2 are referred to as *reaction functions*. They indicate the optimal action of one firm given the output level of the other. The reaction functions in our example are

$$Q_1^* = (475 - 25Q_2)/50 \tag{13.6}$$

and

$$Q_2^* = (450 - 25Q_1)/50 \tag{13.7}$$

Figure 13.3 shows the graph of these expressions.

In an oligopoly, movement toward or away from an equilibrium can thus be thought of as a game proceeding in a sequence of alternating moves. At move one of the game, firm 1 chooses a particular output level; at move two, firm 2 will choose a corresponding output. At move three, firm 1 considers the decision firm 2 made in move two and revises its initial decision accordingly. Firm 2 will base move four on the decision firm 1 made in move three, etc.

Let us trace these moves in Figure 13.3. Suppose that firm 1 starts initially at the output level Q'_1. The reaction curve g_2 indicates that firm 2 will then maximize its profit by choosing Q'_2. Next, firm 1 looks at firm 2's choice and chooses Q''_1. Each successive step moves closer and closer to point A, where the reaction functions intersect. If we had started at an output level for firm 1 to the right of the intersection, like $\bar{Q}_1$, and repeated the same steps, the path of actions and reactions would also lead toward point A. The Cournot equilibrium output pattern is Q^*_1 and Q^*_2. For the numerical example given earlier $Q^*_1 = 7$, $Q^*_2 = 6$.

Point A represents an equilibrium because firm 1 looks at firm 2's output level, Q^*_2, and finds that its optimal level, Q^*_1, is the one it is already producing. Similarly, firm 2 looking at firm 1's output level, Q^*_1, finds that it, too, is already producing its optimal level, namely Q^*_2.

Although each intersection of the reaction curves represents an equilibrium, these equilibria are not necessarily stable, like the one occurring at point A. Satisfy yourself that, while an equilibrium occurs at point B in Figure 13.4, it is not a stable one. If firm 1 is producing at a level a little to the right of point B instead of at Q^0_1, the adjustment process moves away from B toward A.

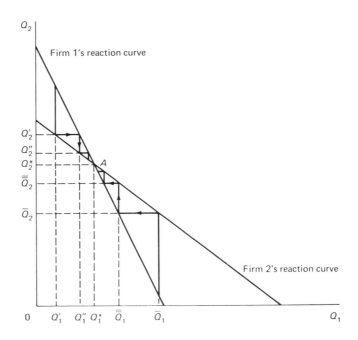

Figure 13.3   Adjustment Toward a Cournot Equilibrium

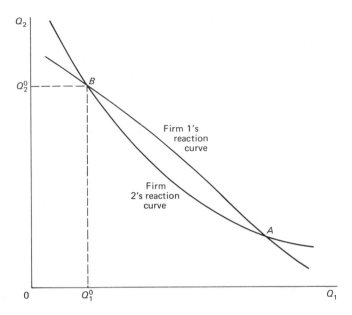

Figure 13.4 An Example of Stable and Unstable Equilibra for the Cournot Model

Variants of the Cournot Model

There are two well-known variants of the basic two-firm or duopoly setting: (1) *the Edgeworth/Bertrand model* and (2) *the Chamberlin model.* Instead of treating a competitor's *output* as constant as in the Cournot model, the Edgeworth/Bertrand model assumes that the *price* charged by a competitor does not change. While the Cournot model can yield a stable equilibrium, the Edgeworth/Bertrand model may not. Since consumers presumably buy from the least expensive source, there is a constant tendency toward price instability. Firms may increase profits by raising prices simultaneously, but eventually the temptation for one firm to grab the whole market by price cutting will become too great to resist.

The Chamberlin model is distinguished from the Cournot model by its assumption that a firm chooses its output taking the reactions of its competitors fully into account. Firm behavior is not predicated on an assumption of blind faith in the independence of competitor decisions. Practicality suggests that firms recognize interdependence and simply reach an agreeable way of carving up the monopoly profit pie that they can secure for themselves by joint action. The resulting market price may be the same one a monopolist would set.

The Chamberlin model, like the Cournot model, is set up in terms of the actions and reactions of existing firms. Ignoring the threat posed to such firms by potential entry is an important defect of these models. At the end of this chapter we will return to the Chamberlin model and consider the effect of uncertain entry on current pricing and capacity decisions.

Price and Output Stability: The Kinked Demand Curve

Over long periods of time firms in an oligopoly appear to maintain stable price and output levels, with an absence of price competition, even though the prices of inputs are changing. Under normal conditions we would expect a firm faced with changing costs to change its output and pricing policy in order to maximize profits. What is the explanation for this phenomenon?

Suppose a firm in an oligopoly is initially selling at a market price P^0, as in Figure 13.5, and producing an output level Q^0. One way of describing the strategic environment of the firm is to say that if the firm considers changing its price from the prevailing price of P^0, the firm would be confronted with an *asymmetry* in the reactions its competitors would follow. If the firm

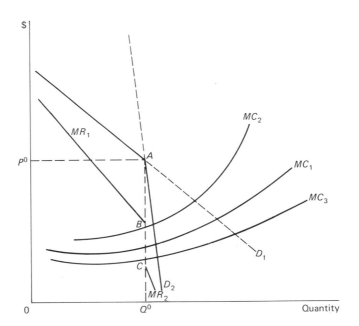

Figure 13.5 Price and Output Stability with a Kinked Demand Curve

lowers its prices and its competitors do not follow suit, it stands to gain substantial portions of the market shares held by its competitors, since the firms in the oligopoly are all producing essentially identical products. The resulting demand curve for the firm will be similar to D_1 below point A.

On the other hand, if competitors react by instituting their own price cuts, the firm will not stand to gain the market shares that its competitors have. In this case the firm's demand curve will be similar to D_2 below point A. Since firms are not likely to stand by and see their market stolen by a competitor, we can anticipate that price decreases below P^0 will result in the demand schedule represented by the curve D_2 below point A.

The reactions of the firm's competitors to price increases will be *asymmetrical* to their reactions to decreases. This comes about in the following way. If a firm increases its price, its competitors can either follow by raising their prices or else make no change. The portion of the demand curve D_1 above point A describes the result for the firm if competitors do not follow increases. On the other hand, the segment of demand curve D_2 above A describes the result if competitors do follow increases. There is no reason for a firm to assume that its competitors will necessarily follow its lead in making price increases, as they stand to gain increased market shares simply by doing nothing.

The asymmetry between competitors' reactions to price increases and decreases produces a demand curve which is *kinked* at the prevailing market price. Since the demand curve in Figure 13.5 has a kink at point A, the associated marginal revenue schedule shows a discontinuity at the quantity level Q^0. For output below Q^0, the marginal revenue schedule is MR_1; for output above Q^0, it is MR_2, which is based on demand curve D_2. It would be purely by accident if the two marginal revenue schedules were to meet at Q^0. The discontinuity in the marginal revenue schedule is represented by the vertical segment BC in Figure 13.5 at output level Q^0.

Suppose the firm initially has marginal costs described by the marginal cost schedule MC_1. Subsequently a new technology comes into use which gives the firm marginal costs substantially below those described by MC_1, say MC_3. Notice that the profit-maximizing output level, i.e., the level that equates marginal revenue and marginal cost, remains at Q^0. The same reasoning applies to higher marginal costs resulting from input cost increases, which might produce a curve like MC_2. Unless the cost difference is dramatic it will not lead to any change in the firm's price and output policies. Observe that though the discontinuity in the marginal revenue schedules arises from the threat of competition, it ultimately produces a stability in the firm's behavior, showing that a potential threat can be a stabilizing force.

Unfortunately, stability is the only characteristic highlighted by the kinked demand curve model. The model provides no information as to why P^0 is the initial price.

Spatial Competition: Optimal Location as a Competitive Strategy

Among the important dimensions of marketing policy are product characteristics and the physical location of production and warehousing facilities. (The latter affects such factors as production cost, transportation cost, and delivery time.) The Hotelling model of spatial competition provides a one-dimensional model to determine the optimal location for a firm, but it can also be used to find optimal commodity characteristics.

A spatial competition model in two dimensions can be used to find the optimal location of plants over geographical areas, to locate warehouses so that transportation costs for serving particular marketing areas will be minimized, and to describe regions in which a firm has a protected market by virtue of transport cost or some other impediment that prevents its competitors from intruding. Three-dimensional models, with the third dimension representing time, can be used to determine the optimal moment for each optimal location. Thus a firm might secure optimal expansion by locating at point A at time t_1, at point B at time t_2, and at point C at time t_3. These could correspond to the same firm having a single plant that changes locations over time or, perhaps more importantly, the time-phasing of the optimal expansion and growth of a firm. The one-dimensional location problem is the basic building block for these more elaborate models.

Suppose two firms must choose a location on the line $\overline{OL}$ as shown in Figure 13.6. The location of a hotel or restaurant along a highway is an example. Assume that at each point along $\overline{OL}$ there is one customer with a perfectly inelastic demand for one unit of the commodity. Since we are dealing with an oligopoly setting, we shall assume that the two firms produce

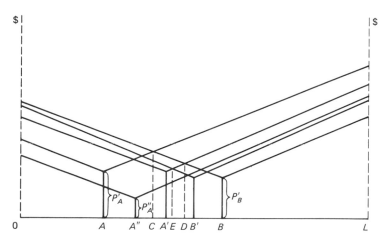

Figure 13.6 Optimal Location and Price Policy for Two Firms (A and B)

an identical commodity and that consumers purchase from the firm that offers the lowest delivered price. Firm A is initially located at point A charging a base price of P'_A and firm B is located at point B charging a base price of P'_B. For this example, base price is defined as average revenue less average total cost.

Along the line segment $\overline{OL}$ the firms seek their optimal location so as to maximize profit (i.e., market share, in this case). They have to solve not only an optimal location problem, but an optimal pricing problem at the same time. The delivered price from firm A, P^D_A, is equal to its base price plus a transport cost per unit distance, r, times the distance from point A to the customer, $P^D_A = P'_A + rd$, where d is the distance from A to the customer. In the same way, the delivered price from firm B is the base price firm B charges plus the transport rate, r, times the distance, d, from the location of firm B to the consumer, $P^D_B = P'_B + rd$. Thus a customer buying from firm A pays a price described by a straight line beginning at P'_A and rising on either side of point A. The slope of the line is the transport charge per unit distance, r. Similarly, customers buying from firm B must pay a delivered price described by a line whose slope is r and which starts at P'_B and rises on either side of point B.

Initially, the total market $\overline{OL}$ will divide at point C, giving firm A a protected market for all consumers that lie between zero and C, because in this area its delivered price is less than firm B's, and firm B a protected market for all those consumers that lie between C and L, because in that interval its delivered price is less than firm A's. This initial division is not a stable one, however. Although it is true that initially we find the firms located at points A and B, notice that if both firms are attempting to maximize net profits this is equivalent to trying to maximize their market share. The initial locations A and B are not stable because firm A could jump to the point A' (Figure 13.6), and even if it maintained its initial price P'_A it can enlarge its market share to $\overline{OD}$. There are two dimensions to marketing policy: a price policy and a location policy. Physical location is a very real part of the marketing policies open to a firm. Figure 13.6 illustrates this facet.

Firm B, on the other hand, is not going to remain at B if firm A jumps to A'. It may move to B', increasing its market share to $\overline{EL}$. At the next stage of the game firm A might attempt to improve its position not only by changing its location but also by decreasing its price to P''_A. The firms will continue in this manner until they arrive ultimately at the midpoint of the line. Once at the center, each firm will still find it advantageous to cut prices, but then the other firm must retaliate, as shown in Figure 13.7. A stable solution will only occur when both firms locate at the center and charge the same base price.

The solution depicted in Figure 13.7 can be interpreted in several ways. In terms of physical location, the solution indicates that two firms should

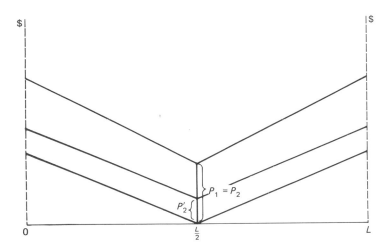

Figure 13.7   Price Cutting by Firms at the Same Location

move to the same place. However, three or more firms should be located at
equal distances from one another.

Alternatively, the linear segment from O to L could represent an index
measuring some commodity attribute, such as weight, from O (light) to
L (heavy), or scent, from O (no fragrance) to L (very pungent). Interpreted
in this way, the equilibrium solution in Figure 13.7 describes a tendency
toward homogeneity. The fact that the firms are drawn to a common equilibrium point is interpreted in this characteristic framework to mean that
competition among firms produces commodities whose characteristics turn
out to be very similar. Such a tendency toward homogeneity would imply
that one of the theoretical advantages of a monopolistically competitive
market setting could, over a period of time, be eroded.

Instead of representing two different firms, points A and B could represent
two different product lines of the same firm. The optimal market division
then provides a rationale for producing a low-grade product and a high-
grade product, in order to siphon off more profit from the market. This
interpretation gives a single firm justification for price lining or tailoring
products for particular classes of customers. The spatial competition interpretation is similar to the optimality of price discrimination. This policy uses
product grade differentiation to divide the market, much as a monopoly
divides it by price discrimination. The old military maxim "divide and
conquer" may have a practical analog in business!

A centralized location will be optimal only in a riskless setting, where it
gives one firm one half of the customers and the other firm the other half.
If the probability that a customer buys from either firm is $\frac{1}{2}$, then even though

this gives the firm an expected profit which is the same as in the riskless situation, there is now a variance about expected profit. Where consumers buy randomly from one seller or the other (provided delivered prices are the same), actual profit for the individual firm may be less than under certainty.

In an uncertain setting it is no longer necessarily optimal to locate in the center. The optimal location for a risk-averting firm is at the quartiles. By moving away from the center the firm secures a protected market. The protected market reduces the variance of profits back to zero. If firm A moves to the first quartile and firm B to the third, their expected profits will be the same as if they were located at the center. Firm A will be assured of the market from O to $L/2$, since its price is lower in that area, and firm B will be assured of the market from $L/2$ to L. If a firm is willing to assume some risk, then its optimal location will depend on how expected profit and variance are weighted.

In an uncertainty context, product lining may be basically a risk-averting strategy aimed at reducing brand switching by customers. Marketers imbue their product with a minimum perceived difference from other products on the market (in the eyes of consumers) in an attempt to secure brand preference or loyalty, and thereby reduce sales risk—particularly for products where repeat sales are important.

Gaming Strategies

One of the most interesting models that can be applied to oligopoly markets treats interdependent decisions as a game. While each of the models of firm behavior discussed earlier was typically cast in an environment of complete information, using game theory allows a firm to take into account the uncertainty of its opponents' behavior.

Any game can be broken down into certain basic components. First, we must specify the *players* in the game. In the following examples, the players will usually be two or more business firms, but a firm might play against the government in a regulatory game, or against an adverse natural environment in an agricultural setting. Or countries might be the players in a game of politics.

The second element is a *set of alternative strategies for each player*. A *strategy* is simply a rule for making individual decisions. The third element is the *information set open to each player*. The information set might include the decisions that opponents made at prior moves in the games, the number of opponents and their alternative strategies, or, in an economic setting, the history of price or advertising policies in a given industry. The information set of each player is not necessarily the same, is not necessarily complete, and does not necessarily reflect accurate information. Thus, games can be a model for decision making based on incomplete or inaccurate information.

The fourth component of a game is a *payoff matrix*. The payoff matrix is a rule which assigns a payoff to each player after each player specifies the strategy it has chosen. For example, a payoff rule would specify the profits of firm A and firm B if firm A establishes a specific marketing policy and firm B a specific price policy. The final component of a game is a specification of the *rules of play*. These rules determine whether the game is played sequentially in a series of moves or entirely in one move. They might permit a player to make decisions with knowledge of its opponent's moves, or require that each player make its decision without knowing what its opponents are doing. Rules of play may also specify whether or not side payments or bribes are allowed in the game—an important point for both political and economic games—and whether or not the players are permitted to communicate or collude with one another. Communication is an element that was absent from our previous description of decision-making settings.

There are two main classifications of games: (1) zero-sum games as opposed to non-zero-sum games and (2) strictly determined games as opposed to non-strictly determined games. A game is a *zero-sum game* when the sum of the amounts won by all winners is equal to the sum of the amounts lost by all losers. If in order for one firm to make $1 million in profits all other firms in competition with it must lose a total of $1 million, the firms are playing a zero-sum game. However, most descriptions of business environments are not in terms of zero-sum games. Games are said to be *strictly determined* if the optimal strategy for each player is to play one particular strategy consistently throughout the game. In a non-strictly determined game players may find it optimal to play different strategies at different times. Strategies of this kind are called *mixed strategies*. In a mixed strategy, each individual strategy is played with a specified probability.

As we have seen, a pure competitor or monopolist can simply choose its price or output policy and directly calculate the resulting gain or loss. In an oligopoly setting, the choice of a price, output, or other marketing policy does not uniquely determine profit, because the outcome for each firm depends on what its opponents decide to do. The Cournot and Chamberlin descriptions of oligopoly suggest the kind of interdependence that arises explicitly here, but do not take into account uncertainty about an opponent's decisions.

To introduce a game model for business decisions, let us use the example shown in Table 13.1. Firm A has three strategies available, S_1^A, S_2^A, and S_3^A. S_1^A might correspond to entering market 1 with a new product; S_2^A to entering market 2 with a new product; and S_3^A to entering both markets. Firm B has two strategies available. Strategy S_1^B might correspond to entering market 1, and S_2^B to beginning an advertising campaign. The entries in the table represent the payoffs to each firm measured as millions of dollars of profits. The first term in each square is the payoff to firm A, and the second term is the payoff to firm B. As an example, if firm A chooses to play strategy

Table 13.1 An Example of Payoffs in a Two-Person Non-Zero-Sum Game

		Firm A				
		S_1^A	S_2^A	S_3^A		
Firm B	S_1^B	A B (1, 2)	(2, 50)	(21, 18)	2	B's minimum
	S_2^B	(8, 3)	(6, 75)	(3, 13)	3	profits
		1	2	3		
			A's minimum profits			

S_2^A and firm B chooses to play strategy S_1^B, then the payoff to firm A is a profit of $2 million and firm B a profit of $50 million. If firm A plays strategy S_1^A and firm B plays strategy S_2^B, then firm A receives profits of $8 million and firm B receives profits of $3 million.

Suppose both firms know the information described in the payoff matrix and the rules of the game specify that the firms must make their decisions simultaneously and independently, without colluding or communicating with one another. The basic character of this decision problem depends crucially on communication. If firm B knows that firm A is going to play strategy S_3^A, then there really is no decision problem since firm B would simply choose to play strategy S_1^B and receive a profit of $18 million. Notice that the decision problem is *created by imperfect information*. The inability to collude might be caused by a very stringent antitrust law. Alternatively, we could impose the no-collusion rule on the game merely by making the payoff for colluding an enormously high penalty, which automatically introduces an economic disincentive to collude. Antitrust laws currently in effect in the United States permit the injured party to recover treble damages, which is equivalent to a penalty in an economic game.

How should a firm play the game, i.e., make a management decision? One possible strategy is to make the decision with the maximum potential return disregarding any other possible consequences. This game plan is too risky to be popular with any but confirmed gamblers. The alternative which has received the most extensive attention is called the *minimax decision rule*. Using this rule, the firm determines the worst possible outcome for each decision, over all possible decisions its opponents might make. It then makes the decision whose worst possible outcome will be the least prejudicial to its goals.

Suppose in Table 13.1 firm A may choose the alternative strategies S_1^A, S_2^A, or S_3^A, but not a combination of them. Looking at strategy S_1^A, firm A sees that the worst that can happen, over all possible alternatives open to firm B, is a profit of $1 million. With S_2^A the worst outcome is a profit of $2 million, and with S_3^A the worst outcome is a profit of $3 million. Firm B

Table 13.2 The Payoff Matrix for the Prisoner's Dilemma Game

		Player A		
		S_1^A	S_2^A	
		A B		B's minimums for each strategy
Player B	S_1^B	$(-10, -10)$	$(-15, -5)$	-10
	S_2^B	$(-6, -12)$	$(4, 4)$	-12
		-10	-15	
		A's minimums for each strategy		

asks the same set of questions. The worst that can happen from following strategy S_1^B is a profit of \$2 million; the worst outcome if strategy S_2^B is chosen is a profit of \$3 million.

Firm A chooses strategy S_3^A and B chooses S_2^B. Firm A receives profits of \$3 million while B receives \$13 million. Notice that this outcome does not represent the maximum profits that either player might have received. Firm A could obviously have obtained much more by playing strategy S_3^A if firm B had played strategy S_1^B and firm B could have received more by playing other strategies provided that A had also played others. Although neither firm is achieving the maximum payoff it could get over all possibilities, each is receiving the *largest minimum* payoff available.

The minimax rule thus describes a very conservative type of management strategy. Let us apply it now to the game described in Table 13.2. While this game can be interpreted as a business example, other two-person, two-strategy interpretations include (1) country A and country B with strategies of war and peace, (2) firm A and firm B with strategies of collusion and noncollusion, (3) student A and student B with choices of cooperation or noncooperation on homework or examinations, (4) Republican Party and Democratic Party with strategies left to your imagination, or (5) prisoner A and prisoner B with strategies of confession or silence.

Table 13.2 represents possible payoffs in a famous game called the Prisoners' Dilemma. Two criminals have just been apprehended. We know they actually committed the crime for which they have been apprehended, but the authorities do not. They are taken into custody and the choices open to them are to talk or to remain quiet. Lack of communication is an essential element of this game. If the prisoners can communicate with one another there is *no* game! But if neither knows what the other one is doing each may adopt a defensive attitude, and try a psychological defense that takes the form of acting in such a way as to minimize the worst that can happen faced with uncertainty. In other words each prisoner will play the game according to the minimax behavior rule.

For prisoners A and B, the negative quantities refer to years in prison while the positive ones correspond to being set free. If both talk, both will be found guilty and receive a 10-year sentence. The structure of the other pay-offs incorporates the well-known cops-and-robbers proposition: "Tell on your buddy and I'll make a deal for you with the D.A." If A remains quiet while B talks, A gets fifteen years while B gets a reduced sentence, with roughly corresponding results if A talks. The structure of the payoffs provides an incentive for each player to talk before the other does. Analogies to this incentive in other settings might include a payoff for being aggressive instead of passive or for beating a competitor to the market with a new product.

The worst that can happen to A if he talks is a 10-year sentence, while the worst that can happen to him if he remains quiet is a 15-year sentence. The worst that can happen to B if he talks is a 10-year sentence, while the worst that can happen if he remains quiet is a 12-year sentence. If A and B each knew with perfect certainty that their pal in the next room would be faithful to the bitter end (even though the bitter end might be 15 years in jail), neither would talk and both would go free. It turns out paradoxically that the mini-max solution is for each individual to talk, so that they are convicted and sentenced to 10 years each.

The dilemma of the game is that the lack of information generated by the environment of uncertainty pyschologically traps the players. Obviously both want to go free. This is not a situation where one individual would gain and one would lose, i.e., this is not a game of opposition of interests of the players, yet the gaming situation precludes cooperation. This type of decision making under uncertainty traps decision makers into making decisions that are nonoptimal from the point of view of *all* the players. Notice that the dilemma is created solely by a lack of information through noncommuni-cation. Such an impact arising from noncommunication is not unique for business problems. Students of group psychology, interpersonal relationships, or politics know it only too well.

Both the preceding games prohibited communication and side-payments, i.e., payments from one player to another. To see the way in which these factors alter the outcome let us solve a third game, initially with no com-munication, no side-payments, and no collusion and then re-solve it allowing communication, side-payments, and collusion. We will be able to see very clearly how the choice of marketing, pricing, or output policies is altered by the firms' collusion.

Table 13.3 shows the basic decisions available and the resulting payoffs. Playing independently and using the minimax rule, A chooses S_1^A, B chooses S_3^B and the payoffs are \$7 million for A and \$17 million for B. Both will do better if they can collude since the largest total profit for the two firms results from using strategies S_2^A and S_3^B. B would choose S_3^B in any case, but A will require some inducement to move to S_2^A, since playing S_1^A against S_3^B gives

Table 13.3   Another Example of Strategy and Payoff
in a Two-Person, Non-Zero-Sum Game

		Firm A		
		S_1^A	S_2^A	
	S_1^B	A B (6, 10)	(10, −1)	−1 B's
Firm B	S_2^B	(9, −3)	(4, 3)	−3 minimum payoffs
	S_3^B	(7, 17)	(5, 30)	17
		6	4	
		A's minimum payoffs		

Table 13.4   Alternative Collusive Shares

FIRM A	FIRM B
8	27
9	26
10	25
11	24
12	23
13	22
14	21
15	20
16	19
17	18

A $7 million as opposed to $5 million. Table 13.4 shows all the possible shares in the $35 million total profits which would make it worthwhile for both players to enter a collusive agreement. Both communication between the players and a side-payment would be necessary to arrive at a viable agreement.

Games with Mixed Strategies

In the previous discussion a firm played one and only one strategy throughout the game. In practice, this policy might well enable competitors to seize the advantage. A firm (or any game player) might do better by using mixed strategies, just as in a football game it is not too wise for the quarterback to call a pass play on every down.

Suppose two firms are confronted by the strategy choices and payoffs for a zero-sum game shown in Table 13.5. The entries represent the payoffs to firm A. Firm B will have to pay the negatives of these entries. Obviously

Table 13.5 Payoffs in a Two-Person, Zero-Sum Game

	S_1^B	S_2^B
S_1^A	$15,000	$5,000
S_2^A	$10,000	$20,000

firm A wishes to maximize these payments while firm B wishes to minimize them.

According to the minimax rule firm A secures the highest minimum payoff by playing S_2^A, while firm B secures the lowest maximum payoff by playing S_1^B. Thus A receives $10,000, which B pays.

Suppose that instead of committing itself to one strategy, A considers playing S_1^A with probability α and S_2^A with probability $(1 - \alpha)$, $0 \leq \alpha \leq 1$. Notice that $\alpha = 1$ is equivalent to the result achieved by applying the minimax rule. Firm B can also randomize its choices by playing S_1^B with probability β and S_2^B with probability $(1 - \beta)$, $0 \leq \beta \leq 1$. The expected value of the payoff to A is

$$V_A = \alpha\beta15{,}000 + \alpha(1 - \beta)5{,}000 + (1 - \alpha)\beta10{,}000$$
$$+ (1 - \alpha)(1 - \beta)20{,}000 \tag{13.8}$$

and the value of the payoff to B is

$$V_B = -V_A \tag{13.9}$$

The optimal rule of play for A can be found by maximizing Equation (13.8) with respect to α, which leads to the condition

$$\frac{\partial V_A}{\partial \alpha} = \beta15{,}000 + (1 - \beta)5{,}000 - \beta10{,}000$$
$$- (1 - \beta)20{,}000 = 0 \tag{13.10}$$

which implies

$$\beta = \frac{20{,}000 - 5{,}000}{15{,}000 - 15{,}000 - 5{,}000 + 20{,}000} = 0.75 \tag{13.11}$$

Similarly, minimization of V_B with respect to β implies

$$\alpha = \frac{20{,}000 - 10{,}000}{15{,}000 - 15{,}000 - 5{,}000 + 20{,}000} = 0.50 \tag{13.12}$$

Using these values for α and β it is clear that A can improve the expected value of his gains from $10,000 (achieved with certainty) to

$$V_A = (.5)(.75)15{,}000 + (.5)(.25)(5{,}000)$$
$$+ (.5)(.75)(10{,}000) + (.5)(.25)20{,}000 = \$12{,}500 \tag{13.13}$$

Cartels and Price Leadership

A *cartel* is essentially a collusive arrangement in an oligopoly of which *price leadership* is a variant. Because of legal restrictions within the United States, cartels are usually international, since there are no enforceable international restrictions on their use. From time to time cartels have been alleged to exist for coffee, tea, and copper, among others. In a price leadership situation, large firms lead the industry in setting market prices, and the many smaller producers in the industry follow suit. Steel is a good example.

A simplified picture of cartel pricing and output policy is shown in Figure 13.8. Assume that a cartel agreement—explicit or implicit—gives a firm $\alpha\%$ of the market where D represents the total market demand. The firm's own demand schedule is D'_α and its marginal revenue schedule is MR'. Profit maximization within the cartel agreement leads to a price of P' and output Q'. Note, however, that there is an economic incentive to break the cartel agreement. Profit can be increased by cutting price to P'' and expanding output.

Game theory provides a partial explanation for the observed instability of cartels. In a business setting it is rarely possible to use explicit side-payments. A cartel agreement without side-payments is likely to lose its stability as soon as one or more of the participants finds that it can make greater profits

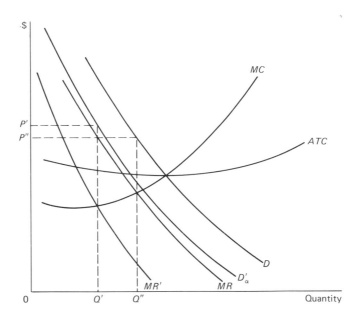

Figure 13.8 Determining Cartel Pricing with Agreed-upon Market Shares

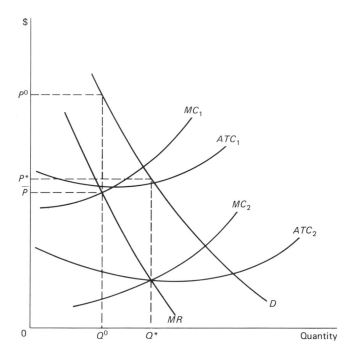

Figure 13.9   Price Leadership by Lowest-Cost Firm

by violating it. Each firm has an economic incentive to make side deals which are unauthorized by the collusive agreement, in order to gain larger market shares for itself.

A firm may achieve price leadership by being able to produce at lower costs than others, or by an explicit or implicit agreement assigning to it the dominant role in price setting. Figure 13.9 illustrates an example of price leadership by the firm with the lowest costs. Assume MC_1 and ATC_1 represent the costs of other firms in an industry while MC_2 and ATC_2 represent the costs for the lowest-cost firm. D and MR represent market demand and marginal revenue. Since the other firms have higher costs, the price which would maximize their profits is P^0. The profit-maximizing price for the lowest-cost firm, on the other hand, is P^*. If all firms are compelled to sell at the same price, the higher-cost firms must use P^* as well. Only the lowest-cost firm, therefore, has a chance to maximize profits.

Nothing explicitly limits the price set by the lowest-cost firm. However, a price below $\bar{P}$ will drive other firms out of the industry or compel them to adopt different technologies. Notice that in market settings like oligopoly in which free entry is impeded the firms remaining in an industry in the long run are not necessarily led to maximize efficiency. Even if the lowest-cost firm's optimal price turned out to be below $\bar{P}$, it might still prefer to charge a higher price, rather than driving its competitors out of business and coming under the scrutiny of the antitrust investigators. Survival of the fittest may work quite well in nature, but in a business setting that includes laws and the watchful eye of tax auditors it may be a fool's operating rule. "Live and let live" may be a better strategy for protecting sustained long-term gains.

While in a lowest-cost price leadership model the other firms in the industry are obliged to follow the leader's price, a dominant-firm price leadership model allows other firms to sell as much as they find desirable at the leader's price. The demand for the leader's output is total market demand (D in Figure 13.10) less what other firms sell. Assume MC_1 represents the marginal cost schedule for the price leader while MC_2 represents the supply schedule formed from the horizontal summation of the marginal cost curves of all other firms. At a price of P' the nonleader firms would supply the whole market quantity Q', and for any price above P' they would consider it profitable to do the same. For prices below P' the demand for the leader's output is found by equating price with MC_2 and subtracting the corresponding quantity from the market quantity demanded at that price. Schedule D' and associated marginal revenue MR' represent demand as seen by the price leader.

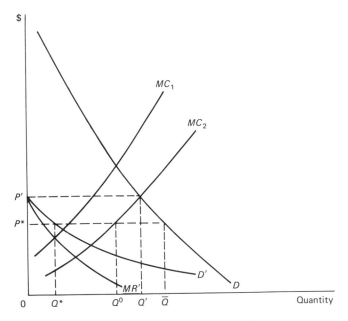

Figure 13.10   Price Leadership by Dominant Firm

Using MR' and MC_1 the leader finds its most profitable price to be P^*. At this price, the other firms sell a total of Q^0, while the price leader sells Q^*. As in the lowest-cost price leadership model, the leader can generally maximize profits based on a derived demand schedule, while followers can only maximize their profits within the limits set by the leader's price policy.

Empirical Evidence on Price Leadership and the Administered Price Thesis

Now that we have developed theoretical descriptions of two forms of price leadership we shall turn to market data to discover the extent to which price leadership appears to prevail.

Consider the automobile price change example given at the beginning of the chapter.[1] On Tuesday, September 30, 1967, Ford announced price increases averaging $105–$113 on new models. On Wednesday, October 1, Chrysler announced increases of $92. Later the same day General Motors announced price increases averaging only $56. A short while afterwards Ford revised its price increases to an average of $70 while Chrysler revised its price to an average of $68. The 1967 model prices are not an isolated exception. Table 13.6 shows the end result of the price juggling on 1968 models. The marked conformity in the price changes leaves little room for doubt about the pressure exerted by competitors' policies.

Table 13.6 Automobile Average Price Changes for 1968 Models

ANNOUNCEMENT DATE	FIRM	AVERAGE PRICE CHANGE	AVERAGE PERCENTAGE CHANGE
September 16	Chrysler (original price)	+$84	2.9%
September 23	GM	+49	1.6
September 25	Ford	+47	1.6
September 26	Chrysler (revised)	+52	1.8
September 27	AMC	+37	1.5

SOURCE: *The Automobile Industry: A Case Study in Competition*, General Motors Corporation (October, 1968).

[1] Adapted from "GM Sets Off Rollbacks in Prices," *Business Week*, October 1, 1966, and *The Automobile Industry: A Case Study of Competition* by General Motors Corporation (October, 1968).

Table 13.7 An Illustration of Price Leadership in Cigarette Pricing

| | Successful Leads | | Unsuccessful Leads | |
	UP	DOWN	UP	DOWN
1924–1939				
Reynolds Tobacco	4	1	0	0
American Tobacco	0	2	0	0
Ligget & Myers	0	0	0	0
1940–1950				
Reynolds Tobacco	2	0	0	0
American Tobacco	2	0	1	0
Ligget & Myers	0	0	2	0

SOURCE: W. H. Nicholls, *Price Policy in the Cigarette Industry*, 1951.

Among several large firms, there may be more than one price leader. Table 13.7 gives the history of price leadership in the cigarette industry. "Successful leads" are ones in which competitors followed suit.

Famous price-fixing scandals have included conspiracies among manufacturers of electrical equipment and of cement, and the price roll-back fight between President Kennedy and U.S. Steel. These events reflect the tendency of firms within an industry to avoid price competition with each other. The prevalence of large amounts of advertising that omit any mention of price provides added evidence that firms prefer to compete along other dimensions. Where price competition is ruled out by regulation as in the case of commercial airlines, the firms affected have instituted a multiplicity of nonprice competition devices, including frequency of flights, amount and type of liquor, games in flight, and choice of meals.

The ability of a single price leader or a small group of firms to control prices for a given product has been cited as a major cause of the upward drift of prices over time. The proponents of the *administered price thesis* argue that firms raise their prices not only when demand is expanding, but also when it subsequently contracts. They note that firms frequently set prices on a *cost-plus basis*; in other words, the selling price provides a specified margin over cost at the anticipated sales volume. During periods of demand expansion, profits come easily and management tends to let "fat" creep into the production process. This results in increased average costs which are translated into increased prices.

When demand contracts, some of the "fat" may be trimmed. However, prices will now rise for a different reason. Markets served by only a small number of firms often employ large-scale technologies with decreasing average costs for higher output. A contraction of output causes increases in average costs and corresponding increases in prices.

The empirical evidence is inconclusive. A sequence of contractions and expansions between 1959 and 1970 suggests that about one-half to two-thirds of the price changes observed in concentrated industries conform to the administered price thesis. The size of the samples is typically too small to give unambiguous answers. Further work in this area may provide guidelines for evaluating policies designed to control inflation.

Industrial Concentration, Barriers to Entry, and Profits

In economics it is often important to determine how large any one firm or group is relative to the market. This is most easily accomplished by using a *measure of concentration*. The most popular concentration index compares the ratio of sales for individual firms or groups of firms to total sales over an industry or other similar grouping. Table 13.8 shows the degree of industrial concentration in the United States, measured in terms of sales and total assets.

Individual industries, however, may exhibit a much higher degree of concentration. Table 13.9 provides some examples illustrating the wide variation from one industry to another. The trend toward concentration appears to have declined since World War II. The rapid merger activity of the late 19th and early 20th century has been replaced by diversification, producing the modern conglomerates. It is not clear whether this stabilization of concentration has been caused by antitrust regulation, increased gains resulting from diversification of financial risk, or other influences.

The barriers to entry which create and sustain oligopolies can take the form of product differentiation, large capital requirements to set up production, absolute cost advantages stemming from special patent or resource ownership, or large-scale techniques required in order to achieve production costs low enough to compete with existing firms. Table 13.10 illustrates profit rates obtained by limiting entry.

Table 13.8 Industrial Concentration Measures for All of United States in 1964

NUMBER OF CORPORATIONS	SALES	PERCENTAGE OF TOTAL SALES	TOTAL ASSETS (MILLIONS $)	PERCENTAGE OF TOTAL ASSETS
100 Largest	$172.6	36.1%	$150.3	43.8%
200 Largest	214.8	44.9	183.6	53.5
500 Largest	266.5	55.7	224.7	65.5
All Corporations	478.1	100.0	342.9	100.0

SOURCE: *Statistical Abstract of the U.S.*

Table 13.9   Sales Concentration Ratios for Selected U.S. Industries 1963

INDUSTRY	4-FIRM RATIO[a]	8-FIRM RATIO[a]
Automobiles	99%	100%
Flat glass	94	99
Cigarettes	80	100
Soaps and detergents	72	80
Motors and generators	50	59
Textile machinery	35	52
Shoes	25	32
Newspapers	15	22
Bottled and canned soft drinks	12	17

SOURCE: F. M. Scherer, *Industrial Market Structure and Economic Performance.*
Rand McNally, 1970.
[a]Ratio of sales for 4 (or 8) largest firms to total industry sales.

Table 13.10   Average Profit Rates on Stockholders' Equity 1950–1960

	VERY HIGH BARRIERS	SUBSTANTIAL BARRIERS	MODERATE TO LOW BARRIERS
High concentration	16.4%	11.1%	11.9%
Moderate concentration	—	12.2	8.6

SOURCE: F. M. Scherer, *Industrial Market Structure and Economic Performance.* Rand McNally, 1970.

Uncertain Entry and Strategic Price Policy

The Chamberlin model of oligopoly confines itself to consideration of those firms already existing within an industry. If the barriers to entry are absolute, then the high profit rates produced by cooperation among the firms will not create new entrants, and economic life will be serene. In most markets however, potential entry poses a very real threat. If the existing firms price high enough to maximize current profits, they may be extending an open invitation to enter the industry.

To take into account the influence of the probability of entry on current price and profit rates, we can use a modified view of price and capacity policy formulation known as the *limit pricing model.*[2] The future is divided into two periods: (1) from now until entry occurs and (2) from the point of entry on. If the exact date of entry is known and is independent of current

[2] Extended developments of limit pricing are contained in the D. Baron, M. Kamien and N. Schwartz, and F. Hahn materials cited in the References.

policy choice, the firm maximizes profits in both periods. Typically, however, current choice may influence the date of entry. In that case, instead of maximizing only current profits, the firm maximizes the present value[3] of the stream of future profits. The resulting limit price policy dictates a lower price than would result from maximization of current profits alone. The more risk-averse the firm the lower it will set the current price to inhibit entry.

This lower limit price forestalls the time at which competitors will appear in a riskless model or decreases the probability that entry will occur in an uncertainty model. In either view the basic economic force at work is a trade off of current benefits for long-term gains.

Summary

An oligopoly model fits many economically powerful industries, including automobiles, steel, air transportation, heavy machinery, glass, etc.

The interdependence of decisions in an oligopoly setting was emphasized in the Cournot and Chamberlin models and in the gaming formulation, which also illustrated the influence of communication, information, and the ability to collude on actual market outcomes.

Further work on the theory of oligopoly as a tool for studying competitive struggles between small numbers of powerful firms may provide an improved picture of the interaction of politics and economics in shaping an economy. The empirical evidence on concentration makes the importance of oligopoly markets quite clear. This is particularly true of the administered price thesis, which has a direct bearing on the choice of policies for curbing inflation.

Questions for Study or Class Discussion

1. List at least three measures of the degree of industrial concentration. What aspects of concentration might they mask?
2. Using one or more measures of industrial concentration, analyze data from at least one industry for the last 15 to 25 years. Are there any trends toward concentration? Check your results against trends toward concentration in other industries.
3. Potential entry threats may cause firms to lower their prices. Determine how other aspects of decision making might be affected by the entry threats (e.g., new product plans, introduction of technological change, plant size, etc.).
4. Find empirical data for one or more industries indicating whether price leadership or tacit price agreements exist. You will need data for several firms in each industry over a period of time.
5. List as many elements as you can that might tend to create a barrier to entry. Compare your ideas with some of the studies listed in the References.

[3] The concept of present value is elaborated in Chapter 16.

References

Adelman, M., "The Measurement of Industrial Concentration," *Review of Economics and Statistics*, 33 (November, 1951), 269–296.

———, "Changes in Industrial Concentration," in *Monopoly Power and Economic Performance*, E. Mansfield, ed. W. W. Norton, 1968.

Bain, J., *Barriers to New Competition*. Harvard University Press, 1956.

———, *Industrial Organization*. J. Wiley & Sons, 1968.

———, "Economics of Scale, Concentration, and the Conditions of Entry in Twenty Manufacturing Industries," *American Economic Review*, 44 (March, 1954), 15–39.

Baron, D., "Limit Pricing, Potential Entry, and Barriers to Entry," *American Economic Review*, 63 (September, 1973), 666–674.

Fellner, W., *Competition Among the Few: Oligopoly and Similar Market Structures*. Knopf, 1949.

Hahn, F., "Excess Capacity and Imperfect Competition," *Oxford Economic Papers*, 7 (October, 1955), 229–240.

Hotelling, H., "Stability in Competition," *Economic Journal*, 39 (1929), 41–57.

Kamien, M., and N. Schwartz, "Uncertain Entry and Excess Capacity," *American Economic Review*, 62 (December, 1972), 918–927.

Machlup, F., *The Economics of Sellers' Competition*. The Johns Hopkins Press, 1952.

Mann, H., "Seller Concentration, Barriers to Entry, and Rates of Return in Thirty Industries, 1959–1960," *Review of Economics and Statistics*, 48 (August, 1966), 296–307.

Mansfield, M., *Monopoly Power and Economic Performance*. W. W. Norton, 1968.

Means, G., "The Administered–Price Thesis Reconfirmed," *American Economic Review*, 62 (June, 1972), 292–306.

Scherer, F. M., *Industrial Market Structure and Economic Performance*. Rand McNally, 1971.

Shubik, M., *Strategy and Market Structure*. J. Wiley & Sons, 1959.

Siegel, S., and L. Fouraker, *Bargaining Behavior*. McGraw-Hill, 1963.

Smith, Adam, *The Wealth of Nations*. Random House edition, 1937.

Stigler, G., "Administered Prices and Oligopolistic Inflation," *Journal of Business*, 35 (June, 1962), 1–13.

———, "The Kinky Oligopoly Demand Curve and Rigid Prices," *Journal of Political Economy*, 55 (October, 1947), 432–449.

———, "Monopoly and Oligopoly by Merger," *American Economic Review Proceedings and Papers*, 40 (May, 1950), 23–34.

Sweezy, P., "Demand Under Conditions of Oligopoly," *Journal of Political Economy*, 67 (1939), 568–573.

von Neumann, J., and O. Morgenstern, *Theory of Games and Economic Behavior*. Princeton University Press, 1944.

Weston, J. F., S. Lustgarten, and N. Grottke, "The Administered–Price Thesis Denied: Note," *American Economic Review*, 64 (March, 1974), 232–234.

Chapter 14   Markets for Inputs to the Productive Process: Perfect Competition

Introduction

Our analysis of input markets will closely parallel the one we applied to output markets. The simple reason is that most commodities which are outputs in one industry will be inputs for another. However, there are two important distinctions. In the analysis of output markets demand schedules were treated as if they were derived solely from individual consumption decisions. In fact, total market demand is usually composed of both demand for consumption and demand for further production. The latter type of demand is referred to as a *derived demand* because the market value of the inputs depends on the goods they can be transformed into. Similarly, we must extend the concept of supply. Not all inputs are produced by some other industry—some may be owned, such as labor services or natural resources. Thus the concept of supply needs to be revised to incorporate preferences of resources owners.

Input market analysis can clarify policy issues, such as the influence of minimum wage legislation on the labor market or of allocation plans for natural resources. Even more important, input prices are the key link in completing the chain of income flow in a market system. Up to this point consumer income has been taken as given. In studying input markets, we can now focus on some of the economic determinants of consumer income. An economic system can be represented by a circular flow. Ownership rights to resources, together with the market price of each resource, determine consumer income. Consumer income, in turn, influences demand; demand influences product prices; product prices influence the amount firms are willing to pay for inputs, which determines their market price, thus completing the circle. Prices for inputs determine, in effect, incomes to individuals. Commodity and input prices determine incomes to firms.

  This chapter deals with input demand and supply and input prices in perfectly competitive markets and the next chapter with imperfect market settings. We shall first develop the concepts of short-run and long-run input demand, followed by a discussion of short-run and long-run input supply.

Short-Run Demand for a Variable Input

The demand for inputs to the productive process depends upon the behavior of individual firms. If firms attempt to make decisions about inputs, outputs, and prices in such a way as to maximize profits, then we can use the profit maximizing behavior as a vehicle for obtaining each firm's derived demand schedule for each input.

  A demand schedule for an input describes the price per unit that a firm is willing to offer for various quantities of the inputs. This price depends on two basic pieces of information: (1) the price of the commodities the input can produce and (2) the available technologies, which set an upper limit on the productivity of each input. As mentioned in the Introduction, the demand schedule for an input is frequently referred to as a *derived demand schedule*. Resources (inputs) do *not* have a value in and of themselves; their market value is *derived* from the value of the goods they can be converted into.

  Table 14.1 provides data from a situation where a firm is using two inputs, capital and labor, which are converted into a single output. The quantity of output attainable from the various combinations of capital and labor is shown in the third column. Since the amount of capital is held constant and only the labor input is being varied, the marginal physical product given

Table 14.1   The Derived Demand for Labor (Output Price = $2)

AMOUNT OF LABOR	AMOUNT OF CAPITAL	OUTPUT PER WEEK	MPP_L	MRP_L	VMP_L
0	3	0	—	—	—
1	3	40	40	$ 80	$ 80
2	3	90	50	$100	$100
3	3	275	175	$350	$350
4	3	380	105	$210	$210
5	3	440	60	$120	$120
6	3	475	35	$ 70	$ 70
7	3	500	25	$ 50	$ 50

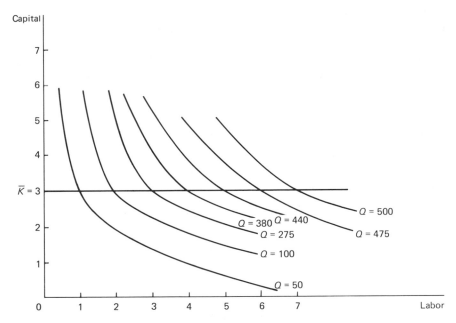

Figure 14.1 Short-Run Production Possibilities with One Variable Input

in the fourth column is the marginal physical product of labor, MPP_L. Figure 14.1 shows the underlying short-run production relationship.

Marginal revenue product

Suppose that a firm is selling in a perfectly competitive output market where it is obtaining \$2 for each unit sold. This means that total revenue is found by simply multiplying output by \$2. To determine optimal quantities of a given input we use an important new concept called the *marginal revenue product*, *MRP*. Marginal revenue product for an input is defined as the change in total revenue associated with a change in the amount of input employed; for labor $MRP_L = \Delta TR/\Delta L$. To compute marginal revenue product we first change the amount of a given input and employ it in the production process to obtain a change in output, and then sell the output on the market. The change in total revenue obtained from each additional unit of input is the marginal revenue product of that unit.

Assuming that the firm can sell an unlimited quantity output for \$2 per unit, marginal revenue product can be computed simply. Since selling more output does *not* mean that the firm has to lower selling price, the marginal revenue product for labor can be found by multiplying marginal physical product by market price.[1] When the first unit of labor is added, output increases by 40. When this increment is sold on the market for $2 per unit this leads to a marginal revenue product of $80. Hiring the second unit of labor leads to a 50-unit increase in output and when this is sold at a price of $2 total revenue increases by $100. The marginal revenue product of the second unit of labor is thus $100.

If the firm desires to maximize profits, it will be willing to hire more labor, provided that the added revenue it obtains from hiring one more unit is at least as great as the added cost of hiring that unit; in other words, it will hire inputs up to the point where marginal revenue product is equal to the marginal input cost. With a wage rate of $120 per week, the firm in Table 14.1 would certainly be willing to hire the third unit of labor, since that unit would contribute $350 to total revenue, thus increasing profits by $230. Hiring the fourth person leads to a smaller marginal revenue product of $210, but total cost rises by only $120, so profits would still increase by $90. The firm will hire no more than five people, since hiring the sixth would cost $120, but would add only $70 to revenues. In essence, the declining portion of the *MRP* schedule for each input represents its derived demand schedule.

Input demand and the stages of production

Figure 14.2 illustrates the marginal physical product data described in Table 14.1. Notice that like the marginal physical product curve discussed in Chapter 6, this curve rises, reaches a maximum, declines, and may actually become negative. In Chapter 6 we described these short-run phases of the marginal and average physical product curves by the term "stages of production." We can now link this behavior of output to input demand.

The range in which it will be economically feasible for a firm to hire an input, if it is maximizing profits, is always Stage 2. Stage 3 is out of the question, since an increase in employment of the input in that stage leads to a decrease in total output. On the other hand, the firm will be forgoing profits if it confines its hiring to Stage 1. To see why, use the information in Table 14.1.

---

[1] If we let $Q = F(X)$ denote the production function, then marginal revenue product can be represented as the derivative of total revenue with respect to the single variable input, X:

$$MRP_X = \frac{dTR}{dX} = \frac{d}{dX}\left[P \cdot F(X)\right] = P \cdot \frac{dF}{dX} + F(X) \cdot \frac{dP}{dQ} \cdot \frac{dF}{dX} = P\left(1 + \frac{1}{\eta}\right)\frac{dF}{dX}$$

where $\eta = dD/dP \cdot P/D$ is the elasticity of demand and $D(P)$ is the demand function. Since $\eta \to \infty$ in the competitive case and $dF/dX \equiv MPP_X$ one obtains

$$MRP_X = P \cdot MPP_X$$

When there is more than one variable input the same procedure will give

$$MRP_i = P \cdot MPP_i \qquad i = 1, \ldots, n.$$

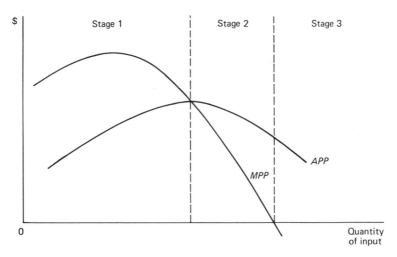

Figure 14.2 Input Productivity and the Stages of Production

In Figure 14.3 the marginal revenue product curve was found by multiplying marginal physical product in Table 14.1 by $2. We know that the firm will hire inputs up to the point where marginal revenue product is equal to the cost of an additional unit of the input, but in Figure 14.3 there are two such points. A level like $\overline{X}$ where the marginal revenue product curve is rising can never represent an optimal level of employment, because a slight increase in employment will increase revenue by more than $120, the cost of an additional unit of input. Increasing employment to the $\overline{X}$ + 1st unit will therefore increase profits. At the employment level X^0, the added revenue from increasing employment is less than the added cost and vice versa for a decrease from X^0.

Marginal cost and marginal physical product

The marginal physical product of an input is directly related to its marginal cost. If the firm is employing only one variable input, the marginal cost of one more unit of output is equal to the price per unit of the input divided by the marginal physical product of the input. For example, if an input costs $30 per unit and one more unit of the input will yield 60 additional units of output (in other words, if the marginal physical product of hiring one more input is 60), then the marginal cost of output is $0.50.

Using $MC =$ Input Price/MPP and recalling that a competitive firm's optimal production rule requires it to produce up to the point where $P = MC$, we can develop a symmetry between profit-maximizing output decisions and

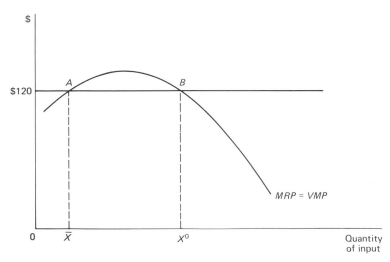

Figure 14.3   Short-Run Derived Demand for One Variable Input

profit-maximizing input decisions. Optimal input decisions use the rule

$$MRP = MIC \qquad (14.1)$$

where MIC stands for marginal input cost. Optimal output decisions involve using the rule

$$MR = MC \qquad (14.2)$$

In perfectly competitive input and output markets MIC and MR are constant and equal to the respective market prices, thus

$$MRP = MIC = P = MR = MC \qquad (14.3)$$

from which

$$P = MC \qquad (14.4)$$

But notice that since

$$MC = P_X/MPP_X \qquad (14.5)$$

where P_X is the price of a unit of input X, we can substitute Equation (14.5) into Equation (14.4) and obtain

$$P = P_X/MPP_X$$

or

$$P \cdot MPP_X = P_X \qquad (14.6)$$

This illustrates that the optimal input hiring rule (14.6) can be derived from the profit-maximizing output rule (14.4) and vice versa.

The above discussion can readily be extended to obtain the short-run derived demand functions for several variable inputs.

Value of the marginal product

Table 14.1 contains an additional piece of information—the *value of the marginal product*. The value of a marginal product is defined as the marginal physical product times the price at which it is sold. In Table 14.1 this turns out to be identical with the marginal revenue product since the output price is always $2 per unit regardless of how much we sell. However, this is a special case. A more general relationship will be developed in the next chapter.

Long-Run Input Demand

Although in the short run changes in the relative cost of variable inputs can lead to a change in the extent of their short-run use, the firm cannot respond to changes in the relative cost of fixed inputs. In the short run, of course, at least one input must be held to a fixed level. As soon as we allow *all* inputs to vary we can develop the *long-run input demand*.

Figure 14.4 illustrates a set of isoquants and a solution to the least-cost input mix problem at point A given a particular set of relative prices for the inputs X_1 and X_2. Successive reductions of the price of input X_1 while maintaining the same level of total expenditures can be represented by the sequence of isocost curves fanning out from the X_2 axis. This leads to a succession of

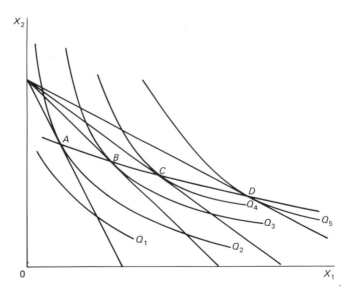

Figure 14.4   Deriving Long-Run Input Demand

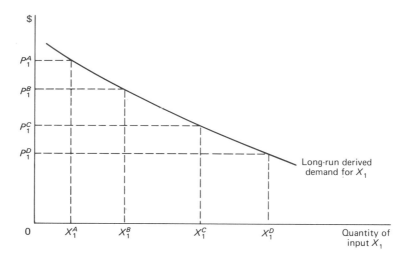

Figure 14.5   The Long-Run Derived Demand for an Input

least-cost input choices at points B, C, and D. The influence of the changing input price has two separate parts—a substitution effect and an output effect. The method of separating these influences is the same as that used in Chapter 4 for the analysis of substitution and income effects. If X_2 is a fixed input, any substitution effect between X_1 and X_2 is blocked although an output effect can occur along a line parallel to the X_1 axis.

The data in Figure 14.4 can be used to obtain the long-run demand schedule for input X_1. At each input price for X_1, P_1^A, P_1^B, etc., we can see how much X_1 will be chosen. This data is plotted in Figure 14.5. The resulting curve is the derived demand schedule for X_1, given the price of input X_2 and the available techniques of production. When the relative price of X_1 decreases the firm will increase the quantity it uses relative to X_2; furthermore, the decrease in price has decreased marginal cost, so that it is profitable for the firm to expand output. These two results are the input substitution and output effects of a change in input price.

The relationship between short-run marginal cost and short-run profit-maximizing decision rules for output and input choice carries over to the long run. The firm whose production function uses n inputs could expand production by increasing any one of the n possible inputs. Dividing the marginal physical product for each input into the price of hiring one more unit of that input, we can calculate the marginal cost of an additional unit of output resulting from varying any particular input. From the alternative input mixes, the firm will choose the mix which keeps the marginal cost of producing that extra unit to a minimum, i.e., the one that follows the expansion path shown in Chapter 6.

Short-Run and Long-Run Input Demand Elasticity

The elasticity of input demand depends on (1) the number and quantity of substitutes available, (2) the degree to which one input may be substituted for another in production, (3) the number of alternative uses in which an input may be employed and (4) the length of time permitted for adjustment. In the short run, the first three influences dominate. Over a longer period of time demand is likely to be more elastic since firms may take advantage of input price declines by adjusting their production methods. Short-run input price increases may not produce immediate adjustments, but may spur research into alternatives.

Short-Run and Long-Run Input Supply

The supply side of the market of a commodity used as an input is not qualitatively different from the supply of any other commodity, with the exception of labor and other owned resources. For inputs produced in other industries, the conditions of supply faced by an industry in a competitive market correspond to the short-run and long-run market supply conditions analyzed in Chapter 7. Although it might seem that supply to a competitive industry would be perfectly elastic, this is not necessarily so. Long-run supply to a given industry could take place under increasing, constant, or decreasing cost conditions.

The development of a supply concept when individual preferences are added parallels the discussion of preference and choice in Chapter 2. Let us use the supply of labor as an example.

Assume an individual has a set of indifference curves between leisure (X_1) and all other goods as illustrated in Figure 14.6 and is initially at an equilibrium point such as A. The slope of the individual's budget constraint is $-W/P_2$, where W is the wage rate (i.e., the opportunity cost of leisure) and P_2 is the price of all other goods. We will assume that income is derived solely from working. If the time available for working is B, income is $W(B - X_1)$. Each hour of leisure reduces income by W. The maximum income is WB (when $X_1 = 0$) and the maximum number of units of X_2 that the individual can consume is WB/P_2 (Figure 14.6).

If the wage rate undergoes successive increases, the individual will be subject to new budget constraints that might resemble the ones in Figure 14.7. In each case we can observe the way in which the individual changes his/her choice. The information in Figure 14.7 can be translated into a schedule indicating the individual's supply schedule for work. As the wage rate, i.e., the price of leisure, increases there will be successive decreases in the amount of leisure. Decreases in the amount of leisure consumed are equivalent to

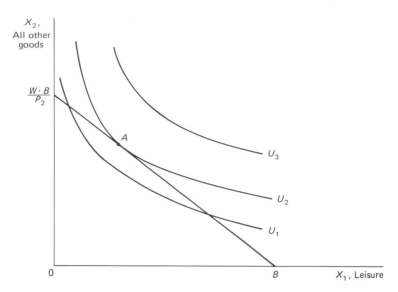

Figure 14.6   Choice Between Leisure and Other Consumption Goods

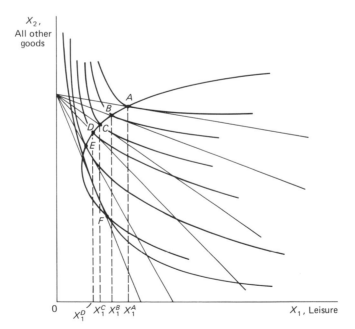

Figure 14.7   Changing Wage Rates and Changing
Leisure Choice

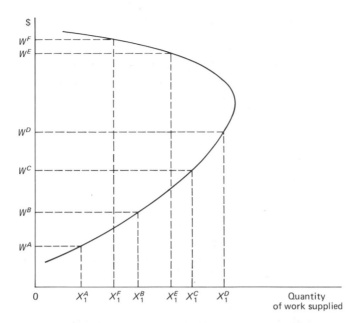

Figure 14.8   Derived Individual Supply Schedule for Labor

increases in the amount of work. At wage rates W^A, W^B, and W^C we can plot the amount an individual will work (Figure 14.8). The supply schedule of any owned input can be built up in the same way by constructing indifference curves based on the resource owner's desire to realize income now or to continue to hold the resources. Holding a resource such as timber, oil, or coal is essentially a decision to forgo current income for future income.

It is quite possible that continued increases in the price of an input, in particular the wage rate, may not continue indefinitely to produce increases in the amount offered. In fact, this can lead to a paradoxical situation known as the *backward bending supply curve* for an input. A backward bending supply curve for labor would indicate that as wages continue to rise the worker may eventually earn a sufficiently high income so that he or she will prefer to take the benefit of higher wage rates in the form of more leisure; thus at a higher wage the worker will actually work *less*! Figure 14.8 illustrates this possibility.

The market supply schedule is obtained by summing the amount supplied at each price over all suppliers.[2]

---

[2] Simple direct summation is, of course, valid only when the various suppliers act independently of each other. See the footnotes to Chapter 3 for modifications in cases of interdependent preferences.

Short-Run and Long-Run Input Supply Elasticity

Input supply, like input demand, shows different tendencies in the short run and in the long run. The elasticity of input supply will depend on: (1) the length of time needed to produce the input, (2) the technology and cost conditions under which the input is produced, and (3) the preferences of resource owners. In general, the longer the period permitted for adjustment, the more elastic supply becomes.

Equilibrium and Disequilibrium in Input Markets

In a perfectly competitive riskless market setting, input and output prices adjust until they produce an equilibrium where there are sufficient goods for any consumer willing to pay the going market price, and where no firm sells more or less than it finds profitable. Perfect competition in riskless input markets leads to analogous equilibrium conditions.

A perfectly competitive input market may occur in practice for certain natural resources or agricultural products where changes in short-run demand produce substantial price changes. In such a setting, fluctuations in the short-run demand for a commodity *may* cause instability in the employment of an input and consequent volatility in the income received by the input. Unstable product demands may show up as unstable employment and/or unstable incomes. An example of the policy problems arising from labor market adjustment is given in the next chapter.

The presence of uncertainty, particularly when it is caused by imperfect information, again requires a revision of the concept of equilibrium price. As we saw in Chapter 9, a large portion of contemporary research is concerned with the equilibrium distribution of prices, with the focus shifting more and more to the analysis of disequilibrium phenomena rather than concentrating solely on *equilibrium* conditions.

Marginal Productivity and Income Distribution

In this section, we shall show the effect of the marginal revenue product and the conditions for hiring inputs by profit-maximizing firms on the distribution of incomes among owners of resources.

Efficiency conditions for resource use by a firm operating in a perfectly competitive output and input market require extending use up to the point where the marginal revenue product of each input multiplied by the output price is equal to the market price of that input. This can be expressed by the condition

$$P \cdot MPP_i = v_i \qquad i = 1, \ldots, n \tag{14.7}$$

where P is the market price of output, MPP_i is the marginal physical product of input i, and v_i is the market price of input i. If none of input i is employed then the value of one unit of its services, as represented by the left-hand side of Equation (14.7), is less than or equal to its market price, v_i, at a zero level of use.

Every firm operates under a technological constraint given by a production function relating the amount of each input to total output. Extensive attention has been given to a class of production functions referred to as *homogeneous of degree one*. These production functions have the property that the level of output can be expressed as the sum of the quantity of each input times its marginal physical product.

$$Q = \sum_{i=1}^{n} X_i \cdot MPP_i \tag{14.8}$$

Multiplying both sides of Equation (14.8) by output price we obtain

$$PQ = \sum_{i=1}^{n} X_i \cdot P \cdot MPP_i \tag{14.9}$$

but since Equation (14.7) states that $P \cdot MPP_i = v_i$ for all $X_i > 0$, Equation (14.9) can be written

$$PQ = \sum_{i=1}^{n} X_i v_i \tag{14.10}$$

The left-hand side of Equation (14.10) is total revenue for the firm. The quantity of an input hired, X_i, times its market price, v_i, is the total expenditure on input i. The sum which is the right-hand side of Equation (14.10) therefore represents total expenditure, i.e., total cost.

Equation (14.10) states that if a firm has a production function of the form given by Equation (14.8), then hiring each input for an amount equal to its marginal revenue product, $P \cdot MPP_i$, leads to zero economic profits for the firm. This basic result is referred to as the *Product Exhaustion Theorem* because, as Equation (14.10) shows, total revenue is exhausted by total input expenditures. The right-hand side of Equation (14.9) shows the basic determinants of income distribution in a perfectly competitive market system: (1) the amount of each resource an individual owns, (2) the market price of the outputs that can be produced from the owned resources, and (3) the marginal physical product of each resource achievable with existing technologies.

Unemployment, Welfare Payments, and Incentives to Work: Some Problems of Public Policy

Unemployment compensation, welfare payments, a proposal for a negative income tax, and job retraining programs are major economic policy issues

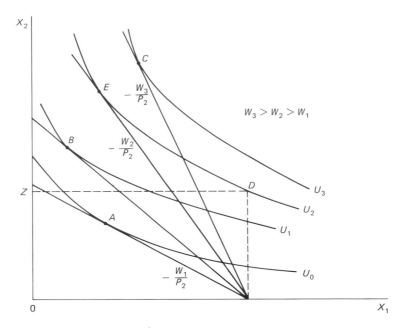

Figure 14.9 Analyzing the Effect of Unemployment Compensation and Inflation on Income-Leisure Choice

relating to labor markets. The first of these issues can be studied with the aid of the income-leisure choice problem illustrated in Figure 14.9, where X_1 represents leisure and X_2 represents all other goods.

Suppose the prevailing level of unemployment compensation gives an individual all other goods in an amount Z. An unemployed individual will therefore reach indifference curve U_2. The individual's budget constraint is based on the wage rate, W, and the price of all other goods, P_2. Maximum income is obtained by working all of the hours available and consuming zero leisure time. An unemployed person consumes as leisure all of the time available. Does this situation create economic incentives to be unemployed? If so, this may contradict a policy goal of providing income stability and social security for the family.

With a wage rate W_1 the best choice is at point A where the budget constraint is tangent to indifference curve U_0. Notice that the level of utility achieved by working is *lower* than the level of utility achieved by taking unemployment compensation. With unemployment compensation, an individual will have all the available leisure time and the best choice will be at point D.

When the wage rate increases the budget constraint becomes steeper. Notice the wage rate may have to rise substantially before an individual will choose to go off unemployment compensation. In Figure 14.9, for example, a wage rate higher than W_2 is required to put an individual on the indifference curve achieved by taking unemployment compensation.

The slope of the budget constraint is the ratio of the money wage, W, to the price of all other goods, P_2; in other words, the slope of the budget constraint represents the real wage. If initially one has a high *real* money wage, say W_3 with prices P_2, a decline in real wages may make it economically optimal to go off employment and into an unemployment status! Since the real wage is the money wage divided by price, if prices go up faster than the money wage rate is going up, then real wages decline. Inflation and changes in nominal wage rates—particularly minimum wage rates—directly influence the type of economic influence created in the market. The description shown in Figure 14.9 sets up the employment versus unemployment problem in strictly economic terms and suppresses the sociological and psychological aspects associated with working. Yet the information contained there does give one some insight into the economic incentives to choose unemployment compensation over employment. Several problems arise from trying to provide an adequate level of unemployment compensation and yet keep total costs down. Generally the value of Z increases over time and this tends to produce a rapidly expanding level of expenditure which is difficult to control. One of the problems is creating incentives to get people off unemployment rolls. Several plans have been suggested. One plan implemented for several years is job training or retraining designed to equip individuals with sufficient skills to raise the wage rate they can command high enough, relative to the level of prices, to make their real wages rise to the point where working yields more utility than unemployment.

A second, more recent proposal is the negative income tax. This arrangement would pay individuals an amount sufficient to bring their "after tax" income up to some specified level. The tax would be zero if income is already at some cut-off level. The cut-off level could change according to a person's marital status and number of dependents. The negative income tax is intended to bridge the gap between working and being unemployed. It is scaled so that as an individual begins earning wages, support from unemployment compensation is gradually phased down to zero, instead of being cut off abruptly. For example, unemployment compensation might be reduced dollar for dollar with increased wage income. However, this scheme offers no incentive to work, since working adds nothing to net income. The individual must feel that working will produce a tangible economic benefit. As long as there is *some* positive remuneration for working, part of the problem of the work disincentive quality of unemployment compensation is mitigated.

Taxing Inputs or Outputs: A Problem in Policy Application

Coping with air and water pollution is an issue which has attracted considerable attention from layperson and politician alike. Both air and water are products which can be directly consumed, but they also represent important inputs to production activity. Taxes, such as excises, have been proposed for curtailing production processes which lead to extensive pollution. We might put a direct tax on inputs that cause pollution to curtail their use, or try to cut back production by taxing the output.[3] These two alternatives have different economic effects.

A tax placed on a particular input creates an incentive to substitute other inputs, if this is technologically feasible. If the tax causes substantial changes in relative input prices, it might even lead to investment in alternative production techniques. On the other hand, as we have seen, when demand is inelastic the use of particular products cannot always be effectively curtailed by taxing particular inputs. Taxing inputs leads to a shift toward use of untaxed substitutes, but taxing an output directly may lead to a worse rather than better situation.

If the production of a particular product introduces undesirable by-products, it appears reasonable that taxing the output itself will cut down

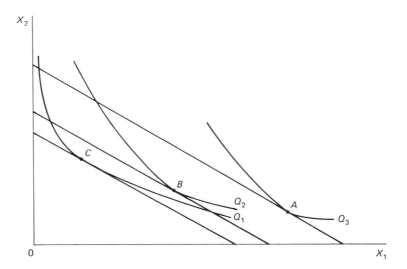

Figure 14.10 An Example of Increased Input Use Associated with Decreased Output

[3] Adapted from C. R. Plott, "Externalities and Corrective Taxes," *Economica*, 33 (February, 1966), 84–87.

the offending by-product. Unfortunately this is not necessarily true. Taxing an output and thus forcing a curtailment of production still leaves a firm free to use the least-cost method of producing its optimal output. This process can be illustrated by the isoquants and isocost curves in Figure 14.10. Notice that when output is reduced from Q_3 to Q_2 or from Q_2 to Q_1 the optimal input mix shifts from A to B and from B to C. Although the optimal amount of X_1 decreases as output declines, the optimal amount of X_2 increases. If X_2 is creating a polluting by-product, we may produce more pollution by taxing the output rather than the offending input. Treating symptoms rather than causes can lead one just as far astray in economic policy as it can in medicine—the patient can even die from the treatment!

Some Empirical Evidence on Returns to Education and Experience

All inputs are not created equal. Mineral samples come in different grades; so do agricultural products; so does labor. Wage rates vary with amount of education, years of experience, and type of employment. Table 14.2 gives an empirical example of wage variation for economists. Observe that there is a 50% difference in annual salary between the highest and lowest salary for a Ph.D. and a 49% difference for holders of a Master's degree, depending on the nature of the employer.

These data might also suggest an investigation of the return available from investing in various levels of education. Salaries eventually earned are not an adequate basis of comparison, because they fail to take into account the opportunity cost of education, which takes the form of income forgone while attending school. The comparison must therefore be based on the present value of the expected lifetime stream of income.[4]

Table 14.2 Annual Wage Variation for Economists by Education and Employment

Employment	*Education*		
	PH.D.	MASTER'S	BACHELOR'S
Educational Institution	$10,000	$ 8,300	Not available
Federal Government	13,000	11,000	$9,300
Business	15,600	12,400	9,600

SOURCE: *Studies of the Structure of Economists' Salaries and Income.* American Economic Association, 1968.

[4] The concepts of present value and rate of return are developed in further detail in Chapter 16.

Table 14.3   Some Estimates of the Return to Graduate Education

YEARS IN GRADUATE SCHOOL	ESTIMATED RATE OF RETURN
2	14.0%
3	10.1
4	7.8
5	6.2
6	5.0

Previous studies suggest that the rate of return on investment in an under-graduate degree is over 10% per year.[5] Table 14.3 gives estimates of the rate of return over cost resulting from various numbers of years in graduate school. These estimates suggest that the return to getting a Master's degree (such as the popular MBA) may be quite high. On the other hand, the typical four-year Ph.D. program appears to yield lower returns than a Bachelor's degree![6]

These comparisons have implications not only for individual educational choice but also for governmental allocation of educational funds. If these figures accurately reflect relative *market* returns and *market* signals are used as a guide to resource allocation, then a declining relative rate of return to higher education might imply a shift in emphasis toward undergraduate education and away from graduate training.

Summary

The analysis of competitive input markets provides a starting point for probing practical problems ranging from fuel or power shortages to un-employment compensation and pollution.

The basic concepts introduced in this chapter are: (1) marginal revenue product and (2) marginal value product. Marginal revenue product is particularly important since it forms the basis for the derived demand for inputs arising from firms seeking to maximize profits. The Product Exhaustion Theorem establishes a relationship between production technologies and income distribution.

However, competitive input markets exist for only a limited range of inputs. The next chapter deals with the behavior of inputs in imperfect markets.

[5] Adapted from D. Bailey and C. Schotta, "Private and Social Rates of Return to Education of Academicians," *American Economic Review*, 62 (March, 1972), 19–31.

[6] Quantification and inclusion of nonmonetary benefits such as social prestige might significantly alter these returns.

Questions for Study or Class Discussion

1. Using the work versus leisure model, show how the effect of overtime premiums can be illustrated. Assume a worker receives a wage rate of W_1 per hour up to L_1 hours of work and $W_2 > W_1$ per hour after that.
2. Using the work versus leisure model, show the effect of levying an income tax of $\alpha\%$. Then analyze the income and substitution effects of a change in the tax rate from α to α'.
3. Write out the derived demand for an input used by a perfectly competitive firm to produce n different outputs.
4. How does technological change affect input prices and use? Since input prices represent incomes, how does technological change affect income distribution to owners of different inputs?
5. The distribution of ownership and the institution of a private property legal concept are important factors in explaining the distribution of nonwage income. Look up the major sources of nonwage income. How large are they? Who owns corporate businesses? What is the concentration of share ownership?

References

Cartter, A., *Theory of Wages and Employment*. R. D. Irwin, 1959.
Hicks, J. R., *The Theory of Wages*. Macmillan, 1932.
——, *Value and Capital*. Oxford University Press, 1946.
Marshall, A., *Principles of Economics*. Macmillan, 1920.

Chapter 15   Markets for Inputs to the Productive Process: Imperfect Competition

Introduction

Common causes of imperfections in input markets include the presence of labor unions, a less than perfectly elastic demand for products, and discrimination on either the demand or supply side. The economic motives for price discrimination are much the same as in a monopoly setting. Discrimination permits employers to reduce costs and input suppliers to increase revenues. Price discrimination in labor markets is the economic issue at the heart of the current "equal pay for equal work" movement on the part of women, blacks, and other minority groups.

Organized labor includes not only such familiar unions as the United Auto Workers and United Steel Workers, but also doctors belonging to the AMA, lawyers belonging to a bar association, and teachers belonging to various collective bargaining groups. In each case, organization prevents the supply side of the labor market from being a perfectly competitive one. Individuals do not negotiate separately with employers to determine wages, nor are wages set solely by demand and supply. In addition, employment in monopolies, oligopolies, or monopolistically competitive industries far exceeds employment in perfectly competitive industries.

For all these reasons, the economic forces at work in imperfectly competitive input markets are of substantial importance.

Derived Demand for a Single Variable Input

We shall first consider the demand side of an imperfect input market. When we studied the behavior of marginal physical product and total revenue for a firm in Chapter 14, we found that the derived demand for an input was represented by the decreasing segment of its marginal revenue product schedule. In the case where the firm is selling in a perfectly competitive market at a constant output price, marginal revenue product is marginal physical product times product price and is equal to value of the marginal product; $P \cdot MPP = MRP = VMP$.

When a firm is not facing a perfectly elastic demand, marginal revenue product is usually less than the value of the marginal product, because the firm must lower prices in order to sell more output. Marginal revenue product is given by

$$MRP_X = \frac{\Delta TR}{\Delta X} = \frac{\Delta(P \cdot F(X))}{\Delta X} = P \cdot \frac{\Delta F(X)}{\Delta X}$$

$$+ F(X) \cdot \frac{\Delta P}{\Delta F} \cdot \frac{\Delta F(X)}{\Delta X} \tag{15.1}$$

where X represents the variable input and $F(X)$ is the production function. Since $\Delta F(X)/\Delta X = MPP_X$, we can rewrite Equation (15.1) as

$$MRP_X = MPP_X\left(P + F(X) \cdot \frac{\Delta P}{\Delta F}\right) \tag{15.2}$$

Using the expression $MR = P(1 + 1/\eta)$, Equation (15.2) becomes

$$MRP_X = MPP_X \cdot MR \tag{15.3}$$

Marginal revenue product depends on the change in total revenue and in this situation the only way to sell added output is to lower prices.

The numerical example in Table 15.1 illustrates the influence of the product market in which a firm sells. Column 4 is the price that the firm must accept in order to sell the various levels of output shown in column 3. The value of marginal product, which is equal to market price times marginal physical product, is shown in the last column. This is not the same as marginal revenue product. The total revenues for each input combination are $175, $250, $366, etc. The marginal revenue product of labor is the change in total revenue divided by the number of units of labor added. Column 7 gives the *MRP*.

Notice that this confirms our earlier statement that in an imperfect setting as a general rule the marginal revenue product is always equal to or less than the value of the marginal product. *MRP* is the same as *VMP* only when unlimited quantities can be sold at the same market price. If the firm has to lower price in order to sell more, then the added revenue it gets from producing more output is not in general as large as if it could keep price the same. Instead of having marginal revenue product equal to marginal physical product times output price, we have a new relationship where marginal revenue product is equal to marginal physical product times marginal revenue,

Table 15.1   Derived Demand for Labor with an Imperfect Output Market

AMOUNT OF LABOR	AMOUNT OF CAPITAL	OUTPUT PER WEEK	SELLING PRICE	TOTAL REVENUE	MPP	MRP	VMP
1	3	50	3.50	$175	—	—	—
2	3	100	2.50	250	50	$75	$125.00
3	3	200	1.83	366	100	116	183.00
4	3	380	1.28	486	180	120	230.40
5	3	440	1.22	537	60	51	73.20
6	3	475	1.20	570	35	33	42.00
7	3	500	1.18	590	25	20	29.50

$MRP = MR \cdot MPP$.[1] Notice that when demand is perfectly elastic, price and marginal revenue are the same, so that this new expression for marginal revenue product returns to the one developed in Chapter 14.

Comparing the data in Table 15.1 to those in Table 14.1, we can see how the demand for labor and the resulting level of employment in an imperfect market differs from the case where the firm faced a perfectly elastic output demand. At a wage rate of $120 per week the marginal revenue product for labor indicates four men should be hired rather than five as in Table 14.1.

A similar analysis applies to other inputs in an imperfect setting.

Derived Demand with Several Variable Inputs

Table 15.2 provides a numerical example of production and input demand where two inputs X_1 and X_2 are involved. The basic concepts developed in the previous section for a single input apply directly to settings involving

[1] This result can be derived formally by considering a situation in which a firm produces a single output, Q, and uses a single variable input, X. Total revenue, TR, can be written $TR = PQ$ where $P = D(Q)$ is the inverse demand relationship and $Q = F(X)$ is the firm's production function. Marginal revenue product is

$$\frac{dTR}{dX} = P \cdot \frac{dF}{dX} + Q \cdot \frac{dP}{dQ} \cdot \frac{dF}{dX} = P\left(1 + \frac{Q}{P} \cdot \frac{dP}{dQ}\right) \cdot \frac{dF}{dX}$$

Since

$$P\left(1 + \frac{Q}{P}\frac{dP}{dQ}\right) = P\left(1 + \frac{1}{\eta}\right) = MR$$

and $MPP_X = dF/dX$, dTR/dX reduces to

$$MRP_X = \frac{dTR}{dX} = MR \cdot MPP_X$$

If there is only one variable input and the demand relationship is constant over time, then this derivation yields the long-run derived demand schedule for X. If multiple inputs are used, but only X is varied, then the derivation yields a short-run derived demand for X. In the discussion above simply replace $Q = F(X)$ by $Q = F(X_1, X_2, \ldots, X_n)$, then

$$MRP_{X_i} = \frac{\partial TR}{\partial X_i} = P \cdot \frac{\partial F}{\partial X_i} + Q \frac{dP}{dQ} \cdot \frac{\partial F}{\partial X_i} = MR \cdot MPP_{X_i}$$

with some (or none) of the inputs held constant to obtain the short-run (long-run) derived demand schedules.

two or more inputs. The firm's derived demand schedule (in other words, its marginal revenue product curve) can be readily found by using the formula $MRP = MR \cdot MPP_i$.[2] The last two columns of Table 15.2 show the results of this calculation. With input prices $P_1 = \$84$ and $P_2 = \$142$, the firm will find it profitable to expand production to 400 units of output by hiring 15 units of X_1 and 27 units of X_2.

If all inputs are variable and product demand is constant over time, the resulting derived demand functions represent long-run influences. If at least one input is constant, the resulting derived demand functions represent short-run influences.

Monopsony

If an input market is perfectly competitive, then a firm can purchase as much of any input as it wants at a given price, at least in the short run.[3] It is more realistic, however, to suppose that the firm must pay a higher price per unit as it purchases more of an input. Table 15.3 describes this situation.

Table 15.3 illustrates the quantities of an input a firm can purchase and the various prices that it would have to bid to obtain them. Total expenditure for various levels of input is given in column 3. The firm has to decide how much of the input to employ using the marginal revenue product data already available. We shall assume that the firm is precluded from using discrimination in its purchasing, that is, each time it hires more of an input, it pays more per unit not only for the additional units but for all the units it is hiring. This means that the relevant figure is not the average cost per unit given in column 2, but rather the marginal cost given in column 4. This added cost is sometimes referred to as *marginal expenditure* or *marginal outlay*.

Table 15.2   Derived Demand for Two Inputs with an Imperfect Output Market

UNITS OF INPUT X_1	UNITS OF INPUT X_2	TOTAL OUTPUT	OUTPUT SELLING PRICE	TOTAL REVENUE	MARGINAL REVENUE	MPP_1^a	MPP_2^a	MRP_1	MRP_2
5	15	100	$172.85	$17,285	$11.15	20	35	$223.00	$390.25
8	19	200	91.13	18,226	9.41	18	30	169.38	282.30
10	22	300	63.17	18,951	7.25	16	27	115.84	195.48
15	27	400	49.00	19,600	6.49	13	22	84.37	142.78
25	30	500	40.00	20,000	4.00	10	19	40.00	76.00

[a] Assume these are known from an analysis of the related production function. If only one input at a time had been varied, they could have been calculated from the data in the first three columns.

[2] Long-run supply schedules include the same type of cost considerations mentioned in Chapter 14 as well as elements reflecting imperfect aspects.
    [3] This statement assumes that *all* units of an input must be paid the *same* per unit price, i.e., no discriminatory purchasing is permitted.

Table 15.3   Rising Supply Price and Marginal Input Cost

QUANTITY SUPPLIED	PRICE	TOTAL EXPENDITURE	MARGINAL EXPENDITURE
150	$ 2	$ 300	—
190	4	760	$11.50 = $460/40
220	6	1,320	18.67 = $560/30
235	8	1,880	37.33 = $560/15
245	10	2,450	57.00 = $570/10

Marginal expenditure is the change in total expenditure divided by the change in the number of units hired. To find the marginal cost of hiring an added unit of input when moving from 150 units to 190 units in Table 15.3 we have to divide the difference in total expenditure, $460, by the number of additional units acquired, 40. The marginal expenditure for each additional unit is thus $460/40 = $11.50. Notice that this is substantially greater than the average cost of $4. When the firm expands from 190 units of input to 220 units, it has to spend $1,320, representing an increase of $560 for 30 additional units. Marginal expenditure is $560/30 = $18.67. There is thus an even greater discrepancy between marginal expenditure and average input price. The supply schedule given in columns 1 and 2 of Table 15.3 and the marginal expenditure at each input level is graphed in Figure 15.1. Schedule D represents the firm's demand schedule for the input, or the marginal revenue product of the input. What decision will a firm make about employment and input price when confronted with this information?

If the firm takes into account the fact that its own actions influence input price, then the relevant schedule for the firm to use is not the supply schedule, but rather the marginal expenditure schedule. Profit maximizing dictates extending input acquisition up to the point where the marginal expenditure is just equal to marginal revenue product. Optimal employment will be E^*, which is generally less than the purely competitive level E^0. The price per unit of E^* units is P^*. Thus the firm arrives at a level of employment below what would be achieved in a purely competitive market and at a lower market price for the input.

The foregoing model of input purchase behavior takes place in a setting called *monopsony*. Monopsony is defined by the presence of a single buyer, in contrast to monopoly with its single seller. Although less prevalent today, monopsony still occurs in rural areas where there is a single saw mill in a town, in timber country where a single logging operation provides the only employment opportunity or where a single coal mining firm dominates an entire region.

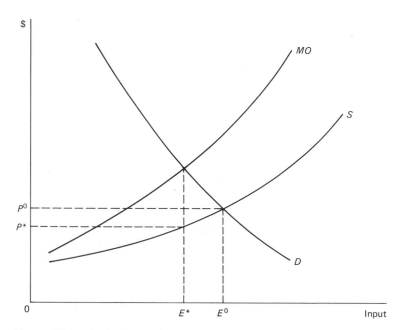

Figure 15.1 Analyzing the Impact of Rising Marginal Input Cost

The Role of Unions

Labor unions certainly have an impetus for developing in a situation of monopsony. However, even without monopsony present, the economic and/or sociological incentives that bring unions into existence arise from the fact that labor has certain peculiarities associated with it that are not generally true of other resources. For example, labor skills tend to become *job specific*, that is, skills which substantially narrow the range of alternative employments. In fact, high salaries are often based on a high degree of technical proficiency in very specific tasks. In addition, labor may be *immobile*. This immobility may be geographical, depending on the location of different industries, or sociological. Families, friends, and other social and psychological factors build rigidities into labor that are not necessarily associated with other inputs. When labor or other inputs are immobile, firms frequently will enjoy a degree of monopsony power, permitting partial control of rates of remuneration, working conditions, and fringe benefits in the short run.

The power of labor unions is based on the threat of bringing the employer's business to a standstill. As we saw earlier in studying oligopoly, threat potential is an important element in gaming situations. Bringing a union into a bargaining picture results in a gaming situation—the management–union game. The extreme situation with a single union acting as the supplier and a single bargaining agent representing the employers is referred to as a *bilateral monopoly* situation. Negotiations between the United Auto Workers Union and the four major United States automobile makers are an example of bilateral monopoly, although in practice negotiations are carried on with one firm at a time.

Union members frequently contribute to a union strike fund which provides supplemental unemployment compensation. Without these added funds, a strike might not be economically viable for the employee because the alternative to a wage of perhaps $175 per week might be unemployment compensation of only $80 per week. Such a prospect provides quite an incentive not to strike! The larger the union's strike fund the more credible the threat of a strike becomes. If a firm and a labor union are negotiating over a new contract that would increase the firm's cost by $30 million a year and if shutting down the plant would cost the firm $1.5 million a day in lost profits, a strike fund covering twenty days out of work would probably force the firm to agree to the $30 million increase in cost. The opportunity cost of a strike is the lost profit, and an astute management will not allow a strike to continue more than twenty days. Agreeing to a $30 million increase in cost may be preferable (from the point of view of management, not of the consumer) to shutting down for twenty-one days and losing $31.5 million in profits.

Through collective bargaining, unions provide employees with a means of protecting their real wage, for example, by negotiating cost of living adjustments which tie wage increases to increases in consumer prices. Another possibility, and one easily overlooked, is the advantage that unions have to perform a tax planning service for employees such as deferred income through retirement plans, typically unavailable to a single individual. Fringe benefits such as annuity plans and medical insurance protect an individual's income well beyond the period of actual employment.

Labor unions influence wage rates in another way by controlling the supply of specific types of labor. Unions cannot effectively control the demand for the products that gives rise to the derived demand for labor, but they can have an effect on supply conditions. The supply of doctors is controlled by the American Medical Association (AMA) through its recognition of universities and hospitals for training doctors and by licensing requirements. Craft unions require apprenticeships and journeymanships prior to arrival at mastercraftsmen status, thereby controlling the number of skilled workers in each category. If labor contracts specify the employment of union craftsmen and the demand for their services grows faster than the supply, equilibrium wage rates for union members are bound to increase.

Although unions may increase the incomes of particular labor groups, they do not necessarily increase the income of labor in the economy as a whole, and the gains they achieve may be limited to the short run. The reason is, for a period of time, restricting the supply of labor may cause an increase in equilibrium wage rates, but if the equilibrium price of capital goods or other inputs does not rise at least as fast, labor will become relatively more expensive. This sets up an economic incentive to substitute capital or other inputs for labor—to innovate in ways aimed at reducing relatively costly inputs. Unions, therefore, have a long history of fighting the introduction of new types of technology.

It is natural to ask whether unions actually cause increased wages. This is not an easy question. Ideally we would like to compare incomes and employment in the same setting with and without the presence of a union. In practice we must be content with comparisons of union and nonunion settings which are not strictly identical. Recent studies have suggested that union wages are from 5 to 15% higher than nonunion wages.[4]

Labor Market Adjustments: An Example Drawn from the Supply of Teachers

Within the market period the quantity supplied of a particular input is fixed in amount. For example, suppose the supply of teachers at a particular point in time is $\overline{X}$ in Figure 15.2. The time required to produce new teachers is so long that supply is quite inelastic in the short run. In a perfectly competitive market setting the marginal revenue product of teachers would be the sole determinant of short-run income.

In recent years the demand for teachers has remained relatively stable while supply has expanded, let us say from $\overline{X}$ to $\overline{\overline{X}}$. In a perfectly competitive market, the increase in supply would cause a short-run income to decrease from M_1 to M_2. Such a decline in short-run income is ordinarily a deterrent to entry into the teaching profession and may encourage some teachers to leave it.

A perfectly competitive input market is subject to the same adjustment processes studied in Chapter 9. It transmits price information through the economy so that labor resources facing a declining demand in a given occupation will receive two types of signals—signals to those already employed in that occupation to move into other areas and signals deterring potential entrants from coming into the industry. The economic selection at work may be such that individuals with the greatest skills (thus highest alternative MRP) leave first.

Unfortunately(?) labor markets do not typically operate in this way. In most labor markets, there is a downward rigidity to wages. As a result,

[4] See the article by H. Johnson and P. Mieszkowski cited in the References for an example of recent work in this area.

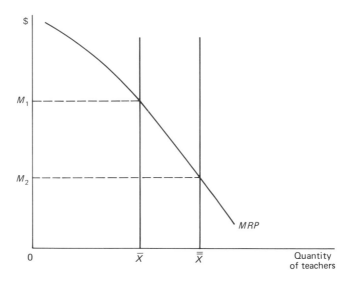

Figure 15.2   Changes in Derived Demand and Its Impact When
Wages Are Inflexible

declining demand does not produce a decline in wage rates, followed by an
adjustment process. Instead, the brunt of the decline in demand is absorbed
in the form of unemployment. Falling incomes would cause substantial
hardship for the individuals involved, but would permit all individuals to
remain employed. The result of rigidity is a group of highly trained individuals,
many of whom are unemployed, and a very uneven distribution of the
economic as well as psychological benefits of employment.

Unemployment thus does not necessarily mean that there is insufficient
demand for a particular input, but rather that there is an insufficient quantity
demanded of that input at the prevailing market price. The same analysis
applies to other input or output markets which exhibit price rigidity problems.

Minimum Wage Legislation: An Example of Policy Impact

Minimum wage legislation is directly associated with public policy relating
to unemployment. The effects of minimum wage legislation can be broken
down into the impact on employment, work, and income, and impact on
product prices and input substitution by firms.

Figure 15.3 illustrates a market setting with a derived demand for labor
and a market supply. Assume that the market is initially in equilibrium with
wage rate W^0 and employment L^0. A minimum wage law at level $\overline{W}$ would
have no effect whatever, since the prevailing wage rate is already greater

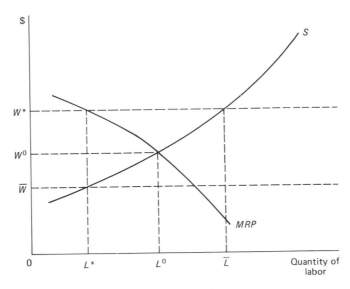

Figure 15.3 Analyzing the Impact of Minimum Wage
Legislation

than $\bar{W}$. Minimum wage legislation, if it is going to have any impact, must set a real wage higher than the market has otherwise achieved. However, raising the minimum wage to W^* will cause employment to fall to L^*, provided no other inputs are substituted for labor. If input substitution is possible, the MRP curve will probably shift down, leading to an even greater curtailment of employment.

Notice that a minimum wage above the normal market equilibrium price generates unemployment at the minimum wage W^* of $\bar{L} - L^*$ (Figure 15.3). This measured unemployment is in a sense artificial since it is created by specifying a minimum wage above the wage prevailing in the market as a whole.

Minimum wage legislation has both a short-run and a long-run effect on employment. In the short run, if firms are not able to substitute other inputs for labor, i.e., if the available technologies for production permit only limited input substitution, then the change in relative input prices will not cause marked input substitution and the incomes of laborers will rise. In the long run, however, if possibilities exist to technologically substitute other inputs for labor, for example, capital, then a rise in the wage rate caused by an increase in the minimum wage makes labor relatively more expensive. This creates an economic incentive for firms to substitute capital for labor and, in fact, if labor becomes costly enough, it will encourage research to find equipment capable of economizing on labor even further. These statements are true not only of labor but of any input to the production process.

Let us now consider the impact of minimum wage legislation on the labor force itself. If firms are hiring inputs in order to maximize profits, they will hire up to the point where marginal revenue product is equal to marginal expenditure. Raising the minimum wage above the equilibrium market wage will generally lead to decreased employment. The fact that aggregate employment may fall, however, masks some important side effects.

The potential decline in aggregate employment caused by minimum wage legislation is far less important than the *distribution* of the increased unemployment. Empirical observations reveal systematic differences in unemployment rates according to education, race, sex, age, etc. Increasing minimum wages creates an economic incentive for firms to reduce hiring, but this influence is not uniform across individuals. The individuals likely to bear the brunt of the unemployment resulting from an increased minimum wage are those whose marginal revenue product is relatively low. Employment of a highly skilled carpenter, a machinist, or a railroad engineer is not directly affected. The most dramatic impact is on the employment of individuals who have relatively few skills, are handicapped, or possess other characteristics that do not make them highly productive. The distribution of employment in a market system is geared to hiring those individuals who are relatively most productive.

The goals of raising the minimum wage and of other programs for social well-being, such as reducing unemployment among minority groups, may be in conflict with one another. Trying to increase individual incomes by increasing the minimum wage operates on the supply side of the market. On the demand side of the market increasing the wage rate presents firms with the problem of remaining an economically viable unit and therefore choosing inputs that are most productive.

The impact of minimum wages on product prices and input substitution results from increasing average costs and marginal costs of production. Rising costs cause rising output prices. An increased minimum wage must be absorbed in one of two ways. The impact of increasing the minimum wage is either to increase unemployment or commodity prices (and probably some combination of both effects) or reduce returns to other production inputs like capital. Increased consumer prices drive the real wage back down. This can result in a wage-price spiral in which prices and wages undergo successive increases, with little long-run impact on real wages.

Rent Controls and Other Price Ceilings

Minimum wage legislation has a direct parallel in rent control legislation and maximum price legislation, such as the price control phases of 1973. Legislation of this kind tends to produce a "dual" market in the controlled commodity, in which buyers pay premiums over and above the legislated maximum price in order to obtain commodities. Prior to the law providing for vacancy decontrol, rent control for apartments in New York City created two separate sets of prices. To obtain a rent-controlled apartment it was necessary to make an under-the-table payment to the lessor or to the previous lessee, which might be as much as $1000, simply for the privilege of renting at the rent control price!

Whether for apartment rents or other commodities, in the short run price ceilings typically necessitate some other scheme of rationing—explicit or implicit—since market price is inhibited from performing its normal allocative role. If continued over longer periods of time, they lead to a curtailment of investment which will further aggravate the shortage that originally existed—particularly if demand continues to grow.

Capital Market Imperfections Induced by Income Taxes

Individuals and corporations both pay income taxes. Tax provisions which discriminate between different types of firms or individuals can be a direct cause of market imperfections.

Suppose for purposes of argument that loans are available at 8% interest to all who wish to borrow. Interest payments are tax deductible, thus paying 8% interest on a $2,000 loan provides a tax deduction of $160. Assuming that taxable income exceeds all available deductions, this deduction yields a tax benefit equal to the difference between the taxes payable with and without using the $160 deduction. This benefit is approximately equal to $160 times the taxpayer's marginal tax rate.

With a progressive income tax schedule higher taxable incomes are subject to higher marginal tax rates and therefore realize higher tax benefits from the interest deduction. The actual cost of the loan is $160 minus the tax benefit. Thus higher income individuals acquire the loan at a lower effective cost, as illustrated in Table 15.4.

Table 15.4 Tax Benefits and Effective Loan Cost Differences

MARGINAL TAX RATE	TAX SAVING	EFFECTIVE LOAN COST	EFFECTIVE INTEREST RATE
15%	$ 24	$136	6.8%
30	48	112	5.6
50	80	80	4.0
75	120	40	2.0

A similar analysis can be used to obtain the equivalent *taxable* yield required on bonds or other securities for a given *nontaxable* yield for individuals in different tax brackets.

Discriminatory tax provisions for firms create differences in the effective tax rates for firms in different industries. While exact numerical estimates of such differences are complicated by a myriad of tax regulations, their effect may be substantial and important for resource allocation questions.

Summary

Imperfections in input markets abound. Input markets play a crucial role in an economic system by acting as a vehicle for distributing part of the value added by production activities to resource owners. At the same time, they transfer control over resources from owners to those who will make productive use of them.

This chapter has traced the impact of imperfect product markets on the derived demand for variable inputs. From this discussion we obtained a more general expression for the marginal revenue product, which includes the result developed in Chapter 14 as a special case. A useful new tool is the concept of marginal expenditure which was illustrated in the context of monopsony.

Study has traditionally focused on labor markets and unemployment, with a more recent emphasis on electricity, petroleum, and natural gas. The crucial public policy issues in these markets should encourage further research.

Questions for Study or Class Discussion

1. Collect data on annual wages for several unions and some nonunion wage data. Compare your findings to the consumer price index. Do unions do a better job of increasing their members' real wages than would be possible without a union? What aspects of employment are not reflected in wage figures?
2. Some union contracts limit employee layoffs. Assume that certain groups of employees cannot be laid off unless a business closes down completely. How will this affect the derived demand for other inputs? Could the employment stability of other inputs be affected? How? Why?
3. Collect data on employment and unemployment by age, sex, years of schooling, race, etc., for several years. What are the characteristics of unemployed persons? What policies might improve their ability to find and keep employment?
4. Look up the history of minimum wage legislation and gather data on price indices over a period including several changes in the minimum wage. Compute and graph the real wage implied by the minimum wage. What do you conclude? Is it possible to raise the real wage in an economy? Has the distribution of income changed over time? If so, how? What factors are producing change?

5. Natural resources—particularly energy resources such as natural gas, coal, and oil—are not produced under competitive conditions. In some countries one or more natural resource industries are nationalized. List several arguments for and against nationalizing an industry.

References

Cartter, A., *Theory of Wages and Employment*. R. D. Irwin, 1959.

Hicks, J. R., *The Theory of Wages*. Macmillan, 1932.

Johnson, H., and P. Mieszkowski, "The Effects of Unionization on the Distribution of Income: A General Equilibrium Approach," *Quarterly Journal of Economics*, 84 (November, 1970), 539–561.

Reynolds, L., *Labor Economics and Labor Relations*. Prentice-Hall, 1959.

Siegel, S., and L. Fouraker, *Bargaining and Group Decision Making: Experiments in Bilateral Monopoly*. McGraw-Hill, 1960.

Chapter 16   Investment by the Firm, Capital Budgeting, and Financial Markets

Introduction

Among the inputs acquired by a firm, capital investments play a particularly important role. Investment decisions lock the firm into costs it cannot avoid in the short run; thus there is a risk attached to them. Derived demand for capital goods has a dynamic character that is worth exploring.[1] The discussion that follows includes financial markets, markets for capital goods, and investment decision analysis.

A firm deals with two basic types of capital markets: the *capital goods market*, in which a firm purchases capital goods, and *markets for loan funds*. The term *capital* can refer to fixed assets such as buildings and equipment, as well as to financial capital. Investment decisions can thus involve both physical acquisition decisions and financing decisions. Firms commonly finance the acquisition of capital assets from internal funds generated by retained profits or depreciation reserves or from the sale of bonds or equity shares of common or preferred stock.

Demand for Capital Goods

The demand for capital goods differs markedly from the demand for other inputs, primarily because capital goods have useful lives that cover considerable periods. Their contribution to profit, therefore, is not limited to any one point in time. The passage of time becomes a crucial element for analysis.

---

[1] Labor markets, particularly the supply side, also have a dynamic aspect, since decisions about building "human capital," e.g., job training, education, etc., involve costs and potential returns over a period of time.

Evaluating Streams of Revenues over Time

Figure 16.1 shows three possible streams of net revenues a firm might realize from three different investment projects. One project offers a stream of net revenues, i.e., gross revenues minus payments to all other factors except capital, that is constant over time, represented by π_1. Another alternative, π_2, offers very high short-term gains; then net revenues gradually diminish as time elapses. A third possibility, π_3, offers net returns that are fairly low, possibly even negative, to start with, and high net revenues later in its economic life. Supposing that all three projects have the same investment cost, how are we to evaluate the net revenues for each one, since they are received at different points in time?

Investment Criteria

Selection among alternative investment projects with or without limitations on available funds is frequently referred to as the problem of *capital budgeting*. This problem can be discussed in either a riskless or risky setting with reference to projects which are either independent of one another or interdependent. We shall start by evaluating riskless independent projects and then extend the discussion to a risky interdependent setting at the end of the

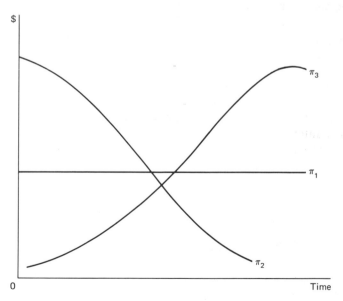

Figure 16.1 Alternative Time Streams of Net Revenues

chapter. There are several investment criteria the firm might use to make a selection among alternative projects.

The first investment criterion, which is also probably the most widely used, is based on the *discounted present value method* of evaluation. This method takes as given the net returns $R_1, R_2, R_3, \ldots, R_N$ expected over the life of the project, say N years, and the investment costs that must be laid out in each year, $C_1, C_2, C_3, \ldots, C_N$. If the full investment cost is borne at the outset, it will be represented by C_1 and the terms $C_2, C_3, \ldots, C_N$ will be zero. It may be, however, that a firm incurs an added investment cost in one or more of the subsequent years and this can be handled quite easily.

The next step is to calculate the *net present value* of an investment. The present value method evaluates time streams of receipts and outlay by expressing all earnings and costs in terms of their dollar equivalents at the initial point in time. In other words, the future returns and future costs are *discounted*. A dollar received now is not equivalent to one dollar received one or more years in the future. Suppose that we wish to receive one dollar a year from now and that the interest rate is r per year. We want to find the amount of money, X, to invest now. One year hence we shall get back our original investment plus the interest earned during the period, rX. These terms must add up to one dollar, $X + rX = X(1 + r) = \$1.00$. The present value of one dollar discounted at the rate r is $X = \$1/(1 + r)$.

If we want to find the present value of a dollar that will be received two periods from now, we start at period 2 in Figure 16.2 and discount the dollar back to the end of period 1 by dividing by $1 + r$. We discount the quotient back one more period, by dividing once more by $1 + r$.

The present value of one dollar discounted back two time periods at the rate r is thus $\$1/(1 + r)^2$. The present value of $\$1$ three periods hence is $\$1/(1 + r)^3$, etc. The present value of a stream of earnings is calculated by using $R_1/(1 + r) + R_2/(1 + r)^2 + \cdots + R_N/(1 + r)^N$. In the same way, we can discount a stream of costs back to time zero by dividing C_1 by $(1 + r)$, C_2 by $(1 + r)^2$, etc. The sum of these adjusted cost terms represents the present value of the outlay stream associated with the investment project, again discounted at the rate r.

To find the net present value of a project, subtract the present value of the net revenue stream from the present value of the cost stream. Choose the investment project that has the highest net value, up to the limits set by

Figure 16.2   Finding the Present Value of $1 to Be Received Two Years Hence

available funds. In a riskless setting choosing projects with maximum net present value maximizes profits and the market value of the firm. Several numerical examples are provided in the next section.

The second investment criterion is based on the *internal rate of return* or the *marginal efficiency of investment method* of evaluation. The marginal efficiency of an investment is calculated by taking the net returns at time 1 and dividing these by an adjustment factor $1 + r$ and adding the result to the net returns to be received at time 2, again divided by an adjustment factor $(1 + r)^2$, and continuing in this way for the life of the investment project:

$$\frac{R_1}{(1 + r)} + \frac{R_2}{(1 + r)^2} + \frac{R_3}{(1 + r)^3} + \cdots + \frac{R_N}{(1 + r)^N} = \sum_{j=1}^{n} \frac{R_j}{(1 + r)^j} \quad (16.1)$$

With $C_1, \ldots, C_N$ representing investment outlays, the internal rate of return r is the solution or solutions to the equation

$$\sum_{j=1}^{n} \frac{(R_j - C_j)}{(1 + r)^j} = 0 \quad (16.2)$$

The internal rate of return can also be defined as the discount rate which yields a net present value of zero.[2]

The investment rule based on the internal rate-of-return method for evaluating investment projects is to undertake an investment project only if the internal rate of return exceeds the opportunity cost of investment funds. If the prevailing interest rate is 8% and the internal rate of return is greater than 8%, then the investment is feasible, since, while it costs 8% to borrow funds, the borrowed funds earn more than 8%, so that there is a net profit remaining after paying interest charges. If the internal rate of return turns out to be less than 8%, a firm would earn more profits by loaning any available funds and earning the market rate of interest.[3]

Both methods require information that may not always be available in accurate form. The following alternatives are frequently used for coping with the problem of imperfect information about revenues and costs. They are rules of thumb criteria that have a practical, not theoretical, origin. The first rule begins by adding a *risk premium* to the discount rate r used in the present value method. For example, instead of using an 8% discount rate we might add a premium of 7% to 12%, arriving at a total discount rate of 15%

---

[2] Unfortunately, Equation (16.2) does not always yield a single unique answer. If multiple solutions occur and some are above the opportunity cost of funds while others are below, the internal rate of return method leads to an ambiguity.

[3] The ranking of projects provided by the internal rate-of-return method is not always the same as that provided by the net present value method. A project with a higher internal rate of return may provide a smaller net present value than a project with a lower internal rate of return. For this reason, the net present value method is generally a more reliable guide for firms maximizing profits.

or 20%. Increasing the discount rate, however, tends to create a bias against investment projects with large payoffs in the future and in favor of projects that pay off relatively early. There are no hard and fast rules for choosing the amount to add as a risk premium, so that a problem can be rigged to give almost any predetermined answer.

A second rule of thumb is the *payback rule*. This rule is based on the period of time that it will take to earn net revenues just sufficient to cover the investment cost of a project. For example, if a project is expected to cost $75,000 and have net earnings of approximately $25,000 per year, the pay-back period would be three years. Among projects that are regarded as essentially equivalent, the payback rule points to another dimension of an investment decision. All other things being equal, the faster a firm can retrieve its investment outlay, the sooner these funds can be reinvested.[4]

Some Illustrations of Present Value Calculations

Example 1

Assume the data in Table 16.1 represent the net revenues a firm expects to receive from an investment project over its three-year life. The firm invests in the project at the *beginning* of year 1 and at the *end* of year 1 receives $20,000; at the *end* of year 2 it receives $30,000; and at the *end* of year 3 it receives $35,000. What is the present value of this net revenue for the firm? The present value is *not* found by simply summing the net revenues in each year. The fact that time has elapsed, i.e., that the firm must wait for the payoff from its investment, means it has lost the opportunity to use these funds in some other manner. It cannot value a dollar received several years in the future as being the same as a dollar received now because it has forgone an opportunity to invest the dollar elsewhere.

Using a discount rate of 10%, the net present value of the revenue stream given in Table 16.1 is $20,000/(1.10) + $30,000/(1.10)^2 + $35,000/(1.10)^3 = $69,971. The direct sum of the net revenues is $85,000—a substantial difference! If we have a 20% discount rate, the present value of the same stream decreases to $57,755 = $20,000/(1.20) + $30,000/(1.20)^2 + $35,000/(1.20)^3. Higher discount rates give less weight to future revenues.

Table 16.1 Net Revenues from an Investment Project

YEAR 1	YEAR 2	YEAR 3
$20,000	$30,000	$35,000

[4] To compare projects, even if their lives are of equal length, a firm must make assumptions about the rates of return available from reinvestment of net revenues.

We took it for granted that each of the net revenues above included any inflation. Starting with revenues stated at the present currency value, we can build in the notion of inflation by multiplying by 1 plus the inflation rate, s. The present value formula then becomes

$$\frac{(1 + s)R_1}{(1 + r)} + \frac{(1 + s)^2 R_2}{(1 + r)^2} + \cdots \tag{16.3}$$

The way in which future revenues are weighted now depends on both the rate of inflation *and* the discount rate. (In general, interest rates depend on the anticipated rate of inflation, thus r may depend on s.) Notice that when the discount rate is zero and there is no inflation or when the rate of inflation is equal to the discount rate, the present value is simply the sum of the net revenues. The latter case effectively nullifies the postponement in time.

If inflation proceeds rapidly enough, it may create a bias in favor of projects that have high payoffs in the future as opposed to the present. On the other hand, raising the discount rate but keeping the inflation rate constant, creates a bias in favor of investment projects having early payoffs.

Example 2

Table 16.2 shows the net revenue streams and the net investments for two alternative investment projects.

The first project has expected annual payoffs of $20,000, $60,000, and $140,000, and the investment is complete at the beginning of the first year. For the second project, net revenue is higher in the first two years, and the investment cost extends over a longer period. Notice that for both projects, the sum of the net revenues and the sum of the investment costs are identical. The only difference is in the time stream of benefits and the time stream of investment outlays.

If we discount the net revenues from project 1 at 8% the present value will be $181,096. The present value cost for the first project is $100,000 since the

Table 16.2 Net Revenues and Investment Outlays for Two Investment Projects

	YEAR 1	YEAR 2	YEAR 3
PROJECT 1			
Net revenues	$ 20,000	$60,000	$140,000
Investment cost	100,000	—0—	—0—
PROJECT 2			
Net revenues	60,000	80,000	80,000
Investment cost	50,000	25,000	25,000

entire amount is paid at the outset. The present value of the net revenues from project 2 is $187,650, while the present value of the outlays is $87,575. Project 1 therefore yields a net present value of $81,096 while project 2 yields $100,075. Project 2 should be chosen. If sufficient funds are available, both projects are worth undertaking. When choosing among a large number of independent projects, a firm using the net present value criterion will invest in those projects which show positive net present value beginning with the one showing the highest net profit first, then the second, etc., up to the limit of available funds.

The Firm's Derived Demand for Capital Goods

A firm's *derived demand for capital goods* is based on the rate of return it can earn on investment. This depends on the physical productivity of capital goods, the market for output, and the price of capital goods. A firm's demand for investment goods can be represented by a schedule showing the amount of investment that would be undertaken at various rates of return, as shown in Figure 16.3. This is generally a downward sloping schedule because at lower rates of return, a firm will typically find more projects which will earn at least that rate of return. As the opportunity cost of funds increases, the number of investment projects capable of earning such a rate of return declines, and the demand for investment goods decreases. While in the

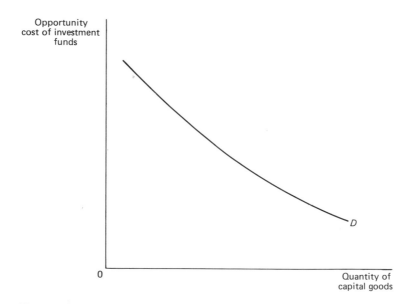

Figure 16.3   A Firm's Derived Demand Schedule for Capital Goods

schedule in Figure 16.3 the price of capital goods is given, the more familiar *demand schedule for capital goods* describes the amounts of capital goods demanded at various capital goods prices.

The User Cost of Capital

A perfectly functioning capital market envisions the firm as able to buy and sell capital goods at the same price and acquire or loan funds at the same price. In other words, in a perfectly functioning capital market, both capital assets and loan money can be purchased and sold freely at constant prices. This assumption is obviously seldom borne out in practice. The cost of financial capital often differs from observed interest rates since firms are usually subject to various forms of capital rationing or loan rationing by financial institutions; in other words, a borrowing rate that increases as the firm attempts to acquire more funds. The cost of capital assets as perceived by a firm depends also on other economic variables, including depreciation provisions and income tax rates.

Suppose that a firm can buy and sell capital goods over time at the prices c_t, c_{t+1}, c_{t+2}, etc. These might be the prices for a particular machine, bought new, at time t, $t + 1$, and $t + 2$. In order to make the input decisions described in Chapter 6, we would like to know the actual cost of using capital goods, that is, an equivalent rental price for each period. The cost of using capital goods is influenced by their market price, as a function of asset age, and by the interest rate.

Suppose now that a firm purchases a machine at time t, at a price c_t. It holds the machine for one period and then sells it at time $t + 1$. The sales price for a new machine would be c_{t+1}. However, in general, the machine will have undergone some depreciation during the period. The firm is therefore selling only a fraction of the original machine, say δ, where $0 < \delta < 1$. The net cost to the firm is thus $c_t - \delta c_{t+1}$. In addition, the firm bears the opportunity cost of tying up c_t dollars for one period. At an interest rate r, the opportunity cost of the investment in the machine for one period is rc_t. The user cost for the machine for one period is the net cost as calculated above, plus the opportunity cost, or $c_t - \delta c_t + rc_t = (1 + r)c_t - \delta c_{t+1}$. This is referred to as the *user cost of capital* and, in general, is not the same as the market price of capital goods.

If the firm is allowed to claim a tax deduction for depreciation we have to make a corresponding adjustment in the user cost of capital. With a profit tax rate of α, the benefit to the firm from a depreciation deduction of D dollars is a reduction in tax payments of αD. Claiming depreciation of $1000 with a tax rate of 25% will reduce the firm's tax payment by $250. The user cost of capital will then be $(1 + r)c_t - \delta c_{t+1} - \alpha D$.

The first thing to notice about this expression is that any reduction in δ will increase the user cost of capital. Decreases in δ might be interpreted either as increases in the physical rate of depreciation or increases in the speed at which technological obsolescence occurs. Rapid technological change makes the cost of capital higher by shortening the economic life of capital goods. Increases in the market rate of interest also tend to increase the user cost of capital because they raise the opportunity cost of funds. On the other hand, increasing the amount of depreciation allowed for tax purposes *decreases* the user cost of capital. This shows why a tax policy allowing increased deductions for depreciation gives firms an added incentive to invest. Increasing D makes investment projects appear more profitable.

Empirical Estimates of the User Cost of Capital

In the foregoing discussion, the user cost of capital was developed for a single capital asset. A more general concept, the yield on the amount invested in a firm, has been used to study the cost of capital. This yield may be roughly measured by the total payments to each class of shareholders divided by the total market value of the equity shares. There are at least two interesting empirical questions: (1) How does the cost of capital differ from one industry to another? and (2) What effect does the firm's choice of borrowing as opposed to equity financing have on its cost of capital?

Some preliminary answers to these questions have been provided in a well-known study by F. Modigliani and M. Miller (M-M) for electric utilities and oil companies.[5] Letting d denote the ratio of debt to the market value of equity, M-M found the following empirical estimates for the cost of capital:

$$\text{Electric Utilities' Cost} = 5.3 + .006d$$
$$\text{of Capital per Dollar} \qquad (\pm.008)$$

$$\text{Oil Companies' Cost} = 8.5 + .006d$$
$$\text{of Capital per Dollar} \qquad (\pm.024) \qquad\qquad (16.4)$$

There is a marked difference between the two industry groups (possibly due to the higher risks experienced by the oil firms) and no statistically discernible effect on average yield from varying the ratio of debt to equity. The constant term is the average return on equity (synonymous with one definition of "cost of capital") observed in the sample data.

This result, however, does not mean that the cost of capital measured as the yield on equity is not influenced by the ratio of debt to *common stock* equity. To test this notion, one estimates the cost of capital using the yield

[5] The Modigliani-Miller results have given rise to a considerable controversy about the definition and measurement of "cost of capital." See the J. Lintner article cited in the References for an extended discussion.

on common stock only and the ratio of debt to common stock market value, h, obtaining:

$$\text{Electric Utilities' Cost} = 6.6 + .017h$$
$$\text{of Capital per Dollar} \qquad (\pm.004)$$

$$\text{Oil Companies' Cost} = 8.9 + .051h$$
$$\text{of Capital per Dollar} \qquad (\pm.012) \qquad (16.5)$$

Notice that the average yield on common stock equity is higher than the average yield on all equity, as shown by a comparison of the constant terms in Equations (16.4) and (16.5). In addition, the debt–equity ratio is now statistically significant. The fact that the coefficients of h are positive indicates that as the ratio of debt to equity rises, so does the cost of capital to the firm. In a rough way these results indicate that as the risk element in the firm's financing choices increases, the yield rises to compensate for the added risk investors must assume.

Interest Rates and the Supply and Demand for Loanable Funds

In any economy, the supply of funds available for loans from the financial sector and the supply of goods available as capital assets are directly linked to the general level of economic activity. The amount of goods available for investment is equal to the aggregate output of goods and services in the economy minus the goods that are consumed either in private households or in the government sector. The total income in an economy can be used for three purposes: (1) consumption, (2) taxes, and (3) savings. Savings, which we are concerned with here, enter into financial markets through financial institutions like commercial banks or savings and loan associations which channel savings between their individual owners and the firms who wish to borrow them.

Figure 16.4 shows a supply schedule for loanable funds. This schedule slopes upward, reflecting the fact that at higher rates of interest individuals can be induced to consume less and save more, thus making a larger quantity of funds available for investment purposes. The loanable funds market is the chief vehicle for determining equilibrium interest rates in the economy by applying basic supply and demand concepts to a different commodity— money. The interest rate is simply the market price of money. As we have seen, the interest rates generated in financial markets are basic to the determination of the discount rate used by firms in applying the present value criterion to particular projects.

In practice, of course, there is no single interest rate in an economy, but a whole spectrum of rates varying with the riskiness and duration of the loan.

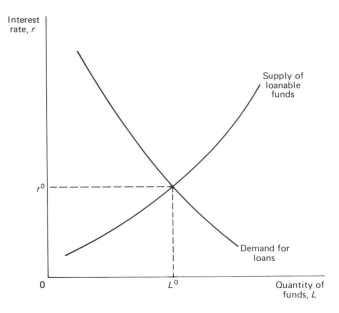

Figure 16.4 The Market for Loanable Funds

The interest cost of short-term loans frequently differs from the cost of the long-term loans desired for investment in plant and equipment. This difference in interest rates associated with different loan maturities is frequently described by a *yield curve* showing the *term structure* of interest rates. Figure 16.5 illustrates a situation where the interest rate on long-term loans is lower than on short-term loans.

From the viewpoint of consumers it is not always optimal to expend all of current income on consumption. In a riskless setting financial market equilibrium determines an interest rate associated with a specified volume of savings. Since savings are simply postponed consumption, this equilibrium interest rate reflects consumers' marginal rate of substitution of current consumption for future consumption.

The preceding discussion shows one link between the physical side of economic activity, sometimes referred to as *real activity* and including production of goods, investment in plant and equipment, and sale of commodities, and the financial sector of the economy that includes the markets in loanable funds such as the markets in bonds, securities, and mortgages. Interest rates in the financial sector directly affect the cost of loans and the cost of capital to a firm. This in turn affects the firm's decisions about investment.

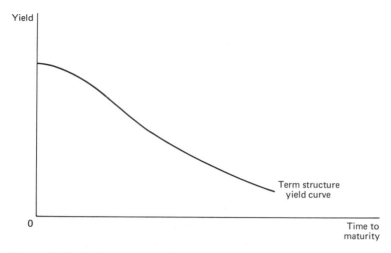

Figure 16.5   An Example of a Term Structure Curve for Interest Rates

Choosing Depreciation Policy and Evaluating the Benefit of Tax Deductions

Suppose that a firm owns a machine that costs $50,000 and has an expected useful life of 25 years. Assume the prevailing interest rate to be used in computing present values is 8% and that the firm pays a profit tax rate of 50%.

The *straight-line method* and the *declining balance method* provide two frequently used formulas for depreciation. Under the straight-line method the firm is allowed to take as a tax deduction in each year of the asset's life an amount equal to investment cost (less salvage value, assumed to be zero here) divided by expected useful life, or $50,000/25 = $2,000. The declining balance method permits a firm to take the largest share of the depreciation in the early years. The depreciation rate for the declining balance method is usually taken as twice the straight-line rate. This rate is then applied to the net book value of the asset. Net book value is defined as initial cost less the depreciation already taken. In this example the straight-line depreciation rate is $2,000/$50,000 = 4%, thus the declining balance rate is 8%.

The importance of these alternative methods of depreciation to a firm is their potential to reduce the present value of the tax payments. Table 16.3 shows the allowable depreciation deductions using each of the two depreciation methods over the first three years of the asset's life. In each year the straight-line depreciation is $2,000, while depreciation under the declining balance method is found by taking 8% of the net book value. For year 1 this gives 0.08($50,000) = $4,000; for year 2: 0.08($50,000 − $4,000) = $3,680;

Table 16.3 Depreciation by Two Alternative Methods

	YEAR 1	YEAR 2	YEAR 3
DEPRECIATION			
Straight-line	$2,000	$2,000	$2,000
Declining balance	4,000	3,680	3,386
TAX SAVING			
Straight-line	1,000	1,000	1,000
Declining balance	2,000	1,840	1,693

and for year 3: $0.08(\$50,000 - \$4,000 - \$3,680) = \$3,386$, etc. The tax benefit of the depreciation deduction is the rate at which profits would be taxed, 50%, times the amount of the deduction. The tax savings for the first three years are shown at the bottom of Table 16.3.

The present value of taking a $1,000 deduction at the end of the first year is $1,000 discounted at 8% or $926 = $1,000/(1.08)$. At the end of two years a $1,000 deduction has a present value of $857 = \$1,000/(1.08)^2$, and for the third year the tax deduction has a present value of $794 = \$1,000/(1.08)^3$. Using the straight-line rate of depreciation for the first three years thus reduces the present value of tax payments by $2,577. Applying the same type of calculation to the declining balance method leads to a present value tax benefit for the first three years of $4,774. The marked difference in the present value of the tax benefits occurs because the firm is allowed to take large deductions very early using the declining balance method. Usually if one is trying to minimize the present value of tax payments, it pays to postpone recognition of revenue and accelerate tax deductions as much as possible.

Decision Rules for Equipment Replacement

Capital budgeting decisions involve investment projects that expand productive capacity, replace existing capital assets, or do both at once.

Decisions relating to equipment replacement basically depend on a comparison of the new capital goods currently on the market and the operating costs for capital goods already in place. The economic life of a piece of equipment is usually quite different from its physical life. Innovations and improvements in productivity typically cause assets to reach the end of their economic life substantially before they reach the end of their physical life. Each improvement that leads to a reduction in the average *total* cost of producing with new equipment as compared to the average *variable* cost of producing with current equipment, adds an incentive for the firm to swap the old equipment in favor of the new. Notice that the initial investment cost of the old equipment is completely disregarded. For old equipment only the salvage value is relevant, not the original cost. Investment costs for the new equipment, however, must be included, since a firm can realize the lower average variable cost only by purchasing it.

Suppose a firm is considering replacing a particular piece of equipment. A new machine costs $2,000 and the salvage value of the old machine is $100. In addition, assume that as each year goes by the average variable cost difference between a new machine and the old one, a difference known as the *operating inferiority gap*, is given by $Z_t = a + bt$, where $a = 12, $b = 20, and t is the time in years. Observe that the gap gradually gets larger over time, either because technological changes make the new machines successively more efficient, or because the old machine is beginning to break down more often, causing higher maintenance costs, or slowing down its rate of productivity. We want to find the point at which it is economically desirable to replace the piece of equipment.

To replace the machine we have to invest net additional capital of $1,900 = $2,000 - 100. The savings in average variable cost is the operating inferiority gap. The change will be worth making when the present value of the savings from changing over are just equal to the present value of the added cost of the change. In other words, as long as the present value of the savings one can achieve is less than the present value of the cost of making the change, one would not replace. On the other hand, if the present value of the potential cost saving is greater than the present value of the cost associated with the changeover, then, of course, there is an advantage to purchasing the new machine.

An appropriate rule for replacement[6] is given by

$$T = \frac{r(C - S) - a}{b} \qquad (16.6)$$

---

[6] If Z_t is the operating inferiority gap, r the interest rate, C_T the new machine cost at time T, and S_T the salvage value of the old machine at time T, then the present value of the cost savings lost from replacing the old machine in T years is

$$\int_0^T Z_t e^{-rt} \, dt$$

and the present value investment cost when replacement occurs is

$$(C_T - S_T)e^{-rT}$$

We choose the replacement time, T, so as to minimize

$$\phi = \int_0^T Z_t e^{-rt} \, dt + (C_T - S_T)e^{-rT}$$

$$\frac{d\phi}{dT} = a + bT - r(C_T - S_T) = 0$$

or

$$T = \frac{r(C_T - S_T) - a}{b}$$

where T is the economic useful life of the machine, r is the interest rate, C is the cost of a new machine, S is the salvage value of the old machine, and a and b are the constants in the formula for the operating inferiority gap. The faster a new machine is outstripping its predecessor in reducing average variable costs, i.e., the larger the value of b, the sooner it is going to pay to replace the old machine. Economic life is prolonged by rising purchase costs for new equipment or by rising opportunity costs for investment funds. Using the data above and $r = 0.08$, the optimal economic life of a machine is seven years. You can carry out optimal replacement time calculations like this for yourself and apply them to common household items such as dish-washers, dryers, or automobiles.

This analysis of replacement might be used, for example, by Hertz or Avis for managing vehicle rental pools. The market value of a used car successively drops every year and every year maintenance expenses rise higher and higher. A new vehicle has a lower maintenance cost but a much higher depreciation, since the depreciation on automobiles is very rapid in the earlier years and then tapers off. Maintenance costs rise very rapidly in the later years but are lower in the beginning years. Total operating costs are the sum of mainte-nance plus the user cost of capital. The firm will choose the replacement policy that minimizes the sum of these costs over the life of the car. Figure 16.6 illustrates one possibility for these cost components. The optimal

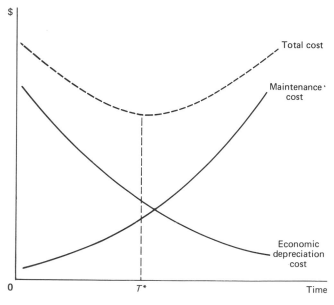

Figure 16.6 Minimizing Equipment Costs by Balancing Maintenance and Depreciation Costs

amount of time to hold the automobile is the period which minimizes total costs, T^*.

Alternative Methods of Financing Investment: The Net Cost of Borrowing

In this section we shall turn from analyzing investment decisions to the problem of financing them. Basically a firm has three sources of funds: loan markets, sale of stock, and retained earnings. An important aspect of alternative sources of funds is their relative cost. Among all available methods of financing, the firm obviously wants to choose the method that provides funds at minimum cost.[7] The following numerical example illustrates the effective cost of borrowing funds.

Suppose a firm is borrowing $100,000 at $6\frac{1}{2}\%$. One year's interest is $6,500. If the firm can take tax deductions for interest payments, the market rate of interest the firm is paying is higher than the actual cost of the loan. If tax rate on profits is 50%, the tax benefit resulting from the added interest deduction is 50% of $6,500 or $3,250. The net interest cost is thus $6,500 minus the tax benefit of $3,250. The *effective* interest rate is thus $3,250/$100,000 = 3.25%. Table 16.4 gives the tax benefit and effective interest rate for various tax rates. Even though the gross interest payment is $6,500 in each case, the net interest payment declines as the tax rate rises, which in turn reduces the cost of borrowed funds.

Financing the Firm: The Problem of Leverage

The preceding example can be thought of as a steppingstone to a more general financing problem for the firm—to find the optimal balance between borrowed funds and equity funds. For a given asset size there are basically two external sources for the financing: debt or equity. To finance assets of $500,000, the firm can either borrow $500,000, have the $500,000 paid by the

Table 16.4   Effective Interest Rates after Profit Taxation

TAX RATE	TAX REDUCTION	NET INTEREST COST	EFFECTIVE INTEREST COST
20%	$1,300	$5,200	5.20%
25	1,625	4,875	4.88
30	1,950	4,550	4.55
50	3,250	3,250	3.25

[7] At least so long as the inherent risk is roughly the same.

owners of the firm in the form of equity, or combine these two sources in some way. The question is whether there is an optimal balancing between them. This is sometimes referred to as the problem of optimal *leverage*.

The concept of leverage can be illustrated by an example showing how the rate of return on equity capital changes as the firm changes the amount it borrows. Assume the firm earns 15% on its total capital assets of $500,000 and loans, L, can be obtained at a before-tax interest rate of $7\frac{1}{4}\%$. We want to calculate the actual return on the owner's equity, E, defined as the total value of assets minus the amount borrowed, $E = \$500,000 - L$. In terms of a balance sheet, total assets are on one side and loans and liabilities plus equity on the other. Equity may, of course, take the form of common shares, preferred shares, or retained earnings.

The rate of return on equity, γ, is the total profit of the firm (15% times $500,000) minus the amount that the firm has to pay in interest ($7\frac{1}{4}\%$ times L), over the value of equity[8] or

$$\gamma = \frac{0.15(\$500,000) - 0.0725L}{E}$$

$$= \frac{0.15(\$500,000) - 0.0725L}{\$500,000 - L} \tag{16.7}$$

Table 16.5 shows the rate of return on equity for different values of L in Equation (16.7).

We can also express the idea of leverage in a more general way. Let ρ represent the rate of earnings on total assets, A the total assets (in dollars), r the interest rate for loans, L the amount of loans, E the equity investment, and γ the rate of earnings on equity. We can then express γ as

$$\gamma = \frac{\rho A - rL}{E} = \frac{\rho A - rL}{A - L} \tag{16.8}$$

Dividing the numerator and denominator of Equation (16.8) by L and using

Table 16.5 Equity Earnings and Leverage

LOAN AMOUNT	γ	DEBT/EQUITY RATIO
$100,000	16.9%	0.25
200,000	20.2	0.67
300,000	26.6	1.50

[8] The rate of return on equity can be calculated using either the book value of equity or the market value of shares. This example uses book value.

the identity $A = L + E$, we can rewrite it as

$$\gamma = \frac{\rho(A/L) - r}{(A/L) - 1} = \rho + \left(\frac{L}{E}\right)(\rho - r) \tag{16.9}$$

Define the debt/equity ratio as λ, then Equation (16.9) becomes

$$\gamma = \rho + \lambda(\rho - r) \tag{16.10}$$

If λ is equal to zero, everything is financed by equity. Larger values of λ indicate that borrowing plays a larger part in the firm's capital structure.

Let us now find the financing arrangement for the firm which secures the highest rate of return on equity. Figure 16.7 illustrates the way the rate of return on equity changes as leverage changes. As long as the firm can borrow at a constant rate of interest and that rate of interest is less than the rate of return on assets, then it pays to continue borrowing more and more. In short, the optimal financing arrangement under such a situation is perfect leverage. The firm will maximize the rate of return on equity by borrowing everything.

A firm is not usually confronted with such a simple situation. Typically, as its borrowings increase the interest rate that creditors require also increases, in other words the cost of borrowed capital rises as λ rises. The empirical tests of the relationship between the cost of capital and the debt/common-stock equity ratio cited earlier in this chapter demonstrate this fact, and the presence of income taxes makes the effect even more pronounced. The more highly levered the firm becomes the greater the risk to creditors, and the higher the potential rate of return to equity shareholders. Figure 16.8 gives a

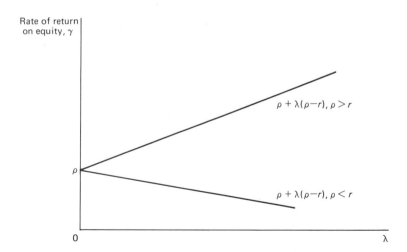

Figure 16.7 The Effect of Leverage on the Rate of Return on Equity

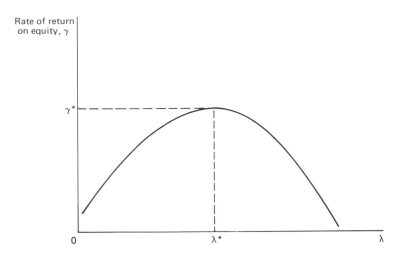

Figure 16.8   The Effect of Leverage on Equity Returns with Rising Borrowing Costs

more realistic picture of the way in which the rate of return on equity might respond to changes in the degree of leverage. Instead of rising continuously as in Figure 16.7, γ typically reaches a maximum, beyond which attempts to apply further leverage produce increased interest costs that cause the rate of return on equity to fall. The optimal degree of leverage, λ^*, produces the maximum rate of return on equity, γ^*.

*Risk, Return, and Optimal Portfolio Selection

This last example is a companion to the optimal leverage problem. It involves a choice among assets with different returns, and although frequently referred to as a *portfolio selection problem*, the same general structure fits a much wider class of problems. Models of portfolio selection can be applied not only to actual stock and bond portfolios for an individual, a firm, or a bank, but also to the management of mutual funds, trust funds, and pension funds, to capital-budget project mix choice, and even to the choice of candidates for merger.

Suppose a firm has P dollars available for investment which it is planning to invest in two classes of assets: X_1, a riskless asset with a very low expected rate of return r_1 and a variance in return of zero, $\sigma_1^2 = 0$; and X_2, a risky asset with a high expected rate of return r_2 and a positive variance about that return, $\sigma_2^2 > 0$. These alternatives might represent putting money in a savings

* Optional material requiring knowledge of probability.

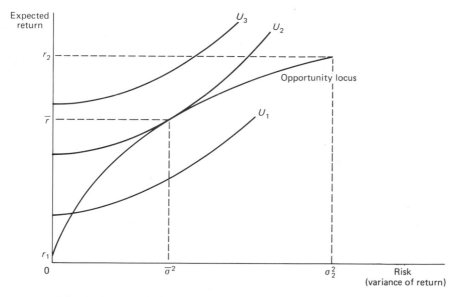

Figure 16.9   Optimal Portfolio Choice Balancing Expected Return
and Risk

account which is guaranteed to pay $5\frac{1}{4}\%$, as opposed to investing in common
stock shares with a potential rate of return ranging from $+150\%$ down to
-80%. Potential gains may be high, but there is a risk of low gain and even
loss. The problem is to find the mix of the assets X_1 and X_2 which best
balances expected return against risk for the portfolio.

Let λ_1 be the percentage of the portfolio in X_1 and λ_2 be the percentage of
the portfolio in X_2. The rate of return on the portfolio is $r = \lambda_1 r_1 + \lambda_2 r_2$.
In addition, the risk associated with the return on any particular portfolio is
the variance about that return, contributed by the assets in the portfolio.
The variance of r can be expressed as $\sigma^2 = \lambda_1^2 \sigma_1^2 + \lambda_2^2 \sigma_2^2$, provided the returns
on X_1 and X_2 are independent of each other, thus their covariance is zero.
We have now two indices of the performance of a particular portfolio mix:
its expected rate of return, r, and its variance, σ^2.

Our problem now is to find a way of evaluating the trade off of risk against
expected return. Suppose that we are given a utility function represented by
a set of indifference curves that look like the ones in Figure 16.9. Notice that
the shape of these indifference curves describes a situation where more risk
will be acceptable only if it is associated with an increase in return.

The last step is to plot the *portfolio opportunity locus* for the various
portfolios that can be bought for P dollars.[9] This opportunity locus describes

---

[9] The opportunity locus can be found by choosing the portfolio mix which minimizes σ^2
for each level of r. Such problems can be solved easily on a computer, particularly with
computational short cuts, as quadratic programming problems.

the highest rate of return achievable for any specified level of risk or, alternatively, the minimum risk associated with a given level of return. As we vary λ_2 from zero to one, r varies from r_1 to r_2 and σ^2 varies from zero to σ_2^2 as shown in Figure 16.9. The optimal portfolio is the one which represents a portfolio mix on the highest possible indifference curve: in this case at $\bar{r}$ and $\bar{\sigma}^2$. Once we have found $\bar{\sigma}^2$, we can find the value of λ_2 from $\lambda_2^* = \bar{\sigma}^2/\sigma_2^2$ and $\lambda_1^* = 1 - \lambda_2^*$. With a total portfolio of P, the firm will invest $\lambda_1^* P = X_1^*$ in asset X_1 and $\lambda_2^* P = X_2^*$ in asset X_2.

*Risk and the Valuation of the Firm

The interest of corporate shareholders is often best served by a management which seeks to maximize the value of the firm, i.e., to maximize the value of outstanding shares. This is particularly true for shareholders in high tax brackets, due to the tax benefit from taking profits in the form of capital gains rather than dividends. In a riskless world with perfect capital markets, maximizing the value of the firm means maximizing the present value of profits, but in a risky setting this is no longer the case.

Superficially it might seem that risk elements could be reflected simply by replacing the objective "profit" by "expected profit." But this ignores the bearing of the degree of risk on the value of the firm. Typically higher degrees of risk require at least the expectation of a higher return. For a given return, the higher the risk the lower the market value of the firm. Under a fairly general set of assumptions,[10] the market value of a firm in a risky setting can be expressed as

$$V = \frac{1}{r} (\mu - R\beta\sigma) \tag{16.11}$$

where V is market value of the firm, μ is expected profit, σ is the standard deviation of profit, r is the discount rate for riskless earnings streams, R is the market value of a "unit of risk" as measured by σ, and β is the correlation between the firm's returns and the return on a portfolio consisting of all other firms in the market. Notice that increasing expected profits will increase the value of the firm only if risk, σ, does not increase too much.

The expression for the value of a firm given in Equation (16.11) is an extension of the portfolio concept to equilibrium values of financial assets. In general, choices of financing method, price and output policy, and the mix of investment projects in a capital budget will alter both return and risk. Many of the pricing, production, and investment rules applicable to a riskless

---

* Optional material requiring knowledge of probability.
[10] See the articles by J. Lintner or W. Sharpe cited in the References for detailed derivations.

setting fail to carry over to a risky setting. As an example, in a riskless world a firm would never undertake a project whose net present value is negative. In a risky setting, it can be optimal to include such a project in a capital budget if returns on the project are negatively correlated with other projects already included in the budget. The decrease in expected return on the whole budget may be more than offset by a reduction in risk. As Equation (16.11) makes clear, a simultaneous reduction in μ and σ may well lead to an increase in market value.

Summary

Investment planning involves two basic problems: the economic evaluation of alternative investments and the evaluation of alternative modes of financing. Demand for capital goods depends on expected input and output prices, the opportunity cost of funds, and the price of capital goods.

The key topics discussed in this chapter are: (1) the concepts of present value and discounting, (2) the role of the market for loanable funds, (3) the user cost of capital, (4) the concept of present value tax benefits, (5) the distinction between market borrowing costs and effective interest rates, and (6) the concept of leverage.

The basic choice of consumption versus investment within an economy has a direct impact on individual firms. Savings are available to potential investors through stock, bond, and loan markets, while at the same time resources must be diverted from the production of consumption goods to make them available for the production of capital goods.

The presence of risk requires a modification of traditional riskless decision rules, as illustrated in the portfolio example.

We have now completed our analysis of individual markets and the economic forces at work in them. The next task is to correlate individual market processes and individual decision makers in order to study a general equilibrium process. The next chapter develops the basic concepts of general equilibrium in a competitive setting. The final chapter explores some of the characteristics of a general equilibrium and their application.

Questions for Study or Class Discussion

1. Look up several empirical studies of the determinants of investment spending for an economy. What appear to be the key factors? How are these factors influenced by: (1) government policy, e.g., taxation, control of interest rates, etc., (2) expectations about future prices?
2. Are the present values of all investment projects affected in the same proportion by increases or decreases in the discount rate? Why?

3. Is the cost of financial capital the same for all firms in an industry? Why? Will the cost of capital be the same for firms in different industries? Why?

4. What does the term *leverage* mean? How does the choice of leverage affect the return for owners of a firm? Can leverage be chosen arbitrarily? If not, what factors would limit choice?

5. Suppose a firm is confronted by two risky investment projects, one yielding an expected return of $500 with a $20 variance and the second an expected return of $800 with a $100 variance. These returns refer to each $5,000 of initial investment. Find the mean and variance of return on a capital budget of $12,000 which consists of 30% spent on project 1 and 70% spent on project 2. Assume the returns on both projects are not correlated to one another.

References

Baumol, W. J., *Economic Theory and Operations Analysis*. Prentice-Hall, 1965.
—————— and B. Malkiel, "The Firm's Optimal Debt–Equity Combination and the Cost of Capital," *Quarterly Journal of Economics*, 18 (November, 1967), 547–578.

Hicks, J. R., *Value and Capital*. Oxford University Press, 1946.

Lintner, J., "The Valuation of Risk Assets and the Selection of Risky Investments in Stock Portfolios and Capital Budgets," *Review of Economics and Statistics*, 47 (February, 1965), 13–37.

Lutz, F. A., and D. C. Hague, eds., *The Theory of Capital*. Macmillan, 1961.

Markowitz, H., *Portfolio Selection*. John Wiley & Sons, 1959.

Masse, P., *Optimal Investment Decisions*. Prentice-Hall, 1962.

Modigliani, F., and M. Miller, "The Cost of Capital, Corporation Finance, and the Theory of Investment," *American Economic Review*, 48 (June, 1958), 261–297.

Mossin, J., "Equilibrium in a Capital Asset Market," *Econometrica*, 34 (October, 1966), 768–783.

Sharpe, W., "Capital Asset Prices: A Theory of Market Equilibrium Under Conditions of Risk," *Journal of Finance*, 19 (September, 1964), 425–442.

Terborgh, G., *Dynamic Equipment Policy*. McGraw-Hill, 1949.

Chapter 17   General Equilibrium

Introduction

In Chapters 10–16 we applied tools of economic analysis to one market at a time. This is referred to as *partial equilibrium analysis*.

General equilibrium analysis considers equilibrium in all markets simultaneously. It therefore provides a greatly expanded scope in which to discuss production and resource allocation. For example, instead of concerning ourselves with the optimal output mix for a single firm, we can ask questions about the optimal mix of outputs for the whole economy. Alternatively, instead of choosing resources for the production of one commodity, we can discuss the distribution of resources in the production of automobiles and televisions, houses and clothes, educational services and airline travel.

Choice problems for the whole economy involve group choice. Up to this point, all of the discussion centered on problems for an *individual* consumer or for an *individual* firm. Even when confronted with only two uses for output, we must make choices between goods produced for the public sector of an economy versus the private sector or between consumption goods and investment goods. We need a way to determine how the productive resources and technological limits of the economy as a whole should be allocated among various alternatives. General equilibrium analysis concerns an important vehicle for coordinating information to solve these allocation problems: markets and the price system.

The main purpose of this chapter is to study the interdependence of the parts of an economy and the character of the equilibrium achieved by a price and market system. We shall also consider whether this method of allocating resources leads to inefficiency or misallocation. In this chapter and the following one, we shall focus on general equilibrium in commodity markets. In practice, general equilibrium must include commodity and financial markets simultaneously. In addition, uncertainty elements intrude in a general equilibrium setting just as they do in partial equilibrium analysis; however, we shall omit them here. The references at the end of Chapter 16 provide extended developments of financial market equilibrium models which parallel the development of commodity market equilibrium.

A Numerical Example of General Equilibrium

Suppose we have two individuals and two commodities, with demand for commodity 1 given by

$$Q_1^d = 50 - 2P_1 + P_2 + M_1 + M_2 \tag{17.1}$$

and demand for commodity 2 given by

$$Q_2^d = 90 - 4P_2 + 2P_1 + M_1 + .5M_2 \tag{17.2}$$

These expressions relate the demand for each good to their market prices, P_1 and P_2, and the incomes of each individual, M_1 and M_2. The supply schedules for the two commodities are

$$Q_1^s = 4 + 3P_1 \tag{17.3}$$

$$Q_2^s = 7 + 4P_2 \tag{17.4}$$

The markets for commodities 1 and 2 are linked to one another through prices and incomes.

A general equilibrium for the economy represented by Equations (17.1)–(17.4) will occur at the prices P_1 and P_2 which simultaneously equate supply and demand in both markets. If we assume that $M_1 = \$10$ and $M_2 = \$14$, then we can substitute into the demand equations and equate supply and demand in market 1 and supply and demand in market 2. This leads to two equations in two unknowns P_1 and P_2:

$$4 + 3P_1 = 74 - 2P_1 + P_2 \tag{17.5}$$

$$7 + 4P_2 = 107 - 4P_2 + 2P_1 \tag{17.6}$$

The prices which simultaneously clear both markets are $P_1^* = \$17.36$ and $P_2^* = \$16.84$. The four pieces of information given by the equilibrium prices P_1^* and P_2^* and the two money incomes, M_1 and M_2, define a general equilibrium for this simple two-market economy.

If there are r consumers and n goods, then we need to specify r incomes and n supply and demand equations involving n prices. Despite the added dimensions, finding a general equilibrium set of prices still implies simultaneously equating supply and demand in each market, subject to the requirement that all of the prices be zero or positive.

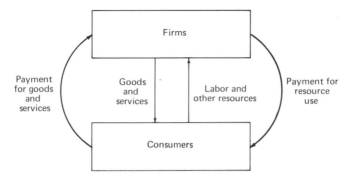

Figure 17.1 An Illustration of the Circular Flow of Income in an Economy

Next, we need to consider how individual incomes are determined. Consumer incomes are generally derived from payments for inputs supplied to the productive process. In general, there is a circular flow of income in the economy as shown in Figure 17.1. Firms derive their incomes from product markets and make expenditures in input markets, while consumers do the exact reverse. Equilibrium market prices for outputs depend on the demand and supply for individual goods, which, in turn, depend on consumer incomes and input prices. Consumer incomes depend on the amount of productive services supplied by each individual, and on the price of inputs. The price of inputs is determined by the prices of commodities, since the value of productive resources is derived from the value of the goods produced.

To illustrate the way in which individual incomes depend on commodity prices, let us suppose that two individuals receive income from the sale of a resource they each own plus a portion of the profits from two firms which they own together. Individual 1 possesses an amount R_1 of the resource and individual 2 possesses R_2. Each person's income is given by the market price of the resource, P_X, times the amount of the resource owned, plus a portion of the profits from firm 1, π_1, and a portion of the profits from firm 2, π_2. Assume the ownership shares are denoted δ_{ij}, which indicates the portion of firm i owned by individual j, where $0 \leq \delta_{ij} \leq 1$, $\delta_{11} + \delta_{12} = 1$, and $\delta_{21} + \delta_{22} = 1$. Their individual incomes can then be written.

$$M_1 = P_X R_1 + \delta_{11}\pi_1 + \delta_{21}\pi_2 \qquad (17.7)$$

$$M_2 = P_X R_2 + \delta_{12}\pi_1 + \delta_{22}\pi_2 \qquad (17.8)$$

Notice that individual incomes are determined by both the price of the resource and the distribution of ownership. A property rights system defining the ownership of resources is a key link between resource prices and the distribution of income. The distribution of income is fixed once the distribution of resources and the input and output prices are fixed.

Profits for each firm are determined by aggregate revenues minus the cost of inputs. Suppose in this case that the two firms use only the resource owned by the two individuals as an input, and that X_1 represents the amount of the resource used by firm 1 to produce output Q_1 and X_2 represents the amount used by firm 2 to produce Q_2. Profits for each firm are then

$$\pi_1 = P_1 Q_1 - P_X X_1 \tag{17.9}$$

$$\pi_2 = P_2 Q_2 - P_X X_2 \tag{17.10}$$

Since there is a limited amount of the single resource, the total amount used, $X_1 + X_2$, must not exceed the total amount available, $R_1 + R_2$. The relationship between output and input for goods 1 and 2 is given by the production functions

$$Q_1 = A_1 X_1 \tag{17.11}$$

and

$$Q_2 = A_2 X_2 \tag{17.12}$$

General equilibrium will occur when the quantities of the resources, X_1 and X_2, used by the two firms, the price for the resource, P_X, and the output prices P_1 and P_2 are such that supply and demand in both input and output markets are equal. Equations (17.1)–(17.2) and (17.7)–(17.12) can be solved to obtain the equilibrium values $P_1^*, P_2^*, X_1^*, X_2^*, P_X^*, Q_1^*, Q_2^*, M_1^*,$ and $M_2^*.$

A Walrasian Description of General Equilibrium

Although we do not have space to give the numerical details of a general equilibrium problem with many consumers, many resources, and many goods, we can provide a formal summary. The following general description is referred to as a *Walrasian general equilibrium model*.

The economy described here has n outputs, r individuals, and m inputs. Demand for each commodity is represented by a demand function which depends on all output prices $P_1, P_2, \ldots, P_n$ and on the level and distribution of consumer incomes, $M_1, M_2, \ldots, M_r$, namely

$$Q_i^d = D_i(P_1, P_2, \ldots, P_n, M_1, M_2, \ldots, M_r) \tag{17.13}$$

This is simply a general way of expressing the demand schedules we have been using all along. The second essential set of information is provided by the supply schedules for each commodity. The quantity supplied will depend on output prices and all input prices, $V_1, V_2, \ldots, V_m$. We will have

$$Q_i^s = S_i(P_1, P_2, \ldots, P_n, V_1, V_2, \ldots, V_m) \tag{17.14}$$

We must also incorporate constraints imposed by resource limitations. If X_{kj} represents the amount of input k used in the production of commodity j, then the available technology is represented by production functions for each input

$$Q_i = f_i(X_{1i}, X_{2i}, \ldots, X_{mi}) \qquad (17.15)$$

In addition, the sum of the amounts of input k used in industry 1, industry 2, and in all other industries must be equal to or less than the total amount of resource k supplied, X_k. In other words,

$$\sum_{j=1}^{n} X_{kj} \leq X_k \qquad (17.16)$$

Resources are owned by individuals. Let Y_{ki} represent the amount of resource k owned by individual i. The next constraint simply requires that the total supply of a resource be equal to or less than the total amount owned:

$$X_k \leq \sum_{i=1}^{r} Y_{ki} \qquad (17.17)$$

The actual amount of resource k supplied will depend on input prices and the level and distribution of ownership:

$$X_k^s = G_k(V_1, V_2, \ldots, V_m, Y_{k1}, Y_{k2}, \ldots, Y_{kr}) \qquad (17.18)$$

and the amount demanded for each resource will depend on output levels, output prices, and input prices, as follows:

$$X_k^d = H_k(Q_1, Q_2, \ldots, Q_n, P_1, P_2, \ldots, P_n, V_1, \ldots, V_m) \qquad (17.19)$$

One last constraint provides the fundamental identity linking all incomes in an economy. It is a mathematical statement of the circular flow relationship described earlier. The price of output i times the quantity of output i in the economy, P_iQ_i, is the total expenditure by individuals on commodity i. Since expenditure by individuals can only arise from their incomes, this means that the total expenditure in the economy has to be equal to the sum of all of the incomes $M_1 + M_2 + \cdots + M_r$ or

$$\sum_{i=1}^{n} P_iQ_i = \sum_{j=1}^{r} M_j \qquad (17.20)$$

Total expenditure is equal to total income because a dollar spent by anyone is always income to someone else.

Incomes for each individual are calculated by multiplying the amount of resource k supplied by individual j, Y_{kj}^s, times the resource price V_k or

$$M_j = \sum_{k=1}^{m} V_k Y_{kj}^s \qquad (17.21)$$

The fundamental identity for the economy, Equation (17.20), thus becomes

$$\sum_{i=1}^{n} P_i Q_i = \sum_{j=1}^{r} \sum_{k=1}^{m} V_k Y_{kj}^s \qquad (17.22)$$

Equation (17.22) shows that prices for resources are directly linked to prices for output. The prices of outputs and the amount sold cannot be determined without implicitly affecting the prices of resources and the amounts supplied. Similarly, we cannot fix the prices of resources and the distribution of ownership without having an implicit effect on the prices of commodities. If all the people in the economy obtain a higher price for the resources they are selling, total income in the economy will increase, but there is only one way this can happen: through an increase in total expenditure. Increasing total expenditure means an increase in either output prices or the volume of output or both.

This system of equations is a way of representing the idea of general equilibrium for the economy in mathematical form. A general equilibrium for an economy occurs at the $n + m$ prices that simultaneously solve the equations. Given sufficient information and a large computer, this is a large, but simple calculation problem. However, more important than the mathematical aspect of the problem is its demonstration of the way in which all the markets of an economy are linked to one another through the dependency of demand in each market on the prices in other markets and the effect of input prices on supply and incomes.

A Basic Description of an Economy

We shall turn now from a mathematical description of a general equilibrium to a geometrical one based on a simple economy with two inputs, two outputs, and two individuals. This two-dimensional economy is convenient to illustrate with graphs, but the basic concepts carry over to settings with multiple inputs and outputs.

The following are the basic components we need to define an economy:

1. A list of *available resources*, sometimes referred to as a list of *initial endowments*. It itemizes the initial number of machines, the amounts of skilled and unskilled labor, the amount of capital, and the amounts of iron ore, copper, etc.

For our economy we will use the symbols X_1 and X_2 to indicate the two resources and assume these are initially given in amounts X_1^0 and X_2^0. Any production use is feasible, subject to the requirement that no more than the amounts X_1^0 and X_2^0 are used.

2. A list of available technologies for production, i.e., the "stock of knowledge" available concerning ways in which one can transform resources into different commodities. We shall assume this information is given by production functions for each output in the form of isoquant maps relating amounts of X_1 and X_2 to output levels.

3. A list of possible outputs. Let the symbol Y_1 denote output 1 and Y_2 denote output 2.

4. Information describing the preferences of our two individuals for different market baskets of goods. Let us suppose this information is given in the form of utility functions described by indifference curves.

5. A description of behavior rules. The behavior rule for each consumer is to choose the market basket of goods which maximizes utility subject to his budget constraint. Each firm chooses input/output configurations which maximize profits subject to technological and resource limitations.

This economy could be a simplified view of a country such as the United States, but the description applies equally well to any physical unit: the world, a particular state, a region, a city, or a town. The size of the physical unit chosen for analysis will depend on the problem to be solved. The management of a firm is obliged to look at the economy as a whole, since the firm's product and the prices it has to pay for inputs are not determined solely within one industry. In fact, effective management planning requires a picture of the economy as a whole, of the industry of which the firm is a part, and ultimately of the firm itself. The picture we are going to sketch of an economy is the beginning of this process.

The economy can be divided into a production sector and a consumption sector. The following discussion first develops the production side, then the consumption side, and finally brings the two together.

Feasible Production Choices and Efficient Production

We begin by considering the limitations on choice imposed by the limitations on resource availability and technological knowledge that will determine the set of feasible productions for our economy. The set of feasible productions is a description of all the combinations of the outputs Y_1 and Y_2 that can be produced, given fixed amounts of the resources and given limits on the ability to translate inputs into outputs through production technologies.

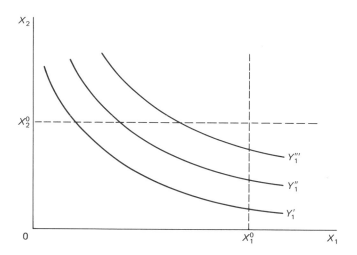

Figure 17.2   Input and Output Limits for Producing Y_1

Figures 17.2 and 17.3 illustrate the production technologies available for producing Y_1 and Y_2. We cannot use more than the amounts X_1^0 and X_2^0 in producing Y_1, thus the only relevant part of the isoquant map for Y_1 is the area below and to the left of the dotted lines in Figure 17.2, which includes all permissible input combinations and output levels for Y_1. In the same way, production of Y_2 is constrained by the limits on the total amounts of X_1 and X_2 available as shown in Figure 17.3. This information can now be translated

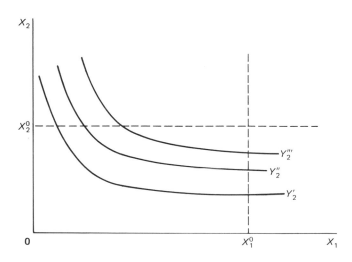

Figure 17.3   Input and Output Limits for Producing Y_2

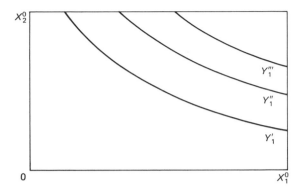

Figure 17.4 Transferring the Relevant Input/Output Combinations for Y_1 into an Edgeworth Box Diagram

into a description of alternative output choices by means of an *Edgeworth box diagram.*

To construct an Edgeworth box diagram, copy the isoquant information in Figure 17.2 bounded by the dotted lines and the axes. Now take the corresponding isoquant map from Figure 17.3 and *turn it upside down* so that the lower left-hand corner of Figure 17.4 is placed at the origin for the isoquants in Figure 17.2. The origin for the isoquants in Figure 17.3 will then be in the upper right-hand corner. The resulting diagram is illustrated in Figure 17.5. The isoquants for Y_2 appear upside down, with the lowest output level at the origin in the upper right corner. The output level for Y_2 rises as we move toward the lower left corner, while the output level for Y_1 rises as we move from the lower left corner toward the upper right corner.

The information in the Edgeworth box diagram describes the fact that the resources in the economy can be used in the production of outputs Y_1 or Y_2 only up to a limit. The distance along the horizontal axis at the bottom of the diagram is X_1^0, the total amount of input X_1 available. Moving from left to right along the horizontal axis represents using more of input X_1 in the production of Y_1. Using resources to produce Y_1, however, has an implicit economic cost measured by the output of Y_2 which could otherwise have been produced. The dimension along the top edge of the box is also X_1^0. Moving along this edge from right to left corresponds to using more of input X_1 in the production of Y_2. Equivalent information for X_2 can be read from the left and right vertical axes.

The information in Figure 17.5 can be used to illustrate the link between production technologies and feasible outputs. First let us define an *efficient production* for Y_1 and Y_2 as an output pair such that for a given amount of one output we obtain the maximum amount of the other. If Y_1 is bread and we fix the amount of bread at 100 loaves, this limits the amount of inputs X_1 and X_2 available for producing Y_2, say cheese. We use the optimal combination of inputs to produce 100 loaves of bread and then use the remaining amounts of X_1 and X_2 to produce cheese. If this yields 215 pounds of cheese, then the production $Y_1 = 100$, $Y_2 = 215$ is an efficient production.

If we fix the amount of output Y_2 at Y_2''', we can find the maximum amount of Y_1 that can be produced by moving along the isoquant Y_2''' to the highest possible isoquant level for Y_1. As we move along isoquant Y_2''' from point A toward B, we successively cut across higher and higher isoquants associated for Y_1. Moving from A toward B one obtains the same amount of Y_2, but a successively larger output for Y_1 (until one reaches point C). Moving along the isoquant Y_2''' from C toward D leads to successively *lower* isoquants for Y_1. In Figure 17.5, the point that represents the maximum amount of Y_1 given an output level of Y_2''' is point C on Y_1'. If we set the amount of Y_2 at Y_2''' the maximum output for Y_1 occurs at the point E with an output of Y_1'' for Y_1. For any given level of output for one of the products, the highest output for the other is geometrically pictured as the highest isoquant just touching the isoquant for the other output. Points like C, E, and F represent efficient productions.

Since the isoquants in Figure 17.5 are smoothly curving, the points C, E, and F are points at which the two isoquants are tangent to one another. Since the slopes of the two isoquants are equal at points of tangency, the marginal rate of substitution between X_1 and X_2 in the production of Y_1 is

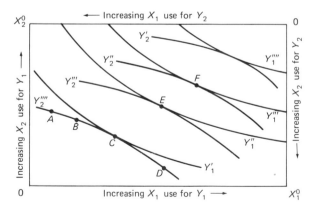

Figure 17.5   An Edgeworth Box Diagram Reflecting Input/Output Choices for Y_1 and Y_2

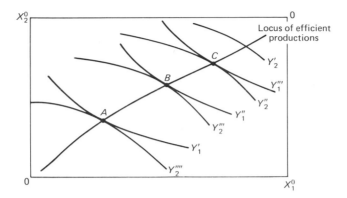

Figure 17.6 Deriving Efficient Productions from Input and Technological Limitations

equal to the marginal rate of substitution between X_1 and X_2 in the production of Y_2 at efficient productions. It is not true, however, that *every* efficient production is characterized by the condition $MRS^1_{X_1, X_2} = MRS^2_{X_1, X_2}$. For example, this condition would be replaced by an inequality if the isoquants touched at a corner or along an edge of the Edgeworth box.

If we repeated this process for each possible level of output, we would obtain a sequence of efficient productions lying on a curve like the one in Figure 17.6. This curve is called the *locus of efficient productions*. The locus of efficient productions indicates the maximum production for any one output given the output of the other good achieved by *efficiently allocating fixed amounts of the inputs* between production for various levels of a second output and fixed amounts of inputs. The information in Figure 17.6 can now be translated into the description of feasible productions we are looking for.

Let us consider the various points on the efficient production locus in Figure 17.6. Point A is associated with the output levels Y'_1 and Y'''_2 which can be plotted in Figure 17.7. Point B is associated with the isoquants Y''_2 and Y''_1 and is also plotted in Figure 17.7. If we repeat this process for each point along the efficient production locus, we shall ultimately obtain the curve ABC in Figure 17.7. This curve is called the *production transformation frontier*. It describes the physical boundaries to production within the economy, determined by the available inputs and the state of technology. The production points on the frontier and beneath it represent the set of feasible productions for the economy. Any output combination that lies outside the feasible production set, regardless of how desirable it might be, is simply not attainable.

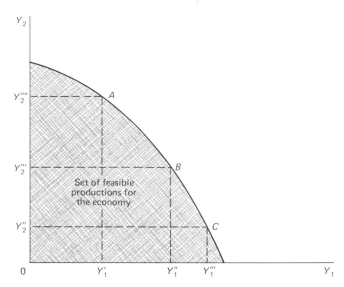

Figure 17.7 The Feasible Production Set for an Economy

Achieving Efficient Productions Through Profit Maximization

In an economy based on markets and a price system, production decisions are made by individual firms. In the economy considered here, each firm's choice of output mix must be made from its feasible production set. The behavior rule states that the firm will choose the mix which maximizes profit. Output prices and input prices are the basic ingredients for output decisions.

Total revenue[1] can be written as $Z = P_1Y_1 + P_2Y_2$. We can rewrite this isorevenue contour as

$$Y_2 = Z/P_2 - (P_1/P_2)Y_1 \qquad (17.23)$$

This curve is graphed in Figure 17.8, initially with $Z = 0$. For $Z = 0$ the only combination of Y_1 and Y_2 in the feasible production set which satisfies Equation (17.23) is $Y_1 = 0$ and $Y_2 = 0$.

Zero total revenues are not the best the economy can achieve. For example, other feasible output levels will produce revenues of Z_1. Maximum revenues are achieved by moving the isorevenue contour away from the origin until it reaches a point on the production transformation frontier, such as E. Notice that, regardless of what the relative profitability of the outputs might be, maximum revenues and profits are achieved with an output mix on the

---

[1] Strictly speaking, profit maximization will utilize commodity price net of input cost, thus P_1 and P_2 should be integrated as *net* output prices.

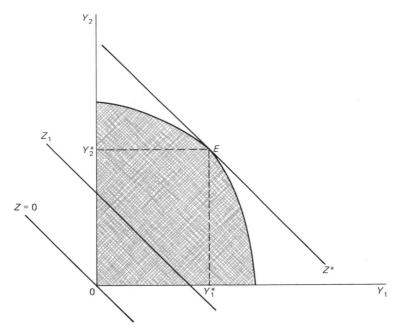

Figure 17.8 Output Choice Through Profit Maximization

production transformation frontier. We know already that all points on the frontier represent efficient productions. In other words, under the assumptions we have used, profit maximization always leads to efficient productions. No resources are left idle that could be employed to produce goods when someone will pay the price for resource use.

Achieving efficient productions may not always be desirable if other criteria are added. However, the efficiency property described here is an important characteristic of the response of a price and market system to the basic problem of resource allocation.

The striking thing about this result is that the information needs are so scant. Decision makers need to know only market prices and their own production transformation possibilities. With this information and a profit-maximizing objective decentralized decision making leads to efficiency for the economy as a whole.

Feasible Consumption Choices and Efficient Allocation of Outputs

The discussion in the previous sections dealt solely with the production side of the economy. The second part of the allocation problem deals with consumption. How are fixed quantities of two or more outputs to be allocated among individuals? In particular, what role do prices play in the operation of a market system in solving the problem of allocating goods among individuals? In this section we will develop a notion of *efficient allocations* parallel to the notion of efficient production. In the following section we will use this concept to examine the process by which commodities are exchanged.

Figures 17.9 and 17.10 show indifference curves representing the preferences of the two individuals in our economy. Given this information, suppose now that we have fixed amounts of two commodities, Y_1^0 and Y_2^0. Initially these amounts may be distributed between the individuals in any manner with y_{11} being the amount of commodity 1 possessed by individual 1 and y_{12} being the amount possessed by individual 2. These must add up to the total amount available, $y_{11} + y_{12} = Y_1^0$. In the same way, the amount of commodity 2 possessed by individual 1, y_{21}, plus the amount possessed by individual 2, y_{22}, must add up to the total amount of commodity 2 in existence, $y_{12} + y_{22} = Y_2^0$. Given any initial distribution of the goods between the individuals, there is nothing to insure that the individuals, if free to choose, might not enter into an agreement to trade and thus change their mix of goods. It is this question of trade that is of particular interest.

The amounts Y_1^0 and Y_2^0 are shown by the dotted lines in Figures 17.9 and 17.10. Preference over distributions of the goods outside the area bounded by the axes and the dotted lines is irrelevant. The relevant parts of Figures 17.9 and 17.10 may be combined through the use of the Edgeworth box notion to isolate efficient allocations of goods between the individuals.

Figure 17.11 is an Edgeworth box diagram built by taking the part of Figure 17.9 bounded by the total amounts of goods available and super-

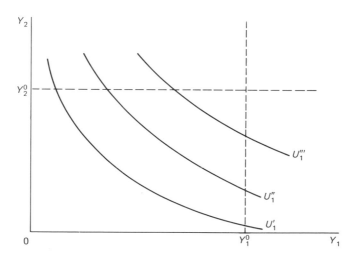

Figure 17.9   Indifference Map for Individual 1

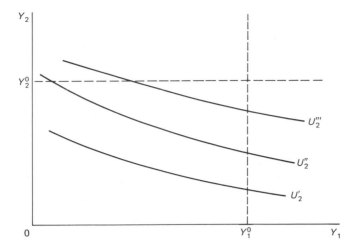

Figure 17.10 Indifference Map for Individual 2

imposing the relevant portion of Figure 17.10, turned upside down so that its origin is in the upper right-hand corner.

We can now define the efficient allocation of goods between individuals. An allocation is said to be efficient if, given a utility level for one individual, the allocation maximizes the utility of the other individual. As an example, if individual 2 is on indifference curve U_2', then an efficient allocation of the goods places individual 1 on the highest possible indifference curve consistent with the available outputs. Starting at a point such as A on U_2', moving toward B successively cuts across higher and higher indifference curves for individual 1, but individual 2 is still at the same level of satisfaction, U_2'. Going past point C leads to lower indifference curves for individual 1. Point C in Figure 17.11 represents an efficient allocation. The resulting allocation of Y_1 and Y_2 gives individual 1 y_{11}^* of Y_1 and y_{21}^* of Y_2, while individual 2 receives y_{12}^* of Y_1 and y_{22}^* of Y_2.

Each point where one individual achieves the highest indifference curve he/she can attain (given the indifference curve the other is on) represents an efficient allocation. In Figure 17.11 the curve CGF represents all efficient allocations of Y_1^0 and Y_2^0 between the two individuals. This curve is referred as the *contract curve* or, alternatively, a *locus of efficient allocations*. If the indifference curves are smoothly curving, these points will occur at tangencies, i.e., situations where the marginal rate of substitution for one individual is the same as the marginal rate of substitution for the other, provided each individual has some of each commodity. If an optimal solution occurs along any edge of the Edgeworth box, the condition of equality for the marginal rates of substitution must be replaced by an inequality.

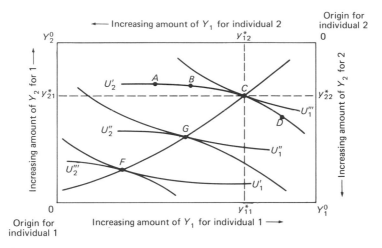

Figure 17.11   An Edgeworth Box Diagram for Describing Alternative Commodity Distributions

Efficient allocations will play an important role in determining the exchange agreements individuals might enter into. If the initial allocation of goods between the individuals is not efficient, there will be an economic incentive to enter at least one trade which will leave at least one individual (and possibly both) better off after the trade.

Exchange of Commodities: A Contrast Between Barter and a Price and Market System

Every point in the Edgeworth box in Figure 17.11 represents the allocation of a certain amount of Y_1 to individual 1, y_{11}, a certain amount of Y_1 to individual 2, y_{12}, a certain amount of Y_2 to individual 1, y_{21}, and a certain amount of Y_2 to individual 2, y_{22}. A point such as E in Figure 17.12 can therefore be taken to represent an initial distribution of goods. Such a point is referred to as an *initial endowment point*. We can now consider the way in which exchange may occur and, in particular, the way in which a price system effects this exchange process.

Assume that individual 1 is initially on indifference curve U_1^0, individual 2 on indifference curve U_2^0, and both individuals are free to enter into agreements with each other, each seeking to maximize utility. Individual 1 will be willing to trade provided that the indifference curve achieved after the trade is at or above U_1^0. Otherwise, the agreement would leave individual 1 worse off than at the initial point E. The set of trades individual 1 will agree to is therefore represented by the indifference curve U_1^0 and the area above it. In

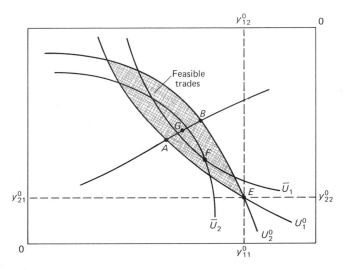

Figure 17.12 Trading Possibilities Beginning from an Arbitrary Initial Distribution of Goods

the same way, individual 2 will enter into any trade that produces a utility higher than or equal to U_2^0. Since individual 2's indifference curves are inverted in Figure 17.12, the higher utilities are toward the lower left.

The set of trades that both individuals will voluntarily enter is the shaded area shaped like a lens in Figure 17.12. The lens represents the distributions of the goods between the two individuals that leave at least one individual better off after the trade and possibly both (i.e., on a higher indifference curve than at E).

If one trade takes the individuals from point E to point F (which lies on the indifference curve $\overline{U}_1$ for individual 1 and on indifference curve $\overline{U}_2$ for individual 2), both individuals are better off than they were originally. Will trading stop at F? No, for there is still a wide range of trades that will leave at least one individual better off than remaining at F. Two individuals, starting off at point E, will voluntarily enter into a sequence of trades until they reach a point that is on the contract curve, such as G.

With any distribution of the goods that is not on the contract curve there will always exist at least one trade that would make one individual better off without making the other worse off. We know that bartering will continue until a point on the contract curve is reached, although it is usually not possible to predict which point along the line segment $\overline{AB}$ will be the stopping point.[2]

---

[2] We are assuming that trading is a costless activity. Obviously transaction costs, and perhaps the opportunity cost of the time spent in trading, may cause trading to stop before the contract curve is reached.

We do know, however, that there are incentives to continually contract and recontract until one reaches *some* point on the contract curve.

The foregoing description was developed solely in a barter context. Now let us return to the point E, in Figure 17.13, and consider the effect of a price system. We wish to determine the optimal prices to assign to the two commodities. Each individual will express different demands for each commodity and be willing to supply different quantities of each good at different prices.

As soon as we name a price P_1 for commodity 1 and a price P_2 for commodity 2, then individual 1's money income, or wealth, M_1, is defined as the price of commodity 1 times the amount owned plus the price of commodity 2 times the amount owned; $M_1^0 = P_1 y_{11}^0 + P_2 y_{21}^0$. The same is true for individual 2; $M_2^0 = P_1 y_{12}^0 + P_2 y_{22}^0$. The budget constraint for individual 1 must pass through the initial endowment point E because money income is computed in such a way that for any set of prices the individual can always afford to own the amounts initially received. The slope of the budget constraint is the negative of the ratio of the prices of the two goods, $-P_1/P_2$.

With a money income M_1^0 and a set of relative prices which make individual 1's budget constraint ($\overline{BB}'$ in Figure 17.14) tangent to the indifference curve U_1^0 at the point E, individual 1's optimal market basket of goods is exactly the one already owned. On the other hand, if the relative prices are slightly different, as indicated by the budget constraint $\overline{CC}'$, individual 1 will choose the market basket on the highest available indifference curve, $\overline{U}_1$, at point F.

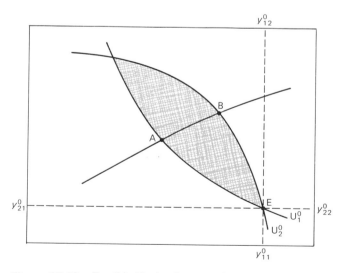

Figure 17.13   Feasible Trades from an Initial Distribution of Goods

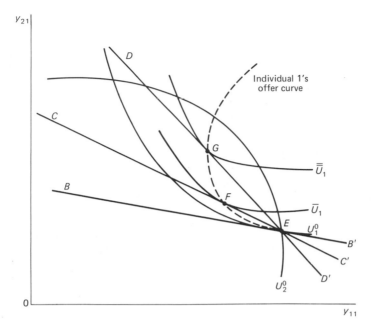

Figure 17.14   Deriving Individual 1's Offer Curve

For still another set of relative prices, described by a third budget constraint $\overline{DD'}$, the optimal bundle of goods to choose is indicated by point G. Each time we change relative prices the budget constraint pivots about point E. Ultimately we will obtain a curve which describes the way in which the optimal market basket for individual 1 responds to changes in the relative prices of the two goods—much like the price–consumption curve introduced in Chapter 3. This curve is called an *offer curve.*

For our hypothetical market to reach equilibrium we have to find a set of prices at which the quantity of Y_1 individual 1 desires is exactly the same as the quantity of Y_1 that individual 2 is willing to supply. In like manner, the price for Y_2 must be set so that the quantity demanded by one individual is equal to the quantity the other individual is willing to supply. In other words, we want a set of prices that will simultaneously equate supply and demand for Y_1 and Y_2.

To complete this search for an equilibrium set of relative prices, we have to plot the offer curve for individual 2. Initially we start with a set of relative prices (represented by budget constraint $\overline{KK'}$ in Figure 17.15) such that point E will be the optimal market basket for individual 2. If we then plot the optimal market baskets for individual 2 at the various sets of relative prices represented by $\overline{LL'}$, $\overline{NN'}$, etc., we shall ultimately obtain individual 2's offer curve.

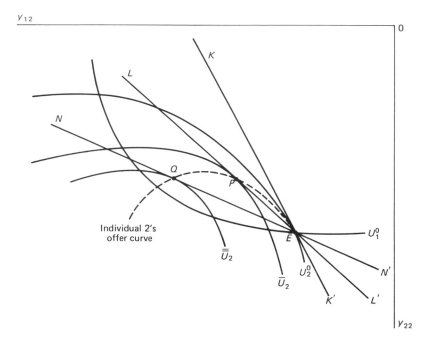

Figure 17.15   Deriving Individual 2's Offer Curve

If the individuals start out at point E, we now vary the relative prices, causing the individuals to trade until they achieve an efficient allocation of the available goods. Point F in Figure 17.16 represents such an allocation, since at this point the supply and demand for Y_1 and Y_2 are equated to one another. In fact, any intersection between the two offer curves represents a market equilibrium condition. It is possible for a pair of offer curves to intersect many times. This simply means there may be multiple market equilibria. In Figure 17.16 the set of relative prices, $-P_1^*/P_2^*$, that produces the single market equilibrium at point F is represented by the slope of the budget constraint $\overline{EE}'$.

The solution illustrated in Figure 17.16 shows that by using an appropriate set of prices a market can achieve an efficient allocation of goods. In other words, we have demonstrated that a market system, using only prices as the information signals, is capable of achieving a distribution of goods between individuals that is in some sense efficient. This is an important property for a market system because we have already established that a barter system is capable of achieving such efficiency also. Since a market system is only one possible alternative method for organizing the exchange of commodities, it is important to know whether or not a market system can be efficient.

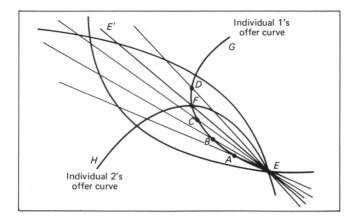

Figure 17.16 Achieving an Efficient Allocation of Goods by a Price and Market System

Summary

General equilibrium involves finding prices for inputs and outputs which simultaneously clear each market. In this chapter we made separate studies of the production side and the consumption side of an economy. Notice that the set of prices that leads to efficient allocation of given quantities of Y_1 and Y_2 is also the signal used by firms to determine the amounts of Y_1 and Y_2 to produce. By considering the exchange and production segments of the economy simultaneously, we can find the set of prices which not only elicits the appropriate aggregate production but also results in an efficient allocation to each consumer of the goods produced.

The key concepts introduced in this chapter are (1) efficient production, (2) the production transformation frontier, (3) the set of feasible productions, (4) efficient allocation or the contract curve and (5) the offer curve. Each of these tools was used to develop a picture of an economy and the role prices play in solving problems relating to the allocation of resources and outputs.

The fact that a price system, coupled with the behavior rules for each individual decision maker, can lead to such a comprehensive coordination of production and consumption appears almost magical, especially since no one person directly controlled more than a small part of the whole process, and each person pursued individual objectives without regard for what others did.

We now want to examine more closely the character of the equilibrium attained and ask another question. While it is true that a price system can get an economy to *some* equilibrium, could we find a set of prices that would efficiently achieve a *prespecified* goal? This is one of the principle questions to be studied in the next chapter.

Questions for Study or Class Discussion

1. Could inefficient production ever be optimal in some sense? Can you think of any examples?
2. If an excise tax makes the price consumers pay different from the price producers receive, thus distorting the market signal quality of prices, what happens when producers attempt to maximize profits through input choices?
3. How could we illustrate technological change in terms of the feasible production set for an economy? Will technological change always alter output? When? Why?
4. If every consumer likes every commodity the economy can produce, will it ever be desirable from the consumer's viewpoint to settle for a production below the production transformation frontier? Why?
5. Suppose externalities cause the production transformation frontier to be cupped toward the origin, at least over a short range. Why might this create a problem for profit-maximizing firms in achieving specified productions on the production possibilities frontier?

References

Bator, F., "The Simple Analytics of Welfare Maximization," *American Economic Review*, 47 (1957), 22–59.

Henderson, J., and R. E. Quandt, *Microeconomic Theory*, Second Edition. McGraw-Hill, 1971.

Samuelson, P.A., *Foundations of Economic Analysis*. Harvard University Press, 1947.

Scitovsky, T., *Welfare and Competition*. R. D. Irwin, 1971.

Chapter 18 Welfare Economics and Group Choice

Introduction

Modern welfare economics deals with choices—choices among alternative goods to be produced, choices among alternative methods for allocating inputs and outputs—and with comparisons between alternative choices. A price and market system is a method for making choices. A price system in which producers make choices among alternative production plans based on the relative profitability of different commodities and consumers use prices as signals to distribute their incomes in order to achieve their greatest satisfaction, is one way of organizing the allocation of resources in the economy. In a sense, a price and market system represents a process of group choice—a voting scheme—only votes are cast with dollars.

Our economy appears to fail occasionally, with respect both to the goods produced and to the allocation of those goods among individuals, in achieving the results desired by a majority of the people. Thus we constantly use government intervention in the form of taxation, welfare payments, and unemployment compensation to redistribute goods among individuals. Each of these interventions occurs because the distribution of inputs determining the choice of goods produced and the distribution of final goods among individuals fails to accord with some implicit norms of how things ought to occur. The recent hue and cry about the environmental impacts of economic activity provides further evidence that a price and market system coupled with certain types of property and other legal rights can produce unsatisfactory results. Let us use the information we have developed about efficient production and allocation to see what alternative distributions of goods can occur in the economy sketched in Chapter 17. From this starting point, we shall study various economic failures and the reasons they take place.

Utility Possibilities

Figure 18.1 illustrates the basic feasible production set for an economy with two goods. Each of the points A, B, C, etc. represents different total quantities of Y_1 and Y_2 that could be produced. Points such as A and B represent inefficient productions. Without introducing the role played by consumer and producer preferences, we cannot say yet whether productions of this are desirable, let alone optimal.

Once we have ascertained the total amount of commodity 1 and commodity 2 in existence, we can use an Edgeworth box diagram to examine the different levels of utility each of two individuals could achieve through various distributions of the goods between them, as shown in Figure 18.2. In general, we will be able to achieve a large number of different utility levels simply by choosing different distributions of the goods, even though we have the same fixed aggregate quantities Y_1^0, Y_2^0. The efficient allocation locus or contract curve describes the various levels of utility for both individuals. At point M individual 1 is on indifference curve U_1' and individual 2 is on indifference curve U_2''. On the other hand, if we choose the distribution of the goods represented by point N, individual 1 reaches indifference curve U_1'' and individual 2 moves to indifference curve U_2''. The movement from M to N puts individual 1 on a higher indifference curve, but at the same time moves individual 2 to a lower indifference curve.

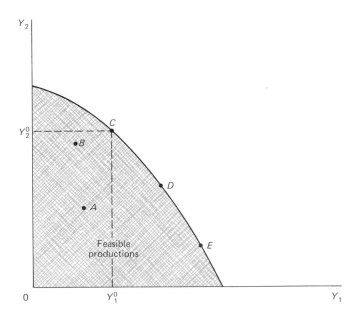

Figure 18.1   The Feasible Production Set for an Economy

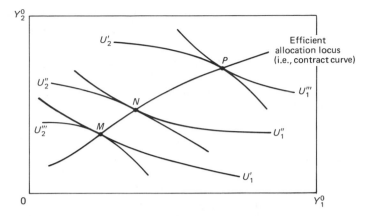

Figure 18.2 Efficiently Allocating Goods Once Total Production
is Known

The information in Figure 18.2 can be used to illustrate the way utility
levels change as commodities are redistributed. Figure 18.3 shows the three
points *M*, *N*, and *P* from Figure 18.2 and the other utility levels for both
individuals along the contract curve. This curve is referred to as a *utility
possibility curve*.

The single point *C* in the feasible production set provides the possibility of
a wide range of alternative utilities for both individuals. A utility possibility

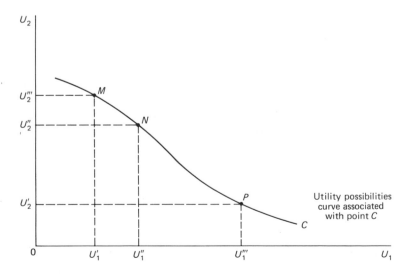

Figure 18.3 Utility Possibilities from Redistributing Commodities

curve gives the outer bound on the utility levels for both individuals given the total amount of goods available. In other words, a utility possibility curve indicates the highest level of utility individual 2 can attain given the level of utility for individual 1 or, alternatively, the highest level of utility individual 1 can attain given the level of utility for individual 2.

Each point in the feasible production set is associated with a utility possibility curve. Figure 18.4 illustrates several utility possibility curves for production at points *A, B, C,* etc. Utility possibility curves may take any shape, so long as they do not slope upward. A positive slope would imply that both individuals are being made better off, and this would contradict the definition of an efficient allocation of commodities. To understand why, look at the efficient allocation locus in Figure 18.2. It is clear that as we move along a contract curve one individual becomes better off if the other one becomes worse off and vice versa. If the individuals start with any distribution of goods off the contract curve, they will always be able to find a mutual ground for agreement to get them to the contract curve. However, once they reach the contract curve any further movement will produce a conflict of interests.

The information in Figure 18.4 can now be used to describe the outermost boundary of the utility levels we can achieve by choosing an appropriate total production point and associated allocation.

The *utility possibility frontier* is defined as the outermost envelope of all of the utility possibility curves, represented by the heavy line in Figure 18.4.

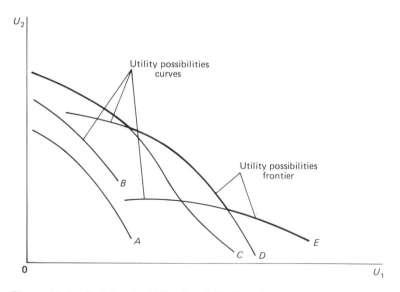

Figure 18.4   Deriving the Utility Possibility Frontier

The utility possibility frontier describes the maximum utility level one individual can achieve given the utility level another person achieves in the present state of this economy. The placement and shape of the possibility frontier depends on (1) individual preferences, (2) the state of technology described by the isoquants, and (3) the amount of inputs available.

Choice Among Utility Possibilities

One of the fundamental problems in general equilibrium discussions is to establish that a set of prices for outputs and inputs can be found which will lead by means of a market system to a situation where the total demand for and supply of each commodity is equal in every market simultaneously. This was illustrated in the last chapter by a numerical example. At the same time, we would like to make sure that resources and outputs are efficiently utilized. The following conditions are prerequisites for efficient utilization: (1) the marginal rate of technical substitution is equal to the ratio of the output prices for all outputs produced, (2) the marginal rate of substitution for each individual is equal to the marginal rate of substitution for every other individual at a particular distribution of commodities, and (3) the common MRS in condition (2) is equal to the $MRTS$ in condition (1); thus $MRS_1 = MRS_2 = MRS = MRTS = P_1/P_2$.[1] If these conditions are satisfied, we say that the given set of prices achieves an efficient outcome. Notice that we have said nothing to imply that a price and market system could or could not achieve a *predetermined* outcome, only that it can achieve an outcome that is efficient in an economic sense.

Instead of just turning the economy loose at some set of relative prices and having it achieve some efficient production and allocation, one of the main problems in welfare economics is to establish whether or not a set of prices can be chosen in a way that a market system leads the economy to a *predetermined* solution. To answer this question, we need to begin with the desired final outcome and work backwards through a general equilibrium system.

To determine a desirable outcome, we need a method for choosing among utility possibilities. This means comparing alternative utility levels for individuals and making a choice based on absolute as well as relative welfare. These choices clearly involve ethical and political questions. Because politics and philosophy are involved in welfare economic choice problems it is important that we introduce information to resolve the economic issue so that we may then evaluate the implications of such choices.

---

[1] Technically, equality conditions are only necessary between pairs of inputs or outputs when strictly positive amounts of both are involved; otherwise, inequalities may replace the equality conditions.

This choice problem is commonly resolved by a device similar to an indifference curve. An indifference curve is a way of representing a ranking among alternatives from least preferred to most preferred. A *welfare function* is introduced here for the same purpose—it enables us to rank alternative utility levels for individuals 1 and 2. Even though we used basic economic principles to determine efficient production and efficient allocation, economic concepts alone cannot resolve problems of ethics. Ethics is what is involved in choosing the distribution of utility between two or more individuals, since basically we are trying to resolve the problem of the distribution of real income.

If we let $W(U_1, U_2)$ be our welfare function, we might represent it in a diagram by the contours W_1, W_2, W_3, etc., in Figure 18.5. The contours of the welfare function are basically indifference curves defined on levels of utility each individual receives, i.e., on distributions of commodities. A welfare function is thus a means of representing an arbitrary ranking for choices that would ordinarily be made on ethical or political grounds.

Point Z in Figure 18.5 represents the highest welfare contour that the economy is capable of achieving given its present body of knowledge and its present resources. Z lies on the utility frontier and also on a utility possibility curve associated with a particular point in the feasible production set, like the point K. Moving from Figure 18.5 to 18.6, we see that point K is associated with the aggregate productions Y_1^* and Y_2^*. If we produce Y_1^* and Y_2^*, then we

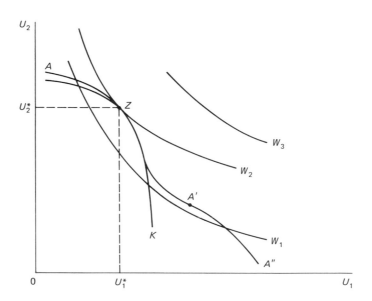

Figure 18.5   Choosing among Alternative Distributions of Welfare (Goods)

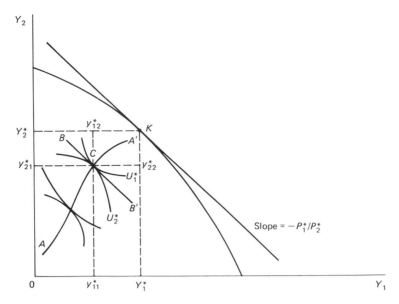

Figure 18.6 Finding Output Prices to Achieve Optimal Production and Distribution

know an allocation can be made between individuals 1 and 2 which will place them at point Z. The required allocation of Y_1^* and Y_2^* is indicated in Figure 18.6. Individual 1 receives y_{11}^* and y_{21}^* while individual 2 receives y_{12}^* and y_{22}^*. We must now ask whether a price and market system is ever capable of achieving the point Z and the allocations y_{11}^*, y_{21}^*, y_{12}^*, and y_{22}^*.

Choosing Prices to Achieve Desired Goals

Prices are the information signals in a market economy. If we want to induce individual firms to produce at point K, we have to choose a set of relative prices which will make Y_1^* and Y_2^* the profit-maximizing combination for Y_1 and Y_2. The slope of the production transformation frontier at K will be the negative of the ratio of the appropriate relative prices P_1^* and P_2^*. These prices cause the market system to achieve a desired goal. First we found the total production we needed to achieve that goal, and now we are choosing the set of output prices which, when transmitted as signals, will lead profit-maximizing firms to produce exactly the quantities Y_1^* and Y_2^*.

The system of prices must also include a choice of input prices for X_1 and X_2. While output prices are seen in two roles—one by consumers and the other by firms—input prices also have two roles. From the point of view of

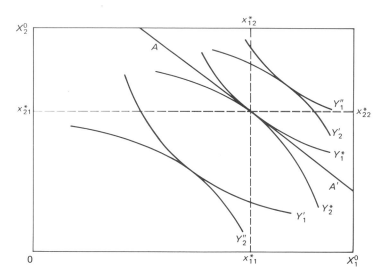

Figure 18.7 Finding Input Prices for Achieving Optimal Production at Least Cost

firms, input prices represent costs while the same prices represent incomes to resource owners. Once an efficient and optimal level of output has been found, we can determine the relative prices for X_1 and X_2 which minimize the cost of producing Y_1^* and Y_2^*. These relative input prices are represented by the negative of the slope of $\overline{AA'}$ in Figure 18.7. Total input quantities are optimally allocated by using x_{11}^* and x_{21}^* to produce Y_1^* and x_{12}^* and x_{22}^* to produce Y_2^*. At the same time, the input prices must yield incomes for each individual sufficient to purchase the consumption mixes represented by point C in Figure 18.6. The height of the budget constraint ($\overline{BB'}$ in Figure 18.6) reflects the appropriate consumer incomes.

Some Rules for Making Choices

As a practical matter, the alteration of prices to achieve predetermined goals, as illustrated in the preceding section, does not play as important a role in national economic policy as decisions which directly or indirectly change the distribution of income.

As the result of a dialogue between several well-known economists,[2] the following criterion, known as the Kaldor-Hicks test, emerged as a possible

---

[2] See the discussions by N. Kaldor, I. M. D. Little, and T. Scitovsky cited in the References.

operational method for evaluating policy changes while avoiding the awkward concept of a welfare function. A policy should be adopted, according to this test, if the resulting increase in aggregate income in the economy is sufficient for all those who are injured by the new policy to be compensated by those who gain, so that in principle no one is left worse off. Notice that no comparison of individual utilities is involved. The test simply requires that the total real income loss of all persons who suffer a loss be less than the total real income gain of those who realize a gain. In principle, those who gain could compensate those who lose real income so losers are at least brought back to their initial level of utility—but notice that those who gain are not required to make good the loss sustained by the losers. As it stands, the test only requires that the loss could be made good with something positive left over.

A curious anomaly can result from applying the Kaldor-Hicks test. It is entirely possible that a policy could be introduced which would move the economy from state A to state B and which would pass the Kaldor-Hicks test. It is also possible, however, that once in state B another policy could be introduced which would move the economy back to state A *and also pass the Kaldor-Hicks Test*! A is preferred to B and B is preferred to A and A is preferred to .... A clear instance where "the grass is always greener on the other side of the fence!"

To avoid this circular possibility a stronger test is required—the Scitovsky test. The Scitovsky test adds to the Kaldor-Hicks test the condition that the losers should not be able to bribe the potential gainers to remain at A. The latter proviso prevents situation A from looking economically desirable once one is at B.

If unanimous agreement on a policy proposal is desired the Kaldor-Hicks-Scitovsky requirement must be pushed one step further and compensation must actually be paid. Otherwise, a redistribution of real income will have occurred which leaves some individuals worse off than before. As a practical matter, of course, compensation is not paid, which means that the policies may have a substantial redistributional impact. Such policies can be implemented because unanimity is not required. Actual changes result from voting schemes in which everyone need not consent.

Voting as a Group Choice Device

Economic decisions which affect two or more individuals involve a group choice process. Group choice processes are frequently carried out by some type of a voting scheme. By far the most popular method of voting is to assign one vote to each eligible voter and to determine the success or failure of a particular proposition by measuring the percentage that must vote for or against the issue. The most common rule, of course, is a majority vote rule, but vote rules requiring a two-thirds majority also occur frequently. These rules belong to a class of voting schemes known as *plurality voting*. Other possibilities include *point voting* and *rank voting*.

Point voting allots a certain number of points to each individual. For example, each person might be given ten points and then confronted with the alternative issues, A, B, and C. Each voter assigns point values to each alternative. A voter who badly wanted proposition A would cast all ten points for proposition A. One who wanted only proposition C could cast all ten points for proposition C. It would also be possible to allocate points among the issues by casting three for proposition A, six for proposition B, and one for proposition C. The winning proposition is the one with the most points.

The advantage point voting offers over majority voting is that it permits voters to express the relative intensity of their preferences. The fact that a voter might strongly dislike a particular proposition or would benefit exceptionally from such a proposition can never be expressed by a bipolar voting scheme.

Rank voting also allows an individual to express relative intensities. In a rank voting scheme, each alternative, say A, B, C, and D, is assigned a value according to its ranking in the voter's scheme of preferences. If alternative B is preferred over the others, it receives rank 1. If alternative B is second best, it receives rank 2. A might be ranked 3 and C ranked 4. One method of determining the winner is to sum the ranks assigned to each alternative. The alternative with the lowest total wins.

A difficulty with both point voting and rank voting is that they create gaming environments where an individual can gain an advantage by using his votes as threats. Voters could threaten to cast all their points for a proposition that another party regards as particularly undesirable. The prevalence of majority voting may result from its apparent avoidance of this particular type of gaming element.

Majority Rule and Arrow's Impossibility Theorem

Despite its widespread use, majority voting has drawbacks. Choice among three or more alternatives is carried out by pairing the winners from the pairings in the previous runoffs, like an athletic tournament. The winners of all of the first set of pairings are then re-paired, and the winners of the second set of pairings again re-paired. Majority voting unfortunately permits the sequence in which choices are presented to individuals to influence the final outcome.

The potential anomaly inherent in majority voting can be illustrated in a situation where we have three possible alternatives x, y, and z, and three individuals. Suppose that we are given the information on individual preferences shown in Table 18.1. Individual 1 has to choose between x and y. He/she prefers x to y, y to z, and x to z. The symbol P is read "is preferred to." Individual 2 prefers y over x, z over x, and y over z. Individual 3 prefers z over y, y over x, and z over x. The preferences shown in Table 18.1 are subject to only one limitation: each individual's choices must be consistent. If an individual prefers x over y and y over z then consistency requires that individual to prefer x over z also. This consistency property is referred to as *transitivity*.

Let us consider the outcome from majority voting. If we pair x and y first, individual 1 prefers x over y; individual 2 prefers y over x, and individual 3 prefers y over x, so y wins.

Another possible initial pairing is y and z. In this case, individual 1 votes for y and individual 2 votes for y, thus y wins. The other possible pairing is x and z. Individual 1 prefers x over z and individuals 2 and 3 would both prefer z over x, so the winner is z. The first-stage eliminations lead to the outcomes shown in Table 18.2.

A runoff election between all possible pairs of first-stage winners will decide the ultimate winner. The winner is y since the only possible pairings are y and y or y and z. In both cases y wins. This example describes a situation in which the process of majority voting leads unambiguously to a single "best" choice, regardless of the sequence in which the alternatives are presented to the voters.

Now assume that the individual preferences are those shown in Table 18.3. The various possible initial pairings lead to the results shown in Table 18.4. We can go through the same majority voting procedure outlined above and see that the winner for the first pairing is x, for the second pairing is z, and

Table 18.1   Individual Preferences over Alternatives x, y, and z

Individual 1	xPy	yPz	xPz
Individual 2	yPx	zPx	yPz
Individual 3	zPy	yPx	zPx

Table 18.2   Results of Majority Voting

PAIRING	WINNER
(1) x, y	y
(2) y, z	y
(3) x, z	z

Table 18.3 Individual Preferences over Alternative *x, y,* and *z*

Individual 1	xPy	yPz	xPz
Individual 2	yPx	zPx	yPz
Individual 3	xPy	zPy	zPx

Table 18.4 Results of Majority Voting

PAIRING	WINNER
(1) x, y	x
(2) x, z	z
(3) y, z	y

for the third pairing is *y*. Taking the first two first-stage results, a second-stage majority vote leads to a choice of *z*, whereas if we pair the second and the third first-stage results it leads to a choice of *y*. One does not have to go any further. The information in Table 18.4 illustrates the possibility that majority voting may lead to an impasse where the actual outcome is dependent on the sequence in which the alternative propositions are paired. In other words, the process can be rigged by merely presenting the opportunities in the appropriate sequence.

The potential ambiguity illustrated in the second example illustrates an important result known as *Arrow's impossibility theorem.* Arrow stipulated five requirements for a group choice process: (1) No dictatorship. One individual's preferences alone do not determine the group choice. (2) Independence of irrelevant alternatives. This property requires that when a group choice comparison is made between two alternatives, *A* and *B*, the relative ranking of other alternatives in terms of individual preferences not be taken into account when comparing *A* and *B*. (3) Each individual has ordered all alternatives according to preference, and votes for the alternative that ranks highest. (4) If everyone unanimously agrees on an alternative, then that is the alternative indicated by the group choice rule. (5) All choices possess the transitivity property. If *A* is preferred to *B* and *B* is preferred to *C*, then *A* is preferred to *C*. The impossibility theorem proves that majority voting does *not* satisfy these characteristics. Even though each individual's preferences satisfy the transitivity requirement, majority voting can lead to group choices which are intransitive.

Group choice questions are important because they are a necessary adjunct to a price system. Taxing people and redistributing income in the form of subsidies to particular individuals is an example of intervention via a group choice system to realign the allocation of goods achieved by the market system. Committees or management teams within a firm are other examples of decision-making units that are not a single individual.

Public Goods: An Example of Market Failure

So far we have always treated market prices as the signals on which choices are based. However, there are commodities that would not be adequately supplied if a market system is used to determine choices. In a market system, individuals express their preferences for goods by their willingness to pay for goods. Expressing a willingness to pay is necessary in order to obtain particular amounts of a commodity, but payment is not always a necessary condition for receiving goods.

A *public good* is a commodity which has the characteristic that a person can consume one more unit of it without decreasing the quantity available for other individuals. Examples of public goods are television or radio broadcasting, clean air, clean water, and to a certain extent, education. Public goods present a difficulty known as the *preference revelation problem*. Each individual who desires to listen to a particular radio program can receive the services of the broadcast simply by turning on the radio, *if* the program is on the air. The decision to produce the program at all depends on whether the sum individuals will pay to hear the program is at least as great as the cost of the resources involved in its production. There is no incentive for individuals to reveal their willingness to pay for television or radio broadcasting simply because as long as the program is broadcast and paid for by someone else, it can be received by them without charge.

With private goods, in contrast to public goods, if one person consumes a unit of the good, then another person cannot consume the same unit. A loaf of bread eaten by one person is physically unavailable for another. Obtaining command over goods requires expressing demand in dollar terms. A price system recognizes only dollar votes. In the case of public goods, there is a definite incentive to mask preferences, because the individual might be asked to back up the preferences expressed by paying taxes or some other price for the commodity. Difficulties with the provision and finance of public services by governmental units and environmental issues such as clean air and water possess a "public good" character.

To illustrate the problem of optimal production as it affects public goods, let us consider the demand for broadcasting a particular program. Suppose that two individuals' demand for a particular quality of broadcasting services is described by the demand curves D_1 and D_2 in Figure 18.8. The broadcasting company must determine how much programming to undertake. Ordinarily the market information expressed by these demand schedules is not available to the firm because of the preference revelation problem. Let us assume for the moment, however, that it is available.

For any given level of programming, say Q^0, the unit price individual 1 is willing to pay, P_1^0, can be read off from the demand schedule D_1. Individual 2 is willing to pay P_2^0 per unit for the same quantity of output. The average

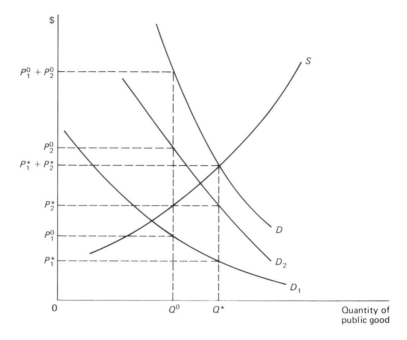

Figure 18.8   Choosing Optimal Production for a Public Good

revenue available from producing Q^0 is therefore $P_1^0 + P_2^0$. If we continue this process for every level of output and ask what is the aggregate amount individuals will pay, we ultimately arrive at an aggregate demand schedule, D, which is formed by vertically adding the demand schedules of each individual. Notice how the public good characteristic changes the way in which one finds market demand. For a private good the demand schedule is formed by horizontally summing the individual demand schedules.

If the supply schedule for producing broadcasting is given by S, then the optimal quantity to supply is Q^*. At the optimal output level Q^* each person's expressed willingness to pay can now be used to charge individual 1 P_1^*, and to charge individual 2 P_2^*. The total charge for individual 1 is $P_1^*Q^*$ and for individual 2 is $P_2^*Q^*$.

The outcome achieved by a market system will typically result in an under-production of commodities that possess this characteristic of public goods. The reason for the underproduction is the incentive people have to mask their preferences in a situation involving public goods. If they express their willingness to pay, they give up the opportunity to receive the commodity free. Understating true demand means that the individual demand schedules are below those illustrated in Figure 18.8 and this fact drives output downward.

Some Other Failures of a Price and Market System

Another group of situations that can lead to a price system breakdown are referred to as *externalities*. Externalities are either interdependencies among individual preferences (externalities in consumption) or interdependencies among the production processes for two or more commodities (externalities in production). Air and water pollution are examples of externalities. Depending upon how one treats them, they could be either production externalities or consumption externalities. In the presence of externalities a market system fails to assign adequate prices to certain inputs or, alternatively, fails to generate output prices which fully reflect the benefits produced. Waste discharged into a river or lake or into the air, permitted by a private property right system unfettered by controls on emission or pollution, creates a situation in which the price system encourages the firm to produce in such a manner that it pollutes heavily simply because one or more of the inputs is not priced. (This case was discussed in detail in Chapter 6.)

On the other hand, some outputs may not be priced. For example, when an individual receives an education that education yields a certain market value to the individual in the form of increasing the value of his/her services; however, it also yields a benefit to the community as a whole. A democratic political system receives the added benefit of an educated electorate and a community gains the advantage of educated participants in the activities or decision processes the community undertakes. These latter benefits, however, are not reflected by a price system. If an individual uses the increment in market value as an indicator of how much education to undertake, without incorporating the value of the benefits received by the community as a whole, then that individual will undervalue the educational services and stop too early. As we saw earlier, this may explain why tuitions are often set at levels substantially below the average total cost of educating an individual and why tuition remissions or grants are typically available to finance education.

The term *externality* is generally applied to any difference between social cost and private cost or between social benefit and private benefit. These differences may result in external economies or diseconomies to third parties. Waste disposal and pollution confer external diseconomies on the community, while education confers external economies. Since the presence of externalities leads to distorted information signals from a price system, it is worthwhile to take a closer look at some of the sources of such market failures.

It is convenient to group externalities into three categories: (1) technological, (2) public goods, and (3) ownership.

Technological externalities

The basic marginal conditions characterizing efficient production ($MRTS = P_1/P_2$) require a nondecreasing $MRTS$ to insure a profit maximum. Notice in Figure 18.1 how the production transformation frontier bends outward away from the origin. The presence of increasing returns to scale may lead to a frontier with inward bending cusps; inputs or outputs may be subject to indivisibilities which further alter the frontier. Interdependence between the technological possibilities open to individual firms can also cause a failure of the basic marginal condition for efficient production. If this occurs, then it is not necessarily possible for the economy to achieve an efficient result via a decentralized decision process using only limited information and price signals.

Public goods

Efficient allocation of goods is also characterized by a marginal condition, $MRS_1 = MRS_2 = MRS = P_1/P_2$. The presence of public goods, however, introduces the need for an additional marginal efficiency rule. Instead of requiring $MRS_1 = MRS_2 = MRS$, optimal provision of public goods requires a summation of willingness to pay as illustrated earlier, i.e., $MRS_1 + MRS_2 = MRS = P_1/P_2$. Needless to say, this latter condition is not satisfied by the basic allocative efficiency condition, except by chance. This failure implies that a set of prices cannot be found to achieve a pre-chosen optimum point by means of a market system.

Ownership externalities

A system of legal and property rights lies at the heart of a market system. Market transactions are contracts; commodities and some form of payment are the objects of contract. Property rights define the objects for which payment can be enforced. A classic example of a situation between a honey bee owner and the owner of an adjacent apple orchard will illustrate the point. The honey bees gather pollen from the apple orchard as part of the honey-making process. While it is true that apple production is the chief motive of the orchard owner, the orchard definitely contributes economic value to the honey. Under existing definitions of property rights it is not possible for the orchard owner to collect for the service provided by the trees, since no market or market price for the service exists. This market failure implies that the input to the productive process which is not paid for may be under-supplied.

Summary

The key concepts of welfare economics introduced in this chapter may be summarized as follows: (1) the utility possibility curve, (2) the utility possibility frontier, (3) the social welfare function, (4) compensation tests, and (5) the concepts of externality and market failure. The last point was illustrated by public goods and pollution examples.

Welfare economics concerns two major topics: (1) the appraisal of a price system in achieving specific results and (2) the evaluation of policy changes.

Our analysis showed that a price system can indeed achieve specified results if prices are chosen appropriately. Market failures caused by ownership, technological, or public goods externalities may, however, destroy the ability of a price system to achieve specified results in an economically efficient manner.

At the level of the whole economy, a basic test for evaluating policy changes is the Kaldor-Hicks-Scitovsky test, which determines whether total benefits measured in dollar terms are at least as great as total losses. Implementation—even without actual payment of compensation from winners to losers—requires information on preferences and data measurements that is not typically available. In addition, there is some incentive to always claim to be "damaged" with the hope of receiving some compensation. Policies, whether desirable or not, are typically subject to some type of voting scheme.

All voting schemes, regardless of type, appear to be susceptible to strategic maneuvering by interested participants. This is clearly possible for point and rank voting schemes, but at present it seems the most prevalent method—majority voting—has been spared such an indictment. Two numerical examples showed this is not always true. However, pending the development of better techniques for formulating group choices, voting remains the most important group choice device.

Questions for Study or Class Discussion

1. Compensation is a key element in the Kaldor-Hicks test. Why? What difference does it make whether compensation is paid or not?
2. Other than voting, what alternatives are there for forming group choices? List some of the strengths and weaknesses of each.
3. Currently, television programming is paid for by advertisers and is essentially free to the consumer. Pay television has been suggested as a better vehicle for allocating the resources devoted to programming. What might be the effects of such a change in market organization and information signaling?
4. List at least five specific examples of market failures. What remedies, if any, exist for these failures?
5. Government policies frequently alter the solution achieved by a market mechanism to the three basic allocation problems. List at least three such policies.

References

Arrow, K. J., *Social Choice and Individual Values.* J. Wiley & Sons, 1951.
Bator, F., "The Simple Analytics of Welfare Maximization," *American Economic Review*, 47 (1957), 22–59.

————, "The Anatomy of Market Failure," *Quarterly Journal of Economics*, 72 (August, 1958), 351–379.

Black D., "On the Rationale of Group Decision Making," *Journal of Political Economy*, 56 (1948), 23–24.

Bowen, H., "The Interpretation of Voting in the Allocation of Economic Resources," *Quarterly Journal of Economics*, 58 (1943), 27–48.

Buchanan, J., and G. Tullock, *The Calculus of Consent*. University of Michigan Press, 1962.

Downs, A., *An Economic Theory of Democracy*. Harper & Row, 1957.

Henderson, J., and R. E. Quandt, *Microeconomic Theory*, Second Edition. McGraw-Hill, 1971.

Kaldor, N., "Welfare Propositions of Economics and Interpersonal Comparisons of Utility," *Economic Journal*, 49 (1939), 549–552.

Lange, O., "The Foundations of Welfare Economics," *Econometrica*, 10 (1942), 215–228.

Little, I. M. D., *A Critique of Welfare Economics*. Clarendon Press, 1950.

Samuelson, P. A., *Foundations of Economic Analysis*. Harvard University Press, 1949.

————, "The Pure Theory of Public Expenditure," *Review of Economics and Statistics*, 36 (1954), 387–389.

Scitovsky, T., *Welfare and Competition*. R. D. Irwin, Inc., 1951.

————, "Two Concepts of External Externality," *Journal of Political Economy*, 17 (1954), 143–151.

Index